COMPLETE MANUAL OF

WHITE COLLAR CRIME
DETECTION
AND
PREVENTION

RUSSELL L. BINTLIFF

PRENTICE HALL
Englewood Cliffs, New Jersey 07632

Prentice-Hall International (UK) Limited, *London*
Prentice-Hall of Australia, Pty. Limited, *Sydney*
Prentice-Hall of Canada, Inc., *Toronto*
Prentice-Hall Hispanoamericana, S.A., *Mexico*
Prentice-Hall of India Private Limited, *New Delhi*
Prentice-Hall of Japan, Inc., *Tokyo*
Simon & Schuster Asia Pte. Ltd., *Singapore*
Editora Prentice-Hall do Brasil, Ltda., *Rio de Janeiro*

© 1993 *by*

PRENTICE-HALL, INC.
Englewood Cliffs, NJ

10 9 8 7 6 5 4 3 2 1

Library of Congress Cataloging-in-Publication Data

Bintliff, Russell L.
    Complete manual of white collar crime : detection and prevention /
by Russell L. Bintliff.
        p.   cm.
    ISBN 0-13-017260-X
    1. White collar crime investigation—United States—Handbooks, manuals, etc.
    2. White collar crimes—United States—Handbooks, manuals, etc   I. Title
    HV8079.W47B56   1993
    364.1′68′0973—dc20   93-4259
                                                                                                CIP

9 780130 172600

PRENTICE HALL
Career and Personal Development
Englewood Cliffs, NJ 07632
Simon & Schuster, A Paramount Communications Company

PRINTED IN THE UNITED STATES OF AMERICA

To my family:
My wife Janie
Our sons Roger and Mark

About the Author

In a career dedicated to law enforcement, **Russell L. Bintliff** has held positions ranging from county deputy sheriff, to criminal and financial investigator for the state of Florida, to Personal Security Officer to the U.S. Secretary of Defense. As a Special Agent (Criminal Investigator) of the Department of the Army, he traveled throughout the world investigating crime both within the Department of Defense and within corporations awarded military contracts. Today he is a licensed private investigator and runs his own agency, which conducts extensive financial and white collar crime investigations for major corporations and the law firms representing them.

Mr. Bintliff's other credentials include degrees in business administration (B.B.A., University of Maryland) and law (J.D., LaSalle University). He has also completed a number of law enforcement courses offered by the FBI, Department of the Army, DEA, and U.S. Secret Service, among others. He is the author of several books, including *Training Manual for Law Enforcement Officers* (Prentice Hall, 1990), *The Complete Manual for Corporate and Industrial Security* (Prentice Hall, 1992), and *Crimeproofing Your Business* (McGraw-Hill, 1993).

Foreword

When the No Name Corporation expanded, diversified, and developed into a major company doing business internationally, it earned a distinction as a model for business scholars. It supplied proof that business giants can grow rapidly from humble beginnings. When the corporation began selling off assets, business scholars lauded the management genius. When the media headlines announced that the No Name Corporation filed for bankruptcy, a shock wave rocked the business world. The same scholars that previously lauded the company now rationalized that the rise and fall was a sign of the times, due to poor management decisions, and a variety of other logical reasons. No one blamed white collar crime—the real reason the No Name Corporation faded from a giant model corporation to extinction.

For a moment, let's look at one day in the former life of the No Name Corporation. This will help us understand why the company's business excelled while profits steadily decreased. We'll learn why, despite cutbacks, selling off assets and a spectrum of traditional business-oriented solutions could not save this company from fading into business world history.

1. In the busy receiving department of the No Name Corporation, Sam Jones, a supervisor, signed an invoice verifying receipt of a truckload of costly tool sets destined for several of the No Name Corporation's facilities around the country. When the truck left the unloading dock, scores of the tool sets remained on board, destined for a back-street buyer. Sam and the driver would meet later at a neighborhood pub as they often did, to split the money from the sale of the No Name Corporation's property.

2. In the shipping department, Jim Smith methodically pasted destination labels on product shipping cartons destined for buyers throughout the world. Only Jim knew how many he diverted to his cousin 2000 miles away. Eventually, weeks or months later, customers would complain about receiving an invoice for products not received. A corporation facility manager would complain later about not receiving a needed tool set. However, no one would blame Jim, since he often received a pat on the back and even pay raises

for the suggestions made to speed shipments and for his meticulous recordkeeping abilities.

3. Margaret Overly, a valued employee in the accounts payable division, worked hard and was lauded for her tough approach in scrutinizing invoices and double checking each item before authorizing payment. No one suspected that increasing numbers of checks going out to suppliers went into several post office box networks she arranged with friends and relatives. The amounts were small by comparison, and she ensured that all the proper entries of accountability went into the data banks. She amended data of the receiving department and inventory and usage data, always ensuring that the products in her private invoice scheme included only expendable materials.

4. In the purchasing department, George Johnson did okay with the No Name Corporation and had a sizable nest egg to prove it. He lived conservatively, drove a well-maintained old car, sported a clearly inexpensive wardrobe, and assured that the corporation got the best deals—or so it seemed. Executives tried to persuade George not to retire. His leaving would create a great loss to the company. However, George cited his wife's failing health and a need to move to a warmer climate. Everyone who knew him sympathized with his hardship. No one suspected that George systematically received kickbacks from suppliers. The company did not suspect that he rigged the bidding or created a variety of schemes that enabled him to amass huge bank accounts at off-shore banks. No one suspected that George's wife had excellent health and spent most of her time managing their considerable investments in the sunny South, where they planned to retire.

5. The No Name Corporation marketing division broke so many sales records that no one complained about the expense accounts that had grown to supply most of the field representatives with a tidy second income. No one noticed the new cars, homes, and life styles that rivaled those of top executives in the company. The devoted sales staff's insistence on staying in field assignments, even when offered promotions, received repeated praise from the boardroom. Insofar as management was concerned, this devotion to company served company interests.

6. A recruiting triumph surrounded the hiring of Mary Stevens, a skilled librarian. Mary created an efficient research department, supplying anyone in the company with accurate information in record time. In the eyes of management she could do no wrong and had whatever access, equipment, or materials she asked for. No one suspected that Mary had a profitable business on the side, supplying No Name Corporation trade information to a variety of competitors, who paid significant cash fees delivered to her home mailbox regularly.

7. A nondescript John Smith worked in the personnel department of the No Name Corporation. Those who knew John defended his integrity, pointing out years of devoted company service, a large family with three boys and two girls in school, and a solid marriage. Each day John arrived at work carrying his worn leather briefcase, and since his job didn't call for one he joked about carrying a large lunch. He made a point regularly of opening the case and taking out his brown bag each day. No one at the company suspected that the briefcase went home each night filled with administrative supplies. He put five children through school using money from the sale of corporation supplies.

8. Pam Roberts and Gail Roney, both divorced with small children and living as suburban neighbors, struggled with prestigious executive secretarial jobs but had a hard time making ends meet on their salaries. One evening Pam read an article about part-time catering to earn extra money. Gail agreed to the plan and they set out to get their new sideline in operation. They would cook in their home kitchens, use their existing cars, and together had enough dishes and other items to make it work. Getting customers was a difficult matter because that meant advertising. After checking the rates of designing, printing, and mailing brochures, the cost far outclassed their budget. Pam and Gail also needed administrative supplies and good mailing lists of the local area. They solved their problem with some ingenuity and the guise of working late a couple of nights each week. The pair created advertising on company computers, printed them on laser printers, and used the copier to make what they needed. Using company envelopes solved other problems involving credibility and cost of postage. Accessing the marketing department mailing lists supplied names, company envelopes allowed them to have mail room post their advertising, and soon the pair had a booming sideline business and continued to use the No Name Corporation's equipment, supplies, and facilities to support it.

The No Name Corporation had far more white collar crime problems than the examples I have given, but by now you see what caused the company's downfall. You might also have a chilling recognition that your company has similar problems. Alone, these examples might seem minimal. However, when you multiply these examples and other white collar crime problems by a hundred, a thousand, or more employees, the cost becomes staggering. Additional threats originate from other companies formed with the express purpose of committing white collar crimes. One of the greatest reasons for the prevalence of this invisible crime in the business world is nonrecognition and the inability of business and security managers to find viable, workable solutions. The law enforcement community also continues to wrestle with white collar crime problems. Investigators believe that only accounting experts can investigate the crimes. Prosecutors are reluctant to bring criminal charges in corporate white collar crimes largely because courts and juries don't understand such crimes or view them as noncrimes. Most people will rarely view a corporation as a real victim of a crime. This attitude also has contributed in recent years to increasing white collar crime. Clearly, trying to control corporate assets and employee conduct with an approach that threatens prosecution does not work. Firing or prosecuting a person caught in the act of a white collar crime (unless in large embezzlement cases where evidence can show intent) often leads to civil suits against the victim company. Courts and juries of civil cases generally lean toward making injury and damage awards to a person and find against a corporation. These decisions not only encourage white collar crime, but convert the victim company into a culprit. Most companies today try to cope by creating an environment quietly called "the cost of doing business." What these companies tell their employees is that it's okay to steal, but keep it within reasonable levels. However, the costs incurred are *not* reasonable.

■ WHAT THIS BOOK WILL DO FOR YOU

How can this seemingly bewildering problem have any viable solution? Your solutions begin with a change in the perceptions of white collar crime. Next, you must break with traditional concepts of dealing with white collar crime that have proven not to work. If the traditional views and countermeasures worked, companies wouldn't lose billions each year from these crimes. Using my book, you'll realize perpetual benefits and advantages for your company. Together, we now have the opportunity to find solutions. I've created a list of possibilities of how we can work together to solve your problems and prevent new ones from emerging within your company.

     1. You supply the goal of shoring up your company's defenses to protect its assets. I will provide you with effective techniques of getting the job done right.

     2. I will show you how to avoid sending the wrong signals to employees that it's okay to convert company assets to their personal gain.

     3. You put aside fears of security and preventive measures that you believe will interfere with company business operations. I will show you how to build in business friendly preventive systems that stop your white collar crime problems.

     4. You view your employees as investments even when you know they're stealing company assets. I will show you how to convert them from white collar crime suspects into valuable, productive employees.

5. When you need to pursue termination, prosecution, or civil litigation involving your white collar crime suspects, take the time to use this book. I will show you how to do it right, preventing liabilities in court that move your company from the position of victim to villain.

In these days of tight budgets, corporate slimdowns, and increased competition, your skill to take on white collar crime and win is critical. It will determine whether your company will thrive—or just survive—or join the ranks of others in history.

◼ HOW TO USE THIS BOOK EFFECTIVELY

I've developed this book to supply you with user-friendly content that will enable you to act effectively in a variety of ways. Your actions involving white collar crime depend on the severity of your problem and how *you* choose to manage it. This book also supplies you with the following benefits and advantages in those chapters examining a specific crime:

1. A reference section that helps you develop a clear understanding of a specific corporate white collar crime problem. (This involves straightforward, accurate discussion of the white collar crime as it is, not as it was fifty years ago).

2. A checklist of qualifiers and essential elements that helps you identify whether your problem qualifies as a white collar crime as opposed to other crimes or noncrimes. This section also helps you later to develop preventive countermeasures using investigative audits.

3. Tested solutions that I've recommended and that are now in use at many major corporations. The solutions probably sound innovative, and they are. Obviously the tired, worn, and ineffective concepts used to combat corporate white collar crime don't work. If they did, companies would not experience losses of $200 billion or more each year. The solutions I show you do work, and companies using them report dramatic results.

4. An investigative section tailored to the specific category of white collar crime, helping you to isolate the problem, develop preventive counter-measures, and take other punitive action.

5. A quick reference review and guide for the chapter. Use it when you are in a hurry to refresh your memory or quickly determine what's in the chapter.

The important investigative section of each white collar crime category supplies you with additional major benefits:

6. Helps you define the current weak points in your company policy and procedures for that category

7. Helps you develop new policies and procedures that effectively end the opportunity for employees and others to commit white collar crimes against the company

8. Helps you take positive, productive action involving
- Making a decision to terminate employment
- Making a decision to file criminal charges
- Making a decision to use civil litigation as a remedy

9. Helps you eliminate company liability or lawsuits by employees by properly documenting and proving the essential elements of the specific white collar crime

10. Helps you create historical files on lessons learned and actions you have taken. These files provide an accurate tracking device to determine effectiveness of action, and they are an invaluable source of information for future management decisions.

This information-packed, solutions-oriented book will supply you with valuable tools of correcting current white collar crime problems and preventing others from occurring in the future. It not only can dramatically change your profit potential and can keep your company in business, but also create actions that prevent employees from becoming white collar criminals. You can develop winning programs that enable corporate management to focus on operations while maintaining tight asset security.

Contents

■ PART TWO   EMBEZZLEMENT: THE PAPER CHASE   141

Chapter Six   Computer Crimes—Hi-Tech Embezzlement   145

Part One
Managing Commonplace White Collar Crime

■ INTRODUCTION

White collar crimes that reach media headlines generally report a dramatic embezzlement using computers or some sensational scheme in the upper echelons of the financial or corporate worlds. These infrequent reports leave many people believing that most executives of high finance and corporate affairs are crooks, because the only time they hear the words *white collar crime* are in relation to such individuals. On the other hand, many people believe that most corporate workers are honest and adhere faithfully to the law and display unquestioning loyalty to their corporate employers. In the real world, they are wrong on both counts.

What the media does not report involves the daily looting of company cash and assets by commonplace corporate and industrial employees—looting that totals tens of billions of dollars each year. Bonding companies and business analysts collect reams of statistics each year disclosing that most corporate employees will steal if they get a chance, another sizable group will steal if they think they can get away with it, and only a few will not steal under any circumstances.

A variety of studies conducted confidentially among corporate workers in a major firm showed that only 36 percent of persons who anonymously admitted theft of their company assets said they felt guilty about their crimes. Sixty-four percent of the employees in the same study said they felt no guilt, and most didn't envision their actions as a crime. Another similar study in England showed that most corporate employees had no guilty feelings about their systematic theft from their companies. A common justification that

1

corporate employees voiced in a variety of studies about their fraud and thefts of company assets is that they believe there's no real victim, because they don't perceive their activities as a real crime. Many employees involved in commonplace white collar crime rationalize that their company takes advantage of people it deals with, so it deserves to be treated in the same way. Others believe that it is okay to break a law that they do not perceive as applicable to corporations. This widespread rationalization seems to be a reason for steady increases of white collar crimes targeting corporations and industry. Other reliable statistics show that annual losses due to white collar crime by corporate employees far exceed annual losses due to street crimes in the United States.

Many business experts believe that massive theft has become so well entrenched and so complex that it's out of control. Others in the business world know from experience that control of white collar crime is possible with the help of one of a handful of experts scattered throughout the United States. However, corporate executives also know that with only a few experts to investigate and to create preventive solutions for white collar crime, they cannot solve problems for several million diversified corporations. This book, however, gives you a way out of that frustrating dilemma. I bring my expertise to you, supplying user-friendly solutions to all of you who have an interest in ending and preventing employee white collar crime.

Many crimes discussed in Part One have become so common in the business world that they're largely unrecognized as criminal activity and are surely not viewed as white collar crimes. However, these commonplace schemes account for about $40 billion or more in corporate losses each year, and they *are* white collar crimes.

In Part One, I offer you viable, business-oriented solutions that end these common crimes and help you transform your company from a beleaguered victim to a bastion of productivity and profit. However, you must first understand what white collar crime really is, not what the confused traditional versions tell you it is. Then you need to know how to understand, identify, investigate, and formulate preventive countermeasures for the primary categories of commonplace white collar crime before moving to other categories.

Chapter One
An Overview of Contemporary White Collar Crime

White collar crime divides into four major types, with each showing us who the victim is: (1) crimes against a corporation or industry, (2) crimes against corporate employees, (3) crimes against corporate customers, and (4) crimes against the general public. This book focuses entirely on white collar crimes against the corporation. White collar crime against corporations or industry originates from its employees, customers, and other businesses.

There are several unique elements about white collar crime that distinguish it from common criminality. The most distinguishable elements include (1) rational execution and (2) resulting personal gain. Equally distinctive but less obvious are (1) the victim company's unwitting cooperation, (2) society's indifference to the crime, and (3) the perpetrator's noncriminal self-image.

The late Edwin H. Sutherland, usually considered the dean of American criminologists, made a major contribution to our understanding of crime as a learned behavior. One of Sutherland's most notable works included his pioneering study of white collar crime. He first coined the term *white collar crime* during a 1939 speech delivered in the American Sociological Society. During the speech and in later works, he tried to frame a general definition of this mysterious crime as it was in 1939 and to identify the class of perpetrators. Sutherland focused attention on corporate and industrial executives, whom he claimed generally were responsible for the problems he outlined. Since these men (women were not considered members of the corporate world in 1939) wore white shirts, as opposed to workers who predominantly wore blue shirts, the term *white collar* emerged. His concept was not altogether new, however, since a short paragraph appeared in a 1935 textbook written by a collection of scholars and contained the phrase "criminals of the upper world," alluding to the executive classes Sutherland targeted. Although he undoubtedly described the situation accurately then, his description has generated debates and arguments ever since, largely by scholars far removed from the business world.

Social and technological changes during the past fifty years have transformed the business world. It bears little resemblance to the corporate and industrial complexes of Sutherland's era. However, the confusion that often surrounds issues of white collar crime in corporations today generally traces back to traditional views of fifty or more years ago. Even scholars have found themselves lost in this time warp, describing the problem of white collar crime much like Sutherland did during a long past era. To prevent your company from becoming a white collar crime victim, and to detect and end any white collar crime currently plaguing your company, you have to begin with a clear understanding of exactly what white collar crime is today opposed to antiquated traditional views that have changed little in the past fifty years.

■ EVOLUTION OF WHITE COLLAR CRIME

An understanding of white collar crime today must begin with Professor Sutherland's views of 1939 and how that opinion emerged from research of earlier years. Sutherland stereotyped the category of corporate and industrial white collar perpetrators as a *privileged few*. In his speech heard around the world, Sutherland said, "White Collar Crime is committed by a person of respectability and high social status during his occupation." During 1939 and into the early 1950s, Sutherland's portrayal of the white collar criminal accurately described the problem as it existed then, but far from how it exists today. Sutherland's limitation of white collar crimes to the upper class's occupational crimes points out a reaction to a socioeconomic situation of the 1930s. In Sutherland's time, only wealthier classes had direct access to and control of corporate assets, a prerequisite for enactment of the crimes described in Sutherland's concept of white collar crime.

In 1939 and over a decade later, blue collar workers were the predominant factor in an industrialized society. Most industrial workers then, compared to contemporary corporate employees today, had minimal education. Furthermore, the industrialization of big business demanded physical labor. Even people who worked in offices generally remained in the blue collar class framework. Office configurations then featured desks lined up in long, neat rows with a teacher-like supervisor seated at a desk on a raised platform. This setup created an administrative, assembly-line atmosphere. In the heat of summer, fans and open windows (not air conditioning) prevailed. In winter, steam radiators supplied noisy winter heat. Clacking manual typewriters and ink pens were the tools of office workers and accountants. The privileged white collars that Sutherland focused attention on reigned from the upper floors. They jealously guarded keys to the executive washroom, and they enjoyed a variety of special privileges including doting female private secretaries that mothered and served them. The white collars that Sutherland indicted in his speech had exclusive control of the company assets in a highly structured business environment.

Contemporary white collar crime can be committed by or perpetrated against (1) corporations, partnerships, professional firms, nonprofit organizations, and governmental units; and/or (2) their executives, principals, and employees and outsiders such as customers, clients, suppliers, and other companies or organizations and individuals. A general failure to review and evaluate this broad range of possibilities is probably contributing to ineffective countermeasures, which have about the same effect on white collar crimes as baseball players whose manager has trained them to cover all bases except home plate.

There is another important factor in this modern equation of white collar crime that Sutherland could not envision in his time. A new trend in the corporate world began subtly with the introduction of women into the blue collar workplace during World War II. When the blue collar men went off to war, women successfully replaced them in corporations and industries. When the war ended and men returned to their blue collar jobs, women had carved out a permanent although uncertain niche in the workplace. The social climate of the mid to late 1940s wasn't favorable for men and women working together in blue collar jobs. So female employees transferred into administrative positions supporting the white collar privileged few. Although these positions were loftier than running lathes and forklifts, they were viewed as blue collar jobs. Thus women continued to work in the equivalent of a blue collar class, primarily as secretaries and in subservient administrative jobs.

The rapid onslaught of technology, spawned largely by the introduction of computers to the business world, started a gradual conversion from a blue collar majority in corporations and industries to a white collar corporate majority. The computer enabled streamlined industrial operations; robot-like equipment rapidly replaced blue collar workers.

Children of blue collar workers also played an important role in the evolution of the business world. Higher education opportunities for blue collar workers' children became a priority for parents, who wanted their children to have a better life. Instead of male children traditionally following their fathers into factories, and females thinking about the little house with a white picket fence, many sons and daughters went off to college. Then the new college graduates went into business management in the growing corporations. The age of the company person and corporate ladder arrived. Retiring blue collar workers were replaced by technology-based equipment and college-educated children. The corporate and industrial workplace changed as the number of new white collar positions grew. Women also participated in this transition, moving into middle management, the professions, and even administrative positions that focused on work and asset control instead of servitude. By the early 1970s, the business world became a white collar–dominated environment; blue collar workers moved into a steadily decreasing minority role.

■ MISCONCEPTIONS AND INACCURATE LABELS

As the Age of Technology and workplace roles within corporations and industry brought sweeping changes in the business world, so did evolving social environments and values. Those changes were reflected in white collar crime. Unfortunately, criminologists, sociologists, business executives, security professionals, and law enforcement officials did not keep pace with the business world changes, and instead became confused about what to call the new onslaught of crimes perpetrated against companies. When people become confused, they often cling to traditional explanations; this is what happened with the white collar crime problem. Even today, most businesses and professions cling to the white collar crime explanation that Sutherland voiced over fifty years ago and often ignore the real problems.

A few people have tried to break out of tradition and the white collar crime mystery. However, even these innovative people often continue with one foot safely on the Sutherland concept of white collar crime and the other foot testing the waters with a series of new titles and labels. Although they are still talking about white collar crime, they replace it with other names. Today, we often see terms like *occupational crimes, corporate crimes, economic crimes, blue collar crimes, financial crimes,* and *business crimes.* Although these labels vaguely, or partly, describe forms of white collar crime, they also add to the confusion factor. In the following brief definitions, I will show you the confusion emerging from their use.

1. *Occupational crimes*: This vague term can mean a variety of things, depending on perceptions and circumstances. Many scholars have tried to equate this term to a prerequisite of white collar crime, reasoning that the person committing the act must become an employee of the victim company. However, placing that label on white collar crime generally perpetuates the same inaccuracies in today's business community as does the Sutherland concept. It disregards the vendors, suppliers, and other companies also targeting corporations, as well as those companies formed solely to steal from other companies with their fraudulent activities. It also disregards the professions such as accounting firms, law firms, computer companies, and others

that may engage in criminal activities. The label also overlooks companies that begin with legitimate intentions and move into criminal or civil crimes before entering bankruptcy or disappearing. Finally, it overlooks persons who take part in collusion with corporate employees (e.g., knowingly receiving stolen assets or information of value from corporate employees).

2. *Corporate crimes*: This term is similar to the term *occupational crime*, but it is vaguer. It might refer specifically to crimes committed *by* corporations, such as dumping toxic waste. It can move in and out of the white collar crime environ. It usually confuses those trying to understand the problem of corporate victims because it has a broad perception according to the person and can involve crimes by the company, crimes against the company and non-white collar crimes.

3. *Economic crimes*: This vague term encompasses any violation of the law that has an economic motive. Even crimes of impulsive passion often have an underlying economic inducement. In realistic terms, this label could describe anything from armed robbery, to murder, burglary, arson, or some white collar crimes. It could describe a white collar crime, but also many others. Thus it's largely an inaccurate term.

4. *Blue collar crimes*: This term clearly delineates the classes and intentionally or unintentionally embraces the concept that only upper class persons commit white collar crime. It normally refers to white collar crime; however, since the perpetrators discussed don't fit into the category Sutherland described, the blue collar label is attached. It is often used by people who do not understand contemporary white collar crime or refuse to accept that times, circumstances, and societies change. The best use of the term *blue collar crime* is in those describing clear statutory crime that does violate an element of trust but does not include use of guile, deception, and concealment, key elements of white collar crime. Blue collar crimes might include pure theft of opportunity (e.g., on waterfront docks where stevedores simply take property from cargo they unload from ships).

5. *Financial crimes*: This common and vague label can mean any offense that involves money or its equivalent. However, it is regularly used to describe specific situations related to financial frauds such as insider trading, stock swindles, major embezzlements, and other high-finance crimes. However, the term *white collar crime* also describes that type of offense, and using one term instead of several generally helps eliminate confusion.

6. *Business crimes*: This term is often used to explain white collar crime; however, it implies that the company is committing the crime. Normally, this term is used to explain crimes committed against business, and it stresses occupation at the company as a prerequisite. It is a vague and misleading term.

■ CONTEMPORARY WHITE COLLAR CRIME —WHAT IS IT?

The essential distinction to remember about white collar crime is this: It is not a specific crime in itself, but rather a "technique" of committing a crime. The technique applied to commit a variety of statutory crimes determines whether it qualifies as a white collar crime.

The technique of committing a white collar crime always remains consistent; however, the term *white collar crime* has a variety of applications. This book focuses *only* on the crimes involving corporations, industries, or businesses that become the victim. An important element of any crime, as noted earlier, involves a *person* as the victim. This stumbling block adds to confusion about white collar crime when corporations become the victims. However, while the traditional victim of a crime is a human being (i.e., natural person), statutes also recognize a *corporation as a person* within the meaning of equal protection and the due process provisions of the United States Constitution. The corporation shares the same equal protection of the law as a person when a white collar crime is committed against it. Within this context, the following definition of white collar crime crafted by the U.S. Department of Justice applies:

> White collar crimes are illegal acts characterized by guile, deceit, and concealment, and not dependent upon the application of physical force or violence or threats thereof. They may be committed by individuals acting independently or by those who are part of a well-planned conspiracy. The objective may be to obtain money, property, or services; to avoid the payment or loss of money, property, or services; or to secure business or personal advantage.

By describing white collar crime as illegal acts, this government definition avoids the implication that only criminal proceedings and sanctions solve the problems of white collar crime. Often, civil proceedings and remedies can be equally, if not more, effective because they may enable recovery of the company's asset loss.

When you focus on the offense, instead of on the offender, the definition of white collar crime is more encompassing and clearer than the traditional one, which concentrates exclusively on offenders. You also need to view white collar crime as a democratic offense. For example, white collar crime committed by a bank teller or a bank president, a corporate employee or a corporate president, has the same weight. A good example of that democratic concept follows: Embezzlements of $100,000 by a corporate vice-president who manipulated accounts payable records are not substantively different from the behavior of a shipping department clerk who stole $100,000 in company products by sending them in his cousin and falsifying records to show that the shipments went to real customers.

■ SIX ESSENTIAL ELEMENTS OF WHITE COLLAR CRIME

I mentioned earlier that the scope of white collar crime clearly includes more than victimizing corporations; however, the parameters of this book focus only on that category. In addition, white collar crime involves a *technique* instead of a specific or statutory crime in itself. To qualify as a white collar crime with a corporation as a victim, the following six elements must be present. When they are not present, the activity or offense is not a white collar crime.

1. *Intent to commit a wrongful act*: Intent is normally inferred from the behavior or statements of the offender and from the presence of proof of a clear effort to avoid detection and clear actions to deceive the victim company.

In every white collar crime it is normally clear that the offender knew he or she was involved in an illegal activity or at least a legally gray area, whether or not the offender has knowledge of the specific statue violated. Implied intent emerges from the following elements that describe white collar crime.

2. *Guileful actions—secrecy and disguise of purpose*: This second element involves the character of the offender's conduct or activity to implement the plan. When a common crime is committed, the wrongful intent is established by some clear overt act (for example, an armed rubbery). There is in that crime an observable act. In a white collar crime situation, a disguise of the purpose or facade of legitimacy become the overt act, although they are more difficult to detect. White collar offenders must plot secret ways of carrying out company asset theft and must often rationalize their acts as noncrimes. Although they may rationalize their acts in that manner, inherently they know that such acts are wrong and technically illegal; this creates the need for guile and secrecy. Guile and secrecy by a white collar crime offender generally help you establish the intent element necessary to prove a criminal offense.

The offender's crime can include either verbal or written disguise. For example, a bank loan officer who creates a fictional borrower complete with promissory note, a borrower financial statement, and false bank background check has created a facade or disguises intended to deceive other bank personnel and examiners. The disguise, plus the officer's position of trust, causes bank personnel to believe the transaction they approve is legitimate. In white collar crime offenses, written communication (e.g., letters) or computer data rarely are what they appear to be, despite their legitimate appearance.

3. *Deception*: The elements of intent and disguise clearly originate with and are controlled by the white collar offender. Both portray the offender's own objective and chosen method of execution. However, the offender must have a positive perception of the victim company's willingness to be a victim of his or her scheme before committing the crime. This confidence normally is grounded in the knowledge that the company cannot or will not fully investigate the accuracy and completeness of every piece of paper, computer entry, or record of accountability.

White collar offenders will create deceptive measures to enable their acts of company asset theft to evade detection. For example, individuals embezzling company funds might work long hours and on weekends to create an image of a devoted company employee. Their real motive in doing so might include manipulating records to cover their activities (when few or no other employees are present). They might also make a considerable effort to appear frugal and create a variety of other deceptive measures to avoid suspicion, especially if shortages or unexplained losses surface. This activity also supports the intent element in proving a criminal offense.

4. *Continued concealment of the act*: This element differs from the disguise element. The reason for disguise is to consummate the crime; it is part of the manner and means by which the fraud is committed. When the white collar crime continues, concealment and disguise will overlap, since postponing pursuit and maintenance of the facade of respectability enable repetitions of fraud. Even when there is no intent by the offender to commit further white collar crimes, concealment will be a continuing element of the original crime. Concealment often results in new crimes to cover old crimes, such as continuous repetitive alteration and falsification of records.

White collar offenders must conceal their offense. This element has special importance to offenders because they operate in the open. They cannot obtain the victim company's cooperation by wearing a mask and brandishing a weapon. The ideal act of concealment for the white collar crime offender is one never recognized as a crime. Instead, if discovered it will appear as an honest error. Examples commonly used by offenders to conceal their acts include altering, destroying, or falsifying documents; conducting inaccurate inventories; padding expense accounts or other expenditures; and representing use of company equipment for business instead of for personal gain. With the proliferation of computerized systems in the business world, offenders might conceal their activities by destroying data or planting computer viruses.

However, the victim company must cooperate in this activity by supplying the white collar crime offender with opportunity. The opportunity to commit a white collar offense is always a necessary condition of the crime. Normally, an operations-oriented company will be so busy trying to make money and expand that opportunities will abound and lead to victim cooperation with the white collar offender.

5. *No use of physical force or threats*: A key element of white collar crime is that there is no hint of physical force or threats. Crimes of extortion or blackmail often are labeled as white collar crime; however, they cannot qualify. Those crimes involve some type of threat to the victim.

6. *An objective of personal or business gain*: Any crime calls for a motive, and white collar crime offenders have a motive or objective of personal gain. This gain might not include money or property; however, the crime is done to create an advantage. For example, two employees are being considered for an important promotion and one decides to create a perception of incompetence or theft implicating the other person. He or she creates that perception by falsifying or altering documents, destroying files, entering inaccurate information, or conducting other activities so it appears that the other person did it. The offender's motive stems from the advantage of a promotion, and there is an underlying financial motive based on the increased salary and benefits. Other examples include obtaining money or other company assets directly or using company assets to make money from some other enterprise not related to the business (for example, two secretaries operating a part-time catering business supported with company equipment and materials).

■ THREE ESSENTIAL ELEMENTS OF PROOF

To help you establish the presence of white collar crime within or against your company, you will need a clear working understanding of the crime's mechanics from a legal viewpoint. This is important when it is necessary to make an official complaint to law enforcement agencies, to terminate the employment of an employee, or to bring a civil suit designed to recover company losses. It is not enough in those circumstances to point out the six essential elements described above, although they must be present.

1. *Intent to commit a crime*: Any crime must have provable intent or legally accepted implied intent based on the offender's actions that clearly shows he or she knew the act was legally wrong.

2. *Verifiable proof of loss*: You must have verifiable proof that some loss recurred resulting from the intentional act of the offender. The loss must have clear documentation, and the more detail the better (such as serial numbers and proof of purchase by the company).

3. *Verifiable value*: You must prove that the loss represents verifiable and reasonable value to the company. For example, if an employee steals a document and sells it to a competitor, did the act create a financial loss to the company? If an employee steals a laptop computer, what is the value? In the latter example, you will need to determine that value based on its worth when stolen, and unless the equipment is new that value will be different from replacement value.

■ USING THE CIVIL LAW AS A REMEDY

Since civil action is simpler and easier than criminal trial, it often supplies the best remedy for recovering property, money, or taking other punitive actions in white collar crime cases. You should always try to document the case with all the elements discussed above; however, the requirements of the court will be less stringent than in criminal prosecutions. Often, your company benefits by using civil court instead of criminal court remedies in dealing with action involving white collar crime.

■ WHICH EMPLOYEE MOST OFTEN PARTICIPATES

An important part of understanding exactly what white collar crime involves stems from knowing who in your company poses the greatest potential of becoming an offender. Statistics and studies, in addition to my personal experience investigating these crimes, clearly defeat the stereotyped, traditional perception based on the Sutherland principles.

Today, most corporate white collar crime offenders are employees regarded as middle class. Predominantly, they appear to qualify as solid, respectable citizens who pay taxes, support their neighborhood little league teams, and voice strong belief in the American way of life. Ironically, they strongly support virtues of hard work and honesty, and they are quick to anger at the mention of welfare chiselers, street hoodlums, and the permissiveness and immorality in society that they believe undermines established social order. Why, then, do these straight-arrows steal?

■ SEVEN ESTABLISHED EXPLANATIONS OF WHY CORPORATE EMPLOYEES STEAL

1. *The corporation is large and impersonal*. The offender's reasons stem from feeling little or no loyalty to the company, and regarding the company as an

abstract entity instead of as comprised of real people. The employee white collar thief, stealing from a large and impersonal corporation, rationalizes his or her act as harmless and victimless. A variety of studies over the years consistently show surprising results. Only 40 percent of corporate employees, including executives, with less than a year on the job view their positions as more than just a job that supplies a paycheck. Follow-up research shows that after employees work two years with the same company, the percentage drops from 40 percent to 20 percent. That leaves about 80 percent of the corporate staff working solely to draw a paycheck and to receive benefits, with no feeling of being a part of the company and with no pride in their work or craft.

2. *Traditional union-management conflict.* Corporations that have union contracts often experience high rates of white collar losses. The thefts stem from those under the union contract who rationalize that the company exploits them and who deeply resent that perceived exploitation. They often use this excuse to rationalize their white collar offenses. In contrast, the non-union employees perceive that the union members have a better position and rationalize their white collar crime activities as a way of rightful compensation. In recent years, white collar unions have experienced steady growth. The old idea of only blue collar workers being in unions is a myth that is opposed to the reality of the corporate business world. The increase of the so-called white collar union stems from a continuing evolution of corporate and industrial work forces from blue to white collar positions; thus we see the evolution of white collar crime as noted earlier in this book.

3. *Perception of being underpaid or abused by the company.* Many white collar offenders become frustrated by a lack of promotions or salary increases and foray into systematic stealing of company assets. They rationalize their activities as not really stealing; instead they perceive their actions as an earned fringe benefit or informal compensation they fully deserve. White collar crime activity becomes a lucrative second income, and the benefits of a better lifestyle realized from it often heighten the offenders' greed and desire to increase their scope of theft.

4. *Corporate theft is a challenge and source of excitement.* Often, at least at first, company employees might steal company assets because they perceive the need for the item or money, but mostly because doing it gives them a thrill. They might feel boredom with their job, or frustration because advancement and a prosperous future seem unlikely to them. Often that feeling can take root among employees when cutbacks, belt-tightening measures, layoffs, and announcements of general austerity programs occur. The act of stealing from the company may fulfill a fantasy or need for excitement (e.g., the offender sees himself or herself as being a secret agent, spy, or daring crime-novel character).

5. *No identity as a real criminal.* This noncriminal self-image is reinforced by the traditional stereotype of real criminals as being those who commit street and violent crimes. These corporate offenders generally rationalize their activities as tolerable by the company for four key reasons: (1) Companies rarely initiate action against white collar crime except in a clear and normally spectacular case. (2) The media rarely takes an interest in corporations unless one becomes involved in a scandal such as dumping toxic waste into a river. (3) Prosecutors and law enforcement show little interest in corporate victims. (4) Few defendants in white collar crime cases receive convictions when the company is the victim because courts and juries traditionally do not perceive the offender as a real criminal.

6. *Regular and unwitting encouragement of white collar crime by the corporation itself.* Companies traditionally have an unwritten, unpublicized policy of acceptable losses each year, as do most government agencies. For example, most companies know that employees and other steal assets, pad expense accounts, and use company equipment and materials. They do not know how to prevent such behavior and often believe that trying to do so will cause problems in daily operation. So they choose to tolerate it—a type of burying the head in the sand and hoping the problem will go away.

To rationalize their problem as allowable, the board of executives (aided by their financial experts who also have no viable solutions) comes up with a tolerated loss percentage. Normally that percentage ranges to 5 percent or more of gross income, depending on the company; often it is much higher and adjusted as needed to avoid admitting a real problem. Once a company admits a problem, the media might find out and spread the word quickly. That causes greater losses from customer and creditor loss of confidence; stocks plummet and disaster lurks in the shadows. So the board finds a way to make the losses tolerable. For example, a company doing $500 million in business each year might tolerate losses of $25 million or more, considering this as the cost of doing business.

Why does this encourage greater white collar crime? The corporate grapevine makes secrets hard to control; people have a strong tendency to talk about business and have a hard time keeping secrets. When word spreads about the year's losses and business continues as usual, the white collar offender knows its okay to continue stealing since no one seemingly cares.

7. *No communication among white collar criminals.* White collar crime offenders who are stealing corporate assets rarely share their secret with anyone else in the company. Normally, although they suspect that others have their own schemes, they do not discuss the subject with others. Few corporate white collar offenders will step back and view the massive amount of theft happening in their company daily.

■ OTHER BUSINESSES AS WHITE COLLAR CRIMINALS

Another type of white collar crime offender that increasingly targets corporations is other businesses acting either as customers or suppliers (see chapter 12). These offenders are divided into two primary categories:

1. *Businesses that rip off other businesses.* These businesses have initial legitimacy and turn to white collar crime in a desperate effort to prevent failure because of financial problems, or to create short-term heavy income for principals before being forced out of business.

2. *Businesses created solely to rip off other businesses.* These offenders are on the increase and often evolve from the ranks of people involved in the old consumer-oriented small-time swindles, such as real estate deals, roofing and driveway repairs, local coupon and merchant advertising scams, and a long list of other popular scams. At some point a few years ago (perhaps because of the proliferation of computers, fax machines, and other fast-moving or instant communications), this type of white collar crime company emerged. Those who run it can create impressive illusions that supply their target with a convincing perception of legitimacy. In the precomputer era, these operations were difficult and costly to create and easier for victim companies to detect. Offenders can now easily move money around from bank to bank electronically, creating an image of affluence and solvency. These white collar crime companies create and expand inventories, develop verifiable sales records (often involving paper companies positioned for this illusion), create long lists of satisfied clients, and more, all an illusion, all by computers, and all designed to rip off legitimate corporations.

■ THE ORGANIZED CRIME PROBLEM

Organized crime groups have infiltrated the world of legitimate business (see Chapter 10). While it is impossible to compile a complete list of businesses involving organized crime, the following have been identified:

Auto sales and leasing	Bakeries
Banking	Beauty and health salons
Construction	Dairy products
Delivery and long-distance hauling	Demolition
Funeral parlors	Garbage and trash collection

Garment manufacture	Horse breeding
Hotels and motels	Insurance
Janitorial services	Laundries and dry cleaning
Linen supply	Lumber
Manufacturing	Meat processing and packing
Nightclubs and restaurants	Paving
Real estate	Stocks and bonds
Tobacco	Vacation resorts
Vending machines	Warehousing

Organized crime has sought involvement in legitimate businesses for several reasons. First, there is the obvious economic incentive: Legitimate businesses can and do make profits, and they supply added sources of income to organized crime's treasury. Second, legitimate businesses can provide a front for illegal activities. Third, legitimate businesses can serve as an important outlet for monies earned through criminal activities. Fourth, organized crime groups have sought holdings in legitimate enterprises to gain respectability. Crime is not respectable work, and the profits from it are dirty money.

However, there is another side to organized crime's involvement in legitimate businesses: the seemingly legitimate daisy chain companies created for the express purpose of bilking legitimate companies. These companies set out to steal corporate assets (involving products or services) and then disappear. This category of white collar crime poses a real threat to your company assets.

■ WHAT DOES WHITE COLLAR CRIME COST YOUR COMPANY?

The exact aggregate cost of white collar crime remains elusive because statistics available show only *known figures*. However, known costs of this crime technique and category (including fraud, embezzlement, swindles, computer crimes, employee theft, and other recurring problems in corporations) exceed a staggering $200 billion annually. Many analysts estimate that at least twice that amount would be accurate. Even the lower figure is three times the cost of organized crime's illegal activities, and ten times the losses sustained from traditional crimes such as theft, burglary, auto theft, forgery, and robbery.

■ FIVE REASONS WHY YOUR COMPANY OFTEN CANNOT DETECT WHITE COLLAR CRIME

Corporations spend hundreds of millions of dollars each year in accounting and auditing programs, but white collar crime prospers and continues to grow (see Chapter 5). Accountants and auditors rarely detect white collar crime for several reasons:

1. *Consistency*: Accountants and auditors look for consistency in the accounting process governed by the Generally Accepted Accounting Principles or Generally Accepted Accounting Standards. These rules are established by the American Institute of Certified Public Accountants and govern what procedures must be present in the recordkeeping and accounting process.

2. *Random samples*: Auditors normally work from random or decided samples instead of reviewing all the books and records. There are two good reasons for that procedure: time and money. A 100 percent audit of a large corporation would take a small army of auditors months or years to complete. Auditors also look for the Generally Accepted Accounting Principles in records they're auditing.

3. *Nonspecific instructions*: The responsibility of accountants and auditors is not specifically to look for criminal activity, although they might rarely stumble onto situations when the offender did not have sufficient concealment skill. They look for and ensure that proper and accurate records of company assets are maintained.

4. *Crime perceived as error*: When a problem appears, auditors most often perceive it as an accounting error instead of a crime.

5. *Company silence*: Employees participating in white collar crime activities perceive company silence or lack of corrective action as implied consent. Keep in mind that perpetrators look for reasons to rationalize their actions even when doing so is absurd in logical terms.

■ THREE TYPES OF WHITE COLLAR CRIMINALS OFTEN DETECTED

Generally, auditors and accountants detect only three types of white collar criminals:

1. *The greedy*: Company employees or others who become greedy and take large amounts of company assets in a short time. This happens when an employee has developed a life style exceeding his or her income and craves even more. The stealing becomes so rewarding, and if it goes undetected the

person begins to increase the amounts and until it finally becomes noticeable in the books and records.

2. *The desperate*: Company employees or others who perceive an immediate need so urgent that they believe it outweighs the risk involved. This offender often has severe financial needs stemming from gambling, drug abuse, creditors ready to sue or foreclose, loan sharks demanding payment, or other compelling reasons.

3. *The mindless*: Company employees who stumble through the motions and make clumsy attempts at the guile, deceit, and concealment elements of white collar crime activity. This person has little understanding of internal accounting procedures, acts impulsively, and hopes to get away with his or her offense.

Clearly, accounting and audits have a necessary role in the business process; however, it is also clear from the staggering and increasing loss totals suffered by corporations each year that neither has much effect in deterring white collar crime. The fault does not fall on accounting professionals, but instead there is a lack of clear company deterrents that deny the offender the opportunity to fulfill the offenses undetected.

■ HOW TO DETECT THE WHITE COLLAR CRIME IN YOUR COMPANY

An important part of preventing your company from becoming a victim of white collar crime involves detecting its presence. You can do that effectively with regular *investigative audits* (see Chapters 9 and 17). These audits differ from conventional concepts of internal or independent audits because you're looking beyond the proper entries, procedures, and accountability factors (see Chapter 5). Your audit *should not* look for *generally accepted accounting standards* but leave that to the accountants and auditors doing conventional audits. Instead, you're verifying authenticity of the records. Whether the columns of numbers add up, or procedures meet all the accounting standards, means nothing since deception and concealment are the mark of a skilled white collar crime offender and normally the perpetrators are good at their fraudulent activities. For example, when an employee files a travel expense reimbursement (see Chapter 2) claim for food, lodging, and customer entertainment, your concern should focus on the following:

1. Do the motels, restaurants, and other expenses supported by receipts really exist?

2. If they do, are the rates and expenses shown accurate or altered?

3. When you find flaws in these areas, you will know an error from a crime by establishing a pattern from other claims.

Your investigative audit also extends to vendors, suppliers, and other companies doing business with your company (see Chapter 12). You're looking for verification and authenticity of their ability to perform as they claim, either supplying products or services or paying for those they purchase from your company. You're interested in several aspects that I will outline later in this book in the appropriate chapters. (See Chapters 5, 9, 12, and 13.)

■ FIVE PREPARATORY STEPS TO AN INVESTIGATIVE AUDIT

Your investigative audit must have four standard elements, which are discussed in the next section. However, begin with research tailored to the specific function or category you're auditing. The research should follow these five steps.

Step 1: Make a needs assessment. When your company doesn't show losses, you still need to audit, looking for weaknesses in your business systems that supply an opportunity for white collar crime. When unexplained losses are known, establish a target priority for the areas where the biggest problems seem to originate.

Step 2: Create a problem definition. Before you continue, know exactly what the problem is. For example, if the losses show that the problem is within the travel section and expense accounts, exactly what is the problem? It could be significant employee fraud, or vague company policy and procedures that employees take advantage of regularly. For instance, when your company policy does not set standards for expenses, employees might stay in expensive hotels instead of comfortable, moderately priced motels. At first glance, it might appear that the employee has padded his or her expense account; however, later you might find that he or she just took advantage of poor company standards and guidance.

Step 3: Conduct primary research. In this step you're nearing the start of an investigative audit; however, you should research all current information such as company policies and procedures, applicable state statutes defining what laws will pertain if any, how the management wants to proceed, and other aspects.

Step 4: Conduct secondary research. You need to take advantage of all available information that embraces the subject you're about to audit. That information might be old files and memos about the same problem, conventional audits, and other notes. Even when conventional audits gave a function a clean bill of health and you suspect fraud is happening but is concealed to fool the auditors, such information might save you time and prove helpful during your investigative audit.

Step 5: Analyze all research. You need to review all your research and determine anything else that might be available. You might already have a good idea of what to look for in your investigative audit from this analysis.

■ FOUR STANDARD PROCEDURES FOR CONDUCTING AN INVESTIGATIVE AUDIT

With your preparatory research steps completed, you're ready to begin the audit. The following standard procedures will guide you through your investigative audit effectively and efficiently.

Procedure 1. Maintain a clear objective. You must maintain a clear objective, including identifying criminal acts and crime-conducive conditions, and identifying persons suspected of engaging in white collar crime activities.

When you conduct your investigative audit, you might find no evidence of criminal activity, but conditions that clearly create an opportunity for criminal activity. That's important in your prevention program because you can formulate new policies and procedures to eliminate that condition. Your audit also must have an objective of identifying employees or persons suspected of engaging in white collar crime activities. That identification supports your next step of conducting a formal criminal investigation, with procedures for collecting and documenting evidence for use in problem management decisions. For example, your management decision (based on the investigative conclusion and founded on evidence collected) supplies justification needed for employee reprimand, termination, prosecution, or civil actions.

Procedure 2. Determine the scope of your investigative audit. Just as conventional accountants and auditors cannot cover all the books and records, neither can your investigative audits. You should create a reasonable scope, normally beginning at the latest date and working back to a predetermined point. For example, if your investigative audit begins today, you might want to go through records from today back to a point six months or a year earlier. Generally, your best interest is with recent happenings or conditions as opposed to those occurring a year or more in the past.

Procedure 3. Plan your investigation audit carefully. This will ensure that you don't waste time with information or documents that cannot serve your objective. You need to plan your investigative audit efforts. One of the greatest problems most people have with investigation of white collar crime stems from trying to encompass the big picture. The white collar offender counts on that confusion in concealing his or her activities. You must keep your objectives clear and move through the investigation looking for violations, not the big picture.

Procedure 4. Create a detailed checklist. Well-planned checklists offer advantages in an investigative audit (see Chapters 16 and 17). First, as you develop your audit plan, you can begin creating a checklist that ensures that you will not overlook some important aspect. Second, the checklist will serve you when analyzing your findings. Third, the checklist will help you conduct the next audit or aid another person later. Fourth, your checklist creates a type of control outline so your audit can proceed systematically in the order it should.

THE FUNCTION OF AN INVESTIGATION

When your investigative audit shows the presence of white collar crime activities, you need to manage the situation in the best interests of the company (see Chapter 16). Just as your investigative audit serves you as a detection device, your criminal investigation narrows attention to any employees that the audit suggests have engaged in fraud, theft, or some other form of white collar crime that victimized the company. Now you need to proceed with a different approach—the criminal investigation.

WHY CONDUCT A CRIMINAL INVESTIGATION?

Your criminal investigation creates several advantages and benefits for both the company and the suspected perpetrator (see Chapter 16). It also places your company in control while eliminating the probability of creating liability with hasty countermeasures or actions not supported by evidence. Your investigation also confirms or disproves the suspicion of a dishonest employee. For example, your investigative audit might disclose the presence of criminal activity and point clearly to the actions of one employee. However, after converting to a criminal investigation, you find that another employee, trying to discredit another for whatever reason, created a situation that made you believe that another employee was stealing or committing some other white collar crime. When you act without an investigation, an innocent employee loses his or her job or is defamed in some way and your company winds up in court without a defensible position. The result can include a devastating loss of both money and company reputation. A thorough criminal investigation that seeks the elements of the crime and supports each with documented proof eliminates that problem and normally will expose the real culprit. However, when you detect and investigate the crime and insufficient evidence prevents any further action against the employee, at least you have a sound basis for developing effective countermeasures to stop the activity and prevent its recurrence.

■ USING YOUR AUDITS AND INVESTIGATIONS TO MAKE MANAGEMENT DECISIONS

Your company policy goal concerning white collar crime should be to prevent it. The only good way to tailor effective countermeasures stems from your investigative activities. They should always become part of your management decision process (such as terminating the employee, filing criminal charges, or pursuing a civil lawsuit remedy). Whatever the intended outcome, your investigation must include important elements that ensure accuracy and reliability for your management decisions.

■ FIVE KEY PRECAUTIONS FOR YOUR CRIMINAL INVESTIGATION

A definition of contemporary white collar crime largely remains elusive in the business world, and confusion persists about how to manage investigations. Each criminal investigation will have specific differences, and I discuss those in each chapter. However, there are five key elements of investigation that must always establish the foundation of an inquiry.

1. *Your investigation must remain specific in intent and limited in objective.* It should always stem from an allegation of a credible person, or from information developed from your investigative audit, conventional audits, or other source. This information or allegation may identify an employee or other person as either probably or possibly responsible for the white collar crime. The object of your criminal investigation is to establish whether a crime has happened, to determine the identity of the person responsible for the crime, and to collect evidence that can stand the test of prosecution even when there's no management intent on prosecuting the employee.

2. *Tailor your investigation to the specific white collar crime. Each white collar crime has its own characteristics.* For example, stealing assets, filing fraudulent expense claims, and altering documents to conceal diverted company prop-

erty have their own complexities. To investigate them properly, you need to tailor the investigative process to that problem.

3. *Properly collect and handle relevant, documented evidence.* The success of your criminal investigation relies upon collecting supporting evidence (normally documents that support your findings). The evidence should always be handled in ways that would serve your case in court or justify terminating an employee without fear of creating liabilities for the company. Each category of white collar crime has its specific rules of evidence collection and handling, and I discuss them in the appropriate chapters of this book.

4. *Establish the essential elements of proof.* When your investigation has collected all available information and evidence, you need to determine if a crime was committed in a legal sense. This is accomplished with a set of legal rules, normally determined by statutes of each state or sometimes by federal laws. When you cannot support these elements, in a legal sense the crime did not happen. Although you know something happened, it might instead fall within the parameters of company policy or may be concealed sufficiently that you cannot determine the elements. For example, when a shipping clerk diverts outgoing packages to a friend, relative, or conspirator, you will have to prove that this happened as well as that the clerk *intended* to commit a crime of theft. When you investigate and cannot prove that he or she did this (beyond information supplied by another employee who witnessed the acts or complaints from the customer who should have received the product), your case will not support action against the employee. You can transfer all you learned into a strong preventive policy and procedure; however, concealment prevented you from collecting and proving the essential elements of proof necessary to establish that a criminal offense happened.

5. *Strive to prove the crime despite your goal.* When your investigation doesn't prove the crime in a legal sense, there should be no other action beyond a new policy and preventive control measures. Often, a company will fire an employee based on information that doesn't prove dishonesty, but only hints at it. When that happens, especially in white collar crime cases, your company has opened itself for a lawsuit that probably will cost much more than the crime. Don't assume; make the evidence establish each element of proof in a legal sense. When it doesn't, you cannot reach a conclusion beyond corrective action to prevent recurrence.

Exhibit 1-1 provides an important white collar crime investigative audit or criminal investigation checklist that always has applicable uses. This checklist also is helpful during creation of stronger policies, procedures, and preventive countermeasures. Although each question might not apply to every given situation, the list creates a systematic test of your investigative activities and will keep you from overlooking some important item.

Exhibit 1-1
White Collar Crime Investigations Checklist

1. *WHO* questions:
   - ☐ Who discovered the crime?
   - ☐ Who reported the crime?
   - ☐ Who saw or heard anything of importance?
   - ☐ Who had a motive for committing the crime?
   - ☐ Who committed the crime?
   - ☐ Who helped the perpetrator?
   - ☐ With whom did the suspect associate?
   - ☐ With whom is the witnesses associated?

2. *WHAT* questions:
   - ☐ What happened?
   - ☐ What crime was committed?
   - ☐ What are the elements of the crime?
   - ☐ What were the actions of the suspect?
   - ☐ What do the witnesses know?
   - ☐ What evidence is available?
   - ☐ What happened to the evidence?
   - ☐ What deception was employed in the crime?
   - ☐ What concealment was used in the crime?
   - ☐ What knowledge, skill, or strength was necessary to commit the crime?
   - ☐ What was the motive?
   - ☐ What was the modus operandi?

3. *WHERE* questions:
   - ☐ Where was the crime discovered?
   - ☐ Where was the crime committed?
   - ☐ Where were the witnesses during the crime?
   - ☐ Where does the suspect live?
   - ☐ Where is the suspect now?
   - ☐ Where is the suspect likely to go?

4. *WHEN* questions:
   - ☐ When was the crime committed?
   - ☐ When was the crime discovered?

5. *HOW* questions:
   - ☐ How was the crime committed?
   - ☐ How did the suspect get access that enabled him or her to commit the crime?
   - ☐ How was the crime discovered?
   - ☐ How much is the company loss?
   - ☐ How much company property was stolen?
   - ☐ How much skill and knowledge were necessary to commit the crime?

6. *WHY* questions:
   - ☐ Why was the crime committed?
   - ☐ Why was the particular method employed?
   - ☐ Why are the witnesses reluctant to talk?
   - ☐ Why was the crime reported?

■ QUICK REFERENCE GUIDE AND REVIEW

- *White collar crime* describes a technique of committing statutory crime.
- White collar crime offenders apply basic and specialized techniques to fulfill their acts.
- White collar crime takes many forms and victims. This book focuses on the corporate and business world as the victim.
- In the years since Sutherland first categorized white collar crime, the perpetrator of the white collar crime problem has evolved dramatically, from the stereotyped privileged few in the executive suite to most average corporate employees.
- The computer, followed by a rush of innovative business technology, triggered a new era in corporate employees' ability and opportunity to commit white collar crimes.

- The misconception of what white collar crime means to the business world, as well as the act of lending a helping hand to offenders by ignoring the problem or establishing acceptable levels of loss, continues to fuel the offender's motivation to steal.
- Seemingly honest, upstanding people commit white collar crime largely because most of them do not perceive it to be a crime or rationalize it as an acceptable action without a real victim.
- Across the board, white collar crime costs corporations billions of dollars each year.
- Detecting the presence of white collar crime in your company begins with investigative audits.
- Use detected white collar crime during audits as your basis for initiating criminal investigations.
- Use investigative findings and conclusions for sound management decisions and preventive actions.

■ IN SUMMARY

In the following chapters, I show you an eyes-open approach to your problems of white collar crime. I present a variety of tested, business-oriented solutions to prevent your company from being victimized from within and outside.

The real questions you need to settle are whether your company (1) wants to bear the cost of subsidizing white collar crime by treating it with kid gloves, or (2) wants to invest in a gloves-off strategy that, although not without cost, promises to earn a higher return over the long run.

The first approach tolerates white collar crime, and the second strategy leads to the development of aggressive policies and procedures that (1) expect and combat white collar crime within your company; (2) weed out, through positive action, problems common to your company; and (3) act to eliminate the opportunities. In the following chapters, I will show you how to accomplish these three goals, starting today.

Chapter Two
How to Control Expense Account and Travel Fraud

Expense account and travel expense reimbursement fraud, especially for corporate employees who travel extensively, are one of the oldest and most common corporate and industrial white collar crimes. This category of white collar crime regularly supplies corporate and industrial employees with a secret and significant tax-free second income. Ironically, this technique of white collar crime has become so tolerated in the business world that it normally goes unnoticed, especially when practiced by old hands who are skilled in the art of reimbursement fraud. So common is this fraud that companies regularly do not think of it as a crime, but only an infringement on company policy.

Normally, those suspected of padding their expense accounts will be cautioned about their extravagance; but there will be no mention of suspicion of fraudulent behavior, although both parties know that's what is happening. When cautioned about their excessive expenses, employees discontinue their fraudulent activities for a while, and then gradually increase their reimbursement claims again. Employees participating in expense account fraud tend to rationalize their fraudulent activities (theft) as deserved extra benefits compensating for their travel, which keeps them away from home and forces them to live out of a suitcase. Most employees also view the company's apathy as authorization, as unofficially telling the employee, "A little theft is okay, but just don't go overboard."

This type of fraud unnecessarily drains billions from corporations each year, and most executives discreetly worry about it. However, typically corporate executives and financial managers will quickly defend their inaction to prevent this type of fraud, proclaiming that there is no effective way to control it.

■ CREATING THE OPPORTUNITY FOR EXPENSE ACCOUNT FRAUD

Corporations often have a vague business-related expense reimbursement policy, and sometimes none beyond some written procedures in an employee handbook. The problem largely stems from the key word *reimbursement*. Unfortunately, when referring to travel expenses, *reimbursement* becomes synonymous with *fraud*. The concept of travel expense reimbursement relinquishes company controls to an employee. It supplies a golden opportunity to commit fraud. Most companies design their travel expense reimbursement policies to meet audit and tax law requirements and not to encourage expense control.

For example, a large, well-known corporation (I'll refer to it as the ABC Corporation) concerned about excessive expenses and unexplained losses asked me to review its controls and make recommendations for improving protection of its assets. After talking with the CEO and other executives, I knew the company was in serious trouble (always true when a company calls in a consultant).

One of the first areas I reviewed involved the company's policies across the board. Often, policies, employee handbooks, and other procedures in a company create hidden agendas for employee white collar crime. I knew the company had many traveling representatives nationwide, with marketing groups operating from corporate headquarters and several satellite offices across the country. After reading company policies, reviewing other procedures dealing with expense accounts, and researching the company's travel costs for the previous year, I decided that the company's policies would supply a good starting point.

I will use that review as well as my recommendations about how to control travel expenses effectively as an example in this chapter. The problems I found in that company were the same or similar to problems I have encountered during assignments over the years for other corporations. My recommendations or solutions proved successful at that company: Expense account costs diminished, and control of the situation returned in the company. Exhibit 2-1 shows an example of that company's policy.

Exhibit 2-1
ABC, Incorporated Travel and Expense Reimbursement Policy

"An employee of ABC, Incorporated required to use his or her automobile for business will be reimbursed at the rate set by the Internal Revenue Service each year for per-mile deductions, provided the employee submits vouchers showing the date(s), miles traveled, and business purpose(s) of each trip.

"Employees authorized by virtue of their positions to entertain nonemployees with meals (customer and liaison entertainment) will be reimbursed for reasonable expenses, if the meal is business related, the employee is present, and the employee submits vouchers showing the date(s), miles traveled, and business purpose(s) of each meal. When the expense totals $25.00 or more, the employee must submit a charge card or restaurant receipt. Similar rules apply to travel and to employee meals and entertaining while traveling.

"Business-related travel expenses will be at the current company per diem rates for lodging, meals, and necessary expenses, or actual expense reimbursement based on receipts from the business establishment (for example, hotels and motels, restaurants, taxis, rental car agencies, and other transportation necessary to accomplish the business purpose). Employees must use ABC, Incorporated Form 39E to document and submit expense reimbursement claims as thought necessary by the employee."

■ HOW A REIMBURSEMENT POLICY CAN CREATE OPPORTUNITIES FOR FRAUD

The company policy shown in Exhibit 2-1 appears as I found it at the ABC Corporation. I will show you the key problems with it, and later in this chapter I will show you the solutions I designed to end these problems. Exhibit 2-2 shows the revised policy designed to reduce opportunities for fraudulent claims and return control of expense accounts to the company.

Although I chose several employees' authorized expense accounts for my investigative audit at ABC, Incorporated, I will portray them collectively as a sales staff employee named John. John travels extensively, leaving ABC corporate headquarters at Any City about noon each Monday after the weekly sales staff meeting, and travels to meet clients and take orders on one of four routine routes. He also works hard to develop additional clients for the company and enjoys success on the job, so he is highly regarded at corporate headquarters. Normally, John arrives back in Any City after office hours and goes directly home. While traveling, John transmits orders and other information back to corporate headquarters with a portable fax machine supplied by the company. On Monday mornings John submits his claims for expense reimbursement for the previous week's mileage, travel expenses (such as lodging, meals, and customer entertainment), and other items authorized by ABC Corporation's policy.

When John started with ABC, Incorporated three years ago, he strove to do everything right and make a good impression. His reimbursed expenses were accurate, and John worked hard to create a solid customer/client base for the company—with significant success. A year after beginning work for ABC, John married. Today he and his wife have two children, a new, well-appointed house in the suburbs, and a new second car for John's wife. John replaces his economy traveling car with a new one each year. Although ABC, Incorporated management has repeatedly offered him promotions to a supervisory desk job in the company, John has declined, citing that he feels the place for him is in the field dealing with people. His record-breaking sales efforts and favorable client response give him the leverage to decline promotion yet stay popular with upper management. Management views John as the ultimate company man.

Why he repeatedly declined the promotion had nothing to do with devotion to the company, however. During my study at ABC, I found his dedication to and interest in traveling had to do with fraud, which supplied him with income beyond what any promotion could offer. As we analyze the ABC, Incorporated policy, you will see why.

◼ ANALYSIS OF EXHIBIT 2-1

Automobile Mileage Reimbursement

(1) The first paragraph of the ABC Incorporated policy discusses employee privately owned automobile mileage reimbursement at the current IRS per-mile deduction rate. Many companies today have moved away from the traditional "company car" concept because the expense and abuse of privilege problems outweigh the advantages. Many government agencies, especially at state levels and local levels, have also followed that course. The ABC corporation moved to use of privately owned automobiles a few years ago instead of traditional company cars furnished to marketing and sales personnel. Although the total expense and problems decreased after that change for a couple of years, they then began to climb and exceeded the cost of the

company car concept. Later in this chapter, I will address the company car concept and problems companies have experienced with this concept, and supply you with effective solutions to curb employee fraud.

(2) In the policy statement in Exhibit 2-1, the employee must show the total number of miles traveled and business purpose of the travel. The ABC corporation reimbursed employees using their privately owned automobiles for company business at 26 cents per mile. Mileage reimbursement proved a lucrative added income for John even at 26 cents per mile (plus parking fees and tolls). On the surface, it might appear that the ABC corporation had a good deal with this arrangement, especially since it has a huge sales staff across the country. The employees using privately owned vehicles to conduct company business did not receive any further compensation beyond mileage for maintenance, insurance, or repairs.

(3) A review of John's mileage reports when he began his job showed that they were about one third of those filed just before my review. To verify John's figures, we dispatched a company nonsales staffer (I will call her Carol) with a rental car to travel a route given to her. We did not tell Carol the real reason for her assignment, to ensure impartial research and avoid either sympathetic or prejudiced views. She followed John's route exactly, including a momentary stop at each address supplied to her. The addresses were near the clients John called on, with many represented in his travel claims and sales records. We also instructed Carol to stay at the same motels and eat at the same restaurants as John claimed he did on a specific week.

John's mileage reports for several months showed that he claimed about 700 miles each week, although he was attentive to make the amounts varied each week (such as 889 or 723). Based on the research Carol supplied, following information exactly as taken from John's expense reimbursement claims, John should have reported about 420 miles per week. Instead of putting in a claim for the 420 miles and receiving a mileage reimbursement of $109.20, John claimed about 700 miles consistently, give or take a few miles, and claimed about $182.00 a week, enabling a profit of $72.80 a week ($291.20 a month—nearly $3,500 each year) from fraudulent mileage reimbursement claims.

(4) For the economical car John drove, we figured his fuel consumption at 20 miles per gallon average. Working from the actual mileage determined from our research done by Carol, about 420 miles per week, John should have used about 1,310 gallons of gas in a year, at $1.20 per gallon, costing $1,572 a year. But John claimed and collected $3,500—a fraudulent profit of approximately $1,928.

(5) John also benefited from the tolls and parking fees clause of the ABC corporate policy. His claim vouchers regularly showed about $50 each week spent for tolls and parking. Our controlled test with employee Carol, how-

ever, showed a maximum of $15 in tolls and parking (most of that unavoidable). Based on Carol's test figures, John added another fraudulent $140 a month ($1,680 each year) from tolls and parking fee reimbursement.

Before moving on to John's other activities, the total fraud stemming from a vague company policy and lack of preventive controls supplied John with the opportunity to make $5,180 a year by padding his mileage, parking, and toll fees. That is just a beginning for John's skillful manipulation of ABC, Incorporated.

Solutions for Controlling Mileage Reimbursement Fraud

When a corporation calls for employees to use their privately owned automobiles to conduct company business, its control over employees and their activities becomes limited.

The odometer mileage shown on a claim form, even when called for, cannot be relied on because the automobile does not belong to the company; nor does the company share liability or responsibility for the car. The owner can use the car as wanted even when on a business trip, although he or she is not authorized to claim the mileage for personal activities. Creating a policy that includes having a company representative check the mileage on a privately owned automobile will probably engender a legal minefield.

The solution we implemented at ABC, Incorporated avoided legal problems, restored company control, and supplied a morale-boosting bonus for honest employees. The new system also enabled a subtle but effective checkpoint for accountants processing the privately owned automobile mileage reimbursement claims.

ABC, Incorporated obtained corporate gasoline credit cards from each of the oil companies common in its sales areas. On the effective date of its new policy, which coincided with the Monday sales meetings, each employee traveling in a privately owned automobile across the country signed for an assortment of gasoline credit cards issued to ABC, Incorporated. The company announced that from that date onward, for all gasoline put in privately owned automobiles used for company business, the owner must use a company credit card. The company also agreed with this policy change to continue paying 26 cents a mile to owners; however, it would also pay for the fuel used during business-related mileage.

Those who inflated mileage could no longer do so unless they could find a way to use an equivalent amount of fuel. With the company agreeing to pay for business-related gasoline, and the credit card hard copies coming to the company and including the employee's vehicle license number, opportunities to cheat on mileage ended. Employees also had to submit their customer receipt from the company credit cards each week. Some cheating could continue, such as taking a five-gallon can along on a trip and filling it a gallon at a time for the lawnmower at home. However, detection of any excessive charges on the credit cards would easily occur, and the employees could envision that.

Each employee receiving the packet of company-issued gasoline credit cards also received a complete briefing on authorized use and signed a statement of understanding that outlined the new company policy on expense accounts. The employee agreed in the statement for a deduction from expense claims or salary of any charge on the credit cards other than gasoline to be used while on verifiable company business. Employees also agreed in the statement that nonbusiness or nonemergency uses of the credit card more than once would result in disciplinary action, including a possibility of termination of employment.

The company took control of the situation, at a cost, but it also realized an important saving over the flood of fraudulent mileage claims. An added control measure including required receipts for parking and toll fees (excluding parking meters) that called for a note on the back, initiated by the claimant, showing the business relationship of the fee. For example, the employee would note: "En route to call on Johnson Industries," or "calling on Acme Supply, Inc." for a parking fee. These claims (as the employee would know) would be compared to orders or other data to detect fraud, and the risk was not worth the benefit. The company reduced opportunities for fraud and regained better control of operating expenses.

Client Entertainment Expenses

The second paragraph of the ABC corporation's lenient expense reimbursement policy shown in Exhibit 2-1 opens a large door for employee reimbursement fraud using customer or liaison entertainment as a tool. Our employee John also made significant added income from this source. My research showed the following disclosures:

John's expense reimbursement claims showed frequent lunches and dinners with customers and clients he called on regularly. Since the company encouraged customer entertainment, especially to regular customers or those businesspersons sought as customers, no one doubted (or checked to verify) the authenticity of John's claims. What also placed John beyond suspicion was that he used his own credit cards to record each entertainment event. He submitted the customer receipt copy of his credit card with his reimbursement claims, properly noting the customer's name on the back and the relationship to business. Since the company did not receive the hard copy of John's personal credit card purchase, no further verification was possible other than calling the client, and that in itself would not be a wise business activity.

Our field research in this area, conducted during the mileage tracking exercise by employee Carol, tipped us that John was also padding the expense account in this area. Carol had instructions while on her mileage research trips to eat at the same restaurants as noted on John's expense claims. We found on her return that two of the restaurants had gone out of business at least a year earlier than John claimed he had dinner there with a client.

A few phone calls revealed that both restaurants sold their fixtures by auction when they went out of business. I found one auctioneer in the firm that handled the auction who remembered seeing a couple of credit card imprint machines in a box of assorted junk sold at the restaurant during the auction. Later, from records supplied by the auctioneer, we found that John had bought the imprint machines, presumably still containing the imprint plates formerly used at the restaurant.

Depending on the area his travel took him to, John could create phony credit card receipts from a restaurant no longer existing, and his receipts showed customer entertainment dinners with clients. He easily obtained the blank credit card forms, imprinted them with the machine, and filled in the blanks to appear genuine. He occasionally submitted a numbered restaurant waiter order card from that restaurant, showing that he paid cash for a customer entertainment dinner. We learned later that he found the dinner order forms in the same box of junk he purchased at the auction. Examining a variety of credit card and cash receipts from other restaurants, and then verifying them by telephone, disclosed that they were also out of business. John had found a person who would duplicate the imprint plate for any business and John would slip in the plate needed at that time. Without question, on these occasions, John probably had a hamburger at a fast food place or a cheap dinner alone. However, the following Monday he claimed reimbursement for a $70 dinner with a customer, at a pricy restaurant 150 miles from corporate headquarters that did not exist. John was clever enough to show that he had entertained a customer who placed a large order that day.

I am sure you noted that ABC corporation's policy made it clear that customer entertainment of $25 or less does not call for any receipts, only a reimbursement claim. That policy created more opportunity for John's fraud and increased his bank account. According to John's expense claims, he had many customer entertainment business lunches that averaged about $20 to $24. With information building, the company sent John to some obscure convention to represent the corporation for a week and invited his wife and children to accompany him, all expenses paid.

During that week, we sent employee Carol to make courtesy calls on a few of John's customers whom he claimed to entertain with a lunch or dinner. On Carol's return, we discovered that John's customers perceived him as a tightwad. That information came easy when Carol genuinely took several customers to lunch and a few to dinner during her whirlwind trip (later, from a criminal investigation, we learned that John took few customers to lunch or dinner, although he claimed many on his expense claims). From that information, and from an attentive review of reimbursement claims, we estimated that John averaged about $100 most weeks from his phony dinners, about $50 a week from his phony lunches, for a yearly total of about $7,500.

Solutions for controlling client entertainment fraud

After identifying the problems created by John and scores of others carrying on similar fraudulent activities, the ABC corporation acted on my advice and created a new policy for customer entertainment.

The new policy, announced the same day as the gasoline card policy noted earlier, involved issuing each authorized employee another corporate credit card for use in customer entertainment (and another purpose discussed later). The employee signed for it by card number and signed a statement affirming that he or she understood company policy on its use. Each employee received a copy of the agreement and a policy handbook.

This credit card was the only authorized way of paying for customer entertainment either at lunches or dinners. Employees learned that the company would not honor a reimbursement claim using cash or personal credit card receipts. The employee-user would continue to submit the customer copy each week from the company credit card showing the name of the customer. That receipt, later matched with the hard copy from the billing statement, authenticated the purchase. A further step included a courtesy letter sent to customers shown on the receipts. It simply said, "Our representative, John, informs us that you and he recently enjoyed a dinner [or lunch] with our compliments at the Snowbird Restaurant, Any City. We value and appreciate your business and always appreciate any suggestions for how we can serve your company better. We are pleased to have the opportunity to show our gratitude."

Should the employee discover a technique of faking the receipt and dinner (for example, taking someone else to dinner who was not a customer) this courtesy letter might well draw a response from the real customer receiving it. Most people like to get something for nothing, and when they believe a company says they paid for a free meal and didn't, the company will often hear of it. Each employee involved in customer entertainment for the ABC company heard about the letters going to their clients. The stated official purpose of the letter did not imply that the company was checking the genuineness of receipts, and instead identified the letter as a new market-ing and commercial relations tool. However, the employee with fraud in mind would know he or she could not go undiscovered with the new credit card policy. The credit and courtesy cards eliminated reimbursement because the employee no longer paid for the lunches or dinners, and the opportunity for fraud ended.

"Actual Expense" Reimbursement Fraud

The third paragraph of the former reimbursable expenses policy at ABC Incorporated also created a gold mine for John and many others. The com-pany offered a standard per diem rate that sufficed twenty years earlier. Instead of increasing the per diem rates, ABC added a clause that authorized and reimbursed for actual expenses. When employees chose to use the actual expense option (and most would do that), they had to submit cash or credit card receipts. Like most reimbursement concepts, the door opened for many to commit white collar crimes of fraud at significant levels.

John (and others) had this opportunity for fraud figured out, too. John could stay in a cheap motel and put in a claim the following Monday for actual expenses at one of the better places to stay, forging a cash receipt and including a forged hotel billing statement. He also added profit after his travel week. Instead of staying out Thursday nights, John would complete his contact list early and drive home, arriving late Thursday night. With his car tucked safely out of sight in the garage, he would fax in orders taken Thursday and dated Friday, giving the appearance that he was somewhere in his sales territory. To avoid someone from the office calling clients looking for him, he would make a couple of calls to the office and inform them of where he was if his boss might want to contact him. However, he would always add that he would be on the road and would call in later. This episode of fraud netted an extra $65 for the bogus Thursday night room, often accompanied by another $50 charge at the motel dining room for a business dinner with a client. His faxed order from home from the same client proved his reasons for the extra expense. That was no problem for John; he would get a blank billing statement from a few motels using some pretext, or he would stay there once and photocopy the legitimate statement. With a personal computer and a dot matrix printer, John easily created a passable forged billing to accompany the fraudulent cash receipt.

Solutions for Controlling Lodging and Travel Fraud

Instead of reimbursing or paying per diem rates, the ABC company adopted my recommendation to allow the use of the same customer entertainment credit card for lodging and meals on an actual expense basis. Certain restrictions applied and were written into the new policy and on the statement of understanding that the employee signed. The company created realistic guidelines regarding amounts authorized for a room and meals by researching rates and prices by telephone at various motels, hotels, and restaurants in the sales areas. Before exceeding the guidelines, the employee must have specific authorization from his or her supervisor. If the extra cost was found to have been unnecessary, the employee agreement cautioned that deduction from salary or commissions could happen. Also, employees learned that repeated problems might lead to termination of employment.

John and others, when confronted with documented proof of their activities, decided to take the option of resigning from the ABC corporation instead of submitting themselves to the risk of prosecution. Some employees had done less cheating than John and were salvaged by reassignment to desk jobs in the company, without the benefit of expense accounts.

■ MODEL TRAVEL AND EXPENSE POLICY STATEMENT

Exhibit 2-2 shows an example of the new company expense account policies integrating the measures and techniques noted in the preceding discussion.

Exhibit 2-2
Revised ABC, Incorporated Travel and Expense Policy

An employee of ABC, Incorporated required to travel and conduct corporate business will follow the procedures outlined in this policy.

Privately Owned Automobiles or Motor Vehicles

A variety of gasoline credit cards with billing direct to the ABC corporation are issued to employees required to travel using their privately owned automobiles or motor vehicles to conduct corporate business. The ABC corporation will be solely responsible for payment of authorized charges on these cards, and employees so authorized will have no liability for the payment. These employees must use the corporate credit cards to purchase all gasoline needed during the time they conduct official company business. No reimbursement is authorized for purchases made with personal credit cards or cash. The corporate credit cards are not authorized for use by employees when not on official company business. The following procedure will apply:

1. The employee is authorized to fill their privately owned motor vehicle with fuel before departing on company business Mondays and upon return Fridays. The dates of use for these cards coupled with reported mileage will be subject to audit.

2. Under emergency or unforeseen circumstances, exceptions to this policy will be granted only with written or verbal approval of the employee's department manager. Before filing the weekly expense report claiming reimbursement under this exception, a letter signed by the employee's manager will accompany any claim within this provision.

3. Each Monday morning or the next business day when Monday falls on a holiday, authorized employees will file expense reports and reimbursement claims for the preceding week when applicable using ABC Form 100-E. They will attach all receipts from the corporate credit cards to the report. Exceptions will be granted only upon verbal permission of the employee's department manager followed by a signed memorandum to the Company Travel Department manager.

4. Mileage reimbursement will remain in effect and be reviewed annually to ensure that the amount coincides with the maximum allowable deduction amount by the Internal Revenue Service.

Lodging and Meals and Client Entertainment Allowances

Certain employees of ABC, Incorporated will be issued a corporate credit card for use in payment for lodging and meals during authorized travel. Use of employee credit cards and cash will not be authorized and not allowed reimbursement. Special arrangements made by the ABC corporation with hospitality services in the cities and areas served by the ABC corporation and attached to this policy will be the only authorized lodging and meals locations (including customer entertainment, unless otherwise stated or authorized by the employee's department manager). Any authorized exception to this policy by a department manager may be verbal to the employee, with a written and signed memorandum about the exception forwarded to the Corporate Travel Department manager, supplying the reasons and purpose. A list of authorized lodging and restaurants for using the corporate credit card is attached to this policy and will be updated and furnished to traveling employees as necessary.

Further guidance regarding meal cost limitations is attached to this policy and will be updated annually or before as necessary and furnished to traveling employees. The following procedures apply for reporting these expenses:

Applicable employees must file a report of corporate credit card usage to the Corporate Travel Department of ABC, Incorporated each Monday morning for travel and expenses of the preceding week. An exception will be when Monday falls on a holiday, with the report due on the next business day after that day.

Employee lodging, meals, and customer entertainment expenses will be filed on ABC, Incorporated Form 101-E. When an employee begins vacation or for other valid reason will not be available on Monday morning or the next business day after, he or she will file expense reports the preceding Friday or business day, or mail them to his or her department manager, who will send them to the Corporate Travel Department.

Client Entertainment Guidelines

1. Customer entertainment will be scheduled by the field representative or other authorized employees of the ABC corporation at least two weeks before and will be approved by the employee's department manager. A copy of the authorized, approved customer entertainment will be forwarded to the Corporate Travel Department for its files and audits. Exceptions are authorized only when the department manager gives verbal approval and submits a written, signed memorandum to the Corporate Travel Department citing the reason for a nonscheduled entertainment or substitution.

2. All customer entertainment costs will remain within the guidelines attached to this policy. These guidelines will be reviewed and updated annually or before when necessary.

3. Each Monday morning or the next business day when Monday falls on a holiday, authorized employees will file expense reports and reimbursement claims for the preceding week when applicable using ABC Form 100-E. Applicable employees will attach all receipts from the corporate credit cards to their report, to be compared with hard copies received by the Company upon billing. Exceptions will be granted only upon verbal permission of the employee's department manager followed by a signed memorandum to the Travel Accounting Department manager.

Air Travel and Related Expenses

Employees of the ABC corporation traveling by commercial aircraft will use the proper issued corporate credit card to purchase tickets. Unless otherwise approved verbally and in a signed memorandum to the Corporate Travel Department, employees authorized to travel by air will purchase only coach class tickets. Other procedures regarding this travel category follow.

1. When employees purchase tickets for authorized travel but their trip is unexpectedly postponed or cancelled, they will deliver the ticket to the Corporate Travel Department immediately through their department manager. When employees prepare to travel on company business by air, they must first contact the Corporate Travel Department if feasible to determine availability of turn-in tickets before purchasing a ticket.

2. Employees traveling on company business by commercial airlines will be authorized to use rental cars from authorized companies as noted in the list attached to this policy, and which is updated annually or as necessary. Employees traveling will be supplied with that list. Using rental cars from other agencies will not be authorized without approval of the employee's department manager verbally followed by a written and signed memorandum to the Company Corporate Travel Department. Unless otherwise approved, employees will only use a corporate credit card to pay for rental cars while traveling. Use of personal credit cards or cash for rental cars used for company business will not be reimbursed.

3. Authorized traveling employees on company business may use taxis for limited travel and will pay cash for that service. The amounts paid will be reimbursed by the Corporate Travel Department, but only when the expense claim includes an attached validated receipt. Extensive use of taxis is discouraged and subject to justification when such use is deemed unnecessary. Exceptions to this policy must have approval by the employee's department manager verbally, followed with a written and signed memorandum to the Corporate Travel Department.

4. Miscellaneous expenses related to business and approved by the employee's department manager will be reimbursed to the employee.

5. Each Monday morning or the next business day when Monday falls on a holiday, authorized employees will file expense reports and reimbursement claims for the preceding week when applicable using ABC Form 102-E. They will attach receipts from corporate credit cards to the report for comparison with hard copies received by the Company when billing arrives from the credit card issuer. Exceptions are granted only upon verbal permission of the employee's department manager followed by a signed memorandum to the Travel Accounting Department manager.

6. Employees not traveling regularly for the Company will be issued the necessary corporate credit cards and guidance before departure by the Corporate Travel Department.

■ EMPLOYEE WHITE COLLAR CRIME IN AIR TRAVEL

I once conducted a white collar crime prevention audit for a major corporation in New York. One of the management executives, proud of his efforts to control fraud, tried to convince me that the company's air travel controls were beyond fraud. He related that all airline tickets issued for crews of technicians sent regularly throughout the country went through the company's personnel travel office. Previously, the manager explained, employees had a prerogative of purchasing their own air travel tickets or having them issued by the personnel travel office. Because of the number of technical crews traveling and because their excuses that coach seats were not available at the time supplied an excuse to fly in first class seats instead of coach, the added cost became excessive as the practice increased. The cost, however, was only a part of the problem for the company. The employees would purchase the first class tickets with their own cash or credit cards, and then also buy a coach ticket for the travel. When they submitted their travel expense reimbursement claims, they included their receipt for the cost of "assignment essential" first class tickets in accordance with company policy at that time.

Using this technique of fraud, employees could accumulate several first class tickets and cash them in, pocketing the difference between the amount they paid for the coach class tickets and those in first class. The company also learned from a former employee that often the technicians would use this technique to trade the first class tickets for enough coach tickets and refunds in cash to take their family on a vacation. With the company's new system requiring issue of air travel tickets and no longer authorizing purchase of air travel tickets with personal funds, the company management believed its problem was solved. However, the problem was *not* solved; only the techniques had changed.

Within the provisions of the new company policy, the personnel travel section made arrangements with a local travel agency to get air travel tickets according to scheduling. The agency also made reservations well before travel and arranged for routing, so coach prices prevailed.

My prevention audit, which included the travel agency, showed that employees continued cashing in the issued tickets or changing them for other tickets issued in other names on other flights. Further research disclosed that on many destinations, the technical crews would receive air travel tickets from the company, through the contract travel agency, but not use them. Instead, they would drive to the location with four employees in each privately owned automobile, allowing nonstop travel to the destination. Dividing the cost of gasoline by four people made the trips inexpensive and enabled transportation fraud.

Related Ground Transportation Fraud

Local ground transportation supplies another form of reimbursable travel expense fraud. What the company authorizes dictates which common fraudulent technique the employee might use to make extra money.

Taxi Use Fraud

Corporations with employees traveling by air expect employees to spend money on taxis and other forms of ground transportation while on company business. Use of taxis allows the greatest opportunity for fraud in travel expense reimbursement. Most taxi drivers supply an informal receipt, normally just a slip of paper with the cab company identified by a rubber stamp. Rarely will a cab driver put the amount on the slip; instead when the rider asks for a receipt, he or she will receive a blank rubber-stamped slip. This enables a person to substitute whatever amount he or she desires.

The technical crews who drove personal cars to their assignment destination, instead of flying, used the cab receipts to add to their fraudulent travel reimbursement claims. For example, the employee knows the company expects taxi receipts unless it has authorized rental cars. In our example employees have saved their air travel tickets and driven a car to their assignment, and they can take a cab periodically while in town although they continue to rely on the personal car for transportation. Asking for receipts each time they take a local taxi, and receiving a variety of receipts from short trips, they acquire the blanks to fill out for amounts normally associated with airport-to-city fares. For example, should the cost of a taxi from the airport to the city be about $25, each of the employees can claim that cost separately for the arrival and return (a total of $200). Taxi fares for local trips can also enable fraud, because riders can ask for receipts and put their own amount of cab fare on the receipt. When the cab driver does show the amount, the employee can change the amount by adding a number. For example, $8.50 can easily convert to $18.50, supplying the employee with a profit of $10 from fraudulent techniques.

Even when the employee travels by air, he or she can use the same techniques discussed above. For example, the employee can take a bus from the airport to the city and submit a travel claim supported by a cab receipt showing use of a taxi as transportation from the airport to the city.

Rental Car Fraud

Companies allowing reimbursement for rental cars paid for by the employee also enable varied dollar amounts of fraud. The most common technique involves altering the carbon printed receipt supplied by the rental agency when returning the car. It's not always possible to do this, and it's difficult with the leading car rental agencies that use sophisticated computerized systems. However, other car rental firms operate on far less capital, and one way for them to save money is to use simple forms. These can be altered by using carbon paper and a dot matrix typewriter or, depending on the situation, changing the amount manually. This employee fraud, often only involving adding a few dollars, builds the collective amount gained through a variety of other activities.

■ SOLUTIONS FOR COMMERCIAL TRANSPORTATION FRAUD

Preventing opportunities for commercial air and ground transportation travel fraud by employees stems largely from establishing effective company controls.

Air Travel

You can control and eliminate employee air travel fraud in three positive ways:

1. *Control the tickets*: First, if you are using a direct or travel agency ticketing arrangement, have the tickets printed in your company name, not the name of the employee who will use them. If the airline needs the employee's name on the ticket, arrange for the agency to stamp the ticket with the word *nonnegotiable* to prevent employees from cashing them in or exchanging them for other tickets. This means that any transaction other than use by the employee must be approved by an authorized representative of the company travel section, on file with the airlines. You should arrange these safeguards with the contract travel agency or directly with the airlines you use. These safeguards are easy to implement and end the opportunity for employee fraud in this category of white collar crime.

2. *Control field purchases*: When your employees need freedom of movement while on the road (for example, they are sent to another assignment not scheduled before they left), then use the company credit card method noted earlier. The employee has specific authorization through a policy and statement of understanding signed by the employee when you issue the card to purchase airline tickets. The employee must turn in the customer copy of the used airline ticket or, if purchased and not used, turn in the entire ticket and the purchaser's receipt from the credit card. This is to ensure that the employee submits this information immediately after he or she returns from travel. You can easily track these purchases and detect any attempt at fraud because the company receives the hard copy of the purchase and other information that will match with the receipts and information filed by the employee.

3. *Create a specific company policy*: White collar crimes committed by employees normally stem from their company giving control or losing control of events. You have an obligation to inform employees exactly what to do in a given situation; this evolves from a clear, specific company policy about the matter coupled with a statement of understanding signed by the employee.

Ground Transportation

You can control and eliminate employee fraud in commercial ground transportation categories with three positive solutions:

1. *Use company-arranged rental cars*: Whenever possible, have the Personnel Travel Section prearrange rental cars and require traveling employees to use them. That process gives you control of employees' transportation.

2. *Use company credit cards or direct billing*: Using a company credit card removes the options for the employee to alter the billing statement.

3. *Use prearranged commercial transportation*: When your employees travel to the same locales regularly, arrange corporate accounts with specific taxi companies. In your arrangement, have the company bill you directly including the name of passenger, pickup and drop-off points, and amount of fare plus gratuity.

■ INVESTIGATIVE AUDITS FOR EXPENSE ACCOUNT FRAUD

Use of company credit cards will normally end your problem of expense fraud because it stops the reimbursement opportunity. However, I also know that many companies won't follow that course and continue as they always have, allowing employees to pay the expenses and claim reimbursement. To compensate for that probability, I am including an investigative section to help you combat the problem (see also Chapters 5 and 17). It's often shrugged off with the pretense that it does not matter much. However, we know otherwise. This category of white collar crime costs corporations billions a year and eats into profits like termites devouring a wooden structure. On the outside, the structure appears sound, until one day it comes crashing down. Expense account fraud alone might not have that devastating effect on your company, but when combined with a variety of other white collar crimes, it can bring down your company.

Expense account fraud also might rank among the toughest to detect, prove, and create viable solutions for unless you can present a solid case to management. The investigative audit helps you do that. Conventional audits look for excesses, wrong addition, lack of receipts, or not following procedures, and when everything is present and accurate they give the appearance of a clean bill of health. Your audit, however, should include that as a first step and then go beyond. A white collar fraud perpetrator will use skill in disguising and concealing his or her activities, and you can be certain that all the receipts and columns add up exactly right. Your job will include verifying the authenticity of the information and receipts. For example, you need to look at reimbursed mileage. Compare it with maps or other information to ensure that it is reasonable. Individuals traveling regularly can total many miles, and adding a few along the way can net them profits and make it hard to prove they padded the amount, unless they become greedy.

Verifying Reimbursable Mileage Claims

You should run a pattern of mileage on each person, going back in the records at least three years. You need to look for dramatic or gradual increases in the mileage that employees claimed. Normally, employees will take vacations. When they do, a temporary company representative will often service their territory. The key to detecting fraudulent mileage reimbursement claims revolves around patterns. For example, you need to

1. Check the mileage claimed by that temporary person compared to the same circuit filed by the person you are auditing. When they differ significantly, you might have a clue to systematic fraud.

2. Review personnel vacation files. When a person does not take any vacations for long periods, or takes short vacations often over holidays when he or she knows no temporary person will travel his or her routes, you might have a clue of fraud. Review the personnel vacation files during your audit. Remember that a white collar crime offender has to continue concealing a crime even when he or she might have stopped committing it.

3. Do not jump to conclusions before you have all the facts. A dramatic or systematic increase in mileage might coincide with an increase in customers, customer development, or instructions from someone in authority. For example, a sales representative's boss tells her to substitute for someone who retired, quit, or became ill. Always check all the possibilities and eliminate all before concluding that the differences show systematic travel fraud.

Verifying Lodging, Food, and Client Entertainment Receipts

This area of reimbursement brings temptation to the employee because receipts substantiate his or her claim. However, genuine receipts can be altered, copied, forged, and padded in other ways. The place the receipt came from might not exist. To verify a receipt's authenticity, you need to take the following steps:

1. *Examine the receipts carefully.* Look for handwriting that appears similar on receipts where it should be different. Ink color might also tip you to altered documents. Remember, white collar crime perpetrators use guile, but after long periods of successfully fooling everyone they might become careless. Also, check the imprints on credit card and hotel receipts. Look at the dates and account numbers or any part of them that might create a suspicious flaw. Check the printing carefully, too. A copy made by a back-street printer will always vary from the real thing, if only slightly (e.g., ink color, type size). Also, compare the printing on a hotel or motel billing and look for variations. Look back in the records. Although you are not checking the authenticity of a receipt filed three years ago, it might supply you with a known standard for comparing key points on receipts you are trying to verify.

2. *Verify the receipts.* Your next step will involve carrying the verification of receipts a step further. You can complete this important task with a few phone calls. Do not tell the business that you are checking on an employee; instead use a pretext when necessary to determine first if the motel, hotel, or restaurant exists.

Tell motels and hotels that a friend recommended their place of business and you would like to know their rates. They will probably ask who your friend is, what company you are with, and a variety of other standard marketing questions. There are times when you need to use a pretext to shield the person you are checking from any inference of wrongdoing. Just say that you are self-employed and might travel in their area. Ask for rate information by telephone, but say you would also like a brochure and rate list sent to you. You may need it later. Always use your home address when requesting information under a pretext.

When your call to the hotel or motel does not seem to give you the right answers, go a step further. Mention the dates of the suspect's receipts for that establishment, keeping your pretext, as though your "friend" had visited during the time frame that includes the receipt. You might get an answer that informs you that there was a management change, renovations, or some other reason that the business was not open on the date of the receipt. You should verify the restaurant and customer entertainment receipts in the same way.

Verifying Air Travel Claims or Issued Ticket Usage

Normally, the company travel claim policy calls for a user's copy of the ticket; however, there are ways of manipulating that seemingly foolproof procedure. The receipt or user's copy of the ticket does not verify who used the ticket.

For example, the employee might have sold the ticket for half price to someone else who traveled using the employee's name. In addition, the employee might claim that he or she lost the user copy, or forgot it and will submit it later. Eventually, its absence will get lost in the shuffle. Since the company paid for the ticket, the employee does not have an interest in reimbursement, only in concealing his or her activities. There are so many possibilities for manipulation that it is not feasible to list them all. However, the following investigative audit techniques will normally supply a clue that fraudulent activity occurred in this area of travel expenses.

1. When the user copy of the airline ticket is attached to the travel claim, examine it for the date stamp of usage. Does that match the time of travel?

2. Next, look at other receipts for that date (for example, a hotel billing coupled with a cash or credit card receipt). Do the dates match with the air travel? The employee might have sold the ticket, for example, and driven to the location but in doing so did not check into the hotel until a later time than he or she would have if traveling by air.

3. Also, look for receipts that show travel from the airport to the hotel, or the time shown on rental car receipts. For example, the person could have driven to the location after selling his or her ticket and, recognizing the need to produce a rental car receipt and reimbursement, parked his or her car and rented a vehicle for the time at that location. If this is the case, the time stamps or entries in these areas probably will not add up as they would if the employee were honest about the travel.

4. When there is no user copy of the company-issued airline ticket, you will have to track it down through the travel agency or airline to get the information and a copy for your files. Although it's possible to lose the ticket receipt, it is unlikely that the employee would have other receipts, especially those calling for employee reimbursement, and would have lost the airline ticket receipt. However, verify that before allowing yourself to jump to a conclusion about the matter.

5. You can also ask the airline to send you copies of the ticket used for comparison with the user receipt. However, getting the ticket from the airline might add another dimension to your audit because it will contain a time and date stamp, plus the flight number or any other changes that may not be reflected in the receipt. That information might also show why the employee conveniently lost the user copy of the airline ticket.

Objective of an Investigative Audit

Your investigative audit for travel fraud has the objective of verifying the information submitted by the employee in a claim for reimbursement or reporting expenses. *Verifying* means that you should examine documents carefully, comparing them with others and conducting follow-up calls as noted earlier.

Your audit also has the objective of detecting ways within the current company policy and procedure that supply employees with opportunities to commit white collar crime. Although you may not find any indication of fraud to date, when the opportunity remains open, fraud can happen later. Your investigative audit enables you to have a solid base for creating better company policies and procedures that eliminate opportunities and thus prevent crimes.

■ WHEN YOU NEED TO BEGIN A CRIMINAL INVESTIGATION OF TRAVEL FRAUD

When unresolved indicators of fraud appear as those noted above or others, you need to transfer the case from an audit or verification to a criminal investigation (see Chapter 16). Initiating a criminal investigation does not ensure that criminal activity did happen; however, the indicators show that there is a good chance it did. As you continue in this manner, your case should narrow to prove or disprove each difference your audit uncovered as a criminal offense. To conduct an effective criminal investigation in travel fraud areas, you need to use the following guidelines.

Guidelines for Conducting a Criminal Investigation of Travel Fraud

First, you need to collect, protect, and preserve the questioned documents. Questioned documents fall into two general classifications: genuine and fraudulent. Travel and expense account fraud will often involve questioned documents in some way, such as those noted earlier and others peculiar to your company and travel situations. Generally, those you will have to deal with include alterations and forgeries. The offenders may repeat their crime many times using the same method of operation (modus operandi). In your criminal investigation, you should give special attention to factors that may link the offense under investigation to other, similar incidents. Although you might recognize the flawed documents, you must prove this to others, perhaps in court. Doing so often hinges on your collection, protection, and preservation techniques supported with an independent laboratory examination and technical expert's confirmation of your suspicions. When experts confirm that the document has flaws and shows forgery or alterations, they supply you with reliable evidence which management can use to make a prudent and confident decision. When corporate management decides to subject an employee to criminal charges or civil litigation stemming from your investigative audit and criminal investigation, it's important to ensure accurate completeness. You want to ensure that the company, prosecutors, and attorneys involved in the matter can proceed with confidence and certainties of success in court, if the case leads to that action.

Six Essential Elements to Prove Forgery

A forgery offense happens when a person attempts to defraud another by falsely making or altering any part of a document that would, if genuine, appear to impose a legal liability on another. To prove forgery in cases of travel fraud, you will have to establish the following essential elements of proof.

1. *The employee or another for and with his or her knowledge and consent altered a document or made a fraudulent document.* This involves the making or alteration of the document not authorized by the original maker or not authorized for duplication (for example, a hotel billing form printed surreptitiously and filled out by an employee to represent that it originated at the hotel).

2. *The altering or making was not authorized and was done to defraud another.* This occurs when a genuine document is altered by an employee or someone else with the employee's consent without the approval of the true original maker.

3. *The altered or fraudulent document will change the right of obligation the company.* For example, the company will have to pay the employee money he or she is not entitled to.

4. *The employee presented the altered or forged document to the company for payment.* This happens when the employee signs a travel expense or reimbursement claim and presents it as true and correct for collecting money for the claim.

5. *The employee knew the document was false.* The term *false* as used in defining forgery does not refer to the truth of facts stated in the document. It refers only to the document not being genuine. For example, a document that has been altered to change the amount or times and dates to conceal another crime or series of events creates the falseness issue. This element supports the employee's intent to commit fraud.

6. *Intent of the employee was to defraud the company.* The employee did this act of forgery or alteration to get something of value, and his or her intent was to defraud or deceive the company.

Four Tips on Preservation of Questioned Documents

1. A questioned document should never be folded, crumpled, or carried unprotected in a pocket. The document should be placed between transparent protective covers. This permits handling for examinations without the direct manipulation of the document itself, and prevents any marring by contamination or destruction by abrasive action.

2. Do not try to restore a torn document. Instead, place the pieces in a protective covering in their most obvious and logical positions.

3. Documents should be handled to avoid destroying or adding any indented markings.

4. It is desirable to make copies of the questioned document for use during your investigation. The original may then be placed in a secure environment. Make reproductions without removal from the protective covering.

Have Questioned Documents Examined by a Laboratory Expert

An effective way of tying up all loose ends during your criminal investigation of travel fraud is to have the questioned documents examined by a laboratory expert. This type examination by an accredited private laboratory will show and prove the following elements.

1. *Confirm that the document has been altered.* Although an alteration of a document might be obvious, you should always seek an expert's opinion using laboratory skills and equipment to certify that fact. Should your company choose to take court action against a person, this strengthens your case. Further, if management decides to terminate the employee, it can have confidence about that action.

2. *Confirm that the employee signed the reimbursement or expense account claim or declaration.* This precaution should always precede any employee termination or court action. This verification can also occur at a laboratory using known standards based on personnel records and other sources within the company.

How to Write a Comprehensive Report

After completing your investigation, you will need to compile your findings and evidence into a comprehensive report. The format shown in Exhibit 2–3 serves the criminal investigation purpose best, especially when you have to file charges with a local prosecutor or supply your conclusions and evidence to the corporate general counsel.

Exhibit 2-3
ASSEMBLING YOUR INVESTIGATIVE FILE INTO A REPORT

Administration	1	Company, Date, Etc.
Basis	2	Why did you investigate?
Offense	3	What is the crime?
Suspect	4	Who committed the crime?
Summary	5	Briefly, what happened?
Support	6	Substantiate your summary.
Witnesses	7	Who has information?
Exhibits	8	Supporting evidence list.
Attached Exhibits		

■ QUICK REFERENCE GUIDE FOR CHAPTER 2

- Review your company policies on travel and expense accounts; they might provide opportunities for employee fraud.
- Take control of your company's expenses and eliminate the opportunity for fraud with corporate credit cards.
- Create revised and detailed company policies for travel expenses.
- Conduct regular investigative audits.
- Conduct criminal investigations when necessary.

Chapter Three
How to Control Pilfering of Office Supplies and Equipment

In a legal sense, an act of pilferage creates a *larceny* which can be qualified as petty larceny, or stealing in small quantities. The word *pilferage* creates confusion in the white collar crime conundrum. It's a word often used to describe a specific crime. However, pilferage instead describes a *technique of theft*, as opposed to a statutory crime. Pilferage is also a first cousin to the white collar crime of embezzlement (another technique of stealing property), which normally describes a white collar crime involving theft of large amounts of money or negotiable financial instruments.

■ THE EXTENSIVE COST OF PILFERAGE

Over thirty years ago, the U.S. Armed Forces created a training film focused on supply conservation awareness among service men and women. The film's title, *The Million Dollar Pencil*, pointed out how seemingly trivial pilferage of pencils could cost the government a million dollars each year (in 1960 dollars). Watching the film years ago left a strong impression on me, because we don't often think about pilferage in that way.

Traditionally, people associate the term *pilferage* with warehouses, retail stores, and other areas but not with administrative supplies within a company. Certainly all the traditional areas continue to be at risk, as well as many others I didn't mention. However, in today's economy, we have to see the total spectrum of problems. The million dollar pencil in 1960 would have greater accuracy today as the billion dollar pencil. For example, if a company employed 20,000 persons and each day each employee took home a ball point pen costing 59 cents, the loss to the corporation would total $11,800 each day! That's over $4 million a year lost from a simple ball point pen. That might seem like an exaggeration, because a detractor would quickly point out that each person won't take a pen home each day. However, if employees take home a box of twelve pens twice a week, the cost will remain the same with only a fraction of the total pilfering. When we add in all the paper, staplers and staples, file folders, tape, and other items, the loss eats into company profits at staggering rates.

According to a variety of government and independent studies, about 50 percent of employees working in various types of corporations and industries steal to a greater or lesser extent (casual pilferage), with about 20 percent stealing in volume (systematic pilferage). Collectively, a company otherwise doing well can become mired in internal losses stemming from pilfering employees and may be forced to sell, merge, or declare bankruptcy.

Even financially strong corporations suffer more than anyone in company leadership will admit, often because they do not know why the profits continue to diminish. It sounds naive to believe that corporate leadership with advice from financial experts and conventional security forces would not know what is happening, but that is often the case. Other times, a company might know that pilferage exists and make unskilled business-oriented efforts to stem the tide. However, often the pilferage problem continues and increases. The cost reaches into the high billions each year across the United States. In reality, extensive employee dishonesty is symptomatic of confused management, not indicative of an impossible problem. You can gain control and create effective preventive countermeasures. In this chapter, I will show you tested ways of doing that. I will begin by identifying your threats.

■ FOUR CATEGORIES OF PILFERERS IN A CORPORATE ENVIRONMENT

Four categories of persons supply the threat of pilfering company assets from within your corporate workplace. You might be surprised at who is likely to become a pilferer. The chronic pilferer in corporate or industrial environments rarely fits the traditional perception of a thief. You might be skeptical, but remember that techniques of white collar crime offenders rarely fit the mold that we regularly associate with traditional crime. That confusion often creates a perception that pilferage within the corporate workplace does not qualify as white collar crime. In the following profiles of pilferer candidates, I'll give you a better view of who might be a threat and how they operate.

1. *The casual pilferer*: This person fully intends to steal but rarely develops elaborate schemes to do it. Often called an *opportunity-oriented* thief, the casual pilferer steals from genuine or perceived need, typically unable to resist temptation or an unexpected opportunity. Because few effective safeguards or countermeasures for casual pilferage exist in most companies, the person

has little or no fear of detection. A part of the casual pilferer's theft includes thinking of an excuse for his or her actions should someone in the company (including security officers) question his or her possession of company assets, especially when leaving the workplace. The casual pilferer normally keeps his or her activities personal and secret from other employees.

2. *The conversion pilferer*: Fraudulent conversion has become so commonplace in the business world that it is nearly a tradition. Yet the cost to corporations can develop into staggering dimensions. Conversion happens when a person exercises the right of ownership, including an unauthorized and wrongful exercise of dominion and control over another's property inconsistent with the rights of the owner (for example, when an employee uses company property, facilities, or equipment for personal reasons and gain). When an employee makes copies of personal documents for personal use, or uses a company computer for personal reasons, or borrows a company truck to move household goods, that is conversion and a white collar crime. Such acts qualify as white collar crime because they use the characteristics and techniques of guile, deception, and concealment although they are often done openly. An employee might walk into the reproduction center and run off a hundred copies of some document with other employees present. No one in the room will look over the person's shoulder to check the type document copied (either personal or business), and no one will notice that the employee signed a log showing that he or she made only ten copies. At the end of the day, a person responsible for tallying the count of copies made on the machine adds up the numbers shown on the log. That person just adds something and lets it go at that. Sounds trivial until we add up an office complex that has ten thousand employees and a thousand copy machines and multiply this by the days in a week, month, and year. Conversion pilferage has become so woven into the fabric of day-to-day company operations that it is akin to termites eating away the underpinnings of a house. On the outside, the structure looks fine, but one day the weakened beams will cause the structure to sag and collapse.

3. *The systematic pilferer*. These people take a job so they can steal their company's assets. They use well-developed schemes, well-planned targets, and they normally make more money from stealing in a short time than their salary could supply over the long term. Systematic pilferers always steal for personal gain or advantage and can act independently, but often involve other employees or outside contacts. Their thefts also might include items they can sell or barter for something else, or they may steal to support a part-time or retirement business.

4. *The nonemployee pilferer*: In this case, pilferage of company assets extends beyond employees, but might include their direct or passive assistance. This category of pilferer includes vendors, contractors, maintenance and repair and cleaning crews, and others who have regular access to com-

pany areas, but are not directly employed by the corporation. Often, these persons become so accepted in company areas that they have the same unsuspecting access that employees enjoy.

■ FOUR KEY PROBLEMS PILFERERS MUST OVERCOME

All pilferers have to overcome certain problems to accomplish their pilferage objectives. Understanding these problems helps you to craft effective preventive countermeasures. Four key problems include the following:

1. The pilferer's first requirement is to find the item or items to steal. For the casual pilferer, this might happen by a search or an accidental discovery. The crime of systematic pilferage requires more extensive planning and execution to conduct regular and profitable thievery.

2. The second requirement confronting the potential pilferer is the manner in which he or she can gain access to the desired items and gain possession of them.

3. The third requirement involves a problem of removing stolen items to benefit from the theft and evade detection.

4. Lastly, to derive any benefit from the theft, the pilferer must use the item or dispose of it in some way. The casual pilferage of supplies primarily happens to satisfy the needs or desires of the thief. The systematic pilferer will normally arrange to sell the material discreetly or trade it to someone for other items, or will use it to supply a sideline business.

■ PROFILE OF A PILFERER

To develop awareness and effective preventive countermeasures for pilferage, you need a clear understanding of who in your company might become a pilferer and who will not. Some pilferage stems from those employees who are simply rotten apples. These include the people who seem to have an inborn predisposition to defraud whenever the opportunity presents itself. Some persons, while initially honest, become subjected to pressures originating outside the company and resort to various forms of dishonesty. Examples of these pressures include sudden family expenses, gambling debts, loan shark involvement, problems with a side business, a drug or alcohol problem, or just plain high living. Employees engaged in pilferage often rationalize their activities in a variety of ways (e.g., the company can afford it; the firm makes allowances for a certain amount of dishonesty; the business can always raise prices).

There is an adage that tells us a chain is only as strong as its weakest link. That concept can also adapt to the business environment and pilferage. In a corporate workplace, your weakest link can include the most trusted employee because he or she is in the best position to inflict the greatest damage. My experience when solving internal theft problems for companies has shown that the most unlikely employees often are deeply involved in pilferage.

There is another factor that often tips me off about employees who steal or convert company property. It is the workaholic or person who goes far beyond any job expectations. When a person earns a fixed salary, the company expects him or her to work hard for eight hours, five days a week, and receive certain benefits. When an employee regularly shows up to do work on time off, I become suspicious. I suppose there are people who work for companies, love their work, and have nothing better to do. However, that situation is the exception rather than the rule. People tend to work according to a perceived potential of personal gain. For example, entrepreneurs or self-employed people might put in excessive hours at work because that is their lifeline, they own it. Their income (including business and personal survival) often hinges on aggressive work habits. A company employee might work hard for free during off-hours when he or she knows that doing so might help him or her move up the corporate ladder. Other legitimate reasons could include catching up on work they should have completed during business hours, but did not. We all have our off days when little or nothing gets done.

■ SIX CATEGORIES OF EMPLOYEES WHO WILL NOT BECOME PILFERERS

I have always found an interesting characteristic in most of the companies having problems with pilferage. Security managers, supervisors, and executives tend to look in the wrong places for pilferers, and maybe that is why this white collar crime has steadily increased and in many companies has become a tradition. In the following paragraphs, I identify employees who will not become pilferers and discuss why.

1. *Employees openly irresponsible, goof-offs, and those who do personal business on company time.* A key element of pilferage and any white collar crime includes deception, and that calls for a creation of an illusion. The pilferer clearly wants to discourage attention to him or her and wants to appear as a hard-working, no-nonsense employee. Less than productive employees have an agenda that does not include the best interests of the company, but also does not include white collar crime.

2. *Employees who display arrogance, ego problems, and excessive aggressiveness.* These employees normally suffer from a real or imagined inferior self-image. They purposely draw attention to themselves and their activities, trying to impress others with their competency and loyalty. White collar crime (including pilferage) demands an obscure image. The pilferer tries to appear as just an average person, diligent and courteous, to remove any hint of suspicion. This image also serves the pilferer when he or she is suspected of wrongdoing, because frequently other employees will not disclose their feelings of suspicion because they like the person.

3. *Employees with chronic absenteeism and lateness.* A necessary element of white collar crime offenders includes constant concealment and staying on top of the situation. Often, these crimes (including pilferage) surface when an employee is on vacation, ill, or absent from work for some other reason. Regularly coming to work late also draws attention to the employee and elicits dissatisfaction from supervisors. Employees in this category will not have pilferage or other white collar crime in their agenda.

4. *Employees who do not follow instructions or who ignore company policy.* These employees will have supervisors watching every move—not a conducive climate for pilferage. White collar crime offenders appear to follow instructions to the letter and normally use company policy to their theft advantage.

5. *Employees who whine and complain.* Employees who voice general discontent with their jobs or with company policies will quickly fall from favor in a corporation. Although often tolerated, this person will also receive attention and will normally be the focus of other employees' criticism. Employees who complain disqualify themselves from participating in pilferage.

6. *Employees who are lazy and lack a sense of commitment and dedication.* Pilfering employees will display an overt attentiveness, commitment, and dedication as a facade to disguise their pilferage plans and activities. Those who noticeably act lazy and show no commitment or dedication to company business will not have the disguise necessary to fulfill acts of pilferage or other types of white collar crime.

■ THE MOST COMMON AREAS OF OPPORTUNITY FOR CORPORATE PILFERAGE

Controlling pilferage calls for several preventive elements working together, and when they do, pilferage ends or becomes so insignificant that it doesn't matter. For example, it's difficult if not impossible to prevent employees from sticking a pen in their pocket or purse as they leave the office at the end of the work day. It is, however, possible to prevent them from taking home a box of pens. I'll show you how to do that later in this chapter.

I have found the following windows of opportunity for pilferage in companies with operational expense problems:

Administrative supplies: This is a monstrous problem because these costly items, although seemingly trivial, fall into an expendable category and are difficult to track. This category is also the least protected and rarely has any accountability. When there *is* an effort to control pilferage of administrative supplies, the person responsible has no idea about security of assets and creates some system filled with loopholes, which leads to a facade instead of a control. In addition, smart pilferers will go to an office supply store and buy some duplicate items so if something does go wrong (and there is a slight chance of that happening) they can honestly say they bought the supplies at XYZ Office Supplies. They will often go there to buy trivial items but will go out of their way to become acquainted with clerks and others working there. Should they ever get trapped for alleged stealing at the office, not only can they produce receipts for the items but they can honestly tell their accuser to ask the people at the store—who would presumably say that the employee comes into their store often to buy administrative supplies.

Computer software and support supplies: This ever-increasing pilferage target also rarely has any effective controls. A popular pilferage of software includes making copies, although doing so is illegal and will subject the company to significant trouble and liability if discovered. Next in line for pilferage are blank disks, printer ribbons and paper, and a variety of accessories. Companies that supply laptop computer systems often have so little accountability that the machines occasionally disappear.

Electronic equipment: Offices today have a wide variety of electronic equipment, ranging from calculators to fax machines. Normally, there is little accountability, especially when the novelty of the device wears off and something new arrives to draw everyone's attention. All this equipment, as well as supporting items such as batteries, fax paper, etc., become lucrative items and lucrative pilferage targets.

Corporate information: Few companies relate stealing or pilferage with corporate information. Thus there are few safeguards for company information. Several opportunities exist in this category for the pilferer, including selling client lists to other companies and mailing list providers. Company plans, statistics, strategies, policies and procedures, and a variety of other information-based items would be valuable to a competitor or information broker.

Overtime or compensation time: Depending on the type of company, provisions for overtime work vary. Overtime does not include employees who voluntarily or on their own come into the office or take work home for the weekend. The law normally calls for employees who work over forty hours to receive some type of compensation. That compensation might include time-and-a-half salary when an employer pays by the hour, or the salary is computed by the hour. Often, government agencies and some companies offer an equivalent amount of time off at the same rate, often called "comp" time. In addition, the company may allow the employees to accrue compensation time and use it at their discretion, the company may buy back the compensation time at the end of the year. Some employees will deliberately slow their work pace while ostensibly being frantically busy, thus pilfering time and money from the company.

Petty cash and coffee services: These areas of pilferage vary with each company. Often they are synonymous because employees contribute money each week to pay for a common coffee area and supplies. Other companies supply a vendor coffee service at their expense. Petty cash might also be a company fund maintained to purchase a variety of things, buy gifts for retirees, and so on. Pilferage of coffee supplies (often including tea and soups) and of petty cash used to buy items for personal use under a guise of company use can become significant over time.

Motor fuel and supplies: This problem can amount to large sums when a corporation has, for example, a fleet of company cars, trucks, delivery vans, or other motorized vehicles needing fuel, oil, and other supplies. A skilled pilferer, for example, can carry a three-gallon gasoline container in the vehicle, supposedly for reserve fuel or public relations when finding a stranded motorist out of gas (an employee driving a corporate vehicle who lends a hand generates goodwill for the company). However, the pilferer will also stop at home or at his or her privately owned vehicle before fueling the company vehicle and pour the three gallons into his or her car or another container at home. When the employee buys gas, the reserve can is filled simultaneously and the total gallons are billed to the company. No one will notice a difference of three gallons, or they will attribute the extra amount to vehicle fuel consumption. Occasionally, the pilferer gets an extra bonus by creating a supposed good Samaritan act for a stranded motorist (really his or her car) and refilling just the can. That supplies the pilferer with an extra three gallons for his or her car. Such pilferage of gasoline can amount to large sums each month or year. For example, an employee who steals about three gallons of gasoline a day for five days at $1.20 per gallon costs the company about $18 a week or $936 a year. When a corporation has twenty-five vehicles on the road, the cost of pilferage could cost an extra $23,400 each year for fuel. A company with a hundred company vehicles might easily spend over $100,000 each year for pilfered gasoline. Some employees add to their pilferage by siphoning gas or making a deal with the gas station owner, who agrees to pad the gallons of fuel and give the driver a cash difference. Both make money on the deal. The owner gets added sales volume and profit, and the driver gets the cash (normally at 50 percent of the pump price). Add other costs such as maintenance (e.g., oil, wiper blades, and a variety of other seemingly routine items) and the cost can become staggering.

Vehicle conversion: Other forms of pilferage with a company vehicle include converting the vehicle to sideline business uses, such as a part-time job delivering products. I have found some pilferers using vans and trucks to operate a weekend moving business. The possibilities stem from poor control and management of company assets—the root of all pilferage opportunity.

Office equipment conversion and supply theft: This area of pilferage normally revolves around copy machines, but can extend into laser printers and other items that use toner and other supplies. Employees converting this equipment use the copier for personal uses, and may also steal toner and other supplies to sell, use in their own system, or give to a friend.

The preceding examples occur daily across the United States unless you have established systems to prevent such pilferage. These and a long list of other situations too numerous to list create the windows of opportunity in most corporations. Other opportunities depend on the company and might include tools, books, products, furniture, and anything of value either personally or for resale.

When a company asks me to find solutions for its losses, I often look at the work environment itself. There is a tendency among workers in the business world to *appear* busy, cramming twenty hours of work into eight or ten hours. I have visited offices where employees were seemingly frantically busy, running around for hurried meetings, rushing here and there, and seemingly swamped with work to do.

In Hollywood they call it *hype*, a bit of jargon for making something appear more than it really is. This term applies to many company environments in which everyone rushes around and realistically accomplishes little, sometimes nothing. It is, however, the pilferer's dream to land a job in such a place. Everyone is so busy trying to look, act, and be important that no one notices the thievery occurring, often openly. I have watched employees (including middle management and executives) rushing about, regularly stopping by the supply closet and grabbing a package of lined paper and box of pens, sometimes more. They toss the supplies on their desk, grab a couple of pens and a pad of paper from the package, and rush off to a meeting. A day or two later I have watched the same employees doing the same thing, and the excess seems to vanish. The same employees to tend to carry briefcases when they leave the building, all chattering and talking shop, acting excited about their projects.

Considering that packages of paper cost the company between $12 and $20 each, and pens cost about $10 to $20 a dozen, a busy employee might pilfer $50 a week on the low end. Throw in staplers, staples, tape, and a variety of other items and one employee could walk out with $100 worth of supplies each week. In a company with a few hundred or several thousand employees and with only a small percentage pilfering, the effect becomes staggering. And ironically, the employees who appear the busiest and most committed to their work are the culprits.

At one company that asked me to find solutions for its internal losses, I found employees who reported that their salaries were so low that veteran employees told them that the company expected them to steal as an income supplement. Another said the company sales staff heard unofficially that they should fraudulently inflate their expense accounts to offset the large expense claims of top management. Another said the company had an unwritten policy that allowed executives access to company materials and services for their personal use, and since they could do it, so should all the underlings.

When that type of workplace environment develops, and there are loose controls, employees receive an open invitation to pilfer. I have found over the years that the workplace environment played a larger role in pilferage than a need for money. What can happen in these circumstances contrasts to a company that was victimized by a few employees who were evildoers from their first day on the job: The firm itself often creates excessive stress for honest and well-motivated persons through a variety of subtle and not-so-subtle pressures within the management and operations system that encourage— and often demand—employee misconduct.

■ HOW TO TAKE CONTROL OF YOUR COMPANY'S PILFERAGE PROBLEMS

The dominant factor in taking control of your company's pilferage problems stems from a series of steps instead of any single solution. You want to ensure that you do not create an oppressive work environment, stifle motivation and operations, or create a bureaucratic nightmare. You also need to craft solutions to create a strong preventive effect or deterrent, beginning with the following recommended solutions in each of the pilferage categories. Next, you'll want to establish a preventive program that helps you detect and identify pilferage, and find out where opportunity exists (using thorough investigative audits). Lastly, you'll need to learn how to conduct criminal investigations into pilferage situations so that, if necessary, you can terminate employment of the pilferer, file criminal charges, or pursue a civil remedy to recover losses (especially in some cases of systematic or nonemployee pilferage).

Establish a Preventive Management Program

Your first step for a corporate preventive management program must include establishing a centralized control point. One of the reasons pilferers succeed in their activities is that each section, department, or division handles its own supplies or other items, and there is no company policy regarding management of supplies. If your company has a security director or manager, primary development and management of preventive programs should be his or her responsibility. Operational departments and all elements of the company need to follow the program, and the best way to encourage this is to establish a strong, well-focused policy.

Creating the prevention policy might lead to some dissension in the company because department heads don't like to relinquish their controls. Although you might begin to suspect that the department heads have a personal involvement in pilferage, or are trying to protect someone involved (that might turn out to be true), do not jump to conclusions. Corporations, much like government bureaucracies, don't like to experience adverse publicity or employee-created embarrassment. Executives, department heads, managers, and supervisors don't like to admit or have others imply that there is a problem of pilferage from within their enclave. They may resist a tough policy and preventive management program under a centralized person. However, your persistence and tact will usually prevail. If not, an order from the CEO will do the trick. With a new company policy in force, you are ready to end pilferage.

■ SOLUTIONS FOR CONTROLLING CASUAL PILFERAGE

Casual pilferage will give you the greatest preventive challenge because it's subtle. You will have difficulty distinguishing between operational need and pilferage efforts. In addition, each company has its unique operational requirements, so trying to offer a specific solution for each conceivable situation will not be feasible. However, in any given corporate or industrial environment, the preventive procedure operates in the same way. You can adapt or craft the solutions supplied here to meet your specific requirements.

The key to ending casual pilferage is to eliminate the opportunity. The pilferer relies on stealing company assets with a no-risk or plausible-excuse assurance. When you create accountability, that assurance diminishes and the risk of detection increases. For example, when individuals can no longer go into the supply closet and grab whatever they intend to pilfer, or they face greater accountability for gasoline, tools, equipment, and other common pilferage targets, their activities cease. Your key goal is to create risk too great for the casual pilferer, using the steps discussed next.

Administrative Supply Controls

1. Require employees to sign for administrative supplies. Requiring an employee to sign an accountability log showing what he or she takes from the

supply closets provides you with an audit trail and creates an effective deterrent against pilferage.

2. Designate one primary employee plus an alternate person in each section or division to control administrative supplies. They are responsible for maintaining the accountability log, securing the storage area, conducting inventories, and submitting requests for replacement supplies. Ensure that such employees will not be away from the area simultaneously. Using a third alternate person might serve your situation best; however, there should be only *one* log that is passed to the alternate(s) when necessary.

3. Maintain a daily administrative supplies accountability log. Each day, at the close of business, the log for that day (even when no employee has gotten supplies) is handed to the section or division head, who must immediately send it to a designated person in the company, such as the Security Director. The log will be signed at the bottom of the last page for that day, showing the number of pages for that day and each of the designated responsible employees who had the log in their possession that day. Each time the log passes to an alternate and back to the primary person, the time and signature must appear. When no supplies were issued, a notation to that effect and a signature need to appear in the log.

4. Number each log sheet in sequence and have a section or division head account for it. Whenever a descrepancy is found, the responsible persons must satisfactorily explain the reason.

Always lock the supply closet and keep the key with the accountability log. When employees want supplies, the key is given to them by the person responsible for the log, allowing the employees to obtain whatever they need. When they have these items, they will lock the supply closet and return the key to the log keeper, who will list the items taken on the log. Employees will sign and date the entries, acknowledging their accuracy.

5. At the close of business hours, custody of the key to the supply closet must remain with the department head or, in his or her absence, a designated supervisor or manager. That person will ensure that the supply closet door is secured and the key is in a locked, secure place. The supply closet will not be available except during normal business hours.

6. Inventory the supply closets on the first days of implementing this policy and procedure. Ensure the responsible persons such as a department head and a designated company person (probably the security director) inventories the supply closets to establish a known starting point.

7. Whenever additional supplies are requisitioned, forward a copy of that request to the company's controlling person, such as the security director. A copy of the invoice received when the supplies arrive also needs to go to the same person so their file is complete, including the request and arrival of the supplies. Coupled with the original inventory, and periodic verification

inventories, theft of administrative supplies either through taking them or using them internally for personal use can be detected and corrected.

Objective of Control Log

Establishing this important control log supplies an audit trail, and employees know that, for example, signing for ten pads of paper and a box of ball point pens establishes a time and date of receipt. When the same person returns in a couple of days to get the same type of supplies, he or she needs to account to management with a supported reason. Although the reason might be legitimate, normally it is not. The person couldn't admit taking the items home for his or her school-age children to use. Although these steps might seem complicated, they are not; and they enable you to eliminate opportunites for pilferage.

It's a good deterrent to periodically remove control of the log from the person designated to maintain the log and redesignate that task to another employee. This action prevents one person from becoming sympathetic with a pilferer's story, and relieves the person from being in a position of this added duty too long. When leaving the person in control too long, you might experience an increasing lack of interest and a tendency to neglect this important detection and prevention of theft activity.

Other Casual Pilferage Targets

Each function in your company that supplies casual pilferage opportunities needs the same type of controls as those for administrative supplies. Having employees sign and date logs, with that log signed by a designated person and turned in after each business day, creates a powerful deterrent. Whenever you require accurate accountability logs signed by employees and ensure that control of keys and the log sheets after the close of business don't remain in the possession of one person, you will have a solid deterrent. If an employee continues to steal, you will detect his or her activities and your company will have written records that support prudent decisions about needed disciplinary action.

Model Pilferage Control Log

An example of a control log is shown in Exhibit 3-1. You can use this log as a guide in creating logs to control pilferage problems in any area.

Exhibit 3-1
Model Pilferage Control Log

ABC1234567A ——————— Sequential serial number, issued to each section or division in blocks—the letter *A* at the end designates the year. For example, next year's logs use the same numbers but a suffix of *B*.

Day and Date: Tuesday, July 18, 0000

Designated Custodian: Joan Davis

Items Issued	Issued to: Name, Section, Signature, Date			
1 pkg lined pads (12)	John Smith,	Acct.	John Smith	6/10
1 stapler				
1 box staples				
1 box pens (25)	Jill Black,	Acct.	Jill Black	6/10

　Log given to alternate Sam Jones at 11:30 a.m.

　Log returned to custodian Joan Davis at 1:30 p.m.

　Log delivered to Ms. Johnston, Division Chief, at close of business,

　June 10, 0000

I certify that all entries in this log are true and accurate.

Joan Davis
Custodian

Page ___ of ___ Pages

■ SOLUTIONS FOR CONTROLLING CONVERSION PILFERAGE

Controlling and ending conversion pilferage requires innovative concepts tailored to your situation. Some areas of concern, such as postage stamp machines, can be controlled with logs similar to the example in Exhibit 3-1. Control of unauthorized copy machine, computer, and other equipment use in an office environment occurs through a combination of countermeasures. Some examples follow:

(1) Establish key lock devices on power source switches or boxes for copiers, computers, and fax machines or other equipment.

(2) Establish a central key control cabinet in each section and call for the key to that container to be turned in at the close of business to a security center or designated person. The key to the control container needs to be secured, available on the following business day, or available in the case of an unexpected operational requirement of the company.

Countermeasures that work best for these types of devices will end unauthorized use during nonbusiness hours.

During Business Hours

Controlling unauthorized use of copiers, fax machines, computers, and other similar equipment during business hours requires effective supervision and control logs, which must go to a central control point daily as noted in the preceding casual pilferage solutions. Each copier, for example, should have a counter, and when there is a difference between the log and the counter, no one should change the log to the number shown on the counter. Instead, a note of the discrepancy should appear on the log, and it must be forwarded to the responsible person (probably the Security Director). When daily use logs and counter discrepancies occur regularly, you will have a written record to aid in your investigation.

Vehicles and other Equipment

Ending conversion of company vehicles to personal use begins with control of the vehicles, including keeping them secured during nonbusiness hours in a company parking lot. Effective control measures include a log book for each vehicle that calls for drivers to make entries each day, even when there's no vehicle use. The log book should contain forms that show

- Driver's name
- Time at pick-up and time at close of business for that vehicle
- Beginning and ending mileage
- Gallons of fuel put in vehicle on that day
- Servicing, including oil added
- Repairs or other expenses.

At the close of the day, the vehicle should be fueled and prepared for its next use. The log book and keys should be turned into a central control point, such as a security desk or vehicle pool center. The supervisor must check the log book to ensure completeness and must verify the mileage at least once a week.

Rotate your vehicle drivers weekly, biweekly, or monthly, whichever is the most feasible for your situation. Rotating drivers and tracking the fuel consumption of the same vehicle with different drivers will show the true average mileage and supply an audit trail for those employees who might use a scheme to take fuel from company vehicles for personal use. With this system, drivers recognize the risk of trying to convert the vehicle's use for personal business, and they know supervisors will discover any pilferage scheme that involves the vehicle, its maintenance, or fuel.

Other Conversions

Conversions of other company assets, like those noted earlier, end when logs and controls are established. However, it's important to require that the documentation leave the section or division after the business day and be placed in the hands of others, who will examine it for accuracy or deficiency. This in itself will supply a strong deterrent to conversion or other white collar crimes and enable discovery when such crimes do occur.

■ SOLUTIONS FOR CONTROLLING SYSTEMATIC PILFERAGE

Systematic pilferage creates the greatest losses in a company and is the easiest to discover and eliminate. It is easily discovered because the systematic pilferer deals in quantity, stealing for money. This person will create schemes for stealing, and because the items have value to others (such as a broker in stolen items, also called a fence), you can survey your company for that type of item and establish controls that make the risk high and discovery easier. Some solution techniques follow:

1. Establish security surveillance of all exits from the company area. The systematic pilferer will need to remove quantities of normally costly items. A surveillance effort might point to suspects, and that will help you create effective and tailored preventive measures.

2. Establish an effective package and material control system. In doing so, you can eliminate one method that the systematic pilferer uses to move items from the company and make his or her effort more difficult. Always remember that controls as like this (or any type) rarely catch anyone in the act. However, their use creates a preventive countermeasure, eliminating one avenue of opportunity.

3. Ensure that employee and visitor parking locations are convenient for employees but inconvenient for systematic pilferage. Arranging parking areas so the rows of vehicles will be observable by other employees from the office or other buildings creates an effective deterrent. When security forces are available, locate an officer in an obvious position of observation. This configuration will create an effective deterrent. The systematic pilferer, like a burglar, can only enjoy success when not observed. He or she will recognize that the risk of detection is high, and you will have eliminated another opportunity for pilferage.

4. Establish effective sign-in, sign-out logs for storage areas and warehouses or office areas that contain items of high value and items that the systematic pilferer could assemble and carry off. This control, as well as security officers observing such areas, eliminates opportunity. Also, establish effective key and access controls to vulnerable areas.

5. Post security officer observation posts in shipping and receiving areas when feasible, and develop as many stumbling blocks as possible to reduce opportunity. For example, post someone to make sure that an incoming shipment is completely off-loaded and to ensure that documents do not stay in the receiving areas but are instead forwarded before alteration can happen. Also develop ways to conduct spot, unannounced inventories. These measures deter pilferage and increase the risk of being caught. They might also enable fast discovery of the determined employee or nonemployee who tries to steal despite your countermeasures.

The key element in preventing and detecting systematic pilferage is the aforementioned controls, which create stumbling blocks in layers. When you establish these and other techniques tailored for specific company areas, you might find that several employees will quit and move onto easier pickings. Such employees might say that these controls make working conditions intolerable, but you know these are the systematic pilferers who know they have been outsmarted.

◼ SOLUTIONS FOR CONTROLLING NONEMPLOYEE PILFERAGE

A large portion of corporation losses stems from nonemployee pilferage. Nonemployees include janitorial service workers, vendors, maintenance, repair, and so on. Such individuals come around so often that employees view them as part of the work environment. Although most of these people will be trustworthy, those who are not are in a good position to steal. Even when security forces scrutinize people entering or leaving company areas, these nonemployees have an excuse to come and go (e.g., to retrieve necessary items from their trucks), and they have other reasons to move freely throughout the company, generally unnoticed or unchallenged. For example, vendors servicing machines or other equipment can carry in containers, boxes, and other items and leave with other boxes that supposedly contain only their property. Janitorial workers normally come into the workplace after all employees have left, and if they want to pilfer, they have a free hand. Since office cleaning involves emptying waste baskets into a large container that is later hauled to a dumpster or some other disposal area, janitorial workers have an excellent way of moving company property out of the building, without other members of the cleaning crew aware of what's happening. Solutions to these and other similar problems of nonemployee pilferage follow:

1. At the close of the business day, ensure that employees secure all pilferable items. Desktops should be cleaned off, and all items easily pilfered should be secured in desk drawers, cabinets, or other storage areas. Ensure that desks and storage facilities (including files) are locked and the keys are placed in a central control container. Employees can keep keys to their desks, but they should not take keys to other containers or storage areas.

2. During business hours, vendors and other nonemployees should not be allowed to wander about company areas. A good policy and briefing of these individuals will go far to deter pilferage. Whenever possible, any item taken from the building or area by nonemployees should be inspected, and in certain areas nonemployee access should be allowed only with an escort.

3. Ensure that nonemployee parking areas are convenient but are clearly observable. Just as in dealing with other types of pilferage, create layered stumbling blocks that these persons can notice easily (and may create some

that are not so apparent). In doing so, you're increasing the risk associated with stealing and eliminating the opportunity for unnoticed pilferage.

◼ THE INVESTIGATIVE AUDIT: SEARCHING FOR PILFERAGE OPPORTUNITIES

In addition to looking for differences and patterns in records, observation is one of my favorite and most successful techniques of investigative audits. (See Chapters 5 and 17.) Earlier I supplied an example of a busy employee in a seemingly busy company environment, and I noted that there is often a white collar criminal hiding behind seeming productivity. Stealing becomes easy when it's intertwined with such a facade. I mentioned the employee rushing to a supply closet and grabbing packages of paper and boxes of pens.

When you conduct your investigative audit, don't get caught up in this harried environment. Instead, find a comfortable place to sit and observe what's happening. Note how easy it is for employees to access items that can become pilfered assets. While you're doing that, imagine that you work at the company and you want to steal. Then decide how you would do that under the conditions you observe. You will probably be surprised at how easy it is to steal in many circumstances, and from this observation your audit will gain greater focus. Also, you will have the tools needed to create better preventive countermeasures, in ways that don't interfere with business operations. When your countermeasures have been in place for a while, come back and observe again. My guess is that you'll notice that the hectic environment has settled down significantly, and employees go about their work orderly instead of frantically.

Techniques for Auditing Documents

Documents often supply you with a step-by-step blueprint of pilferage, but you need to ignore whether columns add up properly and all the answers seem to be there. White collar offenders, including pilferers, enjoy continued and increasing success in companies because they know how to manipulate documents and numbers. Another problem you will uncover in an investigative audit of documents includes employees who alter and pad accountability forms, not because they are stealing but because they find it's easier to fix the problem on paper than endure questions for which they have no answers. This problem, although technically a crime in itself, is so common that you can go off into left field and create a suspect of theft that doesn't exist.

Once a corporate comptroller called me into his company because all the numbers added up right, all the documents appeared authentic, yet a surprise inventory showed a huge shortage. He said that the company suspected a major theft had occurred and had reported it to the police. The police, who were not experts on white collar crime, suspected that the security manager and several security officers were involved in some major conspiracy. The detective in charge developed a theory that mapped out how he believed this major theft had happened, down to how the culprits rented several trucks and hauled off the goods in the dark of night. The problem with his theory, according to the comptroller, was that no one could find any supporting evidence (such as rental trucks, the goods, or witnesses). However, the detective was so obsessed with solving the case that he made the evidence fit his theory and persuaded the prosecutor to take the case to a sitting grand jury for indictments of the security officers and manager. The comptroller and other executives deeply regretted reporting the matter to the police (who had held some press conferences to announce their crime-solving prowess).

My first step included reviewing the hard copy documents involved in the operational area of the company where the alleged big theft happened. Before I conducted my audit and reached accurate conclusions, the company's internal auditors and police amateurs had relied on the auditor's findings, which had evolved solely from computer records. Computers remain a favorite concealment tool for pilferers or any white collar offender. My comparison of hard copy, original documents quickly disclosed some manipulation that had been occurring for several months. With that information, I pinned down a supervisor responsible for inventories in an area that had twenty-five employees. Before my interview, no one had talked to him about the problem. I pointed out a variety of discrepancies to the supervisor and reasoned that I believed he had not been stealing, but instead protecting his job by making the figures add up right when he knew honesty would show that they didn't. He admitted that for months the inventories didn't add up, but that he entered figures into his computer terminal that showed shrinkage within the company tolerance.

With new information and the supervisor's cooperation, the internal auditors returned and straightened out the mess so at least the company could begin with a genuine inventory and set of books. The police detective faded from view, and the security officers and manager left the company to file an immense lawsuit against their former employer, the police department, and others. They will probably win a sizable settlement.

Never rely on computer information; instead compare computer information with hard copy documents—and don't be shocked if they differ. We have become so conditioned to believing whatever the computer tells us that we forget that it only reports what a human told it. Although the computer doesn't lie, the people who use it might.

Other elements to look for when reviewing documents include the following:

Look for stains—maybe water or a cup of coffee spilled. See if the numbers were reconstructed accurately after the paper dried. Faking an accidental spill of liquid creates an opportunity to change a document when reconstructing the area damaged by the spill.

Study documents with a good magnifying glass. You might find some variations that are otherwise not noticed without magnification.

Look for ink color variations. An altered document, even in the same color ink, will normally show some variation.

Check for a copy of a copy. Some offenders will mask off figures on an invoice, copy the invoice on a good machine, and have a master to make further copies. With this inventory of blank, seemingly genuine forms, the offender can fill in different numbers.

Compare invoices and other documents known to be genuine with others on file at the company. Since most invoices today are generated by computer and dot matrix printers, offenders need to make them as close as possible to the real thing. They do this in two common ways: (1) using a computer dot matrix printer, although it is difficult to make a matrix that will fit the invoice form; or (2) purchasing an inexpensive dot matrix electronic typewriter (at most discount stores) for about $150 or less. These typewriters use a dot matrix print head as opposed to standard electric typewriters, which use a daisy wheel or round element. The dot matrix typewriter can fill in an invoice and appear genuine. Use a magnifying glass and you'll soon discover the differences between the real thing and the forgery.

Add the invoice or other document numbers. Often, even auditors won't take the time to add the numbers on an invoice or statement, assuming that they're correct. They might be, but they might have been altered (perhaps only the total was altered because the offender fears detection). We have become a bottom-line society, and we take the rest for granted.

■ GUIDELINES FOR CONDUCTING A CRIMINAL INVESTIGATION OF PILFERAGE

When your investigative audit or other information indicates obvious criminal pilferage activity, you need to shift from an audit to a criminal investigation. (see Chapter 16). The difference stems from how you manage the case. Your investigative audit supplies a broad overview and enables you to find weaknesses in control systems as well as detect ongoing theft. Your criminal investigation takes a problem recognition factor, narrows it to a specific offense, and focuses on evidence collection, protection, and preservation, and in so doing enables evidence evaluation that leads to informed management decisions. Although your company might only want to create better controls, fire a pilfering employee, or take other action, you need evidence sufficient for filing criminal charges to eliminate doubt and to give your company the option of filing criminal charges or taking civil court action against the offender.

1. Your first step will include researching your state statutes for applicable laws. Guidelines discussed below will help you ensure that you use the specific statutes and their elements of proof.

2. Second, collect and protect the documents and, when necessary, have an independent laboratory examine and verify your suspicions of alterations or forgery. When your company brings criminal charges, the prosecutor can have the police crime laboratory do the tests.

3. Document each step that led to one or more suspects, and use Exhibit 1-1 as a guide to compiling your report.

Essential Elements of Crime for Pilferage Offenses

The elements of proof or elements of the crime of pilferage often lead to confusion, because in some circumstances there's more than one crime involved. Pilferage often involves inchoate crimes (i.e., pilferage is an incipient crime that generally leads to another crime). For example, an employee steals company assets (larceny) and conceals the theft by altering or forging a document. Added crimes might include selling or receiving stolen company property. The following crimes normally will fall within a pilferage offense, either separately or collectively.

Larceny (theft): "The essential elements of a larceny include an actual or constructive taking away of some property of another (the company) without consent and against the will of the owner (the company). Obtaining possession of property by fraud, trick, or device with preconceived design or intent to appropriate, convert, or steal is larceny. (*John v. United States*, 65 U.S. App. D.C. 11 79 F.2d 136 and *People v. Cook*, 10 Cal. App. 2d 54, 51 P.2d 169, 170)"

Conversion: This is an unauthorized and wrongful exercise of dominion and control over another's (the company's) personal property, to exclusion of or inconsistent with the rights of owner. (*Catania v. Garage De Le Paix, Inc.*, Tex. Civ. App., 542 S.W. 2d 239, 241)

Fraudulent conversion: This involves receiving into possession money or property of another and fraudulently withholding, converting, or applying the same to or for one's own use and benefit, or to use and benefit of any person other than the one to whom the money or property belongs. (*Black's Law Dictionary*)

Fraudulent intent: Such intent exists where one, either with a view of benefiting himself or misleading another into a course of action, makes a representation that he knows to be false or which he does not believe to be true. (*Orenduff*, D.C. Okl., 226, F. Supp. 312, 314)

Fraudulent or dishonest act: This is an act that involves bad faith, a breach of honesty, a want of integrity, or moral turpitude. (*Hartford Accident & Indemnity Company v. Singer*, 185 Va. 620, 39 S.E. 2d 505, 507, 508)

Embezzlement: To embezzle means willfully to take or convert to one's own use another's money or property, of which the wrongdoer acquired possession unlawfully, by reason of some office or employment or position of trust. (*State v. Thyfault*, 121 N.J. Supr. 487, 287 A.2d 873, 879) Also, embezzlement is the fraudulent conversion of the property of another by one who has lawful possession of the property and whose fraudulent conversion has been made punishable by statute.

■ QUICK REFERENCE GUIDE FOR CHAPTER 3

- Pilferage represents one of the major causes of financial loss in the business world.
- Four categories of pilferers exist in a corporate environment.
- The four key problems pilferers must overcome help in preventing pilferage.
- Candidates for pilferage rarely include the perceived stereotypes.
- Use investigative audits to detect and prevent pilferage.
- Convert audits to criminal investigations to eliminate liabilities.
- Research essential elements of state statutes to ensure accurate investigations.

Chapter 4
Bribery, Kickbacks, and Payoffs

Employee bribes, kickbacks, and payoffs within the business world are pervasive. In conservative terms, the cost to corporations from this white collar crime exceeds $20 billion annually. Anyone can be involved—a janitor, a corporate president, and everyone in between. It's often so subtle that employees don't understand they're instruments of the bribe. Other employees have full knowledge, and even solicit bribes in return for abusing delegated authority or influence. You might have thought this problem didn't exist in your company. I'm willing to bet it does. In this chapter you'll learn to understand and recognize this white collar crime, and you'll learn proven techniques for detecting the problem when it exists and solutions for dealing with it effectively.

The traditional concept of bribery often leads us astray when we apply it to the business community. We normally think of bribery as an act of corruption limited to public officials, because when cases involving corporations do find their way into criminal prosecutions or civil actions, they receive little or no publicity. However, those involving public officials make the headlines. That publicity factor also applies to commercial or business bribery when the perpetrator is the corporation. Rarely, if ever, do we hear about bribery in which the company itself becomes the victim. Another reason these cases are elusive is that companies don't understand how to cope with them and are often reluctant to report them to the prosecutor's office or take civil remedies.

■ DEFINING WHAT'S LEGAL

The core characteristic of a commercial bribe, in which the company becomes the victim, involves improper *influencing* of a corporate decision or expenditure by an employee for personal or career gain. Remember that the white collar crime of bribery has many forms, including offers, promises, money, gifts, gratuities, sexual trysts, and whatever means necessary to influence the recipient. Focusing on the legal aspects of any crime, including bribery, goes beyond statutes to *case law precedence*, which develops from court decisions. Two landmark examples of case law about commercial bribery follow:

Commercial bribery: A form of corrupt and unfair trade practice in which an employee accepts a gratuity to act against the best interests of his employer. (*People v. Davis*, 33 Cr. R. 460, 160 N.Y.S. 769)

Commercial bribery: May assume any form of induced corruption where an employee betrays the trust and business interests of his or her employer or in some other form that prevents them from fair competition. (*Freedman v. U.S.*, 437 F. Supp. 1252, 1260)

Distinguishing a Business Gift from a Bribe

Corporate employees who accept gifts from persons who do, or would like to do, business with your company may find themselves in a variety of difficult positions. Gift givers may believe that they (or their company) have earned a favored status when an influential employee accepts a gift from them. Others may assume that employees accepting gifts have agreed to a beholden position and are no longer free to act for their company without prejudice. There is also another peril for employees receiving gifts, especially those gifts having high value. The Internal Revenue Service allows only one $25 business gift per year as a tax exemption. Gifts to employees exceeding that allowance become taxable as income. When employees ignore that rule, they might find themselves in trouble, especially when the donor subtly lets them know that they might report those gifts as a business exemption. Some playing serious hardball might suggest that an anonymous phone call to the IRS might happen if the employee does not reciprocate with favors.

The IRS ruling on this business problem classifies gifts as income. Employee income generated within a corporation beyond that earned legitimately becomes a bribe, kickback, or payoff; and although it may be illegal in a technical sense, even income from illegal sources becomes taxable.

Determining When Conflicts of Interest Become Bribery

Employee involvement in business conflicts of interest often surpasses an ethics problem. Conflicts of interest may involve white collar crimes that include bribes, kickbacks, or misuse of information and may extend into other crimes such as forgery, fraud, and theft. For example, an engineer for a major corporation decides to open a part-time consulting business from his home and develops a client who is his corporation's chief competitor. The engineer, using his consulting business as a cover, receives large fees from the competitor for advice that stems from confidential information he accesses within his company. This is a veiled form of employee bribery, but it qualifies as the crime of information theft. If the engineer alters or forges documents (including computer passwords) to access information later transferred to the competitor, and if doing so supplies an advantage and creates some measurable damage to the engineer's employer, the criminal offenses of forgery, theft, and fraud enter the white collar crimes he commits. He might also copy and remove information from the corporation, or steal or copy prototype trade secrets. Even when the engineer does not steal information, but accepts a competing company as a client, despite either party's intentions, a serious conflict of interest exists. Irrespective of his intent, it is not possible for the engineer to work in his profession for a competitor of his employing company without conveying advantageous information originating from his job. Doing so might create a lucrative opportunity that leads to added conflict and white collar crime activity.

Recruiting Versus Bribery

The crime of bribery can develop from a company offering or promising a job or position to an employee of your corporation when you can show that doing so influenced the employee to act in a way that created injury to the company. For example, XYZ Corporation, a major competitor of ABC Corporation, contacts ABC's director of marketing and offers him or her a vice-presidency position with double the salary. However, XYZ's offer contains certain terms. The director must supply ABC's mailing lists, marketing strategy, plans, budgets, and manuals, plus a complete customer list and other items that would give XYZ Corporation significant advantage over ABC Corporation. This subtle form of recruiting, in which XYZ's primary motive is to obtain confidential information by hiring ABC's marketing director, creates a clear form of bribery, as well as complicity in fraud and theft.

Offers of Bribery Outside Employment

Offers besides employment often come to employees from suppliers who do or want to do business with a corporation who want to edge out their competitors. The benefit that the supplier can gain from bribing a specific employee will figure into the value of the subtle bribe. The employee who is bribed with an offer must have the authority to influence which supplier his or her company buys a certain type of goods or services from. These types of bribes rarely appear as a bribe and often remain hidden unless your company has clear policies about bribery and you conduct regular investigative audits. Both preventive techniques act as a strong deterrent for this subtle form of bribery.

A common example often involves the perpetrating company offering to landscape the area around an employee's new home, or arrange for a new car for the employee's wife, or to "win" a paid vacation to an exotic place. Although sometimes cash will enter the picture, bribes today normally feature creative concealment, and cash does not appear in a bank account. To the casual observer or other employees, the person receiving the bribe bought a new car, had his new home landscaped, or took the family on a vacation, none of which will seem out of the ordinary. Depending on the size of the account, the supplier becomes more generous and might throw in some cash in a brown envelope delivered to the employee's house by courier.

Bribed employees' egos often lead to their apprehension. Bribed employees or their spouses cannot resist bragging about the bribe, or bringing their new-found "wealth" to the forefront to impress others. Take note of those employees in influential positions who earn a moderate salary but seem to enjoy a lifestyle well beyond their known income. Use discreet investigative audits to detect these damaging activities (see Chapter 17). The IRS uses a technique to detect taxpayers who claim that they earn a specific amount yet have demonstrable lifestyles that far exceed their reported income. This technique, commonly called *application of the net-worth-expenditures principle*, described in Appendix C, can be used effectively to detect bribery and a variety of other white collar crimes in your company.

Intangible Asset Bribery: Stocks and Bonds

Another form of contemporary bribery might include intangibles, such as stocks, bonds, or other valuable investments bought by a competitor, contractor, or supplier in an employee's name and often in a family member's name. For example, the bribe offer from a supplier, contractor, or competitor company recruiting a key staff member might include offering them stock in the company. Obviously, when people own stock in a company, they have a personal financial interest in the company and benefit if that stock increases in value. They would normally try to ensure that the stock received as a bribe remains secure. The employee who receives the bribe can do so by increasing the business of the company—arranging large purchases from the company or supplying information that will create a strong marketplace advantage and increased business. Either way, the other company influenced the employee to act based on a bribe.

■ SOLUTIONS TO YOUR CORPORATE EMPLOYEE BRIBERY PROBLEMS

The pervasive commercial bribery problem in corporations has a spectrum of viable solutions. Your first countermeasure to end this often complex white collar crime issue must include revising existing or creating a new series of company policies that deal specifically with the problem of employee bribery and associated offenses. To achieve the maximum benefits of a good company policy program, you must ensure that each employee has access to it (preferably in a handbook). The benefits encompass a strong deterrent effect and reduce confusion about what the company expects from each employee. Clear policy also eliminates the opportunity to rationalize a bribe or related offense or to claim ignorance of wrongdoing. A good rule for creating solutions is that preventing any white collar crime, including bribery offenses, is always better for the corporation than trying to deal with it after the fact. I've supplied examples of deterrent company policy guidelines (see Exhibits 4-1 through 4-3) to help you develop your own specific policies. However, whenever writing a new or revised company policy, ensure that you receive advice on language and restrictions from your corporate legal counsel and personnel specialist.

How to Develop Prevention-Oriented Company Policies

Many companies have no definitive policy about employees receiving gifts. Others create opportunity through loopholes and do little to prevent bribery in any of its forms. If you want employees to make company policies work, give them policies they can work with. Also, ensure that each employee, despite his or her position in the company, reads and signs a statement of understanding acknowledging that he or she has read and fully understands applicable company policies. That action in itself serves as a constructive deterrent. Consider the examples provided in this chapter as guidelines, and tailor your policy according to your specific situation and applicable laws.

Planning pointers include the following:

- Explain the IRS rules on business gifts. Gifts may qualify as reportable income.

- Determine whether inexpensive, impersonal items may be acceptable gifts in your business circles.

- Tell employees why accepting gifts from people who have a special interest in the company is generally unacceptable.

Exhibit 4-1 provides an example of a policy that creates a preventive foundation and enables you to develop further solutions.

Exhibit 4-1
Model Corporation Policy for Employees Receiving Business or Other Gifts and Payments

Employees of the ABC Corporation may not accept personal gifts or gratuities from any business entity that does business with or seeks to do business with ABC Corporation or any of its subsidiaries or interests. Employees must discourage receiving gifts and gratuities as noted above to the extent possible and immediately (within twenty-four hours or the next business day) report any gifts or gratuities received on ABC Form 2200 to the Personnel Director, who will maintain complete records of these transactions. The Personnel Director will take charge of the gift and seek a ruling from the Executive Board regarding its disposition.

As ordered by the ABC Corporation Executive Board, the Personnel Director will be responsible for donating all gifts and gratuities received by employees of ABC Corporation to one of the local charities. When a gift received from a supplier, contractor, or other person or company appears to be an attempt to gain favor, send a letter to the person or company presenting the gift to the ABC Corporation or employee thanking them for their goodwill and explaining the company policy requires all gifts of that type be donated to a local charity. The letter continues with the name of the recipient charity, adding that the donation was carried out in both company names. The Personnel Director will submit a full report to the Corporate Counsel on the fifth business day following the close of each quarter in reference to the gifts and gratuities received by company employees during that time. An annual report provided to the Board of Directors will show all gifts and gratuities received by ABC Corporation and its employees in the previous year, including disposition.

Invoices from suppliers for goods ordered by ABC Corporation must show discounts given to the Corporation. When receiving added goods (as opposed to cash discounts) from suppliers, their invoice should show that type of rebate. Whenever their invoice does not show added goods as discounts in a delivery, the receiving department manager will immediately report the added inventory on ABC Form 2200, forwarding it to the Corporate Comptroller and sending a copy to the Personnel Director.

Policy exceptions:

All gifts received by ABC Corporation employees from other companies that clearly have a primary purpose of advertising and public relations value—such as calendars, pens and pencils, and other items bearing the other company's name—will be exempt from reporting.

Regarding all gifts received by ABC Corporation employees from other companies who do or want to do business with ABC Corporation: If the gift has value no greater than $25, the employee may retain it for personal use or consumption on a one-time basis annually. However, the employee receiving the gift must report it to the Personnel Director on Form 2200 within twenty four hours or on the next business day. All later gifts within the same calendar year from the same or any other person or company will not be exempt.

The manager concerned must file a report for gifts to ABC Corporation or one of its divisions as a whole. However, in certain cases the gift may be shared jointly by ABC Corporation employees when it is to their benefit and morale and will not, in the judgment of the department or division manager, create an obligation or conflict of interest. Examples include candy, flowers, fruit, or other perishable or consumable items.

■ A CORPORATE NONCOMPETITION POLICY: AVOIDING CONFLICT OF INTEREST

A serious conflict of interest occurs when an employee competes with his or her employing company during employment and for a specified period after leaving the employ of the company. This conflict can occur, for example, in a sideline or postemployment consulting business. Your company might create an opportunity for the employee to accept money from competitors veiled as consulting fees, especially when there's no clear policy on this subject. In addition to a comprehensive company policy dealing with conflicts of interest, you should ensure that each employee signs an agreement of understanding about the policy as a prevention countermeasure. Consult your personnel director and corporate legal counsel for guidance on both documents, including the language.

Tips for creating this policy include:

■ Arrange for your corporate legal counsel to develop or review the company policy and written agreement of understanding.

■ Identify employees who should sign noncompetition agreements.

■ Establish a method for securing and maintaining contracts.

■ Review and update the policy as needed by law or circumstances.

Exhibit 4-2 is an example of a company noncompetition policy.

Exhibit 4-2
Model Corporate Noncompetition Policy During
and After Employment

This policy exists to supply protection of ABC Corporation assets. It is necessary for employees to agree to certain conditions that address noncompetition with the company during employment and for a postemployment period dependent on the type of job and level of access to company information experienced during employment.

These conditions will be detailed in a written agreement prepared by the Corporate Legal Counsel, signed by the employee, and maintained in each employee's personnel files.

The Corporate Legal Counsel will review the company's noncompetitive agreements at least twice a year, or as necessary, and inform the Executive Board of the agreements' status. No one is permitted to hold a position in ABC Corporation unless he or she has a signed agreement on file.

■ A CORPORATE NONDISCLOSURE POLICY

Protection of sensitive company information is essential to safeguard against indiscriminate publicity. You need a company policy that clearly informs employees (to put an end to excuses of not knowing) and creates a basis for legal action, should that become necessary. This policy should appear in your employees' handbooks and other department manuals and any written material that addresses the topic within the company. Ensure that you call on your Director of Human Services and Corporate Legal Counsel for help with the language of this policy.

Tips for creating your policy include:

- Determine what company information would supply advantage to a competitor.
- Clearly establish the confidential nature of certain sensitive information.
- Determine rules and procedures limiting access.

Exhibit 4-3 is an example of a corporate nondisclosure policy.

Exhibit 4-3
Model Corporate Nondisclosure Policy

All employees of ABC Corporation should be aware that certain manuals, materials, contracts, designs, and even oral statements are intended for use within the Company and should not be made available to nonemployees. Further, documents marked as restricted information are not authorized for disclosure outside the company or even within the company, unless there is a need for the employee to know that information. Employees should check with department supervisors and managers before conveying any restricted or confidential material to employees outside their departments, unless doing so complies with established and approved workflow needs.

Proprietary information must have labels whenever possible, and access to it will remain limited. This entails using a document vault or safe to store some restricted company materials and information when they are not in use. Also, access codes will be necessary to obtain sensitive computerized information.

Officers and management personnel should view requests for company materials by nonemployees as nonproductive to the company. Officers and management personnel should consult with the company's public relations director and corporate legal counsel and err on the side of caution regarding disclosure.

■ DISCLOSURE DETERRENT TIPS TO DETECT OFFENDERS

One of the best white collar crime deterrents includes a variety of obvious and not-so-obvious stumbling block layers. Employees or nonemployees contemplating a white collar crime will recognize your countermeasures and will suspect that you have other measures that are not so obvious. Using these effective deterrents creates probable detection too high for the employee to risk. Once you have solid company policies like those shown in Exhibits 4-1 through 4-3 in place, you need to create ways of detecting offenders.

Several tips follow:

Number your manuals: An important deterrent that will prevent employees from accepting a bribe for supplying company information to a competitor is to control materials. Manuals setting out operational policies, procedures, and techniques—especially those regarding marketing, research and development, purchasing, and others containing sensitive information—need serial numbers that are provided during the printing or reproduction process. Numbering the manual after it's printed and in the hands of company personnel supplies a weak deterrent. You need to arrange with a printer or internal employee (when using company word processors to produce manuals) to have the serial number appear on each page in the manual.

Number your documents: Each document, memorandum, or other material that contains sensitive information or information that would be helpful to a competitor needs an internal corporate, department, division, or section control number. The company should supply a block of control numbers to each division or department manager, who can further assign blocks of numbers to smaller elements within his or her department if they also generate documents. The documents begin, for example, at AR101ARS, which makes them easily recognized as generated by the Accounting Department (A), Restricted Document (R), Accounts Receivable Section (ARS). The sequential document control number shows between the letters. Should this document (or a copy of it) be in possession of an unauthorized person or in some unauthorized location inside or outside the company, you have reasonable cause to believe that some type of bribery is happening and you have a starting point for investigation.

Use cover sheets for documents: Stapling a distinctive cover sheet on sensitive documents also creates a strong deterrent for employees susceptible to bribery from a competitor. Ensure that you *staple* the cover to the document. Doing so can help detect copying, because you can see if a cover is bent due to placement on a copier machine or if a staple has been removed and replaced.

Have employees sign for manuals and documents: Employees who must sign their name for anything, including manuals and sensitive documents, are less susceptible to a bribe for that information. This requirement increases the risk and supplies an audit trail for detecting and investigating bribe activity.

■ CONTRACTS: A PRIME TARGET FOR EMPLOYEE BRIBERY SCHEMES

Corporate contracts supply a lucrative target for bribery (especially contracts involving large sums of money). Often, naive employees will find themselves unwittingly compromised in a scheme that delivers subtle bribes, kickbacks, or payoffs. Once compromised, the employee will often continue this white collar crime, either accepting more bribes or demanding a kickback in return for influencing your company to do business with a supplier.

Some actual examples demonstrate how bribery can evolve regarding contracts.

(1) Not long ago, a grand jury returned a several-count indictment against George, a contract manager for a major garment manufacturer, DEF Corporation. The indictment charged George with commercial bribery and theft. Later, in criminal court, George received a conviction for his activities and crimes: demanding and receiving kickbacks from industrial sewing companies for hiring them as subcontractors for his company. From the money received in kickbacks, George opened his own garment manufacturing plant and awarded it subcontracted work from his employing company. He also had inside information and often underbid his employing company or competitors, stealing business for the company he owned. He also equipped his plant with machines and fabric stolen from his employing company in a diversion scheme, and he received other materials as payoffs from suppliers who received contracts from his employing company.

(2) Another example involves a corporate customer representative charged with larceny, conspiracy to commit larceny, receiving a commercial bribe, and conspiracy to commit forgery. Ralph, a marketing and contracts manager, had sole authority from his employer, the XYZ Manufacturing Corporation, to administer contracts resulting from orders his department received for the company's electric motors. A particular high-volume distributor, one of XYZ's primary customers, ordered large numbers of electric motors. Using his position, Ralph arranged to ship motors, mixed with legitimate orders, to an electrical motor distributor without billing. According to evidence at Ralph's trial (which resulted in conviction), he shipped free motors valued at $550,000 to the distributor during a three-year period. In

return, Ralph received $250,000 in kickbacks from the distributor. To conceal the scheme, Ralph altered, forged, and destroyed corporate records. When Ralph became ill with the flu and stayed away from his office for two weeks, the distributor approached his replacement with a bribe offer, however, the replacement went directly to the company president. An intensive audit and later investigation showed the crimes, and criminal charges against the distributor and Ralph put an end to the scheme.

■ CREATING A COMPREHENSIVE POLICY ON CONTRACTS

Your preventive strategy for contract bribes, kickbacks, and payoffs must begin with a comprehensive corporate policy that creates awareness and sets up effective countermeasures. Although you should always seek guidance from your company's legal counsel about policy language, I've provided a simple policy (Exhibit 4-4). Use it to help you tailor a policy to suit your company and circumstances.

Three Contract Policy Planning Tips

1. Let employees know that a contract by another name (e.g., a sales agreement) is still a contract.
2. Ensure that customers' signatures are obtained, when appropriate.
3. Provide an avenue for employees to gain immediate legal consultation when needed.

Exhibit 4-4 is a Model Corporate Policy on Contracts.

Exhibit 4-4
Model Corporate Policy on Contracts

ABC Corporation's view is that employees who sign contracts on behalf of the company need training and information showing them the significance of their actions. Also, company sales people and other employees who interact with customers and suppliers must know when to introduce written agreements and obtain appropriate signatures. Because contracts are legal documents that obligate or entitle the company, they must have proper scrutiny before they are signed by a company representative. Employees must consult with department supervisors, managers, and the company's legal counsel before signing any agreement on behalf of the company. A department manager may waive this stipulation for some employees and some agreements (e.g., purchase orders) outlined in a separate company policy.

The corporate legal counsel will review and approve all contracts (e.g., sales agreements) issued by the company. Preprinted contracts commonly sold by office supply vendors are no exception. The legal counsel will initial each applicable contract in the lower right-hand margin of the last page of the contract.

The director of personnel will schedule orientation programs and periodic updated sessions regarding making, negotiating, and signing contracts for employees who have a need to know. He or she will seek company legal counsel advice and assistance in formulating this training.

■ VULNERABILITIES OF CORPORATE PURCHASING ACTIVITIES

Purchasing activities within your company might also create opportunities for employee bribery, especially kickbacks. A supplier eager for your company's account might offer a purchasing representative tempting kickbacks or bribes in return for larger orders. Often a part of the scheme involves substandard or defective commodities, or orders for supplies and materials that exceed needs. The supplier will manipulate the order in ways to ensure that the receiving company pays the kickback.

Real Estate and Building Contracts

Companies involved in building stores or other types of outlets and facilities often buy real estate and contract with builders and suppliers. Each aspect of this process supplies the opportunity for employee bribery, kickbacks, and payoffs. Contractors may feel a need to bribe due to misrepresentation of their capabilities, substandard construction, faulty equipment, problems with the land, or a spectrum of flaws involved with this type of operation. You need to conduct attentive investigative audits and ensure a system of approval and inspection in the contracting process. The more people involved in a systematic process of inspection and approval, the less opportunity for bribery or related offenses.

Other Opportunities for Contract Bribery

The best rule of thumb when deciding when to conduct investigative audits in the contract bribery category is to "follow the money." Whenever you know there are significant amounts of money involved in a company deal (either purchasing or arranging some other situation such as building, real estate, etc.) or a deal involves commodities with a value equivalent to a large sum of money, take note and create layered countermeasures to prevent and detect bribery.

■ HOW TO STRUCTURE AND CONDUCT AN INVESTIGATIVE AUDIT FOR CONTRACTS AND PURCHASING

Detecting a white collar crime of bribery in its diverse forms will prove a significant challenge for you (see Chapters 5 and 17). It's a crime that normally remains deeply hidden, carefully merged with daily business, and regularly is discovered accidentally. Much of the reason that traditional auditors, accountants, and security investigators overlook bribery and other forms of white collar crime stems from a reluctance to accept that people who don't fit the criminal model may become criminals. You need to abandon preconceived notions and approach each audit or investigation from a neutral viewpoint and let the chips fall where they may. Only then will you detect these elusive crimes and establish the best prevention efforts.

For example, how can you know that a purchasing manager takes a kickback on commodities normally purchased by your company? How will you know that a contract manager accepted a bribe to edge out competitors and award a seemingly legitimate contract to a specific company? Even when you know that happened, a crime of bribery can appear so complex and murky that it often discourages adept accountants and auditors, who approach their work from numbers rather than strategy. They can, however, help you uncover these crimes; although you must contribute by showing them specifically which numbers to look for. In the following pages, I'll show you the most common and vulnerable areas of employee bribery and how to use them to conduct your investigative audit. Although it's not possible to list and explain every possible circumstance (because they generally vary depending on your company's business operations) those I do show can be adapted and tailored to your situation.

Determine the Need of the Items Purchased.

Assuming the contracts meet your company's legal specifications, and are cleared by the Corporate Counsel and others in the company, you need to look at them in a different way. Your investigative audit must determine the requirement for the items purchased. For example, did your company need 100,000 widgets when they were purchased? Even when the items bought through a contract involve regular resupply of items (such as in a manufacturing circumstance), you need to look at the justification for the purchase at that time and the reason for purchasing from the supplying company. A good reason might include a meaningful discount by ordering now, instead of waiting until a legitimate need arises and paying a cost increase. Another good reason might include a hint that soon the item will be in short supply (maybe due to a labor strike against your supplier or some other legitimate, reasonable purpose). However, when that's not the case, you might have found a chink in the white collar crime concealment armor. Remember, white collar crime strategy always makes the offense *appear* legitimate. The offender relies on his or her skill to disguise and conceal as well as the company's cooperation by not asking the right questions.

Since your investigative audit happens after the fact, you will have enough facts available to determine if a legitimate need or reasonable logic did exist and if there were any legitimate reasons for the order. For example, you might find no change in prices from a specific purchase compared to later purchases. You might find that at the time of the purchase or contract, your company had no immediate or future need that would call for placing the order. Also, you might find no hints of supplier shortages, strikes, or increased prices that might supply good reasons for the purchase.

Audit the Activities before Purchasing Actions

You should examine this area carefully to determine if the employee(s) used a valid method of determining your company's need for the item and why he or she chose the supplier. You're looking for inconsistent behavior, such as switching to another supplier without any substantiating purpose. Also, you want to know how the purchasing department or personnel decides when to place orders or draw up contracts. Find out if a policy or procedure exists and determine if it's followed attentively. When you learn that in specific instances it is not, and there's no supporting reason for the action, you might have uncovered bribery or kickback activity.

Examine the existing company policy and procedures for purchasing and contracts. You might find one that is outdated, supplies poor parameters, or does not exist. Ironically, I have found in many large companies that the method of purchasing and contracts is handled more frequently with unwritten policy and procedures than with clear, written guidelines. In those companies, I found a long history of bribery, kickbacks, and payoffs. Your investigative audit will also help to create an effective policy and procedure process for purchasing and contracts.

Determine if Contract Specifications Were Met

Your company's contract with a supplier must have specifications, often involving detailed drawings and descriptions. Often, these specifications supply a contractor with information necessary to formulate and submit a realistic bid. They also call for the supplier to meet your company's rigid quality standards in special manufacturing and in stock orders. For example, when your company places orders, the responsible employee must show that he or she understands the importance of receiving exactly what's needed, instead of leaving the decision to a supplier. When you conduct your investigative audit, look at the contracts (including sales agreements and others) to determine if specifications appear. When they do not, you need to develop a new policy and procedure for your company's contracts; and when specifications already exist, the employee who doesn't follow them carefully should become a suspect for possible collusion with a supplier. Even on simple items like office supplies, you should specify exactly what's needed. For example, if you need 20-pound smooth paper for the copier, the responsible employee ordering must show that specification in the contract, purchase order, or sales agreement. Otherwise, the supplier might send 18-pound grained paper simply because it has an excess and can legally fulfill your contracts in this way because they say only "copy machine paper."

This element is important because when specifications are not precise and detailed, the employee purchasing the supplies for the company has a golden opportunity to make an illicit deal. In collusion with a supplier, the employee can place a large, vague order and receive the items (although they are not always usable and not to your company's standards), receive them, and show them on the company inventory, which is normally computerized. When there are complaints from departments about the items, the same employee reorders, and this time the right items arrive and go out to departments. Everyone in the system is happy, and the original substandard items either collect dust in the department store rooms or come back to a central supply center and collect dust.

Although in an honest business environment, the items would return for credit, in dishonest situations they're part of a kickback scheme. You can end that by requiring that every contract, agreement, or purchase order from your company to another have clear specifications and be supported with rigid procedures of returning any item(s) that do not meet those specifications. When you look for this trend during your investigative audit and ensure that traditional internal audits watch for these problems, the opportunity for undetected kickbacks is effectively eliminated. However, even with countermeasures in place, you must stay vigilant.

When a company has rigid rules about specifications on contracts and similar instruments, the employees looking for extra money from kickbacks can make the specifications appear accurate but alter them enough to continue their white collar crime. This is easy if the company readily accepts what appear to be legitimate contracts, agreements, and purchase orders without carefully reading and comparing them. For example, the white collar offender in this situation will not repeatedly submit flawed specifications, but instead slip one in now and then.

Another problem to look for in your investigative audit on specifications includes price increases after a contract is awarded on a bid. Through either neglect or design, persons preparing faulty specifications leave openings for a seemingly legitimate price change after your company awards the contract. For example, in collusion with a contractor, the company employee responsible carefully flaws the specification, which might pass by several people who do not notice the change. The contractor submits a low bid and receives the award from your company. The contractor, knowing the flaw exists, waits until beginning work and then suddenly finds it and submits modification requests with the substantially increased cost. Your company can reject the bid and start again, maybe losing months of time and probably getting involved in a significant lawsuit that it will probably lose. Or, it can agree with the increases. The contractor, having pulled off the scheme, will pay the conspiring employee a sizable kickback.

Other problems to look for include purposely prepared specifications that *imply* a high-cost item when an inexpensive item will meet the company's requirement. A favored contractor, through various illegal methods, participates with the contracting manager to create specifications that enable the contractor to bid on the lowest priced item to ensure that he or she receives the contract. The contracting supplier knows that the other competitive bidders will bid on the high-priced item. I have found a 3000 percent difference in contract cases I've worked on for major corporations between a contractor's low-price bid and the bids of competitors.

The low-priced contractor has control of the specification and edges out competitive bidders. The trick to this scheme is within the contract language (especially for furnishings and other commercial products where "or equal" clauses are within the specifications). The specification that *implies* high cost becomes fulfilled with cheap items supported by the "or equal" clause. The employee creating the specifications can imply the cost in extensive language, and rarely will anyone in the company have time to give it close scrutiny. I've also found specification schemes that list a particular brand name of a small, nearly unknown local firm. What usually results is that the competitive companies are unable to find the firm (to price and identify the item), so they offer no bid on the item.

Scrutinize Solicitations for Bids, Proposals, and Quotations

Solicitation by your company invites the best possible deal for bids on commodities, proposals, and quotations for work or services. Two techniques will normally be used by corporations. Both need your investigative audit scrutiny to detect possible bribery, kickbacks, and payoffs.

(1) In formal advertising, companies solicit bids through dissemination of invitations for bid to sources on file, posting such invitations in public places and advertising in media such as business or trade journals and certain newspapers. You need to audit to determine if the contracting employee has used the widest range of competition available. White collar offenders can use advertising to disguise their real intent of awarding the contract to a specific company. Keep track of how much advertising for bids was carried out in specific terms, and take note of the placement of advertising. For example, offenders might disguise their schemes by showing a list of publications where an invitational ad appeared. You need to see if those publications were the best placement available. If not, then you need to investigate the background of the employee in relationship to experience, past placement of such advertising, etc. You want to develop information that will indicate if this person is incompetent, inexperienced, or involved in a white collar bribery scheme. You also need to examine whatever guidance the employee relied on in this process. Does your company or the contracting and purchasing department maintain research lists and files that help the responsible person choose the right publications, companies, and other techniques that will ensure the best possible deal for your company?

(2) In a negotiation method of purchasing, you don't need dissemination—it's best to encourage competition whenever practical and feasible. You cannot, however, solicit competition from a sole source contractor who, by virtue of a patent on a desired item, is the only source available. Because the sources chosen for solicitation rest solely on your company's contracting employee or manager, you must stay alert during your investigative audit to

the possibilities of collusion, conflict of interest, and acceptance of bribes and gratuities by that employee.

Maintain Security of Bids Before and After Opening

This aspect of contracting and purchasing applies only to those companies that received invitations through formal advertising. After a company or contractor completes price estimates and needed data on the solicitation (e.g., for 100,000 widgets), the bid goes to the contracting office of your company before the deadline set in the advertisement. In your investigative audit, you need to look for accepting late bids, allowing contractors to make corrections to their bids after bid openings, prereleasing purchasing information, surreptitious opening of sealed bids to effect changes for favored contractors, and poor security for sealed or unsealed bids. Each of those conditions supplies the opportunity for bribery or kickbacks by employees (not only those in the contracting and purchasing departments). When poor security of bids exists, other employees might gain access on a weekend or after normal business hours and inform a contractor of bid information. When you discover suspicious activity in these areas, your thinking will often focus on the contracting and purchasing department. When security is tight and well managed, you are right; when it is not, you should look beyond that department to other employees who might have access. If your company has a weekend and evening sign-in log, it might supply leads. However, the perpetrator might have stayed late and not be shown on the log. Other clues might stem from the previous or following areas; however, this element is an important audit feature.

Ensure that Contractor is Qualified to Receive Award

Purchases should normally stem from contracts (or sales agreements) to responsible prospective contractors only. The award of a contract to a supplier based on lowest evaluated price alone can be false economy if there is subsequent default, late delivery, or other unsatisfactory performance resulting in added administrative cost. Your company needs sound policies and procedures for this important aspect, and your audit will determine if such policies are in place and if they're adequate. You can determine how to create such policies and procedures, evaluate existing ones, and audit the validity of the contracting and purchasing department's choices. The latter is significant when you're looking for the following indicators of bribery or kickbacks:

(1) Minimum general standards needed to qualify a contractor (or company) as responsible should include the following elements:

- Adequate financial resources, or the ability to obtain such resources as needed during performance of the contract.

- Ability to follow the required or proposed delivery or performance schedule, considering all existing business commitments.

- A satisfactory record of performance (contractors who are sufficiently deficient in current contract performance, when considering contracts and deficiencies of each, shall without proof to the contrary be presumed to be unable to meet this requirement). Also, you should look for indications of demonstrated nontenacity or nonperseverance to do an acceptable job for your company, which would normally be enough to justify a finding of nonresponsibility.

- A satisfactory record of integrity.

- Be otherwise qualified and eligible to receive a contract from your company under applicable laws and regulations.

(2) Standards for production, maintenance, construction, and research and development contracts are as follows:

- Have the necessary organization, experience, operational controls, and technical skill, or the ability to obtain them including, where appropriate, such elements as production control procedures, property control systems, and quality assurance measures applicable to materials produced or service performed by the prospective contractor and subcontractors.

- Have the necessary production, construction, and technical equipment and facilities, or the ability to obtain them. Where a prospective contractor proposed to use facilities or equipment of another company not a subcontractor or affiliate, all exiting business arrangements, firm or contingent, for the use of the facilities or equipment will be considered in the ability of the prospective contractor to perform the contract.

(3) The inspection conducted by a preaward policy is important in the decision to award a contract. The survey should be complete and thorough to a point where there is no doubt about the ability and competence of a prospective contractor.

(4) In formally advertised contracts, a contractor must be responsive in the bid before qualifying for an award. Responsiveness in purchasing includes the prospective bidder furnishing the necessary details requested in the company's solicitation. Failure to provide or conform to all the required information generally makes the contractor nonresponsive and the contractor becomes ineligible for award.

Ensure Integrity of Award Procedures

Awarding a contract is a formality carried out by the contracting manager, who notifies the successful bidder of the award and signs an agreement with a contractor in a negotiated-type contract. The award should always come after consideration of the previously discussed criteria by the company representative. In your investigative audit, examine the statement and certificate of award that justifies the contracting manager's decision to make the award to the successful bidder.

Monitor Contractor's Production Progress

In this purchasing function, the contractor's production is monitored according to adherence to the contract terms and conditions. An area of interest from your company's viewpoint is timely completion of contracted work, as well as problems that may delay delivery and relate to anticipated delinquency. Your area of concern when conducting investigative audits of past contracts and contractor performance is to determine if timely production reports were submitted and if false, misleading, vague, or inaccurate reports were received. This type of search is especially important in examining delinquent contracts because reports may not reflect expected delinquency, which might have led to possible contractor and contract management collusion. The production reports should be in the contract file, and missing reports may indicate collusion by the contract and purchasing department or other company employees. Also, the possibility of bribery and conflict of interest should not be overlooked.

Monitor Quality Assurance

Quality assurance is a vulnerable area in the contract and purchasing functions. It is the function your company should exploit to determine whether a contractor has fulfilled the contract obligations regarding quality and quantity. This function is related to and generally precedes the act of acceptance. Your investigative audit should look for your company representatives not monitoring quality and allowing contractors to use inferior materials; falsifying inspection reports; permitting contractors to meet weight specifications by adding inferior materials or allowing them to fail in meeting weight, density, and tolerance specifications; accepting rejected items; and accepting less than contract requirements.

Search for Contract Waivers Granted

Your company might supply a contract waiver where a contractor mistakenly made a deviation in the specifications of an item he or she is to produce under contract. The deviation may be of a major nature but the end product still would function in the required manner (e.g., a contractor drills a hole in the wrong place in items he or she is producing for your company and does not notice the mistake until after producing a large quantity of items). The hole can be plugged without affecting the function of the end item.

Justify Contract Delinquency

Delinquencies in a contract between your company and a contractor are due to either (1) the contractor's failure to perform or (2) unanticipated labor problems such as strikes, machinery breakdown, or subcontractor problems. The unanticipated problems are usually acceptable; however, failure to perform should not be tolerated and your primary concern is whether a justification of the delay is justified or deliberate.

Search for any Collusion in Bidding

This is a noncompetitive practice in which prospective contractors get together and plan high bids, allowing one contractor to bid slightly lower and to receive the award at a higher price than if standard, honest bidding occurred. Generally, the awards go from one contractor to another with each subsequent award, and there is someone in your company who influences the awarding of contracts.

Be Alert to "Buying In"

This is a noncompetitive practice in which a contractor bids low, hoping to make his or her profit through change orders or through kickbacks from subcontractors.

■ CONVERTING YOUR INVESTIGATIVE AUDIT INTO A CRIMINAL INVESTIGATION

When your investigative audit discloses probable criminal activity, you need to begin to collect and verify evidence (see Chapters 16 and 17). These offenses always involve some type of documents, including those that emerge from the first transaction. For example, a bribe given to an employee will be one transaction, and the reason for it will normally develop into other types of documents, such as contracts, information, or other illegal or unauthorized activity between the employee offender and the other party (normally a contractor or competitor). Although your audit shows that the activity might have happened regularly, remember that a criminal investigation needs to remain specific and narrow. For example, you need to choose one incident or situation at a time and prove it separately from others.

■ THE USE OF DOCUMENTS IN PROVING A CRIMINAL CASE

Because you will have to prove your case primarily with documents, Exhibit 4-5 will help you understand their importance and take the proper steps.

Exhibit 4-5
Definitions of Terms Regarding Forgery

A document: Any material that bears handwriting, handprinting, print, typewriting, or any type of drawing or mark. Handwriting includes all systems by which words, letters, symbols, or characters are produced on any type of surface, such as walls, blackboards, cardboard, or paper of any kind or description, if the graphic representations are handwritten.

A questioned document: A document whose genuineness is questioned, normally because of origin, authenticity, age, or the circumstances of writing the document.

A holographic document: A document that's wholly in the handwriting of one person.

A standard document: A document recognized as proven, genuine, or acknowledged as obtained from official records, personal letters, and other sources and known to be the product of a particular person or machine.

An exemplar: A document requested by a law enforcement officer that duplicates the text of a questioned document and is known to be the product of a particular person or machine.

Classification of Documents

Questioned documents fall into two general classifications: genuine and fraudulent. It's often of greater importance to prove a document genuine than it is to prove it forged. A genuine document is often disputed because it imposes a liability on the maker. For example, a person who writes a genuine check may later deny that it's genuine in an attempt to avoid financial responsibility.

Guidelines to Discover Repeat Offenses

Offenses involving questioned documents such as forgery and alteration of documents (including making bogus bills of lading) are often recurring offenses. The offender may commit the crime repeatedly using the same method of operation (modus operandi). The guidelines provided in Exhibit 4-6 will help discover repeat offenses.

Exhibit 4-6
Guidelines to Detect Repeat Offenders

☐ You should give special attention to factors that may link the offense under investigation to other, similar incidents.

☐ You must recognize the importance of the laboratory document examiner in processing evidence in fraudulent document cases.

☐ Meet and discuss laboratory procedures and needs with a certified laboratory document examiner.

☐ The techniques used in laboratory processing are equally applicable to writings in any language using an alphabet. The document examiner does not necessarily have to be acquainted with an alphabet (e.g., foreign language or technical data) to reach a firm, scientific finding.

☐ Document examination theory asserts the improbability of any two writings being exactly alike in characteristics such as style, speed, slant, and spacing.

☐ Writing involves a mental process, despite the skill we develop and the habitual, almost automatic nature of it; in addition, writing involves muscular coordination.

☐ Besides the physical characteristics mentioned above, there are other clues to help identify a particular writer.

☐ The terminology used in a letter, or referral to a confidential incident, may provide an insight into the identification of the writer.

☐ The writer may identify with a small group of persons and use highly technical terms.

☐ Punctuation, spelling, grammar, syntax, and style are all valid clues that may lead to the writer's identity.

Checklist of Possible Offenses Involving Questioned Documents

Because questioned document cases arise in many different contexts, you must be able to distinguish among the various offenses to provide the evidence necessary to prove each offense. The offenses discussed below occur most often in cases involving questioned documents. When you find cases not involving any of the situations discussed in this checklist, note that the same process and procedures usually apply to any questioned document case.

Forgery

A person is guilty of forgery if, with purpose to defraud or injure anyone, or with knowledge of facilitating a fraud or injury to be perpetrated by anyone, the actor (1) alters any writing of another without their authority; or (2) makes, completes, executes, authenticates, issues, or transfers any writing so that it purports to be the act of another who did not authorize that act, or to have been executed at a time or place or in a numbered sequence other than true, or supplies a copy of an original document when no such original existed; or (3) utters any writing the person knows to be forged in a manner shown in paragraph (1) or (2). (Model Penal Code, § 2241)

Crime includes both acts of forging handwriting of another and acts of uttering as true and genuine any forged writing knowing them to be forged with intent to prejudice, damage, or defraud any person (*State v. May*, 93 Idaho 343, 461 P. 2d 126, 129).

Crime happens when one makes or passes a false instrument with intent to defraud, and the element of loss or detriment is immaterial. (*People v. McAffery*, 182 Cal. App. 2d 486, 6 Cal. Rptr. 333, 337)

The false making of an instrument, which purports on the face of it to be genuine for purposes intended, with a design to defraud any person or persons. (*State v. Goranson*, 67 Wash. 2d 456, 408 P. 2d 7, 9)

Counterfeiting of Evidence

The fabrication or counterfeiting of evidence involves the artful and fraudulent manipulation of physical objects, or the deceitful arrangement of genuine facts or things, in a manner to create an erroneous impression or a false inference in the minds of those who may observe them.

Falsely Made Instruments

This is an essential element of forgery, not involving material alteration. The term refers to manner of a writing instead of to its substance or effect. A falsely made instrument is one that's fictitious, not genuine, or in some way something other than it purports to be, without regard to the truth or falsity of facts stated in it. (*Wright v. US*, C.A. Ariz. 172 F.2d 310, 311)

Fraud

This is a generic term that embraces all multifarious means that human ingenuity can devise and that one person resorts to in order to get advantage over another by false suggestions or by suppression of truth. Fraud includes all surprise, trick, cunning dissembling, and any unfair way by which another is cheated (*Johnson v. McDonald*, 170 Okl. 117, 39 P. 2d 150)

Rasure

This is the act of scraping, scratching, or shaving the surface of a written instrument to remove certain letters or words from it. It is to be distinguished from obliteration, as the latter word properly denotes the crossing out of a word or letter by drawing a line through it with ink. The two expressions are often used interchangeably.

■ ESSENTIAL ELEMENTS OF PROOF IN A CRIMINAL INVESTIGATION

You need to prove the alleged offender's activity with documents of some type that show clearly the following elements:

(1) *There is a state (or federal) law (or statute) that forbids the employee's or the other party's activity*. When there is no law governing the activity, there can

be no "criminal" offense. There might, however, be a basis for civil court action (a tort), and that should be proved as carefully as a criminal offense to ensure that your company eliminates liability for charges it cannot support to ensure that the court will find for your company if a lawsuit evolves. There might be a company policy regarding the matter, and perhaps a statement signed by the employee acknowledging a clear understanding that the activity is not authorized and that doing so or attempting to do so can lead to termination of employment. However, to fire an employee on those grounds calls for sufficient evidence to prove beyond doubt the policy offense and to protect your company if the fired employee sues for wrongful employment termination or defamation. Whichever course of action your company decides on in a given situation, ensure that you have documented proof equivalent, if possible, to that needed to file criminal charges. In so doing, you will have eliminated the possibility of error and placed yourself and the company in a clear, defensible position should the employee, contractor, or competitor decide to take a counteraction.

(2) *The offense, tort, or company policy violation in some way "injured" the company.* For example, a bribed or influenced employee, by his or her actions, created a monetary loss to your company in some way. A monetary loss could mean that (1) the company suffered an actual loss of money from the activity, (2) the company had to pay more money for goods and services than if the activity hadn't happened, (3) the activity caused a loss of company reputation and credibility that resulted in decreased business, (4) the activity caused the company to spend sums of money to audit, investigate, and take corrective action; or (5) some other legal injury, damage, or loss for the company resulted from the activity.

(3) *There is conclusive proof that the activity happened.* The belief that this type activity happened based on your audit does not prove it did. Having a signed document, for example, will not be conclusive. Having a laboratory examiner skilled in verifying handwriting certify that the document was signed by the employee, contractor, or competitor is necessary to protect the company and your personal interests. For example, you have a signed contract that is the key item of evidence, and the signatures (based on others on file) appear genuine. However, in a court of law, your opinion will not be enough, and you'll need the opinion of a recognized expert in handwriting and document examination. The handwriting expert will need several "known" exemplars of the person whose signature is in question to compare with the signature on the questioned document. You may ask the person to supply the exemplars; but you need to tell the person why you need them, and normally he or she will refuse to supply them, often on the advice of an attorney. However, there remain several sources of known signatures you can legally obtain and use without the person's permission, even in criminal

offenses. The same holds true for the person signing as a contractor or contractor's agent, and the person signing for a competitor, or other circumstances involving handwriting or signatures. When the case involves a company employee present or past, you can obtain original signatures or "known" standards from the employee's personnel records. However, you can also obtain reliable known standards from many other sources listed in Exhibit 4-7.

Exhibit 4-7
A Checklist of Handwriting Standards

1. Account books	54. Leases, real property
2. Affidavits	55. Letters
3. Application forms	56. Library card forms
4. Assignments	57. Light company forms
5. Autographs	58. Life insurance forms
6. Auto insurance forms	59. Loan applications
7. Auto license applications	60. Mail orders
8. Auto title applications	61. Manuscripts
9. Bank deposit slips	62. Marriage records
10. Bank safe deposit box slips	63. Membership cards
11. Bank savings withdrawal slips	64. Memoranda—all kinds
12. Bank signature cards	65. Military papers
13. Bank receipts	66. Mortgages
14. Bible entries	67. Motor vehicle records
15. Bills of sale	68. Newspaper advertising
16. Bonds	69. Occupational writings
17. Books, signature of owner	70. Package receipts
18. Building after hours registers	71. Report card signatures
19. Business license applications	72. Partnership papers
20. Charity pledges	73. Pawn tickets
21. Checkbook stubs	74. Passports
22. Checks, cancelled	75. Payroll receipts
23. Church pledges	76. Pension applications
24. Convention registrations	77. Permit applications
25. Contracts	78. Petitions, referendums
26. Cooking recipes	79. Photograph albums
27. Corporation papers	80. Court pleadings
28. Criminal records	81. Postal cards

29. Credit applications
30. Credit cards
31. Deeds
32. Deeds of trust
33. Depositions
34. Diaries
35. Dog license applications
36. Drafts
37. Drive-it-yourself applications for rental trucks
38. Drivers' licenses/applications
39. Druggists' poison registers
40. Employment applications
41. Envelopes
42. Fishing licenses
43. Funeral attendance registers
44. Gas service applications
45. Gasoline mileage records
46. Gate records at plant
47. Greeting cards
48. Hospital entry applications
49. Hotel/motel guest registers
50. Hunting licenses
51. Identification cards
52. Inventories
53. Employment records

82. Probate court records
83. Promissory notes
84. Property damage reports
85. Recipes
86. Receipts for rent, etc.
87. Registered mail receipts
88. Release of mortgages
89. Rental contracts
90. Reports
91. School/college records
92. Social security cards
93. Sport scoring cards
94. Stock certificates
95. Surety bond application
96. Tax estimates/returns
97. Telegram copies
98. Telephone service applications
99. Time sheets/cards
100. Traffic tickets
101. Vehicle rental forms
102. Voting registrations
103. Water company applications
104. Wills
105. Worker's Compensation Insurance papers

Three Methods of Proving a Handwriting Standard Is Genuine

There is a legal requirement that handwriting standards be proved to be official and genuine. Three methods of proof are

1. By personal acknowledgment of the persons supplying standards
2. By testimony from witnesses who can state from their own knowledge that certain persons supplied the standards
3. By comparison with exemplars known to be written by a certain person.

When the genuineness of a signature is questioned, you should obtain standards of a known signature, especially those in possession of or accessible to a suspect. This enables a laboratory document examiner to determine whether the genuine signature is traced and determine the actual signature traced.

When a suspect agrees to give you handwriting or signature standards, submit standards (obtained from another source but known to be authentic) with collected exemplars. The examiner can then determine the normal handwriting habits of the writer and find attempts to disguise the writing in the exemplars.

■ EXAMINING TYPEWRITTEN AND COMPUTER-PRINTED DOCUMENTS

Often, you must examine many typewriters and printers to determine which one produced a questioned document. You can eliminate many without submitting exemplars of their typewriting to the laboratory. However, always consider the interchangeable elements and daisy wheels on typewriters and printers before reaching a conclusion. For example, a suspect may buy an element or daisy wheel that will work on office typewriters, a home machine, a rental, or one supplied at a center open to the public (libraries), which makes hasty conclusions risky. An element or daisy wheel may be identifiable to a specific machine. Each machine normally has characteristics besides the element, daisy wheel, or typist. For example, a forger or perpetrator of fraud might install an element or daisy wheel in a typewriter or printer for making the document, then remove it and hide it or throw it away. Since the elements are costly and the person may want to use them further, he or she will probably have them and may be hiding them.

If this isn't the case, you can do a process of elimination by comparing certain letters used in the questioned document. For example, examine the lowercase letters *M* and *W* first. Normally, they are the most distinctive in style, and if there are any deviations from this style, you will recognize them easily. See Exhibit 4-8.

Exhibit 4-8
Guidelines for Examining Typewritten Exemplars

Examining the M and W

☐ The bottom of the staffs of the lower case *m* may or may not have serifs (cross strokes at the bottom).

- [ ] The two outside staffs may have serifs, and the center staff may have none.
- [ ] The center v-like formation of the capital *M* may descend to the base line or end at varying distances above it. If it descends to the base line, it may or may not have a serif.
- [ ] The inverted *v* of the center formation of the *W* may or may not extend to the top of the line formed by the outer parts of the letter and may or may not have a serif at the top.

Guidelines for Obtaining Typewritten Exemplars

- [ ] The numerals should be examined on typewriters and printers. Usually, they're distinctive and it's easy to determine differences.
- [ ] The size of type is also easy to see (for example, pica, elite, and many others).
- [ ] When typewritten exemplars appear similar, include them in your submission to a certified laboratory.
- [ ] You should obtain several exemplars from each machine for successful identification.
- [ ] Unless, through excessive abuse, a typewriter produces typing of distinctive individuality, identifying a typed text as produced by one machine is time consuming and calls for the use of precision instruments.
- [ ] Each typist develops certain personal characteristics of typing, which often are easily identified. For example, work produced by different typists can often be differentiated by typists' individually developed techniques, talents, coordination, skill, and aptitude.

Elements Required in a Typewritten Exemplar

- [ ] A heading
- [ ] Name of person producing the exemplar
- [ ] Make of typewriter and its serial number
- [ ] Electric or nonelectric typewriter
- [ ] Computer printer, daisy wheel, or element
- [ ] Place where an exemplar originates
- [ ] The date the exemplar was produced
- [ ] Signature of the person producing the exemplar
- [ ] Your signature for identification purposes

Steps to Take When Obtaining Typewriter and Computer-Printed Exemplars

- ☐ Verify that the exemplar follows the style of the questioned document.
- ☐ Double space the exemplar if the questioned document is double spaced.
- ☐ Make indentations the same.
- ☐ Make the length of and number of words in each line the same as the questioned writing.
- ☐ Duplicate the word or part of a word ending a line on the questioned document.
- ☐ Make the exemplar as close a copy of the questioned document as physically possible.
- ☐ Have the second exemplar typed by someone other than the person typing the first exemplar.
- ☐ Reproduce the complete keyboard for the second exemplar, first in normal order and then with a space between each letter, numeral, and symbol.
- ☐ Include a carbon copy exemplar if the questioned document is a carbon copy.
- ☐ Make a third exemplar by the carbon stencil method.
- ☐ Use a new piece of carbon paper. It's placed in contact with the paper as though the paper will be a carbon copy—for example, with the carbon side of the carbon paper against the paper used to obtain the carbon stencil.
- ☐ Remove the ribbon of the typewriter/printer or set the machine on stencil, if possible.
- ☐ Strike the carbon paper directly.
- ☐ Make sure the spacing, line length, and word composition are the same as the other exemplars.
- ☐ Don't submit the carbon paper with the exemplar.
- ☐ Omit the carbon stencil exemplar if the typewriter/printer normally uses a carbon paper ribbon (film).
- ☐ Reproduce the questioned document in its entirety if it's approximately one-half page in length.
- ☐ Reproduce the first twenty to thirty lines if the document is lengthy.
- ☐ Examine the remainder of the questioned document, adding any words, numerals, or symbols not appearing in the first twenty or thirty lines of the exemplar.

☐ Add the word preceding and following the material typed as it appears in the questioned document.

☐ Compare the exemplars and the questioned document to find out whether the ribbon producing the exemplars appears to have about the same degree of wear and is of the same style and character as the one which produced the questioned document.

☐ Obtain information about when the ribbon on the machine was last changed and when the date of the latest repair work was done on the machine, including the type of repair performed.

Obtaining Typewritten Standards

☐ Determine a typing date of the questioned document. Then try to obtain standards of the work typed on that machine during that period.

☐ Compare the typing produced by a particular machine during a particular time with the typing produced by it later. This will show any other defects, flaws, or changes in its characteristics.

■ PRECAUTIONS TO TAKE WHEN SENDING DOCUMENT EVIDENCE TO A CERTIFIED LABORATORY

Sending document evidence to the certified laboratory for examination doesn't require elaborate preparation, but there are some precautions you should take.

1. Protect the questioned document from damage. This is best accomplished by placing enough heavy wrapping material around it to prevent it from bending, tearing, or folding in transit.

2. Identify the questioned document so it's not confused with any exemplars and standards submitted.

3. Write your laboratory request in a neutral tone so an examiner has no clue about which of several persons you suspect as the author.

4. Word the request properly. Although all laboratory examinations are without bias, the wording of your request may influence a court to believe otherwise.

■ TIPS FOR MISCELLANEOUS DOCUMENT EXAMINATIONS

The following tips will help you collect documents and evaluate the importance of document collection in a white collar crime investigation. In addition, these tips might link persons to the crime who might otherwise escape discovery through clever concealment schemes.

Examination of Indented Writing

Indented writing is the impression made by a typewriter, printer or handheld ballpoint pen or a pencil made under the ink. Although the ink might become obliterated, the indentation or impression into the paper below it might remain readable by a laboratory using special equipment. Other cases arise when the only evidence available are indentations second sheets, which are sheets of paper underlying the one that the original writing was placed on. The pressure of the writing instrument will leave a trace of the writing on a second sheet. If the pressure is great enough, the indented writing might be seen on several underlying sheets. A laboratory examiner can often decipher indented writing by chemical processing, special lighting, and photographic techniques.

Charred Documents

You should understand the following differences between a charred document and ashes:

- A charred document is one that has become blackened and brittle due to burning and an absence of oxygen.
- Documents placed in a container that is involved in a fire might catch fire, but since there's very little oxygen, the paper will normally char instead of burn and turn to ash.
- No restoration of ashes is possible. However, with charred documents laboratory techniques often enable the writing on them to become visible (usually using infrared photography).
- Charred documents are extremely fragile and are destroyed if not handled carefully.
- If feasible, send charred documents to a certified laboratory by courier to prevent needless handling and to prevent destruction.

- In some cases, if the document is fragile, it may be best to ask the laboratory technician to come to the location of the document.
- If neither of these two aforementioned alternatives is practical, package the document carefully to prevent destruction.

Mutilated Documents

Documents torn accidentally or purposefully may be restored with care and time. Documents often become mutilated by being subjected to a washing machine, either by accident or by a person who is trying to make the washing appear as an accident.

Differences in Inks

You might note that samples of ink appear alike; however, a laboratory examination might show that they are different in composition. One technique of laboratory examination is chromatography, a chemical process that separates the compounds into separate, colored layers. You need very little ink for this process—a single capital letter may furnish an enough quantity. However, the removal of this ink from a document may affect the admissibility of the document in court.

Laboratory Analysis of Paper Samples

Laboratory analysis of paper samples to determine similarities or differences in composition may lead to a conclusion about a common origin with other samples. Adhesive used to hold sheets of paper in tablet form, when analyzed, can determine whether two or more sheets of paper could originally have been a part of one tablet. You may examine papers under ultraviolet light to detect similarities or differences in fluorescence or reflectance that may provide you with an investigative lead pending the laboratory analysis.

Other Examinations

In other types of examinations, such as examinations of copying machines, printed products, and office machines, you should contact a certified laboratory for guidance in collecting specimen material.

■ GUIDELINES FOR PRESERVING AND HANDLING DOCUMENT EVIDENCE

1. A questioned document should never be folded, crumpled, or carried unprotected in a pocket. The document should be placed between transparent protective covers, or in a clean paper envelope. You'll want to avoid handling the document and to prevent any marring by contamination or destruction by abrasive action.

2. Don't try to restore a torn document. Place it or the pieces in a protective cover.

3. Handle a document with tweezers to prevent addition of your fingerprints if a document analysis includes examination for latent fingerprints.

Fingerprints often appear on documents when developed through a fuming process. Normally, the developed latent fingerprints become stronger eventually and remain permanent. The advantage of finding identifiable fingerprints on questioned documents is that you can then link the document to a person. This is especially important when the suspect claims no knowledge of the document or denies making the instrument or document and you have no other conclusive proof to counter the suspect's story. However, a person's fingerprints, coupled with a document examiner's expert opinion regarding the identity of a writer, often provide a solid case.

Tips In Handling Evidentiary Documents

1. Always handle documents to preserve indented markings and prevent creating added marks due to handling.

2. Always makes copies of the questioned document for use during your investigation.

3. Place the original document in a secure place (i.e., a safe or vault) and remove it only for laboratory examination or use as an exhibit in court proceedings.

■ INVESTIGATION RESOURCE KIT FOR QUESTIONED DOCUMENTS

When your investigation involves collecting documents that support your conclusions and prove or disprove an offense or other infraction, you should use certain collection techniques and equipment. I've included a checklist of equipment in Exhibit 4-9.

Exhibit 4-9
Checklist of Equipment for a Document Evidence Collection Kit

You should have at least the following equipment to manage questioned documents under normal investigative conditions.

- ☐ Plastic sheet protectors (available at most office supply stores)
- ☐ Solid containers (e.g. large, flat plastic containers, normally used for food storage, of various sizes to accommodate charred or partly burned paper, or documents which have excessive ink or may be damaged in standard protectors by transfer of ink to the protective cover)
- ☐ Paper envelopes of various sizes, from number 10 envelopes to large manila envelopes (available at most office supply stores)
- ☐ Tweezers (stainless steel, long and short)
- ☐ Magnifying glass
- ☐ Hard briefcase or other container for evidence, in which the document will stay the same as when collected.

■ QUICK REFERENCE GUIDE FOR CHAPTER 4

- ■ Bribery, kickbacks, and payoffs stem from employees, contractors, suppliers, and competitors who have personal and business gain as their key motive.

- ■ These white collar crimes often have a semblance of legitimacy and are always concealed in ways that make them appear as errors or good deals for the company. Or they are masked entirely.

- ■ Sometimes the employee doesn't know he or she has been bribed and only realizes it after the fact.

- ■ An effective prevention program for these white collar crimes begins with the creation of clear and specific written company policies.

- ■ Enforce company policies with training, sound management, and control.

- ■ Detect and deter these crimes with systematic investigative audits.

- Convert investigative audits to criminal investigations when necessary—even when the company does not intend to prosecute but wants to take some positive action.

- Narrow your criminal investigation to one specific situation at a time, and follow technical procedures carefully to prove the offense under investigation.

- Use investigative findings and conclusions productively by creating effective deterrents.

Chapter Five
Understanding Accounting and Audits: A Prerequisite to Understanding White Collar Crime

Whether an accountant, auditor, nonaccountant executive or manager, or a corporate security specialist, you need a clear understanding of accounting and auditing as it applies to white collar crime. The purpose of accounting and audits must surpass the traditional concept of focusing on accountability within specified parameters or GAAP (Generally Accepted Accounting Principles). The skilled white collar offender who is victimizing your company works within GAAP, and when the focus of auditing remains on procedure as opposed to substance, white collar crime will persist and prosper.

Nonaccountants also must speak the language of business. This comes from a basic understanding of the mechanics of the language. However, the language of accounting, auditing, and numbers becomes perplexing and tedious for a nonaccountant, especially when each aspect needs translation. White collar crime offenders rely on your having to make management decisions based on translated information. They also depend on accountants and auditors who have a professional aptitude in the language of business but rarely recognize the flaws built into the system that enable and often encourage white collar crime.

My intention in this chapter is to supply a working knowledge of accounting and audits for nonaccountants, and to create an awareness for accountants and auditors that will enable them to look beyond procedure. I will show you the essentials needed to understand GAAP and GAAS (Generally Accepted Audit Standards) and discuss how white collar offenders work within the systems effectively. I'll also show you how to convert these shortcomings to your advantage in detecting, preventing, and acting against white collar crime and offenders in your company. The information I provide coincides with the general approaches of accountants and auditors; however, you should not confuse these approaches with your investigative audits (see Chapter 17). Instead, use this information to enhance your investigations by understanding the fallibility of accounting and auditing.

■ THE PITFALLS OF ACCOUNTING AND AUDIT RESULTS

Auditing procedures consist principally of samples and tests of the company's accounting records. The theory of testing accounting records as distinguished from complete and detailed examination rests on the assumption that the selected samples equal the probable whole (auditor's call the whole a "population") from which the sample is selected. This idea operates much like an opinion poll, which asks a hundred selected people a standardized set of questions and, based on their answers, tells us what several million others have in mind. Although there's some scientific accuracy in this process, it's far from one to rely on in a decision-making process.

The most important aspect to remember about accounting and auditing information is that numbers in the system rely on those "given" to accountants directly or woven into the records. White collar offenders will weave their altered or forged documents into the system, and if you are not aware that what you see is not always what you get from accountants and auditors, you will pass by the crime to criticize a mistake in procedure. Just as an auditor's findings will not always supply them with a true picture, their report to you will not always give you an accurate picture.

■ THE TRUTH ABOUT AUDITS AND SAMPLES

Auditors "sample" the books and records. What you see in their audit reports is an opinion based on a fraction of the entire records system of a department, division, or company. Sampling, as opposed to 100 percent audits, is done to save time and money. However, the true result of an audit tells us only that a department or section audited is or is not complying with generally accepted accounting principles. Skilled white collar crime offenders will easily conceal their activities in ways that confuse or hoodwink auditors and send them off in the wrong direction.

First, the offender can deliberately confuse the books by *not* following the generally accepted accounting principles. The auditor will become totally engrossed with the idea that he or she has encountered an incompetent fool and spend all the allocated audit time for that function recording all the "accounting" flaws while passing over the real problem, white collar crime.

A second method is to have squeaky clean, precise books and records. White collar offenders take extraordinary measures to make sure that they're doing everything exactly right, to impress an auditor with their competence. The idea is to steer the auditor to the right "samples." The general checklist of procedure that auditors use accepts information supplied to auditors as a *postulate* (e.g., the auditor assumes it's true). If all the entries appear in the right places, all the documents support the entries, and the numbers add up correctly, the department gets a clean bill of health while the reality of white collar crime activity remains hidden.

Third, offenders can use a combination of both tactics depending on their needs to disguise and conceal their crimes. Always understand that auditors and accountants deal with information they assume is correct (postulation); they work from samples, not all the records; and when a problem arises their thinking immediately focuses on GAAP error; not white collar crimes.

■ HOW TO TEST AUDIT OBJECTIVES AND SAMPLING

An audit report can be an asset to your white collar crime detection and prevention effort if you know how the auditor arrived at his or her opinion. You need to know how auditors think, and much of their thinking stems from the following sampling procedures:

Protection objective. The objective of an auditor's protective testing is to guard against large dollar value items not being tested. Personal judgment often leads an auditor to select all items over a stated dollar amount and perhaps mix in some smaller items.

Estimation objective. An auditor's objective might be to project the total dollar value of a sample and to compare this estimate with a recorded book value. At other times, an auditor might estimate an occurrence rate of a particular characteristic in a population (the whole). In either type of estimate, an auditor designs a statistical sample allowing a measurement of the *probable difference* between the estimated value and what could develop in a 100 percent sample or audit. That difference is called a *sampling error*.

Discovery objective. An auditor's approach might be to learn whether a precisely defined occurrence does or does not exist with a specified minimum percentage of frequency. The sample size would have to be large enough that the auditor could estimate a specified *probability* of occurrence.

Correction objective. In this approach, an auditor's primary purpose is to examine separate items to find the *maximum number of errors*. Corrective auditing usually is used as follows: (1) when the probable location of errors in the whole (population) is known, (2) for special-purpose examinations, and (3) as an extension of auditing procedures after analyzing errors found in a sample.

Prevention objective. The auditor's concept of prevention stems from a concept of creating an uncertainty about items or samples of items for future testing. In addition to a selected sample, the auditor may choose a few items each year to ensure that certain types of transaction do not escape audit. (Meanwhile, the white collar offender continues to steal company assets and manipulates the records so it doesn't matter which "samples" the auditor examines a year later.)

■ THE DISADVANTAGES OF ACCOUNTING INDEPENDENCE

Independence plays a large role in the perceived effectiveness of accountants and auditors. Their work must avoid internal or outside influences that could breed corruption or falsification of findings. However, there is another side to independence that affects the reliability of the accounting and auditing numbers that these individuals supply in their opinions and involves your white collar crime preventive program. Skilled white collar offenders are familiar with auditors' typical attitude of aloof independence and use it to their advantage. The offender can steer the auditor with a deliberate and overt act to influence the auditor. The auditor becomes defensive (perhaps only mentally) and, in doing so, falls into the trap of looking where the offender wants him or her to look and is steered away from other areas that might create suspicion. Meanwhile, the auditor will believe he or she has out-smarted the offender. Often the offender will "plant" some GAAP errors, and the auditor becomes satisfied that he or she uncovered the truth. Instead, the auditor has been duped by the traditional guile and disguise of white collar crime.

■ THE ACCOUNTING "EVIDENCE" MISCONCEPTION

Accountants and auditors will use the term *evidence* to demonstrate to you that their opinions have absolute validity. Accounting and auditing evidence is a term created by the American Accounting Association's Committee on

Basic Auditing Concepts. It really means supporting "information and documents" to substantiate an auditor's findings and opinions. *It is not evidence in the criminal or civil action sense*. This common misconception adds to the confusion of nonaccounting persons when they receive the accountant's translation of the numbers, and it often creates a false confidence within the accounting profession. The customary meaning of the word *evidence* leads financial professionals to believe that their findings cannot be in error.

Another problem stems from the source of an auditor's evidence. The evidence comes from financial information or documents supplied to auditors and accountants by someone else (maybe one person or a group of skilled white collar offenders who have seeded or planted the evidence in the company's accounting systems). Never assume that an auditor's claims of evidence to support his or her opinions means that your company is free from white collar crime.

In fairness to auditors and the accounting profession, we must understand the time and money restrictions placed on these individuals. For example, if a company needs to keep a tight rein on controls and hire enough accountants and auditors to do so (and most do), the cost would be so great that it would wreak the same financial havoc on the company as white collar crime. Time and money restrictions on accountants and auditors also play a major role in the formulation of GAAP and GAAS. Accountants and auditors must accomplish a certain amount of work in a short time, so they sample and focus on procedure instead of criminal activity. However, you can take action through investigative audits and criminal investigations if you understand the benefits and fallacies of accounting and auditing and use them to your advantage.

Do Not Rely on Opinions from Accountants and Auditors

Auditors give opinions, not conclusions. They demonstrate their opinions with findings they portray as substantiated with "evidence." As I have shown earlier, the reliability of an accountant's information or an auditor's opinion depends on whether the information sampled in the department, facility, or company is accurate. Numbers *do* lie when they're manipulated, and accounting and auditing professionals might deliberately or inadvertently supply you with financial information that has no validity and can devastate your company when you use that information to make important decisions. The problem with opinions is that everyone has one, and you cannot act against white collar crime using opinions that have a shaky foundation. You need to have *real evidence* that's admissible in criminal or civil proceedings. You can begin with audit reports and their working papers when they're available;

however, do not assume everything is okay. You need to develop information from your sources, not rely on information supplied to you by a potential white collar crime offender.

■ GENERALLY ACCEPTED ACCOUNTING PRINCIPLES

The term *generally accepted accounting principles* (GAAP) came into use in the opinions of certified public accountants during the 1930s, after Congress enacted the Securities Act of 1933. The Securities Act gave Congress the legal authority to prescribe methods of accounting used in preparing financial statements for shareholders of publicly owned corporations. Congress delegated these powers to the Securities and Exchange Commission (SEC), and thereafter the accounting profession became active in creating standardization efforts. The GAAP evolved from cooperative work between a committee of the American Institute of Certified Public Accountants and the New York Stock Exchange and others. The watchdog or self-regulating aspect of the accounting and auditing profession comes largely from generally accepted auditing standards (GAAS), which stem from a framework established during the late 1930s. Although accounting and auditing processes encompass a spectrum of business-related activities with many different functions, your interest in them must stay within the parameters of using financial information to detect or find indicators of white collar crime within your corporation.

Generally accepted accounting principles are the accounting methods and procedures used by firms in preparing their financial statements. These principles do not remain rigid, but constantly evolve through a variety of theories developed presumably to supply better accountability in the business world. They do, however, remain within a general framework in which only the methodology of reaching an objective changes as needed.

To understand principles in accounting, contrast them with principles in fields such as physics and mathematics. In physics and other natural sciences, a principle (or theory) is evaluated by asking how well the predictions of the principle correspond with physically observed phenomena. Mathematicians evaluate a principle (or theorem) by comparing its internal consistency with the structure of definitions and underlying axioms. In accounting, principles stand or fall on their general acceptability to preparers and users of accounting reports. Unlike those in the physical sciences, principles in accounting do not exist naturally, merely awaiting discovery. Unlike mathematics, accounting has no structure of definitions and concepts to use unambiguously in developing accounting principles. An accounting principle cannot be "proven" to be correct. It has simply been judged to be the generally acceptable method of accounting for the specific function. Accounting principles might more aptly be called "accounting conventions."

How to Create an Accounting Advantage for Yourself

An accounting advantage begins with a comprehensive understanding of GAAP shortcomings and how you can convert them to your advantage. The strong points of GAAP stem from accountants and auditors collecting and consolidating financial information into a format for your review. The weak points stem from inaccurate numbers that may have been supplied by white collar crime offenders. You need to recognize that the concept of GAAP also provides a means of legitimizing white collar crime activities.

For example, when the manager of a receiving department supplies records carefully manipulated to conceal thefts and diversion, accountants and auditors look for generally accepted accounting principles. When, in their opinion, all the paperwork appears correct, procedures were followed, and the numbers add up, there's no question insofar as they're concerned about asset accountability or the honesty of the persons responsible for receiving. The collective company financial information merges from all departments and makes its way into the corporate balance sheets and other data. White collar crime offenders rely on unquestioned acceptance of their invented information on department records.

However, when you understand how that accounting information evolved, and the methodology is used to create it, you realize that what you see might not be what's real, and the accounting and audit reports take on a new meaning. Why don't accountants and auditors understand the vulnerability of GAAP and GAAS and look for the same inconsistencies? It is not their job. They take what's given them, put it in form, and represent it as true to executives, managers, boards of directors, and stockholders—that's their job. It is *your* job to verify their findings. They have done a fair amount of research, and you can turn that to your advantage. Exhibit 5-1 shows an example of how accountants research to arrive at their opinions in general financial reports.

■ GENERALLY ACCEPTED AUDITING STANDARDS

In 1939, the American Institute of Certified Public Accountants (AICPA) created ten Generally Accepted Auditing Standards (GAAS). The GAAS

Exhibit 5-1
Examples of Corporate Financial Statement Sources

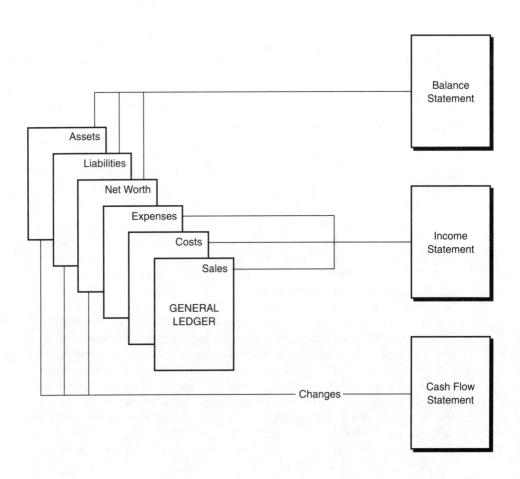

remain intact today and are often augmented with explanations and requirements in publications called Statements on Auditing Standards (SAS), which are issued periodically in a numbered series. Officially, these statements (SAS) serve as interpretations and supplements of the ten basic standards (GAAS). Auditors who do not follow GAAS or SAS directives might find themselves judged by peers to have a performed a deficient audit.

The Ten Generally Accepted Audit Standards

Understanding how auditors reach their conclusions, and how you can use them to advantage in detecting white collar crime (often after auditors have proclaimed a clean bill of health) begins with the ten Generally Accepted Audit Standards listed below.

■ GENERAL STANDARDS

1. The examination is to be performed by a person or persons having adequate technical training and proficiency as an auditor. Auditors are expected to have adequate academic training in accounting and auditing coupled with other areas that relate to their profession. They should also receive further training, both formal and informal, throughout their careers. The standard has several long-range implications for accountants, who should stay abreast of current developments in accounting auditing and other matters.

2. In matters about the assignment, an independence in mental attitude is to be maintained by the auditor or auditors. Auditors must be independent in both fact and appearance. To remain independent in fact, auditors must be intellectually honed; and for recognition as independent, they must not have any direct interest in the location they are auditing (such as friends or relatives).

3. Due professional care is to be exercised in the performance of the examination and the preparation of the report. The typical audit involves the use of tests and samples. Each item chosen for testing must have an attentive examination to ensure that the auditor applied due professional care.

■ FIELD WORK STANDARDS

4. The work is to be adequately planned, and assistants, if any, are to be properly supervised. Adequate planning of the audit is extremely important.

Without careful planning, the auditor becomes more susceptible to unwitting manipulation by a department manager or company employees in the audit.

5. There is to be a proper study and evaluation of existing internal controls as a basis for reliance thereon to determine which auditing procedures will be restricted. From the perspective of the auditor, internal control involves the plans and procedures used by a business to assure that transactions are accurately recorded and assets properly safeguarded. It is also concerned with administrative controls that lead to authorization of transactions.

6. Sufficient competent evidential matter is obtained through inspection, observation, inquiries, and confirmations to afford a reasonable basis for an opinion regarding the financial statements under examination. Following this standard, the auditor must (1) understand his or her assignment completely, (2) follow instructions, (3) use due care in the performance of his or her work, (4) note errors and unusual or questionable items, and (5) prepare complete and self-explanatory working papers.

■ REPORTING STANDARDS

7. The report shall state whether the financial statements are presented according to generally accepted accounting principles.

8. The report shall state whether the principles were consistently observed during the current period related to the preceding period.

9. Informative disclosures in the financial statements will be regarded as adequate unless otherwise stated in the report.

10. The report shall contain either an expression of opinion regarding the financial statements, taken as a whole, or an assertion to the effect that an opinion cannot be expressed. When a general opinion cannot be expressed, the reasons therefore should be stated. When an auditor's name is associated with financial statements, the report should contain a clear-cut indication of the character of the auditor's examination, if any, and the responsibility he or she is taking. Accountants who prepare auditors' reports need to be thoroughly aware of the meaning and implications of generally accepted standards of reporting. They will draw heavily on their knowledge of generally accepted accounting principles.

■ OVERCOMING THE EXPECTATION GAAP: A QUICK REVIEW

- Auditing *standards* are different from auditing *procedures*.

- Auditing procedures explain the particular and specialized actions auditors take to obtain financial information (they call it evidence) in a specific audit assignment.

- Don't confuse the concept behind an auditor's *evidence* and that relevant to *criminal evidence*. Auditors collect evidence (or documented information) to prove *their* accounting opinions, not to help you determine where white collar crime is happening within the company and who's involved in those activities.

- The white collar offender might supply the auditor's evidence, tainted with fraud although appearing genuine.

- Standards are quality guides that remain the same through time and for all audits, including audits of computerized accounting systems.

- Procedures, on the other hand, may vary depending on the complexity of an accounting system (whether manual or computerized), the type of company, and other situation-specific factors.

- This difference is the reason that audit reports refer to an audit as "conducted according to generally accepted auditing standards" rather than according to auditing procedures.

■ HOW TO USE SOURCE DOCUMENTS TO FOLLOW AN AUDIT TRAIL

Every report, financial statement, record, and worksheet an accountant prepares is normally based on documents that show how the estimates and opinions were developed.

One basic concept behind accounting is that numbers in a statement or company books can be traced to a source document. For example, each entry in the general ledger expenses needs to be substantiated with an invoice, statement, receipt, or other voucher. If no voucher is available, a worksheet, memorandum, or other document must be placed in the files to explain the entry. Proof leading to an opinion may also have a contractual obligation. This "audit trail," as it is called, applies not only to the information in the books but also comes into play in the methods accountants use to argue a point or give an opinion. The audit trail is a four-level process described below.

1. *Source documents.* Source documents comprise the first level in the process. These include all vouchers, receipts, and other papers that establish that a transaction happened, tell how much money was exchanged, and show the business nature of the transaction. Source documents are always the starting point for the accounting entry.

2. *Books of original entry.* The second level in the accounting process is the books of original entry, where source documents are recorded and arranged in a consistent, logical format. Accountants normally code transactions from source documents and record them in journals, with coding for eventual posting to the general ledger.

3. *Books of final entry.* Accountants put transactions into proper classifications at the third level. They record information from journals into the general ledger.

4. *Statements.* The fourth level is the financial statement. This is the accountant's report, and it is built on the preceding three levels. Every number on the statement traces back to the other three levels and should be verified with them.

■ HOW TO CREATE AN ADVANTAGE FROM THE AUDITOR'S VERIFICATION LINKS

Auditors traditionally create working papers and files that will help them create an audit trail and can help you significantly when you begin investigative audits or criminal investigations of white collar crimes in your company. Four of the most commonly used verification links are explained below.

1. *Financial records.* Most accounting department records will base findings on financial information, including budgets, financial statements, and other records in the company.

2. *Historical information.* Your company's published statements, the history of the workload in various departments, the development of employee resources, and a view of the markets and competition your company deals with are all examples of historical information that is both financial and nonfinancial.

3. *Analysis.* Many of the opinions that accountants and auditors develop stem from analysis. They define a financial situation or problem by analyzing its importance and effect on the department being audited and on the company generally.

4. *Research.* The fourth common verification link, research, may involve consultation with other departments, employees, or top management. The auditor can often gain a valuable insight into the task from this research and perform a better audit. Keep in mind that audits also uncover a need for better control systems, more training, newer systems, and a variety of ways to enhance recordkeeping through upgrading other aspects of a department.

■ GAAS GENERAL STANDARDS

The three general standards of GAAS relate to the personal integrity and professional qualifications of auditors. The meanings of the three general standards are captured in the theoretical concepts and postulates related to them.

Three of the five concepts of auditing theory provide a primary framework for the general standards. They are (1) ethical conduct, (2) independence, and (3) due audit care. The other two, (4) evidence (supporting the auditor's opinions) and (5) fair presentations, are related to other standards.

(1) *Ethical conduct*: The concept of an auditor's ethical conduct belongs equally to all professional accounting practice, not just to auditing. In addition to the general notions of ethics applicable to all persons, accountants have rules of conduct to guide their behavior. Important rules in this code deal with matters of general standards, independence, and due care.

(2) *Independence*: In auditing theory and practice, independence is a matter of intellectual honesty. Auditors must remain unbiased and impartial on financial statements and other information they audit. They must stay fair both to the companies and executives who issue financial information and to the outside persons who use it.

(3) *Due care*: Due care calls for several important things of accountants. First, accountants should understand what they are doing and why they are doing it. If they are uncertain about any phase of the their assignment, it is their responsibility to seek guidance. Due care also requires that accountants prepare accurate and complete working papers. Working papers prepared in a careless and incomplete way bring into question the supporting information an auditor has supplied.

All general standards are closely related to the concept of due audit care. Auditors must be competent, trained, and independent if they expect to be properly attentive. Their training includes knowledge of computer systems and computer auditing techniques.

Due audit care is best understood in the context of the prudent auditor. The concept of a prudent professional practitioner is present in other social science theories (for example, the "economic person" in economic theory and the "reasonable person" in law). Due audit care is a matter of what auditors do and how well they do it. A determination of proper care must be reached based on all the facts and circumstances in a particular case.

■ HOW TO CREATE AN INVESTIGATIVE ADVANTAGE FROM AUDITS

You notice that there's nothing mentioned in the preceding three standards about white collar crime, or about the auditor having a duty to detect and report crimes. I noted earlier that the misconception about accountants and auditors being able to solve the white collar crime problem works to the offender's advantage, not yours. It's fairly easy to fool auditors; however, you need to debrief them after completing an audit in the company, and in doing so you might learn valuable information. For example, the American Accounting Association, over thirty years ago, developed its own concepts about GAAS as follows:

Procedural Independence

Auditors must remain free from interference by managers who try to restrict, specify, or modify the procedures auditors want to perform, including any attempt to assign personnel or otherwise control the audit work. Occasionally, managers try to limit the number of locations visited and the number of auditors permitted in a location.

    The advantage: During debriefing of an auditor, note his or her impressions about the manager. You will want to know how a specific department manager, or persons within the department, reacted to the presence of an auditor. Nervousness or noncooperation in itself does not always indicate white collar crimes, but it might. For example, a manager, supervisor, or employee might have present or past involvement in a white collar crime, or know someone in the department who's involved, and might believe that giving the auditor a hard time might prevent discovery. Other situations, however, might include one of those persons directly involved in a white collar crime trying to steer the auditor by restricting or modifying his or her procedures. You need to avoid jumping to a conclusion, however, and consider possibilities such as incompetence, a serious management error, or some other problem the person believes can jeopardize his or her job, position, or promotion. This important advantage will serve you well and begins your auditor debriefing checklist.

Investigative Independence

Auditors must have free access to books, records, correspondence, and other evidence (information). They must have the cooperation of management without any attempt to interpret or screen evidence (information). Sometimes, managers refuse auditors' requests for access to necessary information.

The advantage: With a knowledge of how auditors proceed and how white collar offenders use guile, disguise, and concealment to fulfill their activities, you can examine the audit report and often determine what's really happening in a section, department, or company. For example, you know that white collar crime offenders will not allow an auditor or the accounting division to find differences in their recordkeeping or discover what they have done. When an auditor completes his or her work and provides a report detailing his or her opinion, you can generally learn from the auditor whether that opinion was a staged or spontaneous event. Remember, the auditor will not know or believe the event was staged, and will probably believe that he or she controlled the event. Do not argue with the auditor; instead ask him or her exactly what the department head or other responsible person said. How cooperative was the responsible person and employees under his or her supervision? Also, learn whether the auditor noticed excessive interest by employees in the auditor's work (perhaps they were trying to find out what the auditor was doing then or deciding what he or she might look at next time).

Reporting Independence

Auditors must not let any feelings of loyalty to the client or auditee interfere with their obligation to report fully and fairly. Neither should management be allowed to overrule auditors' judgments on the appropriate content of an audit report. Disciplinary actions have been taken against auditors who go to a conference with a preliminary estimate for a financial adjustment and emerge after, agreeing with management to a smaller adjustment.

The advantage: Ask auditors if anyone in the area they worked in has asked, hinted, or implied that the auditor should look the other way or gloss over their report. You might have to remind auditors that the suggestion could have been subtle (may be it was presented in a joking manner).

■ GAAS FIELD WORK STANDARDS

The concept of due audit care is particularly evident in the first of the field standards. Adequate planning and proper supervision indicate care, and their absence indicates careless work. To have time to plan an audit, auditors should begin before the company's fiscal year-end. The more notice auditors have, the better they can provide enough time for planning.

The fourth of the auditing concepts includes evidence. Evidence consists of *all those influences upon the minds of auditors that ultimately guide their decisions*. The second and third field work standards are specifically concerned with gathering evidence.

Relevant evidence may be quantitative or qualitative; it may be objective or subjective; it may be absolutely compelling to a decision or it may be only mildly persuasive. The auditor's task is to collect and evaluate enough competent evidence to afford a reasonable and logical basis for decisions. Evidence has several important dimensions and features, and gathering evidence is a principal feature of audit field work.

■ GAAS REPORTING STANDARDS

The key element for you to note in audit reports concerns the first standard— an opinion. Auditors do not make conclusions, and that reason more than any other demonstrates why white collar crime detection is not within a traditional accounting and auditing agenda. In the opinion paragraph, auditors make a statement of fact about their belief (opinion). Auditors are the professional experts in attestation, so users of financial statements rely on the audit opinion. The standard wording carries the required references to conformity with generally accepted accounting principles and to consistency of application. However, for your purposes of detecting white collar crime, remember that the auditor's opinion and subsequent report stem from information (evidence) available to him or her, not necessarily the correct or accurate information.

■ COMPLIANCE AUDITING

Auditors, especially internal auditing groups, often focus on compliance auditing programs, which consist of compliance-purpose procedures designed to produce evidence (information) about the effectiveness of the company's internal control procedures. The problem with these programs, as noted earlier, stems from the information provided to the auditor.

Checklist for Compliance Audit Procedures

In the following checklist, which is typical of a compliance audit procedure, you will see how vulnerable and fallible this process can be and why white collar crime can prosper despite regular audits.

1. Select a sample of recorded sales invoices and
   - Determine whether a bill of lading is attached (evidence of validity).
   - Determine credit approval process (evidence of authorization).
   - Determine whether product prices on the invoice agree with the approved price list (evidence of authorization and accuracy).
   - Compare the quantity billed to the quantity shipped (evidence of accuracy).
   - Recalculate the invoice arithmetic (evidence of accuracy).
   - Compare the shipment date with the invoice record date (evidence of proper period).
   - Trace the invoice to posting in the general ledger control account and in the correct customer's account (evidence of accounting).
   - Note the type of product shipped and determine proper classification in the right product-line revenue account (evidence of classification).

The first problem with these procedures stems from the postulate (assumption of truth). How does an auditor know the documents come from genuine sources or are accurate? Tracing documents and transactions to all the right places is far different from verifying the validity of the documents. For example, is the invoice or billing from ABC Corporation real or forged? Does ABC Corporation really exist and, if so, did it receive the items or did it send the bill? Auditors taking anything at face value will not only allow white collar crime to prosper, but also encourage it. Therefore, the auditor should also

2. Select a sample of shipping orders and
   - Trace them to recorded sales invoices (evidence of completeness).
   - Perform the appropriate procedures described in Number 1 above on the sales invoices produced by this sample.

However, the shipping orders themselves might be false or altered, and the same problem of validity as noted above exists in this section. The auditor is assuming that the shipping orders are "evidence," although these documents might be false either totally or in part. The auditor must now

3. Select a sample of recorded cash receipts and
   - Trace them to deposits in the bank statement (evidence of validity).
   - Vouch discounts taken by customers to proper approval or policy (evidence of authorization).

- Recalculate the cash summarized for a daily deposit or posting (evidence of accuracy).
- Trace the deposit to the right cash account (evidence of classification).
- Compare the date of receipt to the recording date (evidence of proper period).
- Trace the receipts to postings in the correct customers' accounts (evidence of accounting).

These procedures do not detect skimming when it is done by a skilled white collar offender, and they assume that transactions are accurate. The flaw stems from all the numbers adding up correctly and being posted in the right places. However, the procedures do not establish if the numbers themselves are accurate. The following steps are now necessary:

4. Select a sample of daily cash reports or another source of original cash records and
- Trace to the cash receipts journal (evidence of completeness).
- Perform the appropriate procedures in Number 3 above on this cash receipts sample. However, there's no need for duplication of the work.

5. Scan the accounts receivable for postings from sources other than the sales and cash receipts journals (e.g., general journal adjusting entries, credit memos). Vouch a sample of such entries to supporting documents (evidence of validity, authorization, accuracy, and classification).

In listing the problems associated with compliance auditing I do not mean to criticize the audit method; instead I want to point out the fallibility of these procedures. Except in situations of glaring fraud, auditors must consider that the financial information supplied to them is accurate—and that plays into the hands of a white collar offender.

Using the audit report and working papers compiled by the auditor, you can begin an investigative audit and verify the documents from the originating sources, comparing inventories and goods received with cash receipts and carrying out a variety of other techniques shown in the book to expand and verify the auditor's work or pinpoint flaws.

■ SALES PROCESSING: MANUAL PROCEDURES

The customer's order, usually in the form of a purchase order, is the outside document that starts the sales processing. From then on, the internal data processing system takes over. The flow-chart descriptions of such a sales document processing system begin with the procedures shown in Exhibit 5-2. The customer's written order (or telephone order) provides the information for preparation of the sales order. Note that the sales order is approved by the credit manager, thus authorizing the transaction or cash required before the transaction can continue to be processed. The sales order (with the customer order attached) is used to prepare the invoice.

Sales order forms and invoice blanks should be carefully controlled in the sales order section of a sales department and be issued only on receipt of a customer's written or telephoned purchase order. Use of prenumbered sales invoice forms enables control and monitoring of the numbering sequence for missing invoices.

Copies of the invoice are distributed as authority for other departments to act: (1) Copies 1 and 2 (with customer order and sales order) go to the accounts receivable department as notice that the transaction is in process. (2) Copy 3 (packing list) goes to the shipping dock as notice to expect goods from inventory. (3) Copy 4 (packing list copy) goes to the inventory department as authority to pack and send goods to shipping.

The shipping dock personnel compare the quantities on invoice copies 3 and 4, change the quantities to the actual inventory being shipped, and prepare the bill of lading. Send copies 2 and 4 of the invoice to accounts receivable as notice of shipment. Send copy 3 of the invoice to the person responsible for maintaining inventory records.

■ EVALUATION APPROACHES FOR AUDITING COMPUTER ACCOUNTING SYSTEMS

The evolution of computers as a business tool has had a major impact on how auditors accomplish their objectives. When businesses started using computers, two terms were coined to describe the nature of auditing work on computer systems. The first term, *auditing around the computer*, came to mean that auditors were attempting to isolate the computer and to find audit assurance by vouching and tracing data from output to source documents and from source documents to output. As long as the computer was used as a speedy calculator, this method generally was considered adequate. Nothing is inherently wrong with auditing around the computer if auditors are satisfied with controls and are able to gather sufficient evidence (information). Auditing around the computer becomes unacceptable if this approach is used because of lack of auditor expertise regarding computer processing.

The second term that evolved is *auditing through the computer*. It refers to the auditor's actual evaluation of the hardware and software to determine

Exhibit 5-2
Example of Manual Sales and Shipment Process Flow Chart

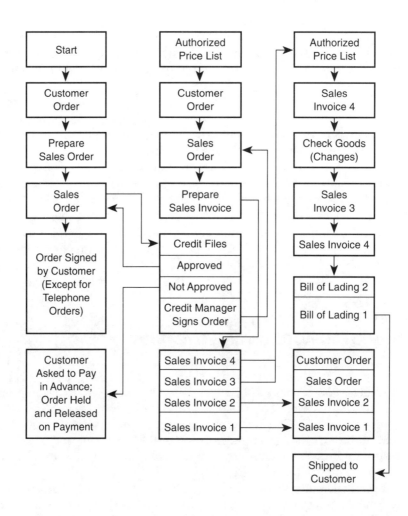

the reliability of operations that could not be viewed by the human eye. Auditing through the computer has become more common in practice because increasingly computer systems do not operate as speedy calculators but have significant control procedures built into their systems. Ignoring a computer system and the controls built into it would amount to ignoring important characteristics of internal control.

Recently, two new terms have been developed to describe an auditor's approach to computer systems: (1) *auditing without the computer* and (2) *auditing with the computer*. The first approach uses visible evidence such as the input source data, the machine-produced error listing, the visible control points (e.g., use of batch totals), and the detailed printed output. The second approach, when auditing a simple computer system, refers to such audit techniques as the use of the company's computer hardware and software to process real or simulated transactions or the use of specialized audit software to perform other audit tasks.

■ COMPLIANCE AUDITING OF ACCOUNTING CONTROLS IN ADVANCED COMPUTER SYSTEMS

The internal controls and audit objectives do not change when the environment changes from manual to computer data processing, or from simple batch computer processing to more advanced computer processing. However, the techniques of control must adapt to different environments, and new audit techniques and procedures must develop. The control features for advanced computer systems are summarized as follows:

1. *User identification*. The system should be able to identify each of the persons using the system.

2. *Request authorization*. The system should be able to determine if the processing or information request of a user is authorized.

3. *Activity logging*. The system should be able to record all user activity (such as attempted log-ons, inquiries, and the like), including recording information about the processes executed.

Audit Tools and Techniques

The tools and techniques applicable to auditing in an advanced computer environment can be classified as those that (1) operate on-line on a real-time basis with live data, (2) operate on historical data, (3) use simulated or dummy data, and (4) use program analysis techniques.

Techniques Using Live Data

Usually, these techniques call for special audit modules designed and coded into programs during development. These audit hooks allow auditors to choose specific transactions of audit interest before or during processing and save them for later audit follow-up. (Program modules solely for audit or maintenance purposes are called *audit hooks*. The same concepts used for fraudulent purposes are called *trap doors*).

Tagging transactions. Transactions elected by the auditor are "tagged" with an indicator at input. A computer audit trail of all processing steps for transactions in the application system can be printed out or stored in computer files for later evaluation.

Audit files. Auditor-selected transactions are written to a special file for later verification. Two methods are used. Systems control audit review file (SCARF) is a method in which auditors build into the data processing programs special limits, reasonableness, or other audit tests. These tests preclude reports of transactions selected according to the auditor's criteria, and reports delivered directly to the auditor for review and follow-up. The SCARF procedure is especially attractive to internal auditors. A sample audit review file (SARF) technique is similar to SCARF, but instead of programming auditors' test criteria, a random sampling selection scheme is programmed. The report of sample transactions can be reviewed by auditors after each production run. The SARF method is efficient for producing representative samples of transactions processed over a period by the computer.

Snapshot. A "picture" records the main transactions memory and database elements before and after performance of computer processing operations. A printout of the picture supplies the auditor with needed information. For example, the method saves the contents of an accounts receivable balance before a sales transaction is posted, and saves the contents again after posting. These balances, plus the sales transactions, show whether update processing was correct. The auditor can trace and verify the decision process using the results.

Monitoring systems activity. Hardware and software are available to analyze activity within a computer. The design of these monitors enable a determination of the computer's efficiency. However, another application includes one for financial audit purposes. With it, the auditor can determine who uses elements of the system and for what operations. For example, a record of passwords used to enter accounting transactions can be captured and compared to the list of employees authorized to enter these transactions.

Extended records. Special programs provide an audit trail of separate transactions by accumulating the results of all application programs that contributed to the processing of a transaction. The accumulated results are stored either as added fields of the transaction record or in a separate audit file. For example, you can add the "snapshot" of accounts receivable balances before and after update processing in the sales transaction, thus making an extended transaction record. Auditors can follow the flow of a transaction without reviewing several files at various times and stages of processing.

Computer Techniques Using Historical Data

These techniques generally give auditors access to data processing allowing them to compare it to original data processing obtained from other sources within a company.

Techniques Using Simulated or Dummy Data

The test data concept explained earlier is a technique that fits in this class. Its use generally remains limited to simple batch computer systems.

■ PROBLEMS OF COMPUTER SYSTEM ACCOUNTING AND AUDITS

Although computer systems might sound confusing and complicated, they are not. However, computerized accounting systems, with all their seemingly impressive safeguards, create more opportunity for the white collar offender. Once the offender understands the system and has access, he or she can create, falsify, erase, and transfer data. When these data are valuable (for example, to a competitor or information broker) or involve tangible and intangible company assets, the damage to the company can be devastating. Documents must be logged and filed, and a variety of manual entries in various ledgers are required. However, when employees use computers to process nearly all company business, detection becomes difficult using only a computer. However, you'll find a variety of computer-related techniques for solving this problem throughout the following chapters.

■ THE REVENUE AND COLLECTION CYCLE COMPUTER PROCESSING

The processing of sales and collection transactions in a manual accounting system can be handled using an advanced computer system, as shown in

Exhibit 5-3. The system example flow chart provides an overview of the sales and accounts receivable computer application system. Note that this is not a "flow of transaction" but a system flow chart indicating the primary inputs, databases (accounting subsidiary and general ledgers), and printed outputs. The auditor would have to prepare the flow of transactions flow charts, with each action on the transaction indicated, and the computer program that processes each action. You should remember that even the most advanced computerized accounting system still processes each transaction sequentially. It is possible to prepare a flow chart of the flow of transactions through computer systems as well as through manual systems.

Refer to Exhibit 5-3 as you consider the following steps in the computer processing of sales and accounts receivable.

1. Customer purchase orders or telephone calls start the manual preparation of a sales order.

2. An employee enters the sales order information through the company billing department with a computer terminal. Only the customer number, inventory number, quantity, and sales order number need to enter the system through the terminal for an existing customer (other necessary information is stored in one of the databases). When the computer system accepts the sales transaction, it creates a record and stores it in the pending order master database, to which other departments can add information on the sale.

3. Computer programs perform a credit check against the credit limit stored in the accounts receivable subsidiary master database. Also, a comparison of the transaction with inventory files determines availability of the ordered items. When an ordered item shows out of stock, an adjustment to the pending order enables the out-of-stock ordered items to be transferred to a back order database or to be deleted per customer instructions stored in the accounts receivable database.

4. After finishing the credit and inventory status checks, the system prepares a packing slip for the stock room to fill the order. After filling the customer's approved order, the stock room clerk enters a command on the terminal in the stock room, updating the pending order database. This command updates the inventory database and triggers the preparation of a bill of lading (according to the customer's shipping instructions stored in the accounts receivable database).

5. The bill of lading is printed at the shipping dock. The shipping clerk recounts the goods to be shipped (as in a manual system), packages the order for shipment, and attaches the bill of lading. When the order is ready for shipment, the clerk enters a command that updates the pending order database, which signals a computer program that the order processing is complete.

Exhibit 5-3
Sales and Accounts. Computer Processing Flow Chart

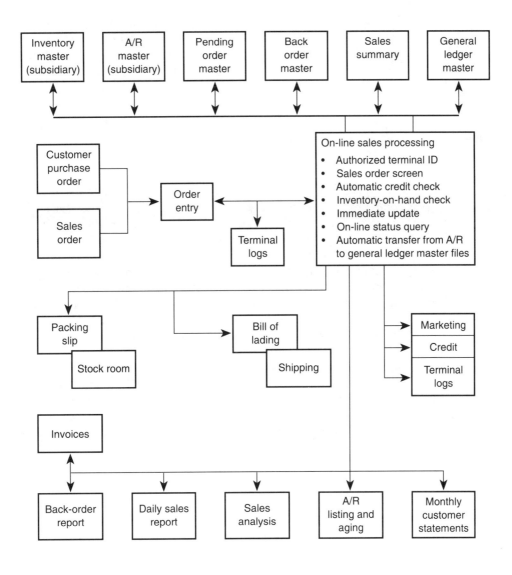

6. The shipping of an order triggers the preparation of the invoice, using the selling prices stored on the inventory database and the sales tax and discount information stored in the customer's record in the accounts receivable database. After preparing an invoice, a record of sale transfers to the accounts receivable database, and the customer's accounts are updated.

7. To monitor the automatic processing of a sales order, the system prepares daily reports of the invoices completed (sales) and items placed on back order. Further, marketing and credit management can determine the exact status of any order from their terminals (but cannot enter any information).

■ AREAS OF COMPUTERIZED SYSTEMS TO MONITOR

Notice in the preceding description that the system sounds efficient and foolproof; however, those working the system will know otherwise. The system becomes effective if there is entry of accurate information and if all the employees along the line do their job properly and honestly. For example, the shipping clerk performs the activity described above but makes a dummy invoice, sending the shipment elsewhere. The computer shows that the shipment went to the correct customer and follows through accordingly. The shipper picking up the item might show it going elsewhere; however, it is billed to the real customer (normally 30 days). The customer complains of nonreceipt, but the computer shows the item going out properly. The next step involves checking the shipper, and that can take maybe ninety days, or at least thirty. Even when all that information comes back, the matter might be old enough and vague enough that no one can resolve it. If a dishonest shipping clerk doesn't get greedy, chances are no one will catch him or her in the act. There are also several other flaws in this system; however, as noted, anyone entering information into the system has an opportunity to take advantage of it in some way to commit an act of white collar crime.

■ QUICK REFERENCE GUIDE TO CHAPTER 5

- Accounting and auditing comprise the "language of business."
- The accounting and audit functions in a corporation serve an accountability function.
- Accounting and audit functions in corporations do little to prevent or detect white collar crime victimizing the company.

- Auditors supply "opinions," not "conclusions."

- The term *evidence*, when used by auditors, means financial information or documents that support their opinions, not the type of evidence relevant to criminal behavior.

- Accountants follow procedures called Generally Accepted Audit Principles (GAAP). These principles involve accountability through procedures and posting but do not prevent white collar crime in themselves; instead they often supply a means for the crimes to remain concealed.

- Auditors follow Generally Accepted Auditing Standards (GAAS) and Statements on Auditing Standards (SAS), which monitor GAAP but do not often detect white collar crimes.

- Computerized accounting systems do not prevent white collar crime victimizing companies and often supply a more efficient, more difficult-to-detect form of white collar crime.

Part Two
Embezzlement:
The Paper Chase

■ INTRODUCTION

The white collar crime of embezzlement developed from a sixteenth-century English Parliament law. Until then, proving a theft called for a person to steal property from the physical possession of another. From that English law, persons entrusted to care or management of another person's money or property legally, but who used or stole it, became known as an "embezzler" and were prosecuted for larceny.

Contemporary embezzlement law evolved from that period; however, in light of the problem of white collar crime throughout the business world, prosecutors rarely use the law. According to a variety of studies by government and private agencies, about 85 percent of known embezzlements with corporations as the victim never get the attention of law enforcement officials. If all existing embezzlements in corporations were discovered, that figure probably would rise dramatically. Companies often do not report the crime for fear of repercussions, including publicizing their vulnerability. Others prefer to administer their own private justice, which includes a pay-back arrangement plus dismissal instead of prosecution. Also, known statistics show that about 30 percent of corporate bankruptcies stem from embezzlement. Although the crime of embezzlement spans a spectrum of circumstances and victims, in Part Two I address only embezzlements in which corporations become the victims through employee schemes designed to loot employer assets systematically. Understanding this crime is important because ironically many executives and employees in the business world continue to have doubts about it. Since each state has its own statutes for this white collar crime, I include the following landmark court decision that will help focus our thinking.

> To embezzle means willfully to take, or convert to one's own use, another's money or property, of which the wrongdoer took possession of or dominion over lawfully, because of some office or employment or position of trust. The elements of embezzlement include a relationship such as employment or agency between the owner of the money or property and the defendant. The money or property embezzled must come into the possession of defendant by virtue of that relationship and there must be an *intentional* and *fraudulent appropriation or conversion* of the money or property. (*State v. Thyfault*, 121 N.J. Super. 487, 297 A. 2d 873, 879)

■ COMMON CHARACTERISTICS OF EMBEZZLERS

There's no such thing as a "typical" embezzler. However, common characteristics among those white collar crime offenders enable you to develop an effective preventive program and identify those who already have an embezzlement scheme in progress. Embezzlers traditionally have appeared as efficient, hard-working, honest people; some are presumed pillars of the community. However, what you see isn't always what you get. Embezzlers most often have outgoing personalities and are sociable people who get along with fellow employees and are generally well regarded by superiors. They normally receive a decent income and are among the employees first considered for promotion within the company. Their positions of trust are often earned fairly by their proven performance, possibly over a long period. Their education level generally is above average, and they possess above average intelligence and mental capacity.

The typical embezzler's shortcomings and vices are few, or well hidden. Often, embezzlers are active in community affairs such as Little League baseball, Sunday school, PTA, Boy or Girl Scouts, and others. They might be the first to volunteer to work on a company picnic or Christmas party or join a company bowling or softball team. On or off the job, embezzlers normally display congeniality, sincerity, and self-confidence. Generally, they are people you would like to have in your home for dinner and an evening of bridge or as companions on a fishing trip.

There's a good reason an embezzler acts like that—such esteem creates the indispensable guise that enables them to plan, disguise, commit, and conceal their scheme of thievery (i.e., Good old Ralph, he wouldn't steal a dime). Often there is substantial evidence that the creation of a false but convincing respectable image is a deliberate and consuming objective for embezzlement.

On the dark side, studies show that embezzlers are scheming and crafty persons, often antisocial loners, avoiding normal social contacts whenever possible. Driven by their insatiable greed, they can and do camouflage their true nature with a deceiving personality. Also, embezzlers often seize an opportunity to create a scheme of collecting embarrassing and probably career-damaging information on key executives, managers, and their families. When they have enough "dirt" about the business and private lives of key people in the company, they implement their embezzlement program. If caught, they can prevent prosecution and often keep their jobs with the damaging information on others.

Often, people who embezzle money from government agencies receive the scorn of courts because this is a crime comparable to reaching into the collective taxpayers' pockets. However, embezzling from a corporation normally brings a different response from courts and juries. Because embezzlers seem like "such nice people," they often receive misplaced sympathy from people who do not or cannot conceive of the enormity of their crimes. Relatives and close friends particularly can become zealously defensive and sometimes abusive in public and published interviews to the point that the victim company becomes the villain. Law enforcement officials also tend to treat crimes of trust violation lightly when it involves a company as the victim. Their rationale seems to be that because the offender had a clear record and was a family person, there was no violence involved in the crime, and no real person was physically or economically damaged by the embezzler's acts, the dimensions of the crime shrink and its importance diminishes.

Corporations might also suffer economically from adverse publicity received when filing charges against any of their employees for embezzlement. Stock holders and stock market participants might wonder if they're hearing the entire story and if other embezzlers continue to operate in the company. Creditors might become nervous about a company's solvency and ability to pay its bills. Other effects include diminished business and public disapproval of a giant corporation picking on a little guy (the public might believe that the corporation wants only to find a scape-goat for other financial problems or to conceal its indiscretions). People rarely trust large companies, especially when they perceive heavy-handed action.

■ FIVE CATEGORIES OF EMBEZZLEMENT

Mention the word *embezzlement* and most people will associate this white collar crime with stealing money through some complex accounting scheme.

Although that happens, embezzlement of money or company funds is only one of a few categories of this increasing corporate problem. The inducement of embezzlement, however, does involve personal gain and financial objectives (not always money in a traditional sense). Five primary categories create the majority of embezzlement problems in corporations, each with several variations or combinations.

1. Computer crimes (hi-tech embezzlement)
2. Intangibles (stocks, bonds, and other negotiable instruments)
3. Commodities (the black market)
4. Corporate time and information
5. Low-tech money (a second occupation income).

■ CREATING EFFECTIVE COUNTERMEASURES TO EMBEZZLEMENT

The white collar crime of embezzlement has the same elements as others included in this book: guile, deceit, and concealment. You can prevent, discover, and take positive action about this problem within your company. The only trick involves understanding how to do so. I've devoted Part Two of this book to discussing valuable techniques that end the embezzlement problem. Remember, the best prevention begins with eliminating opportunity. Without opportunity, a crime cannot happen.

Every embezzlement is a custom-made, one-of-a-kind production. Every embezzlement, every embezzler, and every embezzlement circumstance are different. However, creating effective techniques in the five aforementioned major categories will supply you with ways of combatting whatever type embezzlement situation you will encounter, and you can easily adapt them accordingly. These valuable chapters can increase your profits, create a better working environment, and, most importantly, make the difference between solvency and bankruptcy.

Chapter Six
Computer Crimes—Hi-Tech Embezzlement

The constant growth in computer use throughout the world of business steadily adds new horizons to the problem of white collar crime, including embezzlement. Procedures for keeping business records (including money, securities, titles, money substitutes such as checking accounts and credit cards, letters of credit, money orders, negotiable securities, bank accounts, accounts payable, credit ratings, and other financial data) rely on computer database storage. Financial transactions happen around the clock, transferring assets of all types through computer systems.

In practically all white collar crime, some form of paper serves as a mechanism of deception or as a tool for concealing the true purpose of a transaction. The ability of embezzlers to conceal their transactions becomes enhanced with the proliferation of the computer in the business world. In a matter of seconds a computer can transfer large amounts of money and the instruction can be removed from the system, leaving no trace of the transaction source. A computer can deal with large volumes of data at a very low cost, increasing the possibility of creating large groups of victims in a single act (such as creating large numbers of "personalized" letters, paychecks, or, as in the Equity Funding case discussed below, insurance policies).

Computers now dominate processes for control of inventories and enable large-scale thefts of goods to be executed, manipulated, and concealed through computerized systems. For example, payrolls can be padded with increased salaries or fictitious persons shown as employees, and this information can be supported with entries of false verification documentation in corporate computer systems.

With computers, corporate and financial business employees who perpetrate frauds and embezzlements have found ways to steal larger amounts of money while simultaneously lessening the chance of detection. For example, one case of embezzlement by computer happened over the course of three years, garnered the perpetrator over $1.5 million, and was detected by accident. A chief teller of a New York bank received customer deposits, pocketed the money, and typed into the computer information and instructions necessary to transfer money into the customer's account from one of hundreds of other accounts that had shown little or no activity for several years. Every month the chief teller temporarily transferred the "electronic money" back to the proper interest-bearing accounts to calculate interest and create bogus bank statements. The embezzlement was detected when the New York City Police raided a bookie. They found the teller's name in documents seized, and the bookie's figures showed that the teller was a preferred customer, often betting $30,000 a day. A background check of the names found during the raid by police detectives showed that the high-roller was a chief teller at a New York bank earning a modest yearly salary. Even after the teller admitted his scheme and source of money, he had to explain the process used to auditors and bank examiners, who could not find the hidden transactions and instructions in the computerized system.

I have designed this chapter to cut through the mystery and technical confusion that frequently inhibit executives, security investigators, accountants, auditors, and others who deal with computer issues within corporations. I do not intend to make you an expert on computers or to address the considerable technical issues that computers present. Instead, I want to supply you with a basis coupled with techniques for dealing with computer issues relating to embezzlement of company assets. I will show you how to eliminate opportunities of embezzlement through understanding and recognition, plus ways to prevent these situations, and techniques for conducting investigative audits and criminal investigations involving the white collar crime of embezzlement. This chapter will help to develop your sense of when and where you might need expert computer assistance.

■ TARGETS OF OPPORTUNITY

Business data processing deals with a flow of information needed to run a business. In manufacturing and selling types of businesses, such information might include separately processed elements such as payroll, accounts receivable, accounts payable, inventory control, production scheduling, sales scheduling, production monitoring, sales monitoring, cost analysis, general ledger accounting, and other important areas. Many of the same elements would pertain to banking, insurance securities, publishing, and other businesses that need other specialized types of information such as loan payment accounting, demand deposit accounting, premium payment accounting, policy files, pension payments, customer securities accounts, direct mail addressing, subscription lists, and others. The more information and control systems handled by a computer system, the greater the opportunity for embezzlers to operate complex schemes that often remain undetected. Even when you detect these schemes, it's not always possible in computer systems to determine how many transactions happened, the dollar amount involved, and, more importantly, who conducted the transactions. Computers save time, supply accuracy, and make transactions easier; however, they also supply targets of embezzlement opportunity.

■ DEVELOPING EFFECTIVE COUNTERMEASURES

Protecting your corporation from vulnerabilities created by computerized systems begins with a continuing commitment from company management. Your company must tailor firm, clear policies regarding each aspect of the company's computer system operation and communicate them to employees. Your company must budget the funds to convert those policies into practice and enforce them effectively. You must develop a comprehensive computer system security program that includes a standardized selection process of employees entrusted to access the system and handle vital company data.

Managing the Computer System

Database administration must focus on controlling access to company information. The key technique involves dividing computer system users in ways that would call for collusion between entirely separate groups of employees necessary to compromise the system or fulfill embezzlement schemes.

Another important step includes dividing and restricting knowledge about the system so that few people have enough knowledge to complete a successful compromise. Technical manuals, program descriptions, and computer program listings should remain protected and access should be limited to a specific need to know.

Managing Employees

Recruiting and screening employees who will have access to your computerized systems play a significant role in your prevention program. First, find out and verify how employee candidates learned their computer skills. If you determine that the learned their computer skills while working for another company, you need to research their work performance and reason for leaving. When a company discharges an employee, the reason for dismissal goes on record; and when the company receives calls for references, they will usually reveal that information. However, to avoid possibilities of liability, many companies who catch employees involved in embezzlement or other problems will confront them and offer to allow them to resign without recourse. Later, when you call and ask a personnel specialist for a reference, he or she will pull the file and tell you the employee resigned for "personal reasons," because that's all the file shows. The employee can tell you whatever those "personal reasons" were.

Checking references that an applicant supplies will do little good when you're concerned about integrity, because the applicant will not supply the names of anyone who might give a hostile opinion. Unless you're equipped with a corporate security investigative team, your best action will include hiring a well-established firm that does preemployment screening. If you choose computer system operators from within the company, then create a policy and procedure that calls for the person to apply for the sensitive position. Just because the person has been with your company ten years as a secretary or in some other administrative position does not mean he or she should not take part in a standardized screening process for sensitive positions.

There is also sound reasoning for applying for a sensitive position within the company although working in a different position. First, it establishes some controls, taking the selection process out of the sole discretion of one or two people, and that's always a healthy management step. It removes discrimination or favoritism probability and enables certain legal screening steps, such as credit history research. Credit history becomes important when you're putting employees in a position that would enable them to steal assets to meet obligations or satisfy a vice such as gambling. You should allow the firm hired for screening to conduct and interpret the credit research because there's an art of interpreting the information accurately. For example, situations commonly called "bad credit" can mean several different things. First, the person might have experienced a layoff, become ill, or for some other reason unexpectedly lost an income that he or she anticipated would be consistent for years to come. The result might have been to pay what they could and tell others they would have to wait. Even when agreements between creditors and the borrower work out, an adverse credit report goes into the system. Also, keep in mind that a person who has no credit history or one that's squeaky clean might also have managed that by stealing. Don't always rely on one aspect of a person's background to make a judgment about suitability for sensitive positions.

You should require employees hired or moved to sensitive positions who have access to the computerized systems to sign a statement of confidentiality of information. They also should agree to security updating through background investigations periodically (normally every three to five years). Your company should supply bonding for each employee accessing your company computer systems. The bonding companies also supply varied degrees of background investigations, often corroborating yours. Often, applicants or even current employees seeking a sensitive job will withdraw when they learn that the job requires bonding. When they withdraw, you can feel certain that there's dishonesty or other embarrassing problems somewhere in their past and they suspect it will come out during the bonding process.

The checklist in Exhibit 6-1 coupled with the information above will help you develop a comprehensive program that helps prevent employees with access to your company's computer systems from embezzling assets.

Exhibit 6-1
Checklist for Developing a Program to Prevent Embezzlement of Assets

☐ Are there pertinent policies in force about the database security, privacy, and confidentiality practices of the corporation?

☐ Do employees understand the legal responsibilities, if any, that correlate to information maintained in the computer system databases?

☐ Has your company developed management policy statements on the subject of information privacy and security?

☐ Have all affected personnel signed a statement of their understanding and acceptance of and responsibility for the computer security procedures?

☐ Has your company clearly defined responsibilities for maintaining computer procedures and arranged for auditing the execution of those procedures?

☐ Is there a continuing program of security education for data processing and user personnel?

☐ Is the security education program kept current?

☐ Is adequate background screening performed to determine an applicant's record of general integrity and stability?

☐ Are a prospective candidate's work and academic history checked to determine past levels of responsibility and performance and indications of work attitude?

☐ Are candidates for particularly sensitive positions surety bonded?

☐ Do your company policies and procedures emphasize computer system housekeeping and employee attention in security practices to prevent inadvertent loss or disclosure of database information?

☐ Are periodic security briefing sessions held at your company to continue security education of employees operating computers, including information users, to show a continuing commitment to system security?

☐ Are there periodic follow-up security checks?

☐ Have procedures been established to evaluate employees' performance in assigned functions?

☐ Are company employees who show signs of being disgruntled assigned to noncritical duties and denied access to critical areas in the database?

☐ Are proof and control functions performed by employees other than those assigned as machine operators and programmers?

☐ Are operators assigned to particular jobs or applications subject to periodic rotation?

☐ Are proper machine operation controls and logs maintained?

☐ Is there an independent (disinterested person) check of these controls and computer logs?

■ POSSIBLE EMBEZZLEMENT OPPORTUNITIES: SYSTEM DESIGNS

The structured design and programming approach to project development and the associated concepts of programmer teams, structured walk-through, and development support libraries offer definite benefits to your company in development of new computer applications. Many existing applications developed following bottom-up procedures, where the lowest-level programs have independent designs. During integration, problems often emerge and integration is delayed while data definitions and program interfaces are corrected and programs revised to accommodate the changes. Because of this informal, uncoordinated approach to systems development, management control is often ineffective during much of the traditional development cycle. The most important benefit derived from structured design and programming is that these techniques and their associated concepts provide a formalized, orderly way to develop computer systems.

■ IMPORTANCE OF YOUR SYSTEMS OPERATIONS ENVIRONMENT

A key to eliminating opportunities for embezzlement of company assets stems from not allowing one person to have complete control over the operation of a system. Changes in a computer program or system should require the review and approval of several employees. Such a division of responsibility keeps the authority of programmers and operators within proper limits. It also ensures proper documentation of all changes in computer systems and programs and simplifies the detection of irregularities. By dividing responsibilities you can detect any attempt or actual embezzlement activity and prevent your company from becoming a victim, as those in the following examples did:

1. A payroll programmer chopped a few cents off each paycheck and added them to his own. The company's accounts balanced and employees didn't notice the slight change in their checks.

2. An employee of Encyclopedia Britannica stole the company's computerized most valuable customer list and sold it to a competitor. The list value exceeded $3 million.

3. An employee of British Airways stole (embezzled) the computerized marketing plans and sold them to a competitor for about $5 million.

4. Two clerks in a bank worked in the section that handled mutilated checks. Mutilated checks could not be handled by the computer equipment that reads the magnetic ink character record at the bottom of all checks. The clerks deliberately mutilated their checks so the computer would reject them. When the checks were delivered to their section, they just threw them away so their accounts would not be charged with the checks they had written. This serves as a good example of how computer technology created a new opportunity and lack of controls made it hard, if not impossible, to detect the crime unless large losses were incurred.

5. A bank programmer whose program calculated savings accounts interest, instead of dropping off fractions of pennies had them added to his own account.

6. A computer consultant found a blank form used for adding a new employee to company payrolls. He added his own name to the payroll list and arranged an automatic deposit to his bank account.

7. Two systems analysts started their own company while working for another company that sold metal ores. Their company bought ore from their employer and sold the same ore back to their employer at a profit. The transactions developed entirely through computer systems that they controlled.

8. In the largest known bank embezzlement, an operations officer at a Wells Fargo Bank made bogus deposits in a boxing promotion account at one branch. He used the bank's computerized interbranch account settlement process to withdraw funds from accounts at a different branch. To keep the computer from noticing the imbalance, he created new fraudulent credits to cover the withdrawal. He repeated the process several times, resulting in a loss of $21.3 million.

■ ANCILLARY PROBLEMS OF EMBEZZLEMENT

Embezzlers often need to divert attention from their schemes through a disguise and regularly find ways to destroy evidence of their offenses or conceal who committed the crime. They regularly do that with acts that appear as sabotage, vandalism, or espionage. If your company experiences trouble with its computer systems that stem from any of these three categories, remember that the real problem could include embezzlement.

■ ESPIONAGE AS EMBEZZLEMENT

As more valuable types of information are stored or processed by the computer, the risk of espionage (spying on others) is greater and many businesses need to consider the value of their data. Data relating to oil lease bids were stolen from an oil company during transmission from its computer in Texas to its terminal in Alaska. The victimized company became suspicious when it was narrowly outbid at many oil lease sales. On investigation, the company found that an employee in Alaska tapped the incoming telephone line and received the data on both the company system and his personal computer at his home a few miles away. He sold the information to the competitor for sizable amounts of money. Some areas particularly vulnerable to business espionage (which is embezzlement when it involves a company employee) are

- Sales and service information, market analyses, bid prices
- Corporate finance, stock discussions, stock holder information
- Legal negotiations, plans, policy changes
- Expansion plans, mergers, acquisitions
- Production figures, goals, problems
- Proprietary product developments, tests, processes, formulas
- Personnel changes, payroll data, general administrative matters.

MOST COMMON REASONS FOR EMPLOYEE EMBEZZLEMENT

Money or the equivalent of money remains the key motive for white collar crime and particularly acts of embezzlement. However, studies of computer-related embezzlement have shown that the challenge of embezzling through computer manipulation, often taking advantage of program weaknesses, also plays an important ancillary role.

MOST COMMON COMPUTER EMBEZZLEMENT TECHNIQUES

Manipulation of data for financial gain has become so common that several techniques have evolved to traditional methods. Knowing these techniques and understanding what to look for will help you thwart embezzlement of company assets.

Tampering with Computer Data

This is the simplest, safest, and most common method used in computer-related embezzlement schemes. This technique involves entering erroneous data into a computer, or changing data before or during input. Anyone with access can create changes, including processes of creating, recording, transporting, encoding, examining, checking, converting, and transforming data that ultimately enter a computer. Examples include forging or counterfeiting documents; exchanging valid computer cards or disks with prepared replacements; performing source entry violations; punching extra holes or plugging holes in cards; and neutralizing or avoiding manual controls.

A typical example involved a time-keeping clerk who filled out data forms of hours worked by 300 employees in a department of a railroad company. He noticed that data input to the time-keeping and payroll system on the company computer system included the name and employee number of each worker. However, the computer used only the employee numbers for processing and even for looking up employee names and addresses to print on payroll checks. He also noticed that processing and control outside the computer stemmed only from employee names, with none identified by numbers. He took advantage of the dichotomy of controls by filling out forms for overtime hours worked and using names of employees who often worked overtime by entering his own employee number. His income increased by several thousand dollars a year.

The Trojan Horse: Planting One Program Inside Another

Do you recall the story of how Greece conquered Troy? They presented the walled city with a large wooden horse as a gift—the infamous Trojan horse. After dark, Greek soldiers hidden in the horse slipped out and destroyed the city.

In the world of computer crime and embezzlement, the Trojan horse method involves hiding a small program to fulfill the nefarious deed inside a larger program. Once access is gained through the Trojan horse, the subroutine could use the salami method, plant a logic bomb, or apply some other technique that relates to the crime.

Two Ways to Detect the Trojan Horse Technique

You can probably find a suspected Trojan horse by comparing a copy of the operational program under suspicion with a master or other copy known to be free from unauthorized changes. Backup copies of system programs are routinely kept in safe storage; however, smart perpetrators gain access to them and often will copy their changes in them. Also, unauthorized changes in programs may happen without changing the backup copies, making your comparison possible.

1. A solution to ensuring that investigative audits detect the Trojan horse technique is to have the backup copy of the original program secured in a place unaccessible to computer programmers and operators. For example, the backup or second backup should be stored in a vault controlled by a security force or noncomputer department.

2. Another solution is to test the suspect program with data and under conditions that might reveal why someone placed the Trojan horse in the system. This technique may prove the existence of the Trojan horse but usually will not determine its location.

Salami Technique: Taking a Small Amount from Each Transaction

A worker at a delicatessen meat slicer could slip a single slice from each salami into his apron, and chances are no one would catch on. I'm not sure why a person would want to do this with salami, but it's clear why someone would applying the "salami method" to embezzling company money or property with computer manipulations. When an employee offender takes small amounts from each transaction, chances are no one will catch on. If large numbers of accounts or transactions are processed, even small slices can add up to significant amounts. A good example is the late Senator Everett Dirkson, who once remarked (speaking of federal expenditures), "A billion here, a billion there, and pretty soon you're talking about real money." The amounts for your computerized offender may differ, but the principle stays the same.

Superzapping: Bypassing Security Systems

Occasionally everything goes wrong in a computer and it is necessary to override the running program. At many mainframe installations, an if-all-else-fails utility program called Superzap (IBM)™ serves this purpose. It is like a master key that can open any door on the premises. Superzap programs can spell disaster if misused. An embezzler, for example, can use such a program to bypass whatever security measures you might incorporate in company systems.

A classic example of superzapping occurred at a bank in New Jersey. While using a superzap program to change account balances to correct errors as directed by management, an operations manager realized that the program lent itself to more exotic applications and made off with $120,000 that he had transferred from other accounts into those of his friend, who shared in the new-found wealth with the manager.

Trap Doors: Debugging Computer Programs

In the development of large application and computer operating systems, it is the practice of programmers to insert debugging aids that provide breaks in the code for insertion of added code and intermediate output capabilities. The design of computer operation systems tries to prevent access to them and insertion of code or change of code. System programmers will sometimes insert a code that allows compromise of these requirements during the debugging phases of program development and later when the system is being maintained and improved. These facilities are called trap doors. Normally, programmers eliminate trap doors in their final editing but sometimes overlook them. The programmer might purposely leave them in place to ease future access and modifications. Some unscrupulous programmers may purposely introduce trap doors to compromise computer programs later (such as in embezzlement).

Logic Bombs and Time Bombs

At one company, an in-house programmer inserted a few lines of code in a payroll program that checked for the presence of his own name. Anyone deleting his name would trigger added lines of code, which led to destruction of the company's entire payroll file. A variant of the logic bomb is a time bomb. It waits for the passage of a specified amount of time, the processing of a specified number record, or the running of the program a specified number of times before it wrecks the system. For example, in one case, insertion of secret computer instructions (a Trojan horse) in the computer operating system executed periodically. The instruction would test the year, date, and time of day clock in the computer so that on a specified day of the year two years later at 3:00 P.M. the time bomb, a type of logic bomb, would go off and trigger the printout of a confession of a crime on all the 300 computer terminals on-line then and would make the system crash. This was timed so the perpetrator would geographically be a long distance from the computer and its users.

This system can serve embezzlers especially well in concealing their activities of manipulation of transactions even if they have no access to the computer system. For example, an employee who manages to embezzle money or property through the computer system might plant a logic bomb or time bomb that instructs the computer system to destruct if anyone audits certain parts that would reveal proof of the embezzlement activity.

Piggybacking and Impersonation

To prevent unauthorized access, many corporate high-security computer centers require employees either to punch a sequence of buttons or insert a magnetically coded plastic card in a reader that will open the entrance door.

Many computers now have the card reader system attached to them to guard against piggybacking (i.e., someone is directly behind a person who has just gained authorized access and slips in before the door closes). Electronic piggybacking is another problem (i.e., company employees don't log off a computer terminal when they leave, someone else can use it, piggybacking on their access). Depending on your company's system, this could happen from a different terminal. There are also ways to piggyback via phone lines and satellite communication.

When another person gains access by punching in your sequence code, they have impersonated you. Computer users who have trouble remembering their access number often tape passwords to their desk or computer, and that practice invites unauthorized access and misleads investigators about the identity of an offender. Unauthorized access can also happen as in the movie *War Games* when someone tries various random combinations until he or she hits on the right one. Computer hackers often have programs that automate this method.

Embezzlers look for these types of opportunities that enable them to carry out their schemes without the offense being traceable to them. For example, if an employee in the marketing department learns the system entry code due to the carelessness of a payroll clerk, he or she can access the system either from another terminal or from the same terminal on evenings or weekends, using the clerk's code and setting up instructions for checks to be issued to nonexistent employees (e.g., for nonexistent consulting services) and having them mailed to a post office box or other address where the embezzler can collect them.

Electronic Scavenging

If you have ever walked around the downtown area of New York, Chicago, San Francisco, or other major cities, you've probably seen people scavenging in trash cans for anything of value. One can also scavenge around a computer, scanning discarded output for trade secrets, mailing lists, or other valuable information that is prime for embezzlement and marketing for cash. Electronic scavenging allows employee offenders to tap into your company's computer system and examine memory, or obtain scratch disks or tapes and scan them for items of value. Scavenging is an inefficient method but is often effective for embezzlers of information, especially when company systems have little or no effective security programmed into their systems. This method gives you little to connect the scavenger to embezzled information sold or used for insider deals, especially when entry into the system might include piggybacking or impersonation.

■ CREATING AN EFFECTIVE SYSTEM PREVENTION PROGRAM

How good can protection of your company computer systems become? Regardless of how many measures and countermeasures you take, won't there always be another person who can figure out a way to penetrate them? The answer is yes if you limit your computer system security to system access. Your security must go beyond entry codes. The following solutions will show you a total program to ensure that only the most persistent persons will try to embezzle company assets through the computer system, and that despite their skill, with an effective investigative audit program you will detect them quickly.

■ SIX IMPORTANT CATEGORIES FOR YOUR INVESTIGATIVE AUDIT

Establishing an effective investigative audit program that protects your company from embezzlement schemes that use the computer system also enables protection from system vandalism, sabotage, and information espionage (a form of embezzlement) that might be a disguise for embezzlement activities or separate acts in themselves. (See Chapter 17.)

1. *Physical security.* Tightly control access to company computer equipment and data backups and storage. You will want your investigative audit to begin with this important category. Uncontrolled access or loosely controlled access to these important aspects of your company's computer systems negates any other type of prevention implemented. You must always begin with physical security to make other techniques work effectively.

2. *Internal computer security mechanisms.* You must look for effective devices built into computer equipment, software, and data communication circuits that form the next layer of computer system security. Remember, the layered approach applies to all security, including computer systems. The more stumbling blocks your security program creates, the greater the security and higher the risk to a person who considers embezzlement or other activities not in the company's best interest.

3. *Operational and procedural security measures.* Your investigative audit needs to look for or create a program that limits computer usage that

may connect to important databases. For example, you can have a company policy that limits access only to operators, not programmers, and prevent operators from making program changes. You should also design your prevention program to ensure that certain key systems have further protection. An effective way of protecting payroll databases and programming instructions, for example, is to have computer operators prepare the information or changes but not have an access capability of entering it (input). The input must happen by someone outside the department who can review the input and have the authority to enter the new information or changes. This discourages or eliminates the inclination for covert schemes of asset embezzlement. Conversely, the person authorized to entering data cannot make any changes, only enter the data. This countermeasure would call for expanded collusion for the embezzler. For example, if payroll operators schemed to create padded payrolls, increase salaries, or add fictitious people on the payroll, they would have to share the secret and money embezzled with a person not in their department and whom they might not know personally.

4. *Conventional computer system auditing procedures.* The procedures for auditing computer systems as discussed in Chapter 5 often cannot detect the skilled embezzler unless there is a glaring error. However, as I noted in that chapter, you can use the auditor's work papers and information, when available, to enhance your investigative audit. Often you will see more in the auditor's findings than he or she did. Remember that auditors look for accounting procedure (GAAP) compliance or violations, not intricate embezzlement schemes.

5. *Ethical controls.* The ethical standards of every employee involved in the collection, processing, storage, and communication of data are important; however, as noted earlier, embezzlers traditionally appear as model employees and citizens. A person who seems too perfect probably has a well-crafted agenda of disguise. You need sound company policies on ethical standards as a control element, but persons seemingly following GAAP diligently should not remain beyond your suspicion in an investigative audit.

6. *Legal deterrents.* All employees involved in your company's computer system, and those who aren't, should have the same handbooks, which discuss the legal ramifications of computer use beyond those prescribed by the company show clearly the legal consequences. This in itself probably won't deter the determined, but a clear discussion of the risk involved might convince others that a computer system embezzlement scheme is not worth the pain and hardship that could follow.

■ FIVE IMPORTANT INVESTIGATIVE AUDIT ELEMENTS

Corporate computer systems pose a unique problem for your investigative audit and create the need to approach the audit through a form of risk analysis. Risk assessment and risk analysis involve a process of identifying vulnerabilities of and threats to any system, manual or computerized. Not all risks are unacceptable (such as threats of fire or flood and other uncontrollable factors that endanger life and property). Also unpredictable human errors that may happen so infrequently, with negligible effect on the business operations of the company's computer systems often does not justify extensive and costly countermeasures.

The physical security of a computer system is the type of risk category easily assessed in monetary terms. You can readily determine the cost of neutralizing threats of physical damage by fire, flood, wind, or civil disturbance. However, the prevention of damage to the data assets of your company by either unintentional losses or manipulation (such as embezzlement and malicious human activity) are not so easy to quantify.

How can your concept of risk of loss become workable or quantifiable? Briefly, by developing a systematic method of defining the probability of destruction, modification, disclosure, or misuse of data or equipment, either accidental or intentional. As you design your investigative audit program tailored for your company's computer systems, consider the following key elements:

1. Perform a preliminary risk analysis to identify major problem areas and select urgent "quick fix" security measures as needed to correct major problem areas.

2. Estimate potential losses to the computer system and its users from (a) physical destruction or theft of physical assets, (b) loss or destruction of data and program files, (c) embezzlement of company funds, (d) embezzlement of information, (e) embezzlement of indirect assets, or (f) delay or prevention of computer operation.

3. Estimate the probability, in your best judgment, of potential threat occurrences plus their effect on the computer system, referring to the six aforementioned investigative audit categories.

4. Combine your estimates of loss potential plus threat probability to develop an annual loss expectancy for the company. This estimate creates a cost/benefit assessment that enables you and the company to determine a countermeasure budget.

5. Choose the array of remedial measures that effects the greatest reduction in the annual loss expectancy at the least total cost. Remedial measures will include changes in the company's computer operational environment to reduce exposure, measures to reduce the effect of threats, improved control procedures, early detection, and contingency plans.

■ SEVEN KEY STEPS IN CONDUCTING AN INVESTIGATIVE AUDIT

When you have finished the preparatory work, you're ready to create a checklist for conducting your investigative audits on a routine schedule. The schedule is important because it alerts potential offenders that traditional and investigative audits will detect their embezzlement or other activities quickly.

Step 1: Establish an Inventory of Files

You need an inventory of the files compiled from information supplied by the project managers or sponsors of each database file. At a minimum, this information should include the following:

- File name and other identifiers
- Purpose of the file
- Uses of the file
- Authority for compiling the file (i.e., company policy management directive)
- Essential elements of information, including
  —Personal and separate identifiers
  —Origins of data and frequency of update
  —Type of data (alphabetic, numeric, alphanumeric)
  —Volume (number of records in file and growth rate)
  —Run frequency
- Expected life of the file
- Names of employees authorized to access the file or its products.

If a system of records should spin off a subsystem of records (subfile) for a special purpose, the subsystem must be treated as a "discrete system" in your inventory. The file name should be as descriptive as possible. If no name exists, synthesize a descriptor. Description of the file should include the major outputs, such as reports or displays. Explain uses of the file as either reference, periodic report generation, demand reports, statistical summaries, modeling, and others as well as the application.

When you have completed the inventory, your first classification cut should follow, with each system of records assigned to one of six categories:

1. Files containing proprietary and sensitive information, such as research reports, financial data, plans, and the like
2. Files containing sensitive information involving the general management of your company, such as decisions in process but not concluded
3. Files containing raw transaction information yet unevaluated, such as procurements proceedings, pricing models, results of marketing surveys, or models of marketing strategy
4. Files clearly subject to privacy
5. Files subject to general exemptions from privacy
6. Files subject to specific exemptions from privacy coverage (systems of records called for by statute to be maintained and used solely as statistical records).

Key Terms in Step 1

Data integrity: Exists when computerized data are the same as in the source documents or have been correctly computed from source data and have not been exposed to accidental, intentional, or malicious alteration or destruction. Incomplete data, fictitious changes or additions to the data, and erroneous source data will violate data integrity.

Data confidentiality: The status of data held in confidence and protected from unauthorized disclosure. Misuse of data by employees authorized to use them for limited purposes violates data confidentiality.

Data processing availability: The assurance that data processing services will be available within an acceptable time even under adverse circumstances.

Step 2: Determine the Vulnerabilities

A survey of the vulnerabilities of data generation and capture in remote-terminal facilities and their telecommunication links will catalog the potential for damage to the content of the files identified in step 1. Your audit should cover all the characteristics of an information system, such as generation, collection, processing, storage, and retrieval. Often you must use your imagination to identify potential disruption of operations, disruption of time-dependent services, loss of physical assets, and loss of intellectual assets (such as programs and data) involving computers, manual processing centers, remote terminals, or call-in user locations.

Besides obvious hazards such as flooding, fires, and other weather-related threats to computer systems and data storage, you need to audit carefully the possibilities of surreptitious access. You need to find ways in which a desperate person (maybe an embezzler facing detection) may destroy evidence of the crime. Beyond authorized or surreptitious undetected entry, how could embezzlers force their way into data storage, mainframe centers, and other places and carry out the destruction of evidence?

Step 3: Catalog the Threats

You need to identify threats to the viable operation of the computer systems and categorize them as acute or chronic, serious or minor, and physical or intellectual. In addition, you must assess their probability of happening. Threats stem from acts of God or people. Experience has shown that the disasters resulting from fire, floods, windstorms, power loss, and bombs account for less than 25 percent of losses. More threats to company computer systems stem from human errors of omission or commission caused by lack of training, incompetency, mischief, lack of management interest, concentration of computer activity, no backup and restart plan, and inadequate auditing procedures.

Dishonest or disgruntled former or current employees account for 75 percent or greater of file, program, and data destruction or malicious mischief. Unless information taken from a system of records is convertible to negotiable form through such methods as blackmail, fraud, or embezzlement, there is little purpose in investing time, effort, or money in penetrating systems of records. Yet past incidents show system penetrations made simply to answer a challenge. In cataloging potential threats, these nefarious activities must be recognized but are often ignored during the analysis phase.

Step 4: Quantify the Vulnerabilities and Threats

Reduction of the array of vulnerable areas and their attendant threats to a common unit of measure involves some subjectivity. Since you are concerned with company asset loss, the most logical unit of measure is the dollar, but sometimes the critical unit is time loss.

Step 5: Rank the Annual Loss Expectancies

After you have calculated an annual loss expectancy for threats and vulnerable areas, you need to place them in an action priority. You can then match effective preventive actions with their associated costs for each vulnerability. From this match you can determine whether a potential undesirable event justifies the cost of preventive action.

You will often find that a single preventive action serves to protect many threatened areas of vulnerability. The collective annual loss expectancies of these vulnerable areas need to be compared with the cost of countermeasures. There will be some preventive actions that will cost more than accepting the risk of the threat. Before you dismiss these preventive actions, however, you should guard against a ripple effect stemming from other factors, such as loss of managerial control, that affects another subsystem.

Step 6: Select the Countermeasures

The next step in your risk analysis audit is to categorize the vulnerable areas by priority of protection. Threats to integrity, confidentiality, and availability of data are the types of issues you should consider. You can equate the integrity of data with the validity of data, from source to user. A threat to confidentiality is the unauthorized disclosure or misuse of data by authorized employees. Availability means that computer services are both available and usable within acceptable time frames.

Within the three primary categories, you will find subdivisions in which a severity of effect depends on the application. This point becomes increasingly acute if the computer system operates an integrated database. Data stored only once for multiple use may have its integrity and confidentiality compromised for one purpose to a greater degree than for another. The keys to data element linkage within records can post hazards if tampered with, although the data within the records maintain their integrity and confidentiality. The volatility of files is a time-dependent variable that may affect integrity, confidentiality, and availability. For example, where do you place the vulnerability of programs?

The issue of data processing availability pertains to a computer application that can least tolerate interruption. In an integrated database system, the posting of information reports can endure delay for a reasonable time, but access to a key issue may be critical to the company's interests.

Step 7: Implement Your Security Program

You should prepare a plan and a schedule for implementing selected remedial measures. You should also prepare and maintain a policy and plans handbook that includes a physical security policy statement; mandatory security procedures; security guidelines for system design, programming, testing, and maintenance; contingency plans; security indoctrination material; and a security audit program.

Your investigative audits, coupled with traditional audit procedures, must be scheduled regularly to ensure systematic validation of all critical security and emergency measures. Your audit report should show which measures call for improvement or replacement. To assure prompt resolution, use a check sheet (problem and follow-up) for each major deficiency.

The checklists in Exhibit 6-2 will help you conduct expeditious audits and identify weaknesses and embezzlement opportunities.

Exhibit 6-2
Six Investigative Audit Checklists

1. Employee Management Checklist
   - ☐ Does your company have specific policies and procedures in force that encompass the elements of data security, privacy, and confidentiality practiced by employees?
   - ☐ Do corporate management employees have a clear understanding of their legal responsibilities, if any, that relate to the information within company databases?
   - ☐ Has your company created, published, and disseminated policy statements about database information privacy and security?
   - ☐ Have security procedures been published and responsibilities established?
   - ☐ Have all employees that operate company computers and have access to company databases signed a statement of understanding and responsibility?
   - ☐ Has your company defined procedural responsibility for maintenance procedures and for auditing the execution of these procedures?
   - ☐ Does your company supply a continuing program of security education for data processing and user employees?
   - ☐ Is your company security program kept current?
   - ☐ Are the company security program responsibilities defined for employees to the level needed?
   - ☐ Are the security program responsibilities understood and accepted by applicable employees?
   - ☐ Are the following functional security responsibilities specifically assigned within your company?

     —Security program administration

     —Operating security

—Classification of files and file linkages

—Design and programming security

—Authorization of access

—Technological research

☐ Does your company conduct adequate background investigations to determine the record of general integrity and stability for employee candidates?

☐ Does your company verify an employee candidate's work and academic history, including past levels of responsibility and performance?

☐ Does your company supply surety bonding for sensitive positions for employee candidates?

☐ Are good housekeeping and personal security practices practiced in your company to ensure prevention of careless loss or disclosure of database information?

☐ Are proof and control functions done by employees other than those who normally operate computers and have access to the systems?

☐ Are proper computer access and operation controls maintained?

☐ Is there an independent audit of these controls and computer logs?

2. System Development Checklist

☐ Does your company have an adequate project planning system?

☐ Are company project control reports satisfactory?

☐ Are major company projects subdivided into well-defined phases?

☐ Is documentation of company project work complete and accurate?

☐ Does your company use satisfactory systems testing policies and procedures?

☐ Are all company system changes properly approved and documented?

☐ Does design documentation include a statement explaining the company objectives of the system and its expected benefits?

☐ Does design documentation include a description of the general system concept, including the features that meet the company system objectives?

☐ Does the design documentation define the scope of automated and unautomated system applications and actions?

- ☐ Does design documentation describe the interfacing relationships of the company system with subsystems or other company systems?
- ☐ Does the narrative explain the functions of each system module?
- ☐ Does the design documentation include a flow chart of the general flow of information through the system?
- ☐ Is the flow chart tied in with complete narrative descriptions?
- ☐ Does the flow chart depict all segments of the system and show their interrelationships?
- ☐ Does the flow chart depict the major categories of inputs and outputs and show the general data flow?
- ☐ Does the flow chart depict the interfacing relationships with other company systems?
- ☐ Does the design documentation include a description of company equipment configuration used?
- ☐ Does the description specify the capabilities and limits of the equipment to handle the processing of company data for the system?
- ☐ Is the software planned for use with the company systems identified?
- ☐ Is the computer language used for programming stated?
- ☐ Does the design documentation include flow charts showing the logical data flow and the sequence of operations performed by each computer process (i.e., run or job)?
- ☐ Are all flow charts accompanied by narrative descriptions of the planned computer operations?
- ☐ Are purposes and interrelationships (interfaces) of the various company manual and computer operations clearly identified?
- ☐ Does design documentation include a narrative description of each major computer program that ties in with the flow charts and narrative descriptions?
- ☐ Does design documentation show a description of each process related to processing frequencies, cut-off dates, and resulting reports or other output?
- ☐ Do file and record descriptions identify all inputs and outputs, defining their uses, specifications, contents, formats, and other characteristics as applicable including media used?
- ☐ Do file descriptions identify formats, contents, and blocking factors for each file?

☐ Does design documentation supply a description of input controls, including

— Controls over the submission of source documents?

— Controls over data communications that ensure integrity?

— Controls for identification of separate transactions?

— Controls restricting access to remote input devices?

— Controls over preparation or transcription of machine-readable media?

— Types of edits and other validation routines?

☐ Does the design documentation provide a description of environmental controls, including

— Separation of duties and functional responsibilities of employees?

— Safeguarding of computer programs and program documentation?

— Control of access to data files and records?

— Plans for alternate-site storage of programs to ensure continuity of operations?

☐ Does the design documentation provide a description of the procedures for authorization and approval of program changes?

☐ Does the design documentation provide a historical record (hard copy) of transaction activity and a data retention schedule?

☐ Does the design documentation describe the capability to

— Prepare special listings needed?

— Provide for the interrogation of every data element?

— Periodically print out trial balances of computer-based general ledger and subsidiary ledger information?

☐ Does the design documentation call for transactions to be entered to the system only once for all processing and reporting?

☐ Does the design documentation provide a statement of the audit approach used in the computer environment, including

— The frequency of internal audits and the methods used by internal auditors?

— The identification of specially prepared or general audit programs or packages?

☐ Does the design documentation include a description of the planned methods for testing the logic and reliability of the system?

☐ Are security measures established for the employees and the sensitive data within the system?

☐ Are regular analyses conducted of the system reporting requirements on a need-to-know basis and are distribution procedures based on those analyses?

☐ Does the system design include adequate file backup procedures?

☐ Are procedures included to prevent unauthorized access to on-line systems?

☐ Are procedures included to ensure proper handling of all sensitive company information?

3. Input Controls Checklist

☐ Are responsibilities divided to separate the duties of systems analysts, programmers, and computer operators?

☐ Have time frames been established for the processing of source documents from point of receipt to the input preparation operation?

☐ Are input batches logged and accounted for?

☐ Has authority to start source documents been limited?

☐ Is a number assigned to each key source document for identification purposes?

☐ Is source data information properly verified?

☐ Are source documents controlled after the input operation?

☐ Are operators of the equipment for input preparation prevented from changing data on source documents?

☐ Are operators of input preparation denied access to computer programs?

☐ Has your company developed a system of codes to identify and categorize by reason each reversing entry, whether manual or computer initiated?

☐ Is the identification number of the reversing entry the same as, or cross-referenced to, the original transaction?

☐ Do documents used for beginning error corrections contain adequate justification and proper authorization?

☐ Is a cross-reference file maintained to identify the error correction transaction with the original transaction?

☐ Have procedures been prescribed to prevent duplicate processing of input data?

☐ Has your company planned for a properly controlled library for storage of system tapes and disks?

☐ Are the following edit routines used to detect errors:

—Character checks (checking each character, whether numeric, alphabetic, or blank)?

—Field checks (determining whether all data have been input and are in proper sequence within the transaction)?

—Limit checks (checking certain fields within a transaction to determine whether the data fall within a prescribed range)?

—Validity checks (checking certain fields of known limits, stored information, or computer results)?

—Sequence checks (checking that incoming data records are in proper sequence)?

—Logical relationships (or consistency) checks (determining whether components of input data have a logical relationship among themselves or to a master file)?

—Reasonableness tests (checking for gross errors in calculation or a balance that exceed a predetermined limit)?

—Comparing (checking data fields against each other to prove the accuracy of operations involving matching, merging, coding, balancing, or record selection from files)?

—Batch checks (checking the completeness of input batches)? These checks could include record counts (number of records input), control totals (summation of fields containing quantitative data), and hash totals (summation of fields containing identifying numerical data).

☐ Is a list made of corrections to input data?

☐ When updating balances, is a comparison made by the computer between the first balance plus the current transaction and the afterposting balance?

☐ When tapes are merged or sorted, are control totals checked and the new totals recorded?

☐ When errors or exceptions occur, are they printed out for independent review?

☐ Are manually calculated fields verified by the computer system?

☐ When including balancing totals with input data, is there provision for checking these balances?

☐ When transactions lose their input identification, can a new identification number be developed and cross-referenced to the prior entry?

☐ Are account numbers validated against a chart of accounts?

☐ Have control procedures been adopted to protect against the destruction of tape or disk data?

☐ Are operator actions that affect data processing recorded for audit and review?

☐ Are transaction registers required for input transactions?

☐ Is there satisfactory documentation of the data flow and procedures for the processing and control of input data?

4. On-Line Processing Checklist

☐ Are only certain company employees authorized to operate terminals?

☐ Do access authorization tables restrict terminals and users to the entry of predetermined categories of input?

☐ Is there a record of terminal activity that lists

—Time of request?

—User's identity?

—Authorization code?

—File accessed?

—Function performed?

—Terminal identify?

☐ Are passwords used in sign-on, sign-off procedures?

☐ Is the company procedure for assigning passwords tightly controlled?

☐ Are the company passwords changed periodically?

☐ Are company passwords kept confidential and secure?

☐ Are some terminal users limited in the files that they can access and in the operations that they can perform on files?

☐ Are terminals connected to the system only during certain periods of the day?

☐ Are user identification procedures satisfactory?

☐ Have procedures been established to trace illegal inquiries?

☐ For dial-up facilities, are there controls over the distribution of the computer telephone number?

☐ Are on-line access logs maintained by the system and reviewed regularly by a control group?

☐ Is action taken if the security code is still wrong after a specific number of user attempts to log on?

☐ Are names and passwords of discharged employees promptly deleted from the access authorization tables?

☐ Has your company made a detailed analysis of basic communication system requirements, and is the following information available?

—Sources of transaction data

—Destinations of system outputs

—System processing requirements

—Data formats

—Information volumes

—Message frequencies

—System response requirements

—Reliability requirements

—Security requirements

☐ Have alternative communication network designs that supply a higher level of security been considered?

☐ Are all modem connections and communication line junction and termination points secured to prevent tampering?

☐ Are leased lines used for transmission of sensitive data?

☐ Are encoding or encryption techniques used in the transmission of sensitive data from or to the terminals?

☐ Are terminals in secure areas to prevent access to the terminals or output from the terminals by unauthorized users?

☐ Do terminals include locking devices to prevent unauthorized use?

☐ Are badge readers incorporated into the terminals to permit positive identification of users with a software security system?

☐ Do the terminals transmit a unique electrical signal to permit positive identification of the terminal by the central computer system?

5. Software Safeguards Checklist

☐ Are application programs regularly checked to verify that they are processing accurately?

☐ Are master copies of application programs kept and matched against operational application programs?

☐ Is access to libraries containing operational programs restricted to authorized employees?

☐ Are transactions verified using controlled master files of vendors, customers, employees, and others before they are processed?

☐ Are control totals over key fields and record counts balanced after processing?

☐ Are the counts and totals of input master files reconciled to those of output master files?

☐ Does the application software report all exception conditions, and are these reports reviewed?

☐ Does the computer's operating system maintain an unbroken audit trail?

☐ Are the computer's operating system security features adequate?

☐ Is the software security system for user access to the database adequate?

☐ Are computer projects or jobs put on hold in the case of security violations until the security manager has begun investigative action?

☐ Is prompt action taken on reported violations?

☐ Are security commands that permit changes to the system or its files audited by disinterested persons?

☐ Is the security console kept secure from intrusion, and are console messages secured from disclosure?

☐ Is security documentation maintained in a secure way to prevent disclosure of passwords and other security information?

☐ Are company passwords changed often?

☐ Are passwords assigned to employees in a secure way?

☐ Are records maintained and reports issued on the performance of each user relative to the quantity and type of security violations per time period?

☐ Is there an audit trail of all changes to the database?

☐ Is the database periodically audited and balanced?

☐ Is special attention given to extra shifts run at odd hours?

☐ Are program changes approved by a person of authority in addition to the programmer and system analyst?

☐ Is each change request made in writing?

☐ Is each change well documented as to its reason and effect?

☐ Are periodic checks made to ensure that no unauthorized program changes have been made?

6. Output Controls Checklist

☐ Is there an audit trail from output to original data entry?

☐ Has your company supplied control procedures to protect against accessing incomplete files in producing outputs?

☐ Are there well-defined error detection and correction procedures?

☐ Are exception reports of unusual transactions or abnormal processing results furnished to the proper level of management for necessary action?

☐ Does the system provide for comparison of operating results with physical inventories or confirmations of accounts receivable?

☐ Does the system effectively limit interventions by the console operator, and are all such interventions permanently recorded? Are persons responsible for input transactions prevented from controlling the resultant outputs?

☐ Are transaction registers required for output transactions?

☐ Do reports contain more information than users need?

■ CONVERTING YOUR INVESTIGATIVE AUDIT INTO A CRIMINAL INVESTIGATION

When your investigative audit of company computerized accounting discloses indications of database manipulation or overt embezzlement activity, you need to begin a criminal investigation. (See Chapters 16 and 17.) Remember, a criminal investigation does not require filing charges or prosecuting, but it enables collection of evidence in ways that supply that option. An effective criminal investigation also provides a basis for civil action and liability-free employee termination.

Your first consideration in an embezzlement investigation involving computer manipulation is to establish theft of company assets that have a provable value. When the embezzlement involves money or its equivalent (such as stocks, bonds, etc.), you need to document its existence and company ownership before the theft. That establishes a proof of loss.

Next, you need proof that the theft happened through manipulation of computer records, or that some transaction occurred using the computer, such as an electronic fund transfer. Cash skimming or other thefts might involve concealment by changing records in computer databases. For example, an employee steals cash or commodities and enters false information into the computer or changes inventory databases to disguise or conceal his or her actions. You can document the manipulation by hard copy printouts that show that the transaction happened through a comparison of data printed from a backup source and information in the computer database when you begin your investigation. That's why it's vitally important to maintain a daily backup copy in a secured place where employees with access to the company's computer system cannot change that copy. Normally, companies maintain a backup in a database library, but the offender might also have access to it and change it simultaneously with the operational database.

When you have proven loss and know how the loss happened, you must prove who was responsible. If your company has a well-designed computer system, you might begin with a register of log-ons and maybe the system will show who made the transactions. However, don't jump to conclusions because the employee identified might not be the offender. For example, another employee who is the real offender might have learned the log-on and transaction code of another employee and used it to disguise the crime.

Establishing identity might prove challenging, and you should always surpass the computer system. First, you should establish that the suspect had access to the computer system when the transaction happened, and then verify his or her presence. You might use time cards, other employees as witnesses, or any number of other ways according to your company configuration. When the crime happened from a remote terminal or through a call-in system, your job becomes tougher. However, when you have a suspect for that situation and the call originated from a toll area, telephone bill listings might reveal needed evidence.

Establishing identity beyond doubt in computer crime cases will always be the most difficult task in a criminal investigation. Often you must rely on a series of creative processes when you do not have a clear suspect. The net-worth-expenditure technique described in Chapter 17 will help you identify an embezzlement suspect and might lead to linking the suspect to the database transaction. However, follow all the traditional ways of collecting and maintaining the integrity of the crime evidence (i.e., proof of loss and proof of theft), and then develop admissible ways of identifying the offender and linking him or her conclusively to the crime.

Chapter Seven
Embezzlement in Financial Institutions

The typical U.S. commercial bank is corporate in its structure; like all corporations, its active governing body is its board of directors. Elected by the stock holders, the board is responsible for the proper conduct of the bank's affairs. The growth and diversification of the banking industry today call for lines of communication among the various levels of management that are clear, prompt, and effective. Banks have developed a variety of middle-management levels with fewer line personnel to supervise. However, streamlining and creating efficient operations has not slowed the growth of internal white collar crimes despite efforts to do so. This chapter discusses measures, countermeasures, and effective techniques that will enable you to bring this problem into perspective and then move to reduce and eliminate illegal activities within your bank and the financial industry.

Often, banks and financial institutions are so busy worrying about ways to prevent outsiders from stealing their assets that they forget to look inside the operation—and that's where about 80 percent of the loss problem originates. In this chapter, I will review the most common problems banks and financial institutions experience and discuss how to detect and eliminate losses from them. Embezzlement is limited only by the ingenuity of the embezzlers and the opportunities they're supplied; however, the techniques discussed in this chapter provide an effective way to fight embezzlement.

■ CHARACTERISTICS OF INTERNAL EMBEZZLEMENT

The Federal Bureau of Investigation, Federal Deposit Insurance Corporation, and other financial institution agencies such as the Bank Administration Institute report that at least 80 percent of bank and financial institution losses stem from employee fraud and embezzlement, with the remaining 20 percent stemming from outside schemes. A survey of over 400 banks conducted by the Bank Administration Institute and involving nearly 2000 cases of internal fraud and embezzlement revealed that banks that have total deposits over $1 billion have the highest rates of employee white collar crime. However, the study found that all types and sizes of banks are lucrative targets.

Reliable statistics show that nearly half of reported frauds and embezzlements happened in cash and cash-item functions, and 90 percent of these cases involved losses of less than $5000. The estimated average loss in trust departments totalled over $10,000.

Embezzlement cases involving amounts over $10,000 normally have any of the following characteristics:

- They normally will involve a supervisor or bank officer.
- Concealment of these crimes will normally be successful for a year or more.
- These crimes often involve collusion.
- The most common technique used by offenders included fictitious or irregular accounting entries.

Bank tellers accounted for more than 80 percent of bank employees involved in known embezzlements of cash or cash items. Successful secrecy of these offenses lasted only a few weeks; however, even when the crime became apparent, only a small percentage of these cases were proven. In the commercial and mortgage loan departments, involvement of bank officers topped 75 percent of the reported fraud and embezzlement cases. These statistics involve only known and reported cases, which represent only a fraction of those occurring each year. Often, banks avoid publicly discussing employee dishonesty. Honesty among bank employees has long been a nurtured pillar of the banking system. Dishonesty is contrary to its very concept. Acting as holders for the resources of their depositors and as clearinghouses for business transactions, banks and bankers must display the highest degree of integrity. Without this there would be no banks. The notoriety of dishonest employees can erode the foundation of the banking and financial industry.

■ SIX COMMON CATEGORIES OF BANK EMBEZZLEMENT

Victim banks and financial institutions targeted by employee and outside fraud and embezzlements normally encompass five primary categories, discussed next.

(1) Mysterious Disappearance

This category usually involves the theft of cash, negotiable securities, or credit cards. Cash is the most susceptible to theft and embezzlement because the offender does not need to convert it to other forms or create an investigative trail by deposits in an account. Negotiable securities pose greater challenges for the embezzler because, beyond concealing the crime, it's necessary to leave a trail that a skilled financial investigator can follow during the conversion process. Credit cards and credit card payments normally supply another lucrative target for the embezzler. These opportunities abound in credit card departments of banks and other financial institutions.

The label "mysterious disappearance" or the perception that the loss happened with no apparent reason creates a misnomer. Few managers of banks and financial institutions, accountants and auditors, or others involved in dealing with losses would not admit, at least privately, that a major problem often labeled "mysterious" involves a variety of white collar crime schemes and techniques from inside. Few banks want the public or other commercial enterprises to know they have embezzlement problems. It's clearly not good for business. Although the FDIC insures deposits, the public is skeptical about banks that experience losses after being entrusted with depositors' money. It's easier and safer for a bank or other financial institution to claim "mysterious disappearance" than confess that an employee perpetrated an embezzlement scheme.

(2) Lapping

This embezzling technique encompasses the concealment effort because it involves stealing from one customer's account to cover a theft from another customer's account. This usually requires access to departments of the bank that have daily activity, such as time deposits and demand deposits. Lapping normally involves tellers who conceal the crime by withholding another deposit of an amount equal to or greater than the deposit stolen. The teller must continue this procedure or the embezzlement becomes apparent; however, eventually the teller might receive a deposit for an account that has little or no activity and can clear the deficit. When the shortage appears, maybe one or more years later, it is difficult to prove who was responsible for it, and the bank may drop the matter. An astute teller in a busy bank can research accounts and develop a clever embezzlement plan involving estimated times when nonactive account deposits will arrive and work out accurate embezzlement schedules. These types of embezzlements normally occur periodically, especially when a teller's perception of a need for immediate money outweighs the risk involved. For example, consider the court case of *United States v. Anne DeMeo.* On May 9, 1979, DeMeo waived indictment and entered a plea to a one-count indictment charging the misapplication of $7400 cash of the Westport Bank and Trust Company. She had used various fraudulent bookkeeping entries to transfer small sums to her own account over a six-month period.

Another example is the case of *United States v. Job L. Emerson.* On April 1, 1980, Job L. Emerson, a vice-president and 21-year employee of the Hartford National Bank, was convicted of embezzling $74,530 from that bank. Emerson used his position as manager of Hartford National's Correspondent Banking Department to divert checks from several other banks to his own account. Emerson engaged in the activity to cover personal expenses and poor investments.

(3) Fictitious or Forged Entries

These types of entries occur in several different areas, such as expense accounts, income accounts, loan accounts, and time deposits. Many fictitious or forged entries typically involve loans. Bank loan departments are especially vulnerable to fraud and embezzlements from employees since thousands of transactions pass through these departments. When the bank grants a customer a loan, the customer receives a check, or his or her account is credited with the amount. Other activities of the loan department include collecting and posting principal and interest payments, calculating and paying rebates, accepting and processing various fees, and accepting and holding as collateral stock or other marketable securities.

A prevalent type of embezzlement by bank employees involves creating fictitious loan customers or forging signatures of established customers. An offense running a close third involves employees understanding income received as interest payments made on loans or overstating interest rebates for loans paid before maturity. In this scheme, the employee gains from the difference between the true amount of the rebate and the overstated amount.

Normally, banks pay these funds by check. The employee forges the customer's signature, adds the notation "for deposit only," and deposits the check in his or her account at another bank. When the check returns to the bank, or during audits, it appears to have been endorsed and put in a bank account. Since the customer remains unaware of the money, he or she will not complain, and the auditor's examining records do not detect the data on cancelled checks.

Other schemes involve bank loan officers who establish credit files and loan notes with all appearances of legitimate transactions, but the person applying for the loan does not exist. These "dummy loans" will eventually default and the clever employee will explain the loss as a poor credit decision. Employees participating in this activity will ensure that the loan amount stays within the acceptable loss limits (discussed earlier).

The case *United States v. William Thibadeau, Norman Harris, Patrick Thibadeau, William Pitcher* provides another example. On April 25, 1980, a federal grand jury, after an eighteen-month investigation, returned a 98-count bank fraud indictment involving four persons. One of the persons involved in the scheme was a former board member of the victim bank, and another person in the conspiracy was formerly the bank's chief lending officer. Their scheme involved the submission of inflated retail installment contracts that enabled a rapid buildup of a special dealer account they systematically looted for well over $1 million. The indictment charged sixty-nine counts of submitting false loan documents against William Thibadeau, the former bank director and partner in a truck dealership, whose name appeared on the false documents. It also charged sixty-five false document counts against Norman Harris, a partner of Thibadeau; twenty-two false statement counts against Patrick Thibadeau, an employee of the dealership and the son of William Thibadeau; and an aiding and abetting count against William Pitcher, formerly the chief lending officer of the Guaranty Bank and Trust Company, the victim institution.

A final example is provided by *United States v. C. Marston Ladd*. C. Marston Ladd, a branch manager of the American Savings Bank, of New Britain, Connecticut, was convicted on April 1, 1980, of having embezzled bank money totaling $36,930. Ladd's scheme involved first creating a fictitious loan to cover personal expenses, and then creating a series of four other loans, each used to cover a previous loan.

(4) Asset Embezzlement-Securities

Embezzlement of securities held for customers or diversion embezzlement of income from securities ranks high among the common categories of bank and financial institution employee white collar crimes. In this scheme, the bank employee forges the signature of the customer and temporarily converts the securities to his or her use, either for investment or as collateral for a loan elsewhere.

The creativity of dishonest employees is limitless, and the following example shows how their ingenuity can lead to white collar schemes.

A securities officer in the trust department of a bank stole a large amount of securities through a combination of forgery and address changes for a trustee account. The officer, over time, researched the habits of various trustees holding the largest accounts. He chose one account as his target because the holder generally traveled extensively and over long periods. He mastered the trustee's signature, went a to luxury hotel, obtained a suite, and registered in the trustee's name. Next, the officer submitted a change of address to the bank's trust department, naming the hotel suite as the trustee's new address. The bank officer then began embezzling all the securities (over $500,000) in the targeted account, forging the signature of the customer on all receipts. When the auditing department mailed its audit confirmation, the address on file for the customer remained at the hotel where the officer had established residence in the trustee's name. The officer forged the audit confirmations and returned them to the bank. The officer's scheme involved using the stolen securities as collateral for speculation on the stock market and returning them before the trustee found out they were missing. The bank detected the officer's theft only because the real trustee returned unexpectedly and planned to use the securities as collateral, and the investigators traced them to the bank officer.

(5) Tellers with Sticky Fingers

Bank tellers also resort to "dipping into the till" at banks that do not have strict controls regarding daily shortages in proofs of the day's transactions. Lenient banks stem from the idea that the employee erred instead of embezzled the money. Sometimes a teller has a large difference that is beyond reconciliation at the close of the day's business. These shortages can result from tellers exchanging money, often in the heat of a customer rush and especially in large banks. A dishonest teller "sets up" the banded money in his or her drawer or cabinet, and when another teller calls for "twenties," for example, the dishonest teller volunteers and makes a cash transfer recorded on a log. The dishonest teller has removed a predetermined number of the bills from the banded packet, and when the accepting teller signs for the cash without counting the packet, a "mysterious" shortage will happen at the close of business. Because of many transactions and time lapses, it's nearly impossible to prove that the shortage happened this way or who was responsible.

Bank tellers also steal from their cash position and try to offset the shortage by showing a check cashed in an amount equal to their embezzlement on that day. They often claim that the check went to the bank's transit department but was apparently lost; or because of the large volume of checks processed by the check-processing department, the check probably was misplaced. Tellers might also forge a check against a customer account to obtain funds for their personal use. Often, these transactions will affect dormant accounts so discovery is unlikely.

A notable scheme involving bank tellers demonstrates the ingenuity you're up against and how difficult proving an embezzlement case might be. Two bank tellers with an excellent work record found an opportunity to embezzle a large amount of money from customer accounts. They researched the computer database whenever possible and identified a group of large, inactive savings accounts. Next, the tellers obtained enough signature cards to equal the targeted accounts and recruited a few friends to help in the scheme. Each of the friends filled out a signature card using the inactive savings account number, the customer's social security number, and other information needed. They signed the cards in their handwriting. Then the tellers and friends filled out passbooks in the same way, matching the entries with the database information obtained by the tellers from the bank's computer system. On prearranged dates, the tellers replaced the customer's authentic signature card with those created by their associates in the scheme. An associate would enter the bank, go to another teller, present the passbook, and withdraw most of the money in the account. When the amounts were large, they accepted a cashier's check made out to the customer. After the transaction, the tellers replaced the original customer's signature card and later destroyed the fraudulent copy. The tellers and associates forged customer endorsements on the bank checks and noted that they were for deposit only. They deposited them in a variety of different accounts under several names established in different banks. After looting the accounts for over $5 million, the tellers resigned from their jobs and disappeared. Although the embezzlement scheme eventually surfaced, and investigators suspected the tellers, most of the blame was cast on innocent tellers accused of not verifying the signatures. Actual proof implicating the tellers was never established sufficiently to get them indicted.

(6) Kiting

Individuals and businesses regularly "kite" checks, or write checks on a distant bank with insufficient funds to cover the check, knowing that the check will take several days to clear and planning to make a deposit before the check reaches the bank. For example, a person writes a check for merchandise or some other reason in New York, drawn on a bank in California. Depending on the day of the week the person writes the check, (and on other circumstances such as holidays), it can take as much as ten days or more before the check arrives at the bank for collection. Bank employees know this. After establishing accounts at the most distance places, bank employees (especially tellers or officers who have the right access) may create a large balance in an account and take the money. When the matter finally comes to the attention of the bank, it is nearly impossible to pin the crime on a skilled bank employee. For example, bank teller A has a friend who enters into a conspiracy with the teller. The friend travels to California, Oregon, and Washington during a summer vacation and while there opens three bank accounts using fictitious names, a false local address (often a post office box), and forged ID (which is easily obtained on the backstreets of large cities). Often, the person will use private mailing services. Back home, the person opens three accounts at the bank teller's bank, using the same fictitious names and branch banks around the city. With an investment of a few hundred dollars and six bank accounts plus the teller on the inside, the scheme goes into operation. To maximize profits, the perpetrators work out a schedule, allowing for weekends, national holidays, and bank transaction times known to the teller. These elements supply the most time for the check to float until reaching the bank it's drawn on. With an attentive schedule and accounting, the perpetrators send checks drawn on various accounts as deposits, and with the right timing the checks will often clear. The idea is to build three accounts that the teller can access. When the process reaches its potential before the scheme collapses, again ensuring that the timing allows maximum advantage, the person comes to the teller in the bank and closes the account or accounts simultaneously. With proper timing, the discovery of a problem takes weeks, and meanwhile the smart teller will have to go to a distant city to care for an aging mother or father and will resign, probably with a good record. The two go off to a new place with their fortune and open a business or do whatever they want. This type of scheme netted one pair over $1 million, and since the persons listed in the accounts did not exist, finding them (actually one person) was not possible. In such schemes, considering that the teller did his or her job according to information showing on the computer, it is difficult to prove complicity.

▣ RATIONALIZATION FOR EMPLOYEE THEFT AND FRAUD IN BANKS

Preempting white collar crime in banks and financial institutions often involves understanding why employees get involved in it, beyond personal gain. For example, armed robbery is committed for personal gain, but the robber clearly knows he or she is committing a serious and dangerous crime. Bank employees, however, fall in a different category. They know they are committing a crime, but they rationalize that banks do the same thing legally and can afford the losses.

Depository institutions, including banks, credit unions, savings and loan associations, and mutual savings banks, "create" money each day, and their employees know it. There are many marginal but legal practices conducted by these institutions, at least from a moral point of view. Employees often decide to convert similar practices to illegal, personal gain. The creation of money serves as a good example and is often used to rationalize acts by employees or outsiders who commit crimes in which the bank becomes the victim.

This creation of money occurs when John Doe enters the bank and deposits $1000 cash in his personal account. Federal laws and banking regulations call for the bank to maintain a 20 percent reserve of cash to pay depositors' demands for their money. The law allows the bank to use the remaining 80 percent for loans or investments that create income and profit for the bank. Since $800 of Doe's money is available to the bank's discretionary use, the bank loans it to John Smith, who asks for a loan to buy a used car. Insofar as John Doe is concerned, his $1000 is in the bank vault; however, in reality, only $200 of it is there, and John Smith has the other $800 of Doe's money. Smith deposits the $800 in his bank account at another bank, which has $640 at its discretion after placing the required $160 (20 percent) in its vault. The process continues. Smith, meanwhile, goes to Mary Jones and buys a car she has for sale, and pays her with a check for $800. She deposits the check in her bank. These transactions and money were created out of John Doe's original $1000 deposit. Multiplied by tens of millions of deposits and transactions daily, enormous amounts of money that really do not exist (resulting from the 20 percent reserve rule) continue to create vast wealth for banks and financial institutions.

When employees understand this and see it daily, they easily rationalize kiting and the other five common white collar crimes as being the same thing—using someone else's money. In white collar crime, the offender finds a point of justification and rationalization. When you know what financial institution employee embezzlers probably are doing and how they are rationalizing their illegal actions, you can begin to prevent them from victimizing the bank and others.

■ PROTECTIVE SOLUTION: INVESTIGATIVE CREDIT

Although banks and financial institutions experience some fraud and theft from outside sources, a full 80 percent (according to the FBI) of losses stem from employees and their illegal activities. This fact clearly shows that despite intensive audits and regulatory processes, the problem exists. The key to ending such problems begins with prevention, and preventive techniques must come from regular investigative audits that probe for signs of illicit activity that conventional audits don't detect. It is especially important to find weaknesses in the internal systems that supply the opportunity for employees to exploit their schemes.

Your investigative audit process must keep in mind that embezzlement within any company (including banks and financial institutions) requires opportunity, which stems from access, both initial and continuing. When you audit your bank or other entity, do not view it from a "big picture" point of view; instead, view it just as you would a traditional company. You need to separate and isolate the internal functions and routinely audit each, looking for the opening that an employee might see and use to steal bank assets. Traditional screening processes should always remain in practice; but all banks screen employees, and the 80 percent who embezzle include those who obtained their jobs because of a "squeaky clean" background. Although it's important to begin correctly, there's no assurance that the person hired will not succumb to temptation and rationalize his or her activities as noted earlier.

■ TELLER OPERATIONS: THE STARTING POINT

A good starting point for your investigative audit involves teller or cashier operations. Bank and financial institution tellers are in a position that has the highest rate (about 80 percent) of fraud or embezzlement involving cash and cash items. Statistics of known fraud and embezzlement events in banks across the country show that those crimes are more prevalent among tellers than any other type of bank employee. This is attributable to the position tellers occupy.

Before computer proliferation, the work of tellers was subdivided; one group, called receiving tellers, handled deposits only, while paying tellers were responsible for paying and cashing functions. Today it is far more common to find persons serving as unit tellers, with both functions combined. This gives each teller a far more diversified set of tasks to perform each day and opens a variety of fraud and embezzlement opportunities. This change-over of organization, coupled with the increased activity most banks have experienced, intensifies your need to create excellent controls stemming from investigative audits.

Hundreds of thousands of dollars pass through a teller's hands within a period of several days. Tellers' duties expose them to one of the "richest" areas in a bank for white collar crime activity. Misappropriation of customer deposits occurs more often to customers least likely to detect the loss. However, it's important to note that tellers inclined to victimize their employer, who ultimately has responsibility, rarely work alone. Stealing money or conducting misapplication of funds in itself will not pose a great problem, contrary to the countermeasures banks try to put in place; however, getting that money out of the bank does create a problem for tellers who try to work their illicit schemes alone. This regularly unrecognized problem with tellers accounts for much white collar crime success despite the collective technology, countermeasures, and supervision that banks have in place.

Teller and Outside Complicity

In a Midwestern city, two bank tellers working for a major bank succumbed to the temptations of white collar crime embezzlement in complicity with three friends. Their scheme involved conducting research over time to identify several large inactive savings accounts. To steal the money from these accounts, the tellers prepared a signature card for each targeted account. Their accomplices signed the cards and received a card with the account holder's social security number and spouse's name. The group also obtained forged (but authentic looking) driver's licenses for the accomplices to match each of the names on the savings accounts because they would not have the account passbooks. On a selected date the tellers replaced the genuine account signature cards with those signed by the accomplices. The accomplices (using the account holders' identities and claiming that they misplaced their passbooks) called on the bank and its branches at rotating hours over five days' time and unquestioningly withdrew $5.5 million in cashier's checks. The plan called for cashier's checks rather than cash because of the large withdrawal amounts from each account and to dispel any suspicion that the persons were not genuine. The cashier's checks were immediately deposited in a business account established in a nearby city called "Any City Investments." The following week the tellers, who established the business account in different names and addresses and another similar account in Florida, closed their business account and wire transferred the money to their Florida account. At their employing bank, the tellers replaced the bogus signature cards with the genuine cards and then resigned over the course of three days (one citing a need to care for aging parents, the other for health reasons, and each leaving with good work records).

The white collar scheme became known three years later when two of the genuine depositors tried to withdraw part of their money and found their accounts closed and empty. After several weeks, all such accounts were audited and verified with holders, and the collective scheme and theft surfaced. The cashier's checks were traced to the business account created under fictitious names by the tellers, and the wire transfer to a Florida bank, and another from there to the Bahamas, and still another to the Cayman Islands, where the trail ended. Although investigators found a friend of one of the tellers who knew the whole story, she had no proof, nor was any evidence available. The accomplices were able to withdraw the money with identification and a matched signature. The tellers and their accomplices destroyed both the identification and signature cards, so nothing remained for authorities to determine their identities accurately. According to the teller's friend, each of the accomplices received their cut and went separate ways, but the friend did not know who they were or where they went. The same person told investigators that the tellers also went different ways and were probably in foreign countries. Since there was no conclusive evidence to prove that the scheme happened as the person said it did, or to implicate the tellers or accomplices, the matter closed and statutes of limitations later closed it further.

Preventive Techniques

When your investigative audit shows that situations such as the preceding example can happen at your bank, several preventive techniques must be used. First, ensure that savings and other types of signature cards have serial numbers and are tightly controlled, both those for active accounts and blanks. Banks and financial institutions should not rely on signatures alone. The concept of passbooks and a signature card began decades ago when banks generally knew their customers. Although these items are feasible with strict accountability controls, photo ID cards protect the depositor's account from schemes of impersonators. A duplicate photograph laminated onto the signature card also adds considerable protection. In summary,

(1) Serial number the signature card and maintain strict accountability with an officer outside the teller department and regular audits.

(2) With a passbook, also supply a photo ID card, much like a driver's license.

(3) Place a duplicate photo from the ID card on the signature card and laminate.

Teller Fatigue

One of the challenges that every teller encounters during a day's work is to deal with those customers who try to take advantage of a teller's momentary lapse in concentration or the pressures of an especially hectic hour, when lines are at their longest and the teller inevitably becomes fatigued. Banks often become victims of fraud in this way, even when the transaction involves what appears to be nothing more than a routine cash item.

Split Deposits

A common example of taking advantage of fatigued tellers is the "split deposit," a technique in which a person opens an account and later presents a check to a teller, asking that part of it be deposited and the remainder be in cash. Most banks today enable a teller to access the person's account with a computer terminal at the teller's window to ensure that the person has a balance sufficient to cover the cash amount. However, this transaction does not allow the teller to inform the computer that he or she is paying out a specific amount of cash from that account, because the person is making a deposit. If the check bounces or turns up stolen or forged, then the full amount of the check would be deducted from the account. Smart players know this, so they ensure that they have an adequate balance to get the cash, and then go to a branch bank and withdraw their balance with a check. Several days later, when the bogus check comes back through the system, the depositor's account has little or no money in it and he or she has moved on. The bank has to take the loss because the teller followed directions.

Preventive Techniques

When your investigative audit finds that tellers follow the aforementioned policies, the bank needs to change the policy. Establishing a bank account does not give a customer the right to use it as an automatic medium for cashing checks. The bank policy needs to include a provision for long-term customers who have established themselves as honest persons; however, the split deposit, even when the computer shows enough money in the account to cover the cash amount, should be approved by a bank officer, not the teller. Even an honest customer will simply deposit the check and write another check for cash, drawing on his or her account reserve. Whenever a person has money in the account and wants a split deposit supported by a balance, he or she is probably plotting some type of fraud.

Passing Counterfeit Currency

Often, bank tellers will detect counterfeit currency. Sometimes the forgery is good enough to pass through the hands of a fatigued teller. Once the bank accepts the counterfeit currency, it becomes the bank's property. The bank must turn it in to the Secret Service as required by law, and suffer the loss. Often, the counterfeit currency comes from businesses who accepted it and unknowingly include it in their cash deposit. Or they discover it in their receipts and knowingly include it in their deposit, hoping the teller will accept it so they will not have to suffer the loss. In another case, a criminal element may open several small business accounts around town that may or may not represent a legitimate business. However, the person will appear often and make deposits of cash, mostly small denomination bills and normally a large number of them. The name of the business such people use also has an important psychological effect on tellers. They may use names like "Downtown Amusements" or "Gifts and Things," suggesting that the business handles small denomination cash. Such people know the most hectic time of day at the various banks, and that's when they appear with a wad of ones, fives, tens, and twenties and a completed business deposit slip. These people will often take a moment to scan the tellers to determine which teller appears tired. That's the teller they'll go to. When they get to the window, they hand over a wad of neatly banded money. The teller believes everything is in order and recognizes the person as a regular business customer. There will be a long line behind the person, so the teller does not examine the currency carefully. The person can easily slip in one or two hundred dollars of good-quality counterfeit and do the same at the other banks to create an income of a thousand or more dollars a week.

Preventive Techniques

When you find this opportunity available in your system, even if it has not presented a problem yet, it calls for some procedural changes. For example, when you have a busy bank at a specific hour, use portable signs that designate the windows for personal and business accounts. The tellers assigned to business windows need the greatest amount of experience, especially at detecting counterfeit currency. When you arrange the deposits this way, the teller will have a higher transaction dollar amount but fewer customers. That will offer the teller accepting a large amount of currency for deposit an opportunity to examine the bills as counted. Also, each teller window should have a counterfeit detection light (infrared) that easily and quickly shows the bill as counterfeit or genuine. These easily implemented techniques can serve as an effective deterrent to persons trying to pass counterfeit money to the bank.

■ LENDING AND CREDIT SERVICES ARE OPPORTUNITIES FOR FRAUD

Banks and financial institutions generate profits by rendering services, attracting and retaining deposits, processing payments in a prompt and efficient manner, and putting to profitable use those funds that, in management's judgment, create the best profit advantage for their institution. One of the basic obligations perceived by every bank is the need to serve the credit requirements of customers and the community, and banks translate that credit function into a wide variety of loan and investment operations to meet that obligation. Despite their preeminent position as a source of credit, however, commercial banks face increasing and aggressive competition from many other types of lenders, such as commercial financing firms. Other financial organizations specialize in financing automobiles and fleets of vehicles. Small loan companies accommodate the borrowing needs of persons and some small business ventures, and savings and loan associations focus on housing and commercial building.

Each of these institutions supplies opportunities for the white collar crimes of fraud and embezzlement. One of the glaring examples stems is the infamous savings and loan scandal. Lending and credit often are the cause of bank failures and government takeover. Much of the blame can be placed on economic recession, but a great majority of the contributing factors stem from white collar crimes that are often masked in ways that cannot bring responsible parties to justice. However, prevention of most of these events (and perhaps all of them) is feasible with implementation of varied techniques and programs. Investigation of these frauds and embezzlement crimes will be successful using techniques of criminal investigation too little known or practiced in financial events and institutions.

Bank and financial institution loan and credit departments are extremely vulnerable to internal fraud and embezzlement because thousands of transactions are processed annually and there's strong competition for business accounts. Much of the white collar crime problem emerges from the legal "creation of money" that enables the bank to earn profits but also creates opportunities for a variety of successful schemes by employees.

Loans and Credit

The philosophy or rules of a bank and whether it loans a person or business money depends largely on the person's or business's perceived ability to repay that money and interest as prescribed by the loan contract. The old adage, "Banks only loan money to people when they can prove to the bank they don't need it," has some merit and exemplifies the ways the loan or credit process works. This rigid, strict set of guidelines, however, creates an ideal environment for fraud and embezzlement opportunities. For example, the bank might have a list of qualifiers an applicant for credit must meet. A white collar offender who is a bank officer in a loan department can create authentic-appearing documents to meet these rigid criteria, process the documents, and make the loan without bank management recognizing that the money went to the officer or to an accomplice. Additional loans to pay the first loan can be taken, and the process can continue for extended periods. When skillfully handled, the process can make the bank officer wealthy with the bank's money. When the pyramiding scheme runs its course, the matter can be disposed of as a bad loan to a bankrupt or defunct business, and the bank must write off the amount from its profits. When enough of these situations develop, the bank can fall into decline and even fail.

A Typical Example of Loan Fraud

Most bank embezzlers do not start their fraudulent activity until they have worked in their positions for an extended period. That logic applied to John Smith (not the person's real name) at a large East Coast bank. Smith worked at this bank for several years, working up to one of several commercial loan department managers with a vice-president's title. However, titles don't always supply a salary to support desired lifestyles. Smith needed more to maintain his desired social status, so he decided to use his position to create that added income. He started by testing the water with small loans to "paper corporations" complete with authentic-looking assets, financial statements, and credit reports. He created five corporations in Delaware because he could do so without personally appearing. He used an agent and a fictitious name as the president of each corporation. Smith also developed a system that supplied loans for two of the companies and, later, a loan to another company that paid off the first two loans. The first year, he worked this system to build a credit file that would later justify larger loans with better terms. Finally, when he had established the system, the loan sizes increased and he began investing most of the money.

However, as in most gambling enterprises (especially those that begin with grossly illegal funding), failure and disclosure becomes a matter of "when," not "if." In the case of this officer, however, the faked documents vanished before the collapse because he had access to them. The officer resigned and went off to live and work in the Cayman Islands (in banking). His victim bank and criminal investigators, although fully aware of what happened, had insufficient proof that the loan officer committed illegal acts. Instead they could show only a conflict of interest and violation of the bank's regulations (a civil matter) and suffer the loss with no viable recourse. Banks and regulators usually do not want the negative publicity that such improprieties engender, so they keep things quiet.

Preventive Techniques

A key rule to remember when developing preventive measures is that the scheme will rarely involve multiple persons inside the bank or financial institution because secrecy is essential in this crime, and each person involved reduces the offender's profitably and increases risk. When greed does involve many people inside and the amount of theft is sufficient to make the risk acceptable, the chance of discovery becomes greater and investigation by a skilled financial investigator will usually be successful.

When your investigative audit shows the aforementioned opportunities for embezzlement, you need to create better safeguards of bank assets. For example, the best solution or technique involves splitting the functions of loan processing. You can prevent (and easily detect) fraud and embezzlement by creating an efficient but diversified environment that makes the person who is inclined to commit white collar crimes unable to do so.

For example, in the aforementioned example of the loan officer, the bank should have allowed the officer to make the analysis and approval *only* after others in different sections out of his control conducted the loan application screening, including document validation and credit investigation. I recommend that certain employees (not just one) conduct credit investigations and analysis (usually through credit bureaus and commercial credit reporting agencies). Other employees should be trained and responsible for validating assets and other claims on the loan application. Each of these functions should have, for example, a stamp block (similar to that used by notary publics) showing certification of information and signed by the person who did so. As the separate documents are completed, they funnel back to the loan officer who alone or with others in the loan and credit department makes the decision based on information developed in various sections outside the department. When loans have received approval, the entire packet used to grant or deny the loan should go outside the department again to a reviewing officer (probably a comptroller or accountant) for an immediate audit to ensure that no fraudulent papers have replaced authenticated documents or investigations. When there's any question, the examiner should call the persons responsible for the activity and ask them to verify whether the document came from them or was perhaps forged. This diversification of duties creates a system that clearly prevents employees from committing fraud.

■ THE INVESTIGATIVE AUDIT AS A PREVENTION MODEL

Prevention calls for a sound and continuing program that creates deterrents and establishes controls that disclose improprieties quickly. It also creates a reliable model for bank and financial institution managers, who have ultimate responsibility for safeguarding depositors', investors', and the bank's money and other assets. The prevention program coupled with knowledge of routine investigative audits creates a backdrop for ensuring that honest, hard-working employees receive credit from management for their efforts and assures them that employees who do decide to participate in illicit activities will be identified and stopped. This is done without casting a net of guilt or innuendo over an entire department or professional position. Equally important aspects of your routine investigative audits include continuously updating and disseminating information to employees through awareness programs. These programs can help investigative and traditional audits because employees are alert to current forms of criminality and feel personally responsible for reporting any suspicious activity.

An advantage and benefit of the investigative audit opposed to a criminal investigation is that it keeps diligent employees from having to become a "snitch" in the traditional sense. For example, using investigative audits allows you to receive information without relying on that information as a basis for prosecution. When you hear of possible improprieties or illegal activities in a specific department, the audit will prove or disprove such activities. Through the audit you can obtain the proof needed, and the bank or investigator becomes the complainant.

As a function, investigative auditing embraces many duties, including the design and implementation of the bank's internal control system. The difference between the terms *auditing* and *controls* is important: (1) Internal controls must come first, establishing the guidelines and framework that establish effective, efficient internal operating systems; and (2) auditing is the process that verifies and looks for weaknesses in the system that encourage or supply opportunities for white collar crimes such as fraud and embezzlement. For example, a bank establishes a control over one aspect of its safe deposit operation by requiring every person who wishes to gain access to a box to sign a signature slip. This control prevents unauthorized persons from gaining entry to safe deposit boxes. In your investigative audit, you need to ensure that bank employees follow existing controls and determine if the controls safeguarding the safe deposit boxes are effective. You need to consider any ways within the current system that a criminal element might use to gain unauthorized access. When you find such weaknesses, you must develop measures to close that window of opportunity.

■ THREE BASIC ELEMENTS OF SUCCESSFUL INVESTIGATIVE AUDITING

For assured success, your investigative audit program must include three basic elements:

(1) Independence

Your independence to conduct investigative audits makes it possible to examine part or all the operations of any unit, branch, or department of the bank or financial institution at any time. No member of bank management should have the authority to limit that independence. You alone should have the right to decide which areas to visit and which phases of operation to audit.

(2) Control

You should also exercise full control over your investigative audit. The entire process would fail if a bank officer in charge of a branch or department were to have authority to tell you which records will and will not be made available to you.

(3) Surprise

Often, surprise investigative audits are indispensable in your program, especially when you receive information or circumstances create a suspicion of irregularities or illegal activities. The element of surprise also serves as a strong preventive deterrent because most fraud and embezzlement schemes need time to cover their activities in the record books.

■ VERIFICATION OF INFORMATION WITH CUSTOMERS

An important part of your investigative audit should include, when applicable, verifying all documents and other transactions with customers. However, always take this process one step further and verify that the customer is also legitimate. For example, earlier I discussed the loan officer who embezzled bank money by making loans to "paper" companies he created for that purpose. Sending a letter of verification to that company would only supply a verification that would continue to mask the scheme. You will need to find out if that company does business, what type of business, and other factors to ensure that the loan was a legitimate business loan. Most state and federal agencies can help in this type of inquiry. When you find a transaction that does not fit the traditional or known business, go further and you might uncover illegal activity. Normally, you should use two types of verification techniques, positive and negative.

(1) Positive Verification: Positive verification requires that every customer contacted during your investigative audit sign and return a form letter you prepare and mail, agreeing or disagreeing with the transaction and figures you're inquiring about.

(2) Negative Verification: This concept calls for a reply from the customer only when there is disagreement with the transaction and figures shown in your letter. This method (regularly used by traditional auditors) should not be used in an investigative audit, because it can mislead you. Suppose, for example, you sent a negative verification letter to one or all the companies established by the loan officer in the example shown earlier. The outcome would seem apparent, and no reply would indicate that the transaction was okay.

▣ USING YOUR INVESTIGATIVE AUDITS AS TRAINING INFORMATION SOURCES

Another benefit of investigative audits in banks and financial institutions stems from identifying meaningful training subjects and information. Training bank employees on a continuing basis supplies the best investment and return dollar for dollar. For example, a highly developed scheme (discussed in the next paragraph) could have been avoided with the proper training, coupled with diversified bank policies and procedures as outlined earlier.

Several former bank employees (including middle managers, tellers, and executives) banded together and decided to develop an elaborate scheme that netted them over $500 million. They were so highly organized that those arrested could not be prosecuted for lack of material evidence. This group of white collar offenders, equipped with the latest printing equipment, created a variety of identification items, bought others from backstreet vendors, and converged on the largest banks in pairs armed with an assortment of forged corporate checks, corporate and government bonds, letters of credit, letters of introduction, and banking and insurance company references. The group's credentials were in part valid, and through this mix plus financial statements and stock certificates, they successfully conned the banks for huge loans, operating cash, and negotiable securities.

Organized crime has been highly successful in defrauding the banking and business communities. Persuaded with compensation from prostitution, gambling, loan sharking, bribery, and drugs, many people inside and outside business organizations, banks, and financial institutions may lend their position, influence, and credibility to organized crime. This has resulted in success in opening fraudulent accounts, obtaining loans, and using services of compromised or paid bank employees to hide or disguise illegal financial transactions.

■ CRIMINAL INVESTIGATIONS OF FINANCIAL INSTITUTIONS

After your investigative audit reviews all the facts, figures, and supporting documents, coupled with cooperative assistance and advice of internal conventional auditors, you can bring the information together to begin a criminal investigation of probable white collar crimes.

Each bank and financial institution has an abundance of records, many of which the law requires to be maintained on microfilm. Although often a criminal investigator shudders at the thought of financial investigations, in reality these will prove easiest because of the abundant records. The key to beginning your criminal investigation must always be a clear vision of what crime the offender committed. Each law or statute (and in banking, a variety of punitive federal and state regulations) has elements of proof that establish the probable cause that a crime happened. When those elements are not present, that specific crime (in legal terms) did not happen. However, a different or lesser crime might have happened. Whatever the situation, clearly define the statute that becomes the narrow focus of your criminal investigation. You need to create a matrix that guides your criminal investigation by asking Who? What? When? Where? Why? How? Did this crime happen? When each of these important questions are answered with documented proof and evidence integrity, you can successfully prosecute the crime.

Often, federal and state agencies become involved in prosecuting bank fraud; however, you should also conduct a concurrent or cooperative criminal investigation because even when the matter moves from the jurisdiction or discretion of the bank or financial institution, the lessons learned become invaluable for the management and future investigative audits and criminal investigations. A complete investigative file might become valuable in later civil action by the bank to recover assets.

Commercial banking in the United States and many foreign countries is the most thoroughly regulated, frequently examined, tightly restricted, and closely supervised of all industries. However, losses from fraud and embezzlements continue and climb to billions of dollars each year, primarily because two key aspects don't receive the proper attention: investigative audits and criminal investigations that detect weaknesses and crimes and that document crimes in ways that can enable recovery of losses.

■ FINANCIAL INSTITUTIONS: SECURITIES FRAUD AND EMBEZZLEMENT

Financial institutions other than banks also have problems with fraud (especially involving securities). However, the precise dollar amount remains elusive. In 1973, some 400,000 lost, stolen, or missing securities certificates worth $5.3 billion were listed in a computerized system of a company established to enable members of the security and financial community to validate, within seconds of entering an inquiry, the authenticity or status of securities. However, only 10 percent of the securities industry subscribed to the service, and those listed were securities "known or reported" stolen. In the 1990s, the situation remains largely unchanged, except the number of lost, stolen, or missing securities has more than tripled and the dollar amount tops $50 billion. Whatever the true total and magnitude may be, securities fraud is an alarming problem that nonetheless has viable, effective solutions.

Because the vast majority of thefts involve the cooperation of dishonest employees, most brokerage houses have elaborate security precautions. However, the precautions target conventional thieves, and hardware-oriented measures do not offer protection against embezzlement activities. Some securities thefts stem from robberies of messengers, theft from the mail, or other types of conventional theft. However, even in this category the seemingly overt act of theft might be a technique of concealing embezzlement. You must always consider that the overt theft might not have stolen anything, but instead might be used as an illusion to make others believe that some outside criminal element stole the securities.

At other times, the thefts might include a mix of legitimate outside theft, outside theft with inside collusion, or staged outside theft that enables concealment of embezzlement. Whichever technique fits the event, it's white collar crime. In one instance, a firm treated its securities so that an alarm would ring if someone tried to leave the premises with concealed certificates.

The firm later discovered, to its chagrin, that employees could embezzle certificates by placing them in an envelope and dropping them in a mail chute on the premises. When this problem was corrected, someone stole the outside mailbox used by the firm to mail certificates. Did these events encourage and supply opportunity for embezzlement? The firm doesn't know, and this situation is typical in financial institutions across the United States.

To avoid detection of embezzlement and other thefts, cooperative employees (often pressured by loan sharks) can warn their outside contacts about impending audits. In one case, a brokerage house employee alerted those who owned ABC Bonds stolen from the firm that an audit was scheduled covering securities in the A to M range. ABC Bonds were returned and stolen securities N to Z substituted.

An effective embezzlement method involves stealing a 100-share certificate of XYZ Company from the vault of Broker 1 and substituting that stock for a 100-share certificate of XYZ Company taken from the vault of Broker 2. Broker 1 reports the missing stock, when discovered, but the certificate is safely tucked away among the securities of Broker 2, who usually does not detect the substitution because auditors often only determine whether the number of shares and/or certificates noted on the inventory records corresponds with the number counted during the physical inventory (revealing the weakness of traditional audits).

Occasionally, a brokerage house employee will give a fictitious name to the transfer agent for stock to be "delivered out" to a customer, and will successfully divert the security into the hands of an accomplice. Another problem and embezzlement technique involves bogus and counterfeit certificates that confuse traditional auditors (because the numbers add up). The embezzler steals the genuine certificate and replaces it with counterfeit and successfully conceals the crime.

Often, the embezzler will work out a system whereby an accomplice will direct that his or her purchased stocks be delivered to a home address. Although they receive their certificate, they tell the broker it did not arrive and obtain a replacement. Next, the accomplice presents the first certificate as collateral for a loan, and then sells the replacement certificate and defaults on the loan.

Other schemes may involve stolen stock in combination with counterfeit and bogus securities. A straightforward case involved nine Americans and seven Europeans, caught trying to fence $3.4 million in stocks and U.S. Treasury bills stolen from the mail, a brokerage house, and a bank. The group also possessed $14.5 million of counterfeit corporate bonds. Some securities were sold to banks, others to individuals. Stolen certificates were used as collateral for a loan from a bank in Central America. When the bank learned that the certificates were stolen, it reportedly accepted as replacements $12 million in what turned out to be bogus securities, including worthless notes and shares of other institutions.

Often, embezzlement schemes involving theft of securities involve an international mix of groups. International investigators tracking stolen securities have consistently reported that as many as 200 persons, an additional number of accomplices used occasionally, and several hundred suspect companies create the network that embezzlers can contact to dispose of their securities siphoned from employer corporations, including brokerage houses, banks, and other financial institutions. Single schemes involving three or more countries are not uncommon, and in one case an embezzler's address book carelessly left behind fell into the hands of an investigator. The book listed contacts in Arizona, California, Colorado, Florida, Illinois, Iowa, Michigan, Nevada, New Jersey, New Mexico, New York, Oklahoma, Texas, Utah, and foreign countries including England, Canada, and Switzerland.

Embezzlers also use bogus and stolen securities to shore up the balance sheets in marginal firms they create or have conspired with, to meet asset requirements of state regulatory agencies or to establish an inflated sale price for a prospective buyer of a business. Some embezzlers have also gone into business at locations rented for such purposes.

Same-Name Securities Fraud

A same-name fraud involved securities registered in Panama bearing a name almost identical to a respected Canadian company, as though the Panamanian firm was a subsidiary. An inquiry from a broker in England, where some Panama securities were tendered for sale, triggered an investigation revealing that the securities were also being presented to banks in Germany and Spain. The securities were bogus and had no relationship to the legitimate Canadian firm. The principal perpetrator was traced to Portugal, and this ended the fraud.

Securities Fraud and Organized Crime

Organized crime groups not only commit many securities frauds but also simplify frauds of others by supplying them with needed securities through an efficient fencing network. For example, in one instance, within 48 hours after $21 million of stolen securities and traveler's checks were delivered to a mob fence, many checks surfaced in New York City, Las Vegas, and in several towns in New Jersey. Soon after the embezzlement, the securities and traveler's checks were cashed or presented as collateral at banks in Pennsylvania and Florida. Eventually, other securities appeared in San Diego, Houston, Oklahoma City, Phoenix, Los Angeles, Boston, Mexico City, Chicago, and Toronto.

One of the techniques used by organized crime involves stamping equipment that places a stamp either over or under the signature on the certificate authorizing and guaranteeing it. This automatically creates a negotiable instrument.

An organized crime investment specialist testifying before the Senate Permanent Subcommittee on Banking said that he used embezzled securities to establish margin accounts with Swiss brokers to buy securities for arbitrage, a technique whose profitability was enhanced by his conspiring with members of the U.S. financial community who wanted to avoid the interest equalization tax. His average trading involved about $5 million an hour. This technique, aided by time zone differentials, enabled the specialist to buy, for example, 10,000 shares of ABC at $100 per share in Zurich, Switzerland, with the knowledge that the stock closed at $104 per share the day before in New York. The specialist would sell ABC for close to $104 per share when it next opened in New York. By evading the equalization tax, the specialist could make about $30,000 in this transaction for the mob. Through these manipulations, trades and purchases could be made in Switzerland totaling millions of dollars with no more than $100,000 in cash.

■ SECURITIES FRAUD SCHEMES THAT VICTIMIZE BANKS, FINANCIAL INSTITUTIONS, AND CORPORATIONS

Bogus securities create serious problems for investors, for banks and others who accept them as collateral for loans, and for corporations who invest profits and try to diversify company assets. The themes and variations of securities fraud seem endless. The following examples have successfully victimized banks and corporations:

- "The XYZ Trust Company does hereby irrevocably guarantee the interest and principal payment of this bond." In reality, the bond is counterfeit and the Trust Company is not a bank, but instead a rented office with a telephone in a state that does not regulate use of the term *Trust Company*.

- Oil and gas interests have been popular for fraudulent purposes. In this scheme the promoter gets a 10 percent commission on sales and the buyers get oil (but not in an appreciable quantity or of marketable quality).

- A corporate executive CEO sold his yacht for securities of a corporation in the Bahamas whose assets, in turn, were securities of a nonexistent U.S. corporation.
- Customers of a brokerage house purchased bonds but never received them, or sold securities and never obtained their money.
- A broker creates an artificial demand for a stock through fictitious purchases, often with dummy accounts.
- Forged hypothecation agreements are presented to help explain why securities offered as collateral are not in the name of the borrower (not mentioning that they were embezzled and stolen).
- The certificate number of a stolen stock is carefully altered before used in a fraudulent transaction at a bank.
- A legitimately purchased 1000-share certificate is presented as collateral for a loan. After the bank verifies the certificate's authenticity, a counterfeit bearing the same name and number is substituted.

Sixteen Prevention Techniques for Securities Fraud

Your investigative audits should verify securities already in the banking system, and establish a credible way of verifying each offering before risking bank assets. However, the first objective of investigative audits is to find weaknesses in the system and find viable solutions to protect corporate, banking, and financial institution assets. The following tip-offs of fraud must become a part of your routine training and part of operating policies and procedures.

1. Stock offered as loan collateral is in a street name.
2. Securities are offered for private sale at a large discount from quoted prices. Maybe the seller cites the need to liquidate an estate quickly as the reason for the low price.
3. The balance sheet of an earlier poor credit risk shows a sudden and large increase in securities listed as assets.
4. Financial statements of a firm contain highly questionable entries such as substantial mining interests that, according to "some sources," are valued at $X; or $100,000 worth of notes of an obscure company appear in the asset column.
5. No one has seen, nor knows anyone who has seen, the premises of an unfamiliar company your company or bank is thinking about dealing with.

6. The proper number of shares is accounted for by an inventory check, but certificates in stock do not correspond to records.

7. The transaction involves a numbered Swiss bank account or a secretive foreign trust.

8. The transaction involves trading through a bulk-segregation or omnibus account established in the United States by a foreign financial institution.

9. The insurer, bank, or mutual fund is offshore.

10. An obscure stock displays an unexplained increase in trading activity.

11. A certificate is characterized by any indicator of counterfeit paper:

    —One-color printing is used. Color is muddy.

    —There is no human figure.

    —Border lines are broken in a few places or poorly aligned.

    —The colored dots (planchettes) are missing, or, if present, are erasable or appear in precisely the same location on several certificates.

    —The three-dimensional look is missing.

    —The corporate name does not have a raised feel.

    —Line work is unclear and lines bleed into one another.

    —Certificate numbers are unclear and not distinct.

    —Misspelling is noted.

12. A credit report on a company does not show that the report figures were verified or, if so, to what extent.

13. The statement from the broker does not show that a security held in a street name was "delivered out" to you as requested.

14. The potential borrower who is offering stock as collateral gives a somewhat tortured explanation of why he or she cannot produce satisfactory identification documentation.

15. A security is issued by a company whose name is almost, but not quite, identical to a respected firm.

16. The assets of an unfamiliar firm are chiefly comprised of obscure securities.

Four Key Reasons for Vulnerability to Securities Fraud

There's sufficient evidence that many people within and outside the securities industry painstakingly avoid raising the necessary questions about the legitimacy of the certificates they handle. In one reported case, a bank that learned that it was stuck with a stolen security and palmed it off on another bank, which later found out the true nature of the certificate. Apathy about subjecting securities and those who tender them to a thorough investigation can result in a combination of loss factors. You need to consider these factors as you conduct your investigative audits and develop ways to prevent them from making your company or bank a victim of securities fraud.

1. Naive trust. Securities must be validated before consideration as collateral or investment.

2. Greed that triumphs too often over reason. The commission is too appealing or the deal is too tempting, because no one asks questions that should be answered.

3. Fear of some banks and brokers that by checking the authenticity of certificates with various stolen security master lists (computerized and manual), the protection afforded by the holder-in-due-course doctrine will be jeopardized. In other words, the doctrine can protect a bank or broker from claims of ownership by prior holders of a security if the bank or broker accepts a negotiable instrument in good faith and without knowledge of any problems associated with the security.

4. Fear that a check of an institution's inventory of securities against a list of lost, stolen, and missing certificates would lead to many of these turning up on the premises (having been unwittingly or carelessly accepted during various fraudulent transactions). One respected authority has said that hundred of millions of dollars worth of such securities are probably in the vaults of the nation's financial institutions.

Countermeasures to Prevent Securities Fraud

A key countermeasure for ending securities fraud before it begins (and removing the reasons for the related white collar crimes) stems from a cross-examination of "paper." Ensure that your company, bank, or other financial institution maintains an attitude of constructive skepticism.

-   Transactions involving offshore firms should be viewed with caution.

-   Transactions involving little-known domestic companies whose financial statements show important assets as securities of equally little-known firms may be fraudulent.

-   Credit reports that merely emulate the representation of those reported on should not be regarded as proof of anything.

- Financial institutions and brokerage houses should establish clear lines of accountability for adherence to well-thought-out procedures regarding the handling and storage of securities. When an embezzlement or theft does happen, an accountability audit trail will exist.
- Banks should not accept street-name securities as collateral.
- Brokerage houses should not stamp their street-name endorsements on securities to be held in inventory.
- Physical inventory counts must be compared to records of not only shares in stock but also the identification number on each certificate.
- Proposed transactions involving the sale of securities at bargain-basement prices should be regarded as inherently fraudulent.
- Transactions involving numbered Swiss bank accounts or secretive foreign trusts must be regarded as suspect until proved otherwise.
- Be wary of obscure stock whose price is suddenly increasing, particularly when most of each day's increase happens near the close of trading.

Chapter Eight
Internal Controls to Detect and Prevent Financial Embezzlement

To get a big picture of the role finances play in your company, think about any major decision you or others within your company make. The decisions to hire, fire, buy, sell, start up, or close down are financial in nature. Almost any situation within your company translates into financial terms, including the clandestine business of embezzlement. Embezzlement is one the fastest-growing white collar crimes victimizing corporations and one of the least detected. Uncovering embezzlement schemes within often takes months and years, with little hope of collecting enough evidence to prosecute and often not sufficient grounds to fire the embezzler without creating a situation that enables him or her to sue for defamation or some other civil action. The truth remains that most companies experiencing heavy losses continue to blame malfeasance as opposed to the white collar crime of embezzlement. In this chapter, I'll show you how this clandestine business of siphoning profits from your company will probably happen in the most common specific categories. I'll discuss general characteristics as well as ways to detect, prevent, and effectively investigate this crime.

■ CURBING THE ENTERPRISE SPIRIT OF CORPORATE EMBEZZLERS THROUGH INTERNAL CONTROL SYSTEMS

Virtually every embezzlement has as its basis some negligence, carelessness, or ignorance on the part of the employing corporation, whether the company is small or a huge conglomerate. The shortcomings of the employer can range from plain stupidity to gross negligence or a blind confidence that "it can't happen in this company." Essentially, where no opportunity exists, no white collar crime can happen.

Embezzlers tend to have an entrepreneurial spirit because rarely in the beginning of their illicit enterprise do they need to steal money or convert company property to money. However, once a person becomes accustomed to having more money, giving it up and returning to a legitimate income becomes difficult. In addition, after deciding to become a white collar criminal, the embezzler must practice disguise and concealment which becomes a full-time effort in itself. If a skilled embezzler decides to stop stealing, he or she must continue to conceal their scheme to avoid detection. In time, their embezzlement will fade into the business routine and losses. However, most embezzlers will figure that since they must continue to disguise and conceal their crime, they might as well continue to steal. As a legitimate entrepreneur seizes opportunities to make money, so does the embezzler seek opportunities that take advantage of weaknesses within your company's internal control of corporate assets. If any corporation wants to progress and prosper, it must create and enforce the rules under which it expects to operate and ensure that each employee understands them. Every large company has volumes of policy and operating procedures that govern its every activity. Of the essential minimums, none is more important than the internal controls that cover the company's fiscal affairs. Internal controls are simply a system of mandatory business procedures designed to protect the assets of the corporation and assure the accuracy of its accounting records.

The first premise of any system of internal controls is that responsibility for critical financial procedures will be divided between two or more persons, the more the better. However, corporations rarely follow such ideal division of responsibility, and the problem of embezzlement will inevitably emerge because of the opportunity and the embezzler's entrepreneurial spirit. For example, often simple measures can eliminate opportunity (such as ensuring that all voided checks and numbered invoices and other serial numbered documents go to a clerk who has no opportunity to manipulate them). Separate company employees should receive, open, and reconcile bank statements and cancelled checks, and those employees should not have access to company checks or have any advantage in destroying the checks or otherwise manipulating the account. The concept of effectively preventing embezzlement in certain categories depends on division of certain fiscal-related responsibilities among several different employees. As I noted earlier in this book, an embezzler or any other white collar criminal rarely participates with other employees when engaging in embezzlement activities unless the crime cannot happen in another way and the profits will warrant the risk.

■ THE ROLE OF INVESTIGATIVE AUDITS

The craft of embezzlement of corporate property and money is as complex as your company itself. How embezzlers operate and what they embezzle depend largely on the business your corporation conducts. Only through effective investigative audits can you detect the probability of embezzlement activities, and then isolate them for further investigation. Doing that requires using two common tools of the business world that create your starting point—the balance sheet and financial statement. Although their purpose is to supply decision makers with financial information, you can, with attentive examination, detect the probability of ongoing embezzlement of corporate money, or commodities and other items that easily convert into money. For example, if your company produces widgets, the widget itself does not generate money until sold to a customer. The diversion of company property by an embezzler often applies the same principle of converting it to money illegally.

■ THE BALANCE SHEET: THE STARTING POINT OF THE INVESTIGATIVE AUDIT

The balance sheet of any business is a comprehensive statement of where its financial fortunes stand at a given time. It represents a financial picture of your company on a given date. Normally, every business prepares a balance sheet quarterly or at the close of its fiscal or tax year. The document has two primary sections: (1) the company's assets, and (2) the company's liabilities (or debts), and the accrued equity.

Total liabilities are claims against total assets. A total of these liabilities and equity always equals total assets (assets = liabilities + equity), the formula that creates the name *balance sheet*. Exhibit 8-2 shows a simplified corporate balance sheet. All balance sheets follow the same general format; however, depending on the size, complexity, and type of business, certain elements may be added or the sheet may be called by a different name. Whatever the case, in general the same information is conveyed. The following sections describe each of the basic balance sheet items, many of which will serve to construct the various financial ratios described and applied later in this chapter. You must understand these items if you are to detect embezzlement. Throughout the following discussions, I will supply tips about how you can use these items and the balance sheet to detect embezzlement. You will also learn how to also detect opportunities for embezzlement and how to prevent it.

■ FINANCIAL REPORTING OF CORPORATE ASSETS

Words can be deceiving, and the term *corporate assets* often leads to confusion, even within the company financial circles and among executives who rely on these financial summaries to make crucial decisions. The embezzlers count on this misconception and confusion to disguise and conceal their illegal entrepreneur "profit-sharing" enterprises. For example, the word *asset* suggests concrete wealth—money in the bank, machinery in place, buildings and real estate, and other clearly visible, solid wealth. However, corporate assets in a true sense depend on what your accountants perceive them to be and what they perceive to be present. Accountants in a major corporation rely on the accuracy of figures presented to them by a myriad of sections, departments, divisions, groups, and other elements of the company. They collect these figures and create the balance sheet. However, accountants like their jobs, enjoy receiving a paycheck, and dislike big waves coming out the boardroom that might wash them straight to the unemployment lines. So, even when they don't participate in embezzlement (some do) and are basically honest, diligent, and loyal company persons, accountants tend to fudge a bit on reality so executives won't accuse them of incompetence. Executives also have a tendency to fix blame, because they too enjoy having a job with a sizable paycheck and have to answer to a board of directors and stock holders. This desire for profitability often leads to the creation of corporate assets.

Three Primary Categories of Company Assets

An important step in your investigative audit includes a "true" evaluation of company assets, using the three categories present on balance sheets and asking four key questions.

   (1) Current Assets: Include cash held (primarily in bank balances or money market funds). These assets might also include those that convert to cash in the normal course of business within one business year, such as trade accounts, notes receivable, and inventories. Other assets that conceivably will convert to cash within one year include marketable short-term securities, nontrade debts, or debt installments owed to your company within one year. Other than cash and equivalents, current assets include inventories in various stages of completion, and prepaid expenses such as rent, interest, insurance, or taxes paid before.

(2) Fixed Assets: Include all property, plants, and equipment such as buildings, real estate, machines, transportation equipment, office equipment, furniture, and other items used in the business. The accumulated depreciation on these items is deducted, where applicable, in standard accounting practice. Be attentive in this assessment, however, because fixed assets have value only when it's realistic in the marketplace. For example, costly specialized equipment has value only when a market for that equipment exists. If there's no market, the equipment realistically has no value. This area supplies an excellent opportunity for accountants to "puff" the assets of your corporation and, equally, it can supply the company embezzler with certain opportunities that will be discussed later in this chapter. The best technique for you to realistically assess the true value of your company's fixed assets includes considering what price each item would bring if auctioned. This realistic thinking gives you a far different picture from what you'll probably see in the balance sheets, and you want to get this true picture because of two important factors, sometimes called "tangible assets":

- When you view fixed assets from an auction point of view, you're seeing it the same as the embezzler who considers how to divert fixed assets and converts them into cash.

- If your findings show that the equipment has no true value or little value, the embezzler will reach the same conclusion. When you look for embezzlement problem areas during this initial stage of your investigative audit using balance sheets, income statements, and other financial documents coupled with the two important valuation techniques of fixed asset property, the lucrative areas of embezzlement will become obvious. Embezzlement opportunities and activities will always happen where the best money-making possibilities exist within your company.

(3) Other Assets: All long-term investments, such as securities (including stocks, bonds, and mortgages) and intangible assets (such as goodwill, patents, trademarks, special licenses, and other paper assets that can receive a realistic assigned value) are normally used to determine the total sale price of your company. Other assets identified here will often be called "intangible assets."

Four Key Questions to Ask when Assessing Company Assets

When you begin realistically to assign value to company assets, ask a minimum of four key questions:

(1) Is the value of an asset its original cost (historical cost)? This question leads you to checking the possibility that accountants have inflated values to cover a problem they do not want to deal with or to cover embezzlement losses.

(2) Has the value of the historical cost increased over the years by changes in the general price level? Sometimes assets do increase in value. Examples might include real estate, buildings, and specialized equipment. However, use caution in accepting a cost increase as a fact in financial sheets supplied by accountants.

(3) Should value be the cost of replacing the asset? The best way you can serve your investigative audit is to use the aforementioned auction method and to consider what an insurance company would offer as a fair settlement. Although it's tempting to believe that the value today would be the same as replacing the item, we know that original value is not a realistic figure. One important reason for cost increases is the technology explosion. A five-year-old computer system might have cost $10,000 new, and replacing it might still cost the same. However, the technology gap between a five-year-old computer then and one today would be so great that selling the system at auction or filing an insurance claim for it would probably net no more than 20 percent of the original or replacement cost. However, your company accountants might show that equipment to be worth $10,000. This affects your investigative audit because you see the word *computer* and the value is listed as $10,000. You perceive that the computer might supply a lucrative embezzlement item, especially if your company has several hundred or several thousand of them scattered around. However, before wasting your time, find the real market value easily by checking the item's age first, and see how many generations of the system have evolved since it was new.

(4) Should the value of assets be measured by the price that the market at any given time is willing to pay? This question is the one of most value to your investigative audit. Always take it a few steps farther by determining if a market exists. If so, does that market really pay the assessed value? For example, the market value of a building or vehicle is constantly changing.

The book or assessed value might establish the current market value, or that which people have paid for similar property or property that has a money-making potential. However, market value is established by historical data, and just because people have paid the price for similar items before does not guarantee that they will pay the same price (or market value) today. I continue to prefer the auction or insurance claim figures because that's the formula used by skilled embezzlers to choose their targets.

Goodwill: a Problem Area in Asset Valuation

A favorite and totally unmeasurable asset called "goodwill" is one that accountants like to use when puffing or covering up losses. They may show goodwill as a viable and valuable asset. Goodwill has three basic definitions, none of which will help you conduct your investigative audits and can mislead you when studying the corporate balance sheet and other financial asset documents. Consider the realistic responses to these points in determining goodwill value and how they match with those shown on corporate financial documents:

(1) The business advantage acquired by a firm because of reputation for good business dealings

(2) The excess in purchase price for a corporation over the value of its net assets

(3) The capitalized value of a firm's expected profits more than the rate of return considered normal in the industry in which the firm operates.

■ THE IMPORTANCE AND BENEFITS OF EVALUATING COMPANY LIABILITIES AND EQUITY

As with corporate assets, corporate liabilities are not always—maybe not even usually—what they seem to be. The basic problem is that you can never be sure, from looking at a balance sheet, that all material liability has been disclosed. There's also a problem of classifying liabilities—when it's on the balance sheet, is it in the right place? Often, current liabilities masquerade as long-term debt, and besides creating misleading information for potential investors, this creates fertile ground for embezzlement opportunities. On the liabilities side of the corporate balance sheet, the information splits into four principal categories:

(1) **Current Liabilities**: These include obligations expected to be paid within twelve months. These include items like Trade Payables, Accrued Expenses, Accrued Taxes, and the current part due on any long-term debt.

Current liabilities must be assessed to detect possible embezzlement schemes. For example, compare the reported trade payables with sales and inventory figures. Choose a specific item and total the sales figures, then add the inventory in stock, and you should arrive at the trade payable amount for the specific supplier or suppliers. After running through the entire product line, the figures should match those on the balance sheet. When they don't, or if you find discrepancies en route, the liabilities have been stated incorrectly and create misleading information. In addition, you might have an important lead to an embezzler who reports erroneous information to the accountants, or the accountant preparing the balance sheet might have embezzlement motives. That's easy to determine by reviewing the balance sheet preparers' working papers. When they reflect the information he or she received accurately, then you need to examine the category of information. This often leads you to the section or department supplying the misleading information. I've often gone back to past balance sheets and working papers used to compile them to check a specific department and found consistent manipulation of information supplied to the accountants preparing balance sheets. Whatever the problem you find in this category, it's a simple matter to follow the paper trail back to the root of the problem.

(2) **Long-Term Liabilities**: This category includes obligations expected to be paid over periods of time greater than one year. These debts may include items like a three-year note for equipment, a five-year loan for vehicles, or a fifteen-year mortgage loan for a building.

Manipulation and embezzlement can occur easily in this category, and you can track them. However, you need to approach that task by first determining whether these notes and loans moved around. For example, an embezzler controlling corporate fiduciary systems can deliberately create loans from financial institutions at higher than necessary rates, and then refinance the loan at the same or other financial institution at a lower rate but continue to show payments at the higher rate. The embezzler pockets the difference through a variety of sophisticated methods. A variety of other schemes in long-term liabilities are discussed later in this chapter.

(3) **Equities**: These amounts represent the cash investment(s) contributed by the corporation plus the net earnings retained from operations over the life of the venture. This category has a three-part specific definition:

(1) An interest in the net assets of a corporation

(2) The percentage of investment that an investor has contributed in a margin transaction

(3) The value of a property more than the amount that the company still owes on a mortgage or debt secured by a lien.

This category also creates opportunities for embezzlers because generally there's a lack of management understanding, and that leaves the skill in few hands. Pension funds often receive the most publicity for discovered embezzlement, and frequently poor management and poor judgment or the economy will be blamed. Although this might be the case, embezzlement is often the culprit. You can also track this category by looking carefully at corporate money moved around and verify the interest payments, or to whom the money was loaned.

For example, money legitimately loaned for a short period (the areas where embezzlement is likely to happen) goes to a financial institution or other entity for a specific rate of interest (let's say that the fiduciary reports 7 percent). The short-term loan was really netting 9 percent, with the balance of 2 percent deposited in the embezzler's account. The scheme cost your company money but also paid the embezzler money, and the entity borrowing the short-term money (maybe from a pension fund or other investment fund) profits by paying less interest. When a fiduciary or several in different sections control these activities without stringent controls, the opportunity to embezzle becomes lucrative because the company and traditional audits don't detect a loss. Instead, management often lauds the fiduciary for making the company money when he or she participates in embezzlement. A loss does not show up because the company doesn't monitor what earnings might emerge from the investment or verify what the recipient really paid back. For example, if the corporate fiduciary loans $10 and gets $11 back, the company earns money and doesn't perceive a loss. In reality, the fiduciary loaned $10 and received $12 back, but $1 went into his or her account and the entity receiving the short-term loan should have paid back $13 at the current short-term interest rates. When a fiduciary controls and manipulates millions of dollars regularly, the illicit income and company loss become staggeringly high.

(4) Shareholders' equity (net worth): This is the par value of your corporation's common and preferred stock, plus any paid-in or accumulated capital surplus over this par value, plus any earnings retained for use in business (equity = book value of outstanding stock + capital surplus + retained earnings).

■ RELATIONSHIPS AMONG CORPORATE STATEMENTS

All the numbers in financial statements and documents are related and linked. Specifically, you need to know the following:

- How the corporate financial statements are related to one another as a group
- How the separate component of each financial statement links to others within the same statement
- How the separate component of each financial statement is linked to components with the same or similar names of different statements (e.g., how "cash" on the balance sheet is linked to "cash" on the cash flow statement)
- How the separate component of each financial statement links to different components in other financial statements.

In the latter two cases, you need to know the number of items involved in each linkage and the direction of the association. (For example, the Net Income component of the income statement and Retained Earnings component of the balance sheet are linked.) However, understand that Retained Earnings is derived from Net Income, not vice versa. You also need to know what other variables, if any, are involved (or could be involved) in the calculation (e.g., if Dividends were declared by your company, they would have to be subtracted from Net Income and subtracted from Ending Cash on the cash flow statement).

A set of corporate financial statements becomes easier to understand when you recognize how the income statement and balance sheet are related. Once you understand how these specific linkages work, you will be able to understand better not only what it takes to balance the company balance sheet but also how to identify, trace, and prevent sophisticated corporate embezzlement. Exhibit 8-1 shows the specific relationship between corporate statements. Exhibit 8-2 is a sample corporate balance sheet.

Planning your investigative audit is important and includes isolating the problem and keeping a clear focus on investigating one specific activity at a time. You also need a group of initial techniques or answers to certain questions. In Exhibit 8-3, you will find generally routine questions to answer before proceeding. Often, you may find a "paper error" that appeared to be an embezzlement activity when you started based on assessment of the balance sheet and other financial documents.

Exhibit 8-1
Specific Relationship between Corporate Financial Statements

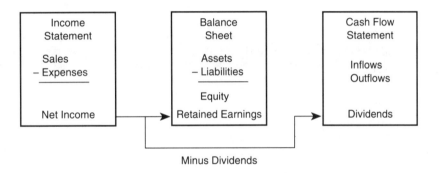

This exhibit is an example of a specific relationship between net income, retained earnings, and dividends.

Exhibit 8-2
Example of Corporate Balance Sheet

Current assets:
  Cash
  Accounts receivable
  (Net of allowance for doubtful accounts)
  Subscriptions receivable: Common stock $
  Inventories (lower of FIFO cost of market)
  Short-term prepayments
    Total current assets

Plant and equipment:
  Land $
  Buildings and equipment $
  Less: Accumulated depreciation $ $
Other assets: Organization costs
Total assets

Current liabilities:
  Accounts payable
  Income taxes payable
  Dividends payable
  Interest payable
    Total current liabilities
Long-term liabilities: Bonds payable, 12%, due Oct. 1, Year 0000
    Total liabilities

Stock holders' equity:
  Cumulative 8% preferred stock
  $100 par, callable at $104, authorized and issued 10,000 shares $
Common stock, $1 par, authorized
1,000,000 shares, issued 600,000 shares $
  Common stock subscribed, 20,000 shares $
  Paid-in capital in excess of par: common $
  Donated capital $
    Total paid-in capital $
Retained earnings $
    Total stock holders' equity
Total liabilities & stock holders' equity

Exhibit 8-3
An Internal Control Checklist for Investigative Audits

1. General Categories
   - ☐ Does your company have master lists of accounts in one central location?
   - ☐ If so, where is this list maintained? Is it current? Who has responsibility for posting the list?
   - ☐ If not, why not? Is there an acceptable reason for a lack of central control?
   - ☐ Is the company's accounting routine set forth in accounting manuals?
   - ☐ If so, are the manuals current and maintained? Who has responsibility for that?
   - ☐ If there are no manuals, or they're not current, why not?
   - ☐ Is there a routine and aggressive traditional internal audit program?
   - ☐ If so, who has responsibility for scheduling? If not, why not?
   - ☐ Do the internal auditors maintain a comprehensive file of working papers?
   - ☐ Is the company general accounting department completely separated from
     —The Purchasing Department?
     —The Marketing and Sales Department?
     —Manufacturing and/or Cost Departments?
     —Cash Receipts and Disbursement?
   - ☐ Are your company fiduciary officers subject to frequent audits? Do the audits measure the market at the time? Do the audits look at the list of loan recipients and verify the interest rates?
   - ☐ Are fiduciary officers and all employees who handle cash, securities, and other convertible assets bonded?
   - ☐ Are all such employees required to take regular vacations, and are their regular duties then assigned to other employees?
   - ☐ Does head office accounting have control over branch offices, and is it adequate to prevent embezzlement?
   - ☐ Are company expenses and costs under strict budgetary control and audited often?

☐ Is company insurance coverage under the supervision of a responsible executive or employee?

☐ Are journal entries checked and approved by

—The controller?

—Other designated accountants?

☐ Are journal entries audited regularly?

☐ Does your company use standard journal entries for the regularly recurring monthly closing entries?

☐ Are your company's journal entries adequately explained or supported by vouchers bearing adequate substantiating data?

☐ Are vouchers, invoices, and other documents verified as legitimate by a second or third party?

☐ Are periodic financial statements prepared for submission to management?

☐ Are the figures on financial statements verified by second and third parties?

☐ Do company financial statements contain sufficient information to support abnormal fluctuation in costs, revenues, inventories, and other discrepancies? Do second and third parties verify this information?

☐ List the names of company executives, officers, and employees responsible for the work listed above:

Company Treasurer:_____

Company Secretary:_____

Corporate Controller:_____

Chief of Internal Audits:_____

Chief Accountant:_____

Chief General Ledger Supervisor:_____

Chief Accounts Receivable Supervisor:_____

Chief Accounts Payable Supervisor:_____

Chief Cashier:_____

Department Heads For:

Purchasing:_____

Marketing and Sales:_____

Credit:_____

Cost Controls:_____

Receiving:_____

Shipping:_____

Payroll:_____

Personnel:_____

Tax:_____

Pension Fund:_____

Investments:_____

Fiduciary:_____

Other:_____

- ☐ Is any one of the above, to the best of your information, a relative of any other, or any other employee in the corporation?
- ☐ Is any one of the above, to the best of your information, a relative of any competing company employee?
- ☐ Do any of the above have personal financial problems?
- ☐ Are all of the above screened thoroughly before hiring or being promoted to their position?
- ☐ Are all of the above persons bonded? By whom? Is the bond commensurate with the position and possible losses?

2. Cash Receipts

- ☐ Is Company mail opened by someone other than the cashier or accounts receivable supervisor or employee he or she designates and supervises?
- ☐ Are pieces of mail counted by one person in the mailroom or detached from cashiers or accounts receivable and opened by another person, with the tally sheets later compared by auditors? Are all pieces of mail accounted for?
- ☐ Does the mail routine prevent the delivery of unopened mail (other than personal mail) to employees having access to the accounting records?
- ☐ Is a record of the money and checks received prepared by the person opening the mail?
- ☐ If so, is this record given to someone other than the cashier for independent verification of the amount recorded?
- ☐ Is this record compared with the cash receipts book regularly?
- ☐ Is the record of money and checks received audited against the incoming mail piece tally often?
- ☐ Are the receipts of currency comparatively insignificant?

- ☐ Are receipts recorded by cash registers or other mechanical devices?
- ☐ If so, are the machine totals checked independently by the accounting department?
- ☐ Are sales books or receipts books used?
- ☐ If so, are the slips or receipts prenumbered?
- ☐ Are the daily totals and numerical sequence checked independently by the accounting department?
- ☐ Are unused books safeguarded and controlled?
- ☐ If neither of the above methods are in use, is some other adequate system of control used? If so, explain.
- ☐ Is there an adequate safeguard against misappropriation of cash through the recording of fictitious discounts or allowances by the cashier?
- ☐ Are miscellaneous receipts, such as from sale of scrap and salvage, reported to the accounting department by the recipient, including the cashier?
- ☐ Does the accounting department verify the reports against the related cash book entries?
- ☐ Are each day's receipts deposited in the bank intact and without delay?
- ☐ Does someone other than the cashier or accounts receivable employee take the deposits to the bank?
- ☐ Is a duplicate deposit slip checked and held for the auditors by someone other than the employee forming the deposit?
- ☐ Are bank debit advices (such for nonsufficient funds checks) delivered directly to a responsible employee (other than the cashier) for investigation?
- ☐ Are the duties of the cashier entirely separate from the recording of notes and accounts receivable?
- ☐ Is the general ledger posted by an employee who is not from the cashier's department?
- ☐ Is the office routine so arranged that the cashier has no access to the accounts receivable ledgers and monthly statements?
- ☐ Are all cash funds, such as other than cash receipts and securities, handled by someone other than the cashier?
- ☐ If the cashier handles such funds, are they carefully examined and audited?

☐ Where branch offices make collections, are such collections deposited in a bank account subjected to withdrawal only by your corporate headquarters?

☐ Are rents, dividends, interest, and like revenues adequately controlled in such a manner that their nonreceipt would be noted and investigated?

☐ Is the cashier responsible for the cash receipts from the time they're received in his or her department until they're sent to the bank?

☐ Are proper physical safeguards and facilities used to protect cash and cash transactions?

☐ Does any employee having custody of company funds also have custody of noncompany funds, such as credit unions, employee benefit associations, and others?

3. Cash Disbursements

☐ Are all disbursements, except for petty cash, made by check?

☐ Are all checks prenumbered?

☐ Are voided checks properly defaced or mutilated and held available for inspection and audit?

☐ Are checks required to be countersigned?

☐ Is the signing of checks in advance prohibited?

☐ Is the countersigning of checks in advance prohibited?

☐ Are authorized signatures limited to corporate officers or employees who have no access to accounting records or to cash?

☐ Is the practice of drafting checks to "cash" or "bearer" prohibited?

☐ If not, are checks so drawn limited to payrolls and/or petty cash reimbursement?

☐ Are monthly bank statements and paid checks received directly by the accounting department?

☐ Are the company bank accounts independently reconciled by someone other than the employees who keep the cash records?

☐ Is the sequence of check numbers accounted for when reconciling the bank accounts?

☐ Is the practice of examining paid checks for date, name, cancellation, and endorsement followed by the employee reconciling the bank accounts, and checked by internal auditors?

☐ Are vouchers or other supporting documents presented with the checks submitted for signature?

☐ Do the signers make adequate investigation before signing checks?

☐ If a check-signing machine is in use, are the machine and signature plates kept under effective control?

☐ Are checks mailed out without allowing them to return to the employee who drew the checks or to the accounts payable accountant?

☐ Are the supporting documents impressed with a "paid" stamp or other mark to prevent their use for duplicate payment?

☐ Are payroll checks drawn against a separate payroll bank account?

☐ Is the payroll bank account on an imprest basis?

☐ Are dividend checks drawn against a separate dividend bank account?

☐ Are transfers from one bank to another under effective accounting department control?

4. Security Investments

☐ Are securities kept in a safe deposit vault in the company's name?

☐ If so, does access to the vault call for the signature or presence of two or more designated company employees?

☐ Is a record maintained by the company of visits to the safe deposit vault?

☐ If not, are securities kept in safekeeping by a disinterested employee or bonded fiduciary?

☐ Are all employees who have access to the safe deposit vault bonded?

☐ Is a record kept by the accounting or the financial department of each security, including certificate numbers?

☐ Are all securities, except "bearer" bonds, in the name of the corporation?

☐ Are securities periodically inspected to ensure that they agree with the record by internal auditors or other designated corporate officers or bonded employees?

☐ Are purchases and sales of securities authorized by the board of directors? A corporate executive? The financial department or fiduciary?

☐ Are securities held for others or as collateral recorded and safeguarded in a manner similar to those owned by the company?

☐ Are security investments already written off or fully reserved and followed through on regarding possible realization?

☐ Are satisfactory records kept to ensure the proper and prompt receipt of income on securities owned?

Only a few sections of a possible all-inclusive internal control checklist are shown above, but the content serves as a guide that you can apply to any activity within your corporation. Other sections of a complete internal control checklist for your investigative audits might also include petty cash fund; notes and accounts receivable; inventories; properties and patents; notes and accounts payable and long-term debt; capital stocks; sales and shipping; purchases and expenses; and payrolls. You need to tailor your investigative audit checklists according to your specific company, its business, size and diversification, and other needs.

■ CORPORATE INVENTORIES: PRIME EMBEZZLEMENT OPPORTUNITIES

Corporate inventories include those items of tangible property held by a company that are (1) held for sale in the ordinary course of business; (2) in the process of production for sale in a business; or (3) to be consumed in the production of goods for sale in a business.

Your investigative audit objective is to determine whether inventories have the control and safeguards necessary to prevent embezzlement and then to detect and act when you discover embezzlement activity. Although it is advantageous for internal auditors to pursue aggressively the control of inventories, they continue to use the generally accepted accounting principles I discussed earlier in this book (see Chapter 5) that view numbers historically instead of looking for criminal activity. Your investigative audit bridges that gap and further tightens the accountability for company money and property, and it detects embezzlers that auditors probably will not detect. Inventories are one of the company assets that embezzlers attack most frequently because they are complex and detection is difficult. However, as this section unfolds, you will learn effective ways to bridge that gap of internal controls, establish accountability, and eliminate losses. Internal control over inventory affects many aspects of a corporation. It includes both safeguarding the inventory from a physical security effort, and safeguarding it from accurate, aggressive accounting procedures.

Safeguarding Corporate Inventory

Safeguarding your company inventory involves control of the various aspects of inventory from the time that raw materials are received until the finished product is shipped. This includes control over the receiving of inventory, store of inventory, movement of inventory within the company, processing and/or production inventory, and ultimately shipping of inventory. From its receipt until its ultimate disposition, inventory must be safeguarded because its nature and movement lead to a spectrum of opportunities for pilferage and sophisticated embezzlement schemes. Losses from these schemes can develop to staggering amounts, yet it is difficult to track or isolate those responsible. This safeguarding must involve the use of a system of documents (always prenumbered) that acknowledge receipt of the goods and then authorize the movement of the goods through the production and shipping processes. These documents include receiving reports, material requisitions, and shipping authorizations. Although computers today normally handle these activities, hard copies remain the only way to validate computer files. Without this checkpoint, your company becomes more vulnerable than ever. Many document requirements at every level, completed by many different employees in separate activities, create a sound deterrent against embezzlement activities by making it difficult and increasing the risk of detection.

Safeguarding inventory also involves assigning selected, bonded employees to be responsible for the inventory at various clearly defined points in the production and shipping process. For example, inventory housed in a storeroom should be the sole responsibility of a designated employee in that storeroom. When strong, clear lines of responsibility are in place, the person knows that his or her embezzlement activities would probably be discovered and will also be quick to report illicit activities.

Accurate Inventory Accounting

An effective system of documentation and of detailed recordkeeping will help produce accurate inventory reporting. You need to investigate the process in your company, asking yourself, "If I were in a specific position within the company, how could I create an effective embezzlement scheme, including disguise and concealment?" You also need to keep in mind that an embezzler gets into the illegal business to make money. Although the controls in a specific area might be inherently weak and supply an opportunity for embezzlement, you need to consider the profit to an embezzler who steals that item. As noted earlier, embezzlers (like entrepreneurs) believe their illegal activities will make money. The items for which you find weak controls may not offer that promise of money, and so the embezzler will probably not waste time and risk detection to steal them. You must concentrate on finding weak areas but also carefully evaluating the likelihood of embezzlement for those items. Normally, you should focus on those items with a high probability of embezzlement instead of those in low probability categories.

The maintenance of reliable, detailed records is enhanced when your company uses a strong perpetual inventory system, especially in lucrative embezzlement areas. Also, accurate accounting regarding the various costs included in the inventory is made possible by a well-conceived and properly functioning cost accounting system.

The detailed records of any perpetual inventory system should agree with the inventory control accounts. Also, businesses with perpetual inventory systems should periodically reconcile the perpetual inventory records with the actual inventory in stock by taking a physical count.

Testing Transactions to Check Inventory

Your company's accounting system needs a design that supplies the information necessary to assign the proper cost to inventory and determine the exact cost of goods sold. Your objective of testing transactions in this area is to ascertain whether employees follow the company's procedures. Two general procedures will help you check inventory transactions:

1. Test postings to detail inventory records for purchases, material requisitions, production, and shipments.

2. Review ledge accounts for periods not tested for unusual entries and investigate any found.

Also, you should examine inventory transactions as part of your investigative audit of cash transactions, vouchers, payrolls, and sales.

■ THIRTEEN KEY ELEMENTS OF REVIEWING YOUR COMPANY'S INVENTORY PLAN

An important part of your investigative audit process includes determining whether your corporation has planned properly for the taking of the physical inventory. For example, in a typical manufacturing company, the inventory may consist of many hundreds or thousands of separate items. These items may be in various stages of completion and may be located in various areas within the company. The count and identification of these items must always remain accountable and might supply the embezzler with fertile ground for carrying out illegal enterprises.

One aspect of your investigative audit techniques that is used to examine company inventory involves reviewing your corporate inventory instructions. Complete corporate inventory instructions should include the following:

1. *Names of the persons drafting and approving the instructions.* Remember that the drafters could have created a system for embezzlement. Usually, the controller or some other responsible executive will approve the instructions. However, do they consider embezzlement in that approval? For example, the corporate embezzler always disguises and conceals, and although on the surface (from an accounting point of view) the instruction might appear sound, from an investigative audit point of view there's a series of loopholes. Part of your scrutiny must focus on the drafters and the approvers and consider possible motives each would have for creating a document that supplies the embezzlement opportunities necessary for theft schemes.

2. *Dates and times of the inventory taking.* Many companies take a complete physical inventory at the end of their fiscal year. The problem is that this procedure notifies the embezzler of exactly how long he or she has to manipulate the figures to disguise and conceal white collar crime. To determine the reliability of inventory controls, your company must use a perpetual inventory system that includes at least periodic inventories by disinterested company employees at unannounced times. The would-be embezzler knows that concealment will be difficult because he or she never knows when an inventory will happen, including the time of day. This creates a powerful prevention effect to keep employees from stealing inventory assets. Another effective deterrent involves the same process, but in the interest of time management the inventories need not include a 100 percent inventory, instead just a "spot" inventory. To avoid a pattern, the employees conducting the spot inventory might check certain items and upon return check the same items or others, and return to the same items later. This will make the employee who is considering embezzlement recognize the probability of detection, and it serves to detect embezzlement schemes.

3. *A record of employees responsible for supervising the taking of the inventories.* I suggest that a random roster of disinterested employees serve to select these supervisors, who should not know the order of their selection. Even the executives choosing them should not decide beforehand, but instead keep records of who has already participated and randomly pick employees from the eligible roster when they're needed. This process again eliminates prenotification or the opportunity for the embezzler to create a collusion offer to the employee scheduled for the next inventory, whenever it will happen.

4. *Plans for rearranging and segregating stock periodically, including the precaution of clearing work in process to natural cut-off points.* Stock arrangement

before the inventory must be orderly so that counts by inventory teams will move quickly and accurately. When different items are intermingled or in difficult to reach locations, the company inventory teams might count the same item twice or overlook items. A favored scheme of an embezzler is to confuse the issue by lumping items together. When a shortage emerges, he or she can claim a miscount, knowing it's unlikely that the company will use the time and commit employees who could otherwise be productive conducting a new inventory.

5. *Provisions for control of receiving and shipping during the inventory count period, and if the plant is not shut down, provision for handling stock movement.* Although not always practical, it is helpful if the receiving and shipping department is cleared of all stock. If items must be transferred between departments, there should be procedures to ensure that each item is counted only once. This problem can produce the musical chairs effect of moving items around to create an illusion of items in place. For example, in a large company, inventory teams can count one floor or section and then move on, and while checking section two, items from section one move to section three before the inventory team arrives.

6. *Instruction about the use of inventory tags or sheets and their distribution, collection, and control.* Generally, I suggest prenumbered tags, and they should have strict accountability after the inventory count ends.

7. *Detailed instructions for accurate description of items and for determination of quantities by count, weight, or other measurement.* Normally, all information recorded on the inventory tag must be examined in a second count by an employee who did not take part in the first count. To ensure that all information is recorded properly, I also recommend a "blind" count. For example, another impartial inventory team compares the two counts and investigates any differences.

8. *Instructions for identifying and segregating obsolete and slow-moving items of inventory.* Watch carefully for substitution opportunities using look-alike (although outdated), obsolete, or slow-moving items. The embezzler might count on the inventory team not recognizing the differences, so it's important to caution against such actions in the company inventory instructions and ensure employees adhere to the procedures.

9. *Plans for determining quantities at outside locations.* This is important when your company has several locations within a geographical area, or supplies components to subcontractors.

10. *Methods of transcribing original counts to final inventory sheets or summaries.*

11. *Methods followed in pricing inventory quantities, including the extent of recheck of prices.*

12. *Instructions for making extensions and footing and for the extent of recheck.*

13. *Instructions for review and approval of inventory by department heads and other supervisory employees.*

◼ CONDUCTING YOUR INVESTIGATIVE AUDIT OF INVENTORY TAKING

When you plan your inventory observation techniques, you need an attentive review of how to proceed. You need to review your company's inventory instructions with particular attention to those sections that describe the company's procedures for the counting of inventory and the control of inventory tags. You should also review the timing and general plans for observing and testing the inventory counts. You need familiarity with your company's inventory, the approximate volume, the proper units of measure, where the valuable items are located, and so on. You need to know when to arrive at the inventory location and who is responsible and the extent of the specific procedures to be performed.

Remember that your position of investigative auditing involves observing and testing the inventory-taking procedures, not taking, determining, or supervising the physical inventory. Ensure that you don't give instructions or suggestions. Your responsibility to the company is to find weaknesses and ways of correcting them at an executive level, not the working level. Your responsibility to "observe" the taking of the inventory involves several important areas, discussed next.

◼ NINE KEY TECHNIQUES TO USE WHEN CHECKING INVENTORIES

1. Determine whether the department subject to inventory, and the inventory teams, prepared adequately for taking the inventory. Stock should be arranged in an orderly manner. Shipping and receiving cut-offs should be established. Movement of stock must remain minimal.

2. Determine whether employees taking inventory appear conscientious and familiar with the stock and their duties, and whether they have adequate supervision.

3. Determine whether the inventory-counting teams follow the company's inventory instructions. Your company procedures may call for two independent counts of each inventory item; the results of these independent counts should receive your attentive review.

4. Stay attentive for any possible double counting of inventory items. Items often will receive a double count when inventory teams skip around instead of counting items in location sequence. The use of inventory tags will aid in avoiding double counting. However, items may still be counted twice when the contents of several bins or boxes are recorded on a single inventory tag or listing.

5. Stay alert for any items not counted. Sometimes entire sections of a department may be inadvertently missed. To prevent this problem, inventory teams should place inventory tags on each item or inventory sheets in each location.

6. Stay alert for "hollow squares" (empty spaces between stacks of boxes) and empty containers. Inventory teams can use a variety of ways to test sealed containers (the easiest is to lift a container or push on it with one hand). When the inventory involves stacks of cartons, pushing on them will quickly develop a feel for the weight of those full, and an empty or half-filled carton (sealed and represented as full) will be detected easily. When a carton's weight is in question, when possible the carton can be weighed or opened and resealed. Remember, the embezzler relies on confusion and complacency, so although thorough inventory teams might take longer and create some inconvenience, the cost will always be minute compared to allowing an embezzlement scheme to continue.

7. Watch for apparently unsalable, damaged, slow-moving, and obsolete items integrated into the regular stock and represented as okay. When this occurs, you'll need to come back and conduct a criminal investigation for embezzlement.

8. Test the effectiveness of the procedures used by the inventory team(s). For example, test the accuracy of the counts made by the team, especially noting how attentively the team counts high-value items. Always keep alert for signs of collusion.

9. Remain attentive to the counting of items that cannot be accumulated as separate items. Special techniques or equipment might include scales, comparison with like items already counted, estimating tonnage of bulk storage items, aerial surveys of timber tracts and log storage ponds, and photographs of construction projects.

■ TWO POINTS TO CONSIDER IN RECEIVING AND SHIPPING CUT-OFF INFORMATION

During your observation of the physical inventory, you should examine and list receiving and shipping cut-off information. Later, you can use that information to trace the company's accounting records to determine:

(1) Whether all items received up to the cut-off date were in the physical inventory and charged to the purchases or inventory accounts (receiving cut-off)

(2) Whether all items shipped to the cut-off date were excluded from the physical inventory and have been credited to the inventory account (shipping cut-off) in sales and cost of goods sold.

■ TWO IMPORTANT CUT-OFF PROCEDURES

You should observe the following cut-off procedures to ensure that inventory remains accurate and to establish a solid preventive countermeasure to embezzlement.

(1) Visit the receiving and shipping areas to observe whether cut-off procedures are being followed so there's a clear separation between items in the physical inventory and those to be excluded. This is important because of items received during the inventory period and those awaiting shipment to customers.

(2) When using prenumbered receiving or shipping tickets in your company, note the last number used preceding the cut-off. Any unused numbers should be noted. If your company receives or ships materials in freight cars, ensure that there's a listing of full and empty cars on the tracks plus needed notations on their inventory status. (This matter needs your special attention because of the large amounts usually involved.)

When your company does not use prenumbered receiving or shipping tickets, you will need to spend extra time later reviewing the recorded sales and purchases to determine whether items recorded as shipped before the physical inventory or recorded as received after the physical inventory were shown in the count.

■ SIX IMPORTANT ELEMENTS OF YOUR INVESTIGATIVE AUDIT REPORT

At the conclusion of your observation and tests, you should prepare an investigative audit report that briefly and accurately describes your conclusions and your recommendations, which supply viable solutions to any discrepancy found during the process. Your report should include information concerning

(1) Location, time of inventories, and departments covered.

(2) Whether the company's employees followed the inventory instructions. Explain any deviations and viable corrective actions.

(3) Comments concerning the company's "housekeeping," such as if the inventory items were neatly arranged, and so on.

(4) Procedures followed in observing and test counting, and the degree of accuracy indicated in your test counts. Note any unusual items or conditions you observed, such as obsolete or slow-moving stock, damaged merchandise, consigned stock, and production and stock movement that occurred during the taking of the physical inventory.

(5) Description of the procedures the company used to get accurate shipping and receiving cut-offs and information you obtained for future testing of the information.

(6) Conclusions and findings based on the results of your tests and observations. Count differences, if any.

Your findings and conclusions serve as a basis for creating preventive measures and for documenting information that merges with other data obtained from balance sheets and the variety of other financial documents and activities discussed in this chapter. They can also serve as the basis for a criminal investigation for embezzlement of company assets.

When completing an inventory, the accounting department will normally price the inventory, extend (multiply) quantities by unit prices, and accumulate the extensions to arrive at a total amount or value for the inventory. Your investigative audit process must determine whether the final inventory was compiled with care and accuracy by tracing test counts, checking cut-offs, and testing their clerical accuracy.

Six Steps for Tracing Test Counts into Final Inventory Listings

The company's inventory account in the general ledger must include all transactions that affect the status of the physical inventory when the count occurred. Otherwise, the financial statements (balance sheet) will become distorted. It's important to find out if proper cut-offs were used. Your tests of the company's receiving and shipping cut-off procedures determine whether

(1) All materials received were in inventories

(2) Liabilities were recorded for materials purchased on account and in the inventories

(3) Liabilities have not been recorded for any items excluded from the inventory

(4) Receivables were charged for products sold on account

(5) All products sold were excluded from inventory

(6) Receivables were not recorded for products in the inventory.

Pay particular attention to inventory in transit, either from vendors or from branches, divisions, or subdivisions of your company. You must determine whether these items were recorded properly in the inventory accounts. As part of your test, you need to note receiving and shipping cut-off data obtained during the physical inventory. The purchasing and receiving records and the sales and shipping records of the company must be included in your tests.

■ TESTING CLERICAL ACCURACY OF INVENTORY ACCOUNTS

Extensions and footings of inventories should always be a part of your accuracy testing. They can supply a means of concealment for corporate embezzlers. Even though the calculations might have been subjected to traditional audits, you must review them carefully combined with all information you've compiled, especially when your observation of the inventory raised suspicions. Your test in this area will depend on factors such as the procedures used by company employees in compiling the final inventory listing, the care used by employees when making and checking the calculations, and the number and dollar amounts of the inventory items.

Common clerical errors in summarizing inventories include

- Transportation errors
- Misplaced decimal points
- Incorrect conversions and/or units of measure
- Errors in extensions (quantity times unit price)
- Failure to carry page totals into the summary sheets
- Errors in footings
- Errors in pricing.

When you perform your tests of clerical accuracy, your primary concern is with substantial errors. Your test will probably be the most efficient and useful when done on an approximate basis, because finding weaknesses and embezzlement schemes will not depend on proving extensions and footings to the exact dollar. For transpositions, misplaced decimals, and errors footings, the time-saving technique of sight testing (i.e., visually noting the reasonableness of the total) will often serve your investigative audit purposes, especially in huge inventories, because your observations supplied you with considerable insight. However, remember to maintain your focus on exactness for those items lucrative to a corporate embezzler, such as large-dollar items and items easily disposed of through the blackmarket. When you find conversions, such as from feet to pounds, you should test the source of information used for the conversion and the conversion conclusion itself. Although not all pages of the inventory detail are footed, all page totals will trace to the summary, which is footed.

When taking physical inventories, as well as pricing and compiling before the balance sheet date, you must learn if the proper adjustments were recorded beginning on the inventory date. Also, you need to test the inventory transactions that happened during the period from the time of the physical inventory to the balance sheet date. Your test of interim transactions normally must include

- A test of entries in the inventory control accounts by reference to purchase journals, labor distributions, overhead allocations, or other records. It's important that you ensure that all products billed have been removed from the inventory at the proper inventory cost amount.
- A comparison of the gross profit margins of the current period with those of prior periods. All unusual variations prompt your investigation.

■ INVENTORY VALUATION TECHNIQUES

An important element of your investigative audit includes determining whether the basis of pricing used by company accountants or others conforms to standards. Your procedure should include

- Examining inventory pricing and cost systems
- Selecting items for a price test
- Pricing of purchased parts and materials
- Pricing of work in process and finished goods.

How to Apply Inventory Pricing and Cost Systems

To test your company's inventory valuation (and compare it with balance sheet and other financial documents produced), you must understand the basic concepts of pricing and the more common cost systems. Common types of cost systems in use include the job order and process cost. Either may be used in combination with a standard cost system. In a job order cost system, you can test the pricing and accumulation of materials and labor used in producing the job lot and test the allocation of overhead. It is important to do so because corporate embezzlers may manipulate these systems to disguise and conceal their illegal activities. You can test the process costs, for example, by reviewing the pricing and accumulation of materials and labor used for each department or process over the accounting period and by testing the assignment of overhead to the units produced. This means testing the computations of equivalent units of production for materials, labor, and overhead. When an embezzler uses these techniques, unexplained differences will begin to surface.

When you use standard costs, you must review the standard costs to determine whether they lead to an acceptable valuation of the company's inventory. The use of out-of-date standards may lead to an important misstatement of the inventory, and you need to watch for that embezzlement technique.

Selecting the Right Items for Your Price Test

When you conduct your price test, select a representative number of the prices of items in inventory. Remember, your investigative audit objective involves ferreting out embezzlement schemes and finding weaknesses in the system that supply opportunities for embezzlement enterprises. In your selection process, choose those items that would create a lucrative or fertile ground for the embezzler, not those items that would have no economical advantage. The prices should conform to an acceptable pricing method (for example, lower of FIFO cost or market). Ordinarily, when you test items of a high dollar amount, you will have maximum assurance with a minimum of time and effort that the inventory is or is not largely overstated.

Techniques for Pricing Purchased Parts and Materials

When you begin preparing your list of items to test, be certain to include a description of the inventory items selected, the stock number, the sheet number or tag number, and the inventory quantity, unit price, and extended amount. Your price test worksheet should provide you with enough space to list several invoices that form the total of the inventory quantity. Once you have selected the test items, you need to consider the following matters:

(1) *Name of vendor for the item.* The vendor should be the usual and regular source of supply. This can be checked by a review of Purchasing Department records.

(2) *Quantity*. Invoices you examine should cover the approximate quantity in inventory.

(3) *Unit price*. The indirect cost of purchases (e.g., freight charges, discounts, insurance) may be accounted for in various ways. Generally, freight charges and insurance are in the cost while rebates and discounts (other than cash discounts) are excluded. A standard conversion table is usually available to help you when invoice prices are based on units that differ from those in the inventory (e.g., steel bought by the pound but priced in linear feet). If there have been no purchases of an item during the current period, the cost used is generally the same as in the prior year, subject to possible adjustment for the reduction in the utility of the goods.

(4) *Date of invoice*. The invoices immediately preceding the inventory date serve as the price test of FIFO values. If no current invoices exist, there is a possibility that the item is obsolete, slow moving, or unsalable—or that you have found traces of an embezzlement scheme.

The lower-of-cost-or-market technique generally serves for valuing inventory in the company's financial statements. A method of testing the market value of purchased items that often proves satisfactory is to review the price paid for recent purchases. However, this procedure will not always prove adequate. For example, if a commodity is subject to declining prices or rapid market fluctuations, supplementary tests and inquires should also be part of your investigative audit. One source of this type of information is published quotations in financial and trade publications; another is suppliers' price lists.

Your company should have adequate procedures to control items removed from inventory. You must also be able to determine the estimated value of obsolete or slow-moving items. Your company's inventory plan should include instructions for reducing such items to their net realizable value. If your company does not have such procedures established, include them in your suggestions.

Six-Step Test for Slow-moving, Obsolete, or Similar Stock Items

A test for slow-moving, obsolete stock and similar items should include the following steps:

1. Define your company's procedures to determine the quantities of such inventory and the related adjustments from cost, and test the reasonableness of the company's determinations.

2. Search for such items during the physical inventory observation, and check later to see whether such items were considered by the company in its determination.

3. Review price-test worksheets for evidence of such items. The lack of recent purchases or the use of old standard costs are indications.

4. Check to determine that the current year's inventory does not include items excluded from the prior year's inventory.

5. Review inventory records on a test basis for items that appear to be inactive.

6. Evaluate inventory quantities based on expected usage to determine that quantities in stock are not excessive. Turnover ratios, sales forecasts, current sales, and unfilled orders will sometimes serve as a basis for estimating usage.

Pricing of Work in Process and Finished Goods

You will determine whether the costs in the final inventory listing agree with those in the supporting cost records, whether detailed cost records have been manipulated or compiled in conformity with your company's cost system, and whether any significant clerical errors were made in accumulating the cost.

As with purchased parts, you usually need to prepare a schedule of the inventory items you select for testing. After choosing the items, examine the cost cards and all supporting data and documents. The test of the cost records will normally include information you compiled on material, labor, and overhead costs. You should test prices of materials by examining the supporting invoices or conducting the purchased parts and materials price test. Test the accuracy of converting purchased units to production units shown in the cost records (for example, converting steel from dollars per purchase price to dollars per hundred pieces of manufactured parts).

You need to test labor costs on separate jobs or for processes or departments by tracing charges to both payroll records and time tickets. Also include both labor rates and hours worked in your test.

To test overhead costs, you need to determine the company procedures to establish rates and test the computation of these rates. Overhead usually will apply because of direct labor hours or direct labor costs, although other bases such as machine hours might serve your examination. All manufacturing costs other than direct materials and direct labor will remain a part of manufacturing overhead. You should test whether a proper disposition occurred for any over- or underapplied manufacturing overhead for the period.

You must also test the market price for items in work in process or for finished products. The price may be the cost of replacement, or it may be the selling price less the cost to complete and sell the item and, sometimes, a normal profit. The selling prices may come from your company's price list, from contracts, from catalogs, or from recent sales invoices. You must stay alert for trade discounts that reduce the listed selling price. As noted earlier, make inquires about damaged, slow-moving, overstocked, and obsolete inventories. You must determine that adequate provision was made for losses in disposing of these inventories, whether in stock or committed to acquisition.

Physical Inventory Adjustments

When adjustment from book to physical inventory is considered abnormal, your company should find the reasons for the adjustment and prepare a summary of the reconciling items. You should review the reconcilement and feel comfortable about the reasonableness of the items. Your review of monthly gross profit margins, standard cost variances, methods of costing sales, provisions for inventory shrinkage, and methods of account for freight and discounts may help explain the adjustment. When the explanation does not satisfy you, an embezzlement disguise and concealment effort might play a role.

Consignments and Purchase and Sales Commitments

You must also determine whether the company has established adequate control over merchandise that was either received or shipped on consignment. Confirmation of quantities in stock may come through requesting that information from outside consignors or consignees. In certain instances, you may also personally observe this inventory. You should ascertain that the consigned stock has been properly included in the inventory if it is a consignment out or excluded if it is a consignment from another firm.

Exhibit 8-4 shows a chronological list of steps for planning and conducting a physical inventory linked to the foregoing detailed explanations. The checklist, in questionnaire form, is broad enough to cover most types of businesses. For smaller companies, the inapplicable techniques can be eliminated. Further, certain of the techniques can be emphasized or deemphasized, depending on the inventory items involved or the existence of alternate procedures. Any questions with a negative response require your immediate investigative attention.

Exhibit 8-4
Checklist for Planning and Conducting a Physical Inventory

1. General Planning

☐ Have the company personnel responsible for the conduct of the count been identified?

Note: Such identification should, at a minimum, name not only the person with overall responsibility for the entire physical inventory but also those persons with supervisory responsibility.

☐ Has a preliminary tour of inventory locations been made by company officials?

Note: A preliminary tour may suggest problems that could arise in the course of the count or matters that should be covered in the instructions (e.g., new locations at which inventory is stored, types of inventory that will require special talents on the part of observers, and areas requiring advance preparation).

☐ Have steps been taken to

—Stack, sort, and clean inventory items?

—Segregate defective and obsolete items?

—Identify slow-moving items?

—Identify consigned or other merchandise on hand belonging to others (including material relating to government contracts)?

☐ Has consideration been given to physically counting inventory that is held by others, such as

—On consignment or approval?

—For processing?

—For storage?

☐ In setting a date for taking the inventory and planning the time sequence of the count, has consideration been given to

—The timing of the count in relation to the balance sheet date?

—The optimum utilization of personnel?

—The needed clearances if overtime is contemplated (e.g., from the appropriate labor unions)?

Note: Sometimes a count is proposed to be made as of a predetermined date within a reasonable time before or after the balance sheet date. If so, careful consideration must be given to the rapidity of inventory turnover and the adequacy of the records supporting the interim changes in evaluating the acceptability of the alternative date.

Setting a date for the inventory also includes fixing a specified time for the job to be completed. This is especially true in a manufacturing operation, where departmental operations must be prescheduled.

Even if overtime for the count crew is not contemplated, it may be wise to anticipate the possibility. A few added overtime hours necessary to complete a count may be critical if goods must be released the following day for production or shipment.

☐ Is a procedure provided that enables the following?

—The progress of the count is reported to responsible company officials during the count.

—Changes in procedures made during the count are communicated to the responsible company officials.

—Upon completion of the count (in specified areas or in total) and before any count records are removed from the inventory items, a tour of the area is made by the company's supervisory personnel to ensure that all inventoriable items have been counted and that all count records are accounted for.

2. Cut-off Procedures

☐ Has the cut-off date and time been established?

Note: The term *cut-off*, when used in connection with a physical inventory, refers to the procedures undertaken by the company to ensure proper correlation of the physical inventory with the accounting records count. This requires procedures designed to

—Stop the flow of materials to permit a cut-off to be established.

—Ensure that transactions are recorded in the appropriate accounting period when they occurred.

☐ Have plans been made for

—Closing down production or suspending or controlling operations?

—Segregating incoming inventory expected to be received during the count?

—Accounting for inventory that must be shipped out during the count?

—Controlling the movement of inventory in process?

☐ Have the applicable departments been alerted to

—Control prenumbered receiving reports (or provide other means) to identify prephysical and postphysical shipments of inventory?

Note: In the case of a multiplant operation, it is important to determine whether there are interplant shipments of goods or materials en route on the inventory date. These shipments are sometimes not recorded by the shipping department in the same manner that shipments to outsiders are. It is important to decide beforehand which plan will record such shipments in inventory.

3. The Count Record

☐ Have the forms for entering the inventory counts been identified?

—Forms of inventory count records can vary greatly. The most widely used are preprinted 8 1/2″ × 11″ sheets on which the counts are recorded directly, or individual tags on which each count is recorded. Both of these types are available commercially. In some industries, counts are recorded on magnetic tape or on calculating machines (with printouts).

—Regardless of the form type used, the count record should ordinarily provide space for recording the following facts:

■ Count record number (if not prenumbered)

■ Description of the item (including size, number, or other identifying characteristics)

■ Quantity and unit of measurement

■ Remarks about the condition of the item

■ Location (building, floor, department or section)

■ Initials of the count team or crew (and second crew, when applicable)

■ Date of the count

■ Cross-reference of the inventory summary (for postinventory use)

☐ Has consideration been given to using count records of different colors, shapes, or sizes for various categories of inventory?

☐ Has provision been made for as many sets of the count record as will be necessary? For providing a visible means of determining that all items have been counted? For providing the company with adequate documentation for the count listing?

Example:

—Three-part tags (or an original and two carbons) serve the multiple purpose of providing both the company and auditors with a set of count tickets and, by the remaining stubs (or second copy) attached to the inventory items, a visible means of determining that all items have been counted. When some form of copy of the count record is not attached to the items, an acceptable alternative procedure must be adopted to make certain that all items have been counted and that there are no duplicate counts.

—When magnetic tapes or calculating machines are the basic count record, you must suitably alter your techniques. For example, you might arrange to receive a magnetic copy of all tapes. From randomly selected tapes, you could use a playback machine to transcribe the information to worksheets. Using these worksheets, you could test check the counts. If tapes are used, some control must be maintained over them in considering test counts.

☐ Will the count record be prenumbered?

☐ Has provision been made to control all count records (issued, returned, unused, and spoiled or voided) and to reconcile them at the end of the inventory count?

4. Instructions for Count Teams or Crews

☐ Have the instructions made clear the terminology to be used in describing the nature, condition, and location of the items being counted?

—To facilitate recognition, meaningful terminology should be established. This should be based on the descriptive characteristics of the inventory items, such as their

■ Nature: description, serial, part or model number, manufacturer

■ Condition: defective, obsolete, slow moving

■ Location: area of plant or building where kept.

The terminology used should avoid similar descriptions especially for items that have different costs. Similar descriptions confuse count crews and facilitate deliberate alteration. In one situation, the word *boxes* (meaning empty containers) was altered in an embezzlement scheme and covered during an inventory by changing the inventory count to show *boxed* (meaning the containers with the finished product).

☐ Have the instructions made clear the units of measurement to be used in recording quantities of various inventory items? Quantity, dimension, and capacity can be stated using various measurements, such as

—*Units*: each, dozen, gross, lot

—*Weight*: Avoirdupois, troy, apothecaries, metric

—*Dimension*: linear, chain, metric

—*Capacity*: dry, liquid, apothecaries, metric

□ Are the terminology and units of measurement compatible with the terms and units used for costing purposes? This compatibility minimizes the possibility of errors (or covering embezzlement activity) in the later entering of pricing information on the count listing.

□ Have the instructions provided guidance to the count crews about the most convenient and reliable methods of counting (consistent with the unit of measurement) various types of inventory items? Sometimes measurements can be accomplished more easily (and with acceptable reliability) by, for example, weighing and then converting to units based on a units-per-pound figure or by rounding off to the nearest pound or foot. Material stored in piles or in barrels, boxes, or bags stacked in solid formation may require special equipment or techniques.

5. Taking the Count

□ Will the count be recorded in ink? Recording in ink minimizes later, unauthorized alteration of the count record.

□ Will counts be made by crews composed of two or more company employees who are not responsible for custody of the items being counted and have no connection that would cause them to gain from altering an inventory count?

□ Will a second count crew doublecheck the accuracy of the count record?

□ Has provision been made to reconcile differences if the second crew finds discrepancies in the count record?

□ Will initials of the count crews (or some other identification) be placed on the count record?

6. The Inventory Summary

□ Has the form of the count listing or summary been identified? The count listing is a summarization of all the separate count records. It should ordinarily provide space for pricing data, dollar extensions, and other identifying comments. In some cases, the count record may also be designed to serve as the listing.

□ Will the count listing provide for identification (or for separate listings) of

—*Classifications of inventory*: raw material, in process, finished goods?

—*Condition*: defective, obsolete, slow moving, excess quantities of active items?

—*Location*: building, floor, department or section, off premises, in transit?

—*Ownership*: inventory on hand belonging to others?

—*Source*: count record number with cross-reference on the count record to count on the listing page?

Note: The identification of the source (count record number) is particularly important in maintaining an audit trail.

7. Work-in-Process Inventories

☐ Has the count been scheduled at a date or time when work in process will be at a minimum? The inventorying of work in process is frequently difficult. If the production cycle is at its lowest point, the problem is minimized.

☐ Is the method of identifying the stage of production related to the cost-accounting system? Variations in cost-accounting systems preclude other than a general question on this point. However, this aspect of inventory requires extensive consideration. In a standard or job cost system, the stage of operations (or percentage of completion) may be identifiable on the basis of standard specification sheets or work orders. In a process cost system, overall movement may be controlled so that input, throughout, and output will be measurable.

☐ Will the count teams (and you) be provided with specification sheets, work orders, or other documentation that will serve to identify stages of production? Not only must the identification be related to the cost-accounting system, but those concerned with the count should have adequate information on which to base their conclusions and record their observations.

QUICK REFERENCE GUIDES FOR CHAPTER 8
CATEGORIES OF EMBEZZLEMENT OPPORTUNITY

Often your financial investigative audit will uncover evidence of inefficiency or weak operating controls and embezzlement activities. In planning your investigative audit, you need to consider the cost versus benefit and focus your attention on the categories within your company most probable to supply a lucrative embezzlement opportunity. Although the following list might not suffice for each category in every company, these categories will in part be present in every company.

- Acquisition and merger policies and procedures
- Budgetary systems and procedures
- Branch officer control procedures
- Capital budgeting procedures
- Contracting policies and procedures
- Credit granting and collection procedures
- Dividend policies and procedures
- Electronic data processing applications
- Energy conservation procedures
- Facilities management
- Fixed-asset control procedures
- Insurance (risk management) procedures
- Inventory planning and control procedures
- Joint venture agreements
- Law and regulation compliance procedures
- Long-range (strategic) planning policies and procedures
- Make or buy procedures, including intercompany practices
- Management information systems
- Manufacturing policies and procedures
- Marketing and advertising planning and control systems
- Office equipment—acquisition and utilization
- Payroll policies and procedures
- Personnel policies
- Policy and procedure manuals
- Product pricing policies and procedures
- Purchasing policies and procedures
- Research and development planning and control systems
- Special projects (such as desirability of specific acquisition or cost-reduction studies)

Your Investigative Audit Work Program Checklist

This checklist supplies you with the minimum investigative audit steps to consider in a plant balance sheet. The extent of the actual work you perform in each case depends on your judgment. Audit steps may be added to those supplied below. Those steps not applicable to your situation can be deleted.

(1) General

- Obtain location balance sheet, exhibits, and vouchers for the month you want to audit.
- Prepare or obtain a balance sheet for work papers and trace it to the plant ledger.
- Review entries to accounts as given in plant exhibits for several months, and question all unusual entries to accounts.
- Prepare summary of approval authorizations.
- Consult the accounting manual and determine whether record retention periods are being followed.

(2) Receivables

- Verify the account balance to detailed records.
- Investigate old items in the balance.
- Determine the types of transactions handled in the account.
- Review procedures for handling miscellaneous sales (e.g., scrap, safety shoes, etc.).
- Investigate noncash credits.
- Determine the sources of charges to the account.
- Obtain order cost schedules and test balance.
- Review sources of charges to the account. Note expense allocations and pricing.
- Investigate order clearances to expense.
- Review credit approvals.
- Determine whether proper controls are in effect for posting receivable registers.
- Consult the account manual and determine whether record retention periods were followed.

(3) Inventories (including product in process)

- Verify the balance of each inventory account to detailed records. This may mean making a test check of the tape of electronic data processing scrolls.
- Review material distributions.
- Examine the balance of the company records for
  —Proper account classification of materials.
  —Application of freight and other costs charged to account.

—Calculation of cost per unit. When standard values are used, note variations from current prices and trace the variance to the cost of shipments.

—Pricing of issues.

—Distribution of separate items:

- Review work papers supporting calculation of usage of bulk materials.
- Check normal usage data with production engineering or another group that supplies the data.
- Test company issues for approval signatures and for information regarding the type of material used.

■ Examine physical inventories.

■ Check adherence to inventory schedules.

■ Review physical inventory sheets. Test check calculations when engineering surveys are made.

■ Trace the disposition of adjustments.

■ Review the procedures involved in taking, reconciling, and adjusting inventories (noting proper division of responsibility).

■ Review the balance of the company's records for slow-moving items. (Compare this with the plant's obsolescence review. Investigate significant items. All appropriate materials should be listed on the "recommended obsolescence" report.)

■ Review last-in, first-out (LIFO).

—Verify entries on the LIFO receipts, production, and inventory report.

—Review LIFO calculations at those locations that carry a LIFO reserve account.

—Review the recosting procedures for product in process, worked materials, and finished goods.

- Note the elimination of the employees' plans expense from the inventory value.
- On a sampling basis, select receipts that involved materials in transit (MIT) at year-end; see that MIT items are not included as receipts in January-March.
- In the costing of crude mixtures of other materials in product in process, see that LIFO value unit pers for December are applied to January inventories per the accounting manual.
- Review the balance of the company's records to see that unloading charges and freight are added to items received from other plants.

—Investigate any writedowns for market depreciation and any inventory revaluation adjustments.

■ Review the cost-accounting system. Determine the reason for making clearances from product in process to accounts other than worked materials or finished goods inventories. Review the following:

—Allocation of expense to product

—Major expense items other than clearances from deferred charge orders

—Procedure for calculating material usage and determining ending inventories

—Handling of variances

—Valuation of material in process.

■ Review the procedures for determination of interdivision profit elimination. This is particularly important in the chemicals and plastics inventories. At chemicals and plastics plants, obtain the report of inventory reserves submitted to headquarters and verify amounts reported under the following captions:

—Direct cost reserve

—Unearned interdivision profits in inventory.

■ Review the gross fixed-investment allocation procedure.

■ Consult the company accounting manual and determine whether record retention periods are being followed.

(4) Special Orders

■ Obtain a copy of all special order summaries, and trace totals to the plant ledger.

■ Obtain a copy of the description of the orders in those special order accounts that do not have summaries.

■ Review authorizations. Check expenditures against the amount authorized.

■ Obtain cost schedules for all active orders for the period you're auditing and for any closed orders of material amounts during the past year.

■ Verify the trial balance or balance tape.

■ Review sources of charges, particularly those clearing through the unclassified account.

■ Review the method of expense allocation.

■ Review the methods and bases of clearances from orders.

■ Review the year-end analysis of special orders.

- Investigate major repair or rearrangement jobs that were authorized on the basis of a cost saving. Review the calculation of cost saving compared to discounted cash flow procedures. Determine the type of follow-up used to compare actual savings with the estimate.
- Consult the company's accounting manual and determine whether the record retention periods are being followed.

(5) Property Orders

Your investigative audit procedures are similar to those outlined under the previous category, "Special Orders," with the addition of the following techniques:

- Review physical completion notices and compare them with clearing notices and acquisition reports.
- Examine retirement reports.
- Review clearing notices and acquisition reports for indication of the certificate of necessity number, property class, date of acquisition, or completion, etc.
- Ascertain that

   Items are promptly and properly cleared.

   Temporary orders are used prior to formal authorizations.

   Proper authorizations are received for overruns in accordance with the procedures of the operating divisions.

Note: In reviewing clearances, the date of acquisition is the date when the property is placed in a condition or state of readiness or availability for a specially assigned function. This includes property that has been installed but requires, for example, painting, outside insulation, testing, or hooking up to adjacent units. This does not include a unit or property that has been delivered but not installed.

- Consult your company's accounting manual and determine whether record retention periods are being followed.

(6) Special Manufacturing Orders

- Determine that the account is authorized in the locations chart of accounts.
- Review and determine whether approvals and instructions for each type of transaction have been complied with.

(7) Materials-in-Transit Accounts

- Reconcile the month-end balance of the account to the date of your audit.
- Examine invoices held pending receipt of the receiving report.
- Investigate items that have been outstanding for 30 days or more.
- Review supplementary invoice payable registers, clearing items from materials-in-transit accounts.
- Examine year-end receipts for items that should appear on the annual statement of MIT.

(8) Accrued Liabilities

- Examine all receiving reports held pending receipt of an invoice.
- Review all accrual registers and trace totals to the plant ledger.
- Investigate old items.
- Examine separate accrual registers for MIT items.

(9) Accrued Vacation and Shutdown Expense

- Verify the accuracy of estimated expense.
- Review accrual calculations and contract charges.

(10) Home Office Entries

- Check monthly reconciliation.
- Review entries. Investigate unusual items. Trace unusual items through the general books.

Chapter Nine
Embezzlement of Corporate Proprietary Information

Historians have labeled previous eras the Agricultural Age or the Industrial Age. They've dubbed our new high-tech era the Information Age. Concurrently, a new white collar crime that emerged that fits into the "gray area" of crimes that victimize corporations and industries: the embezzlement of company information.

Protecting corporations and industry against competitor spying has been emphasized in recent years and probably will continue to be a serious problem because of technological advances. Although computers, facsimile machines, and sophisticated communications advance the business community, they also make stealing information easier. However, corporate fears focus on outside intrusions, with little or no focus on internal information embezzlement. This neglected category of embezzlement often surpasses other categories of employee embezzlement in regard to participation opportunity and corporate financial losses.

It's hard to place a specific value on corporate information for several reasons. One key reason stems from trying to define or prove that company information losses have monetary value and, if so, how much. Prosecutors generally refuse to consider prosecution of employees proven to have participated in handing over information to a competing company or an information broker, even when they received money from the transfer of information. The primary reason is the statutes of larceny, which require elements of proof that a crime happened. One of those elements involves clearly proving a legitimate monetary value, a second involves proving ownership of the item stolen, and a third involves proving that the accused stole the item or property. The crime of larceny (theft) deals with tangible property, while information in itself has an abstract value and falls in an intangible category.

The value of information stems from its use, and the loss factor stemming from the loss must emerge largely from conjecture. A corporation can claim, for instance, that research and development information stolen by an employee and sold to a competitor (who then used the information to create a similar product and introduce it into the marketplace) cost the victim company a certain amount of money. Civil court litigation probably will reach the same conclusion when the victimized company sues a competitor or the information embezzler.

As with most white collar crime within companies, 80 percent or more of the problem stems from within the company, and about 20 percent from outside sources. Information embezzlement, however, has another characteristic often not found in other forms of embezzlement—outside collusion. Stealing information in itself cannot benefit the embezzler (for example, like stealing money or property for personal use). The corporate information brings personal gain to the embezzler only when he or she can sell it, receive a regular income from the buyer, or take part in the conspiracy in an agreement of later employment by the recipient. Some embezzlement occurs when the employee plans to use the information to create his or her own company or service; however, that type of information will normally not have any appreciable effect on corporate profits.

■ IDENTIFYING THE RISK: WHO STEALS INFORMATION?

Earlier in this book, I discussed surveys that revealed that there's little real loyalty within corporations, including those in foreign countries. I also looked at the idea that most white collar crime offenders rationalize their acts, viewing them as victimless acts, and most do not perceive them to be crimes. Or they do not admit that their activities are crimes even though they know they are morally and legally wrong. Stealing information moves us into an even more unclear area of employees who victimize their employers. Within most companies, nearly every employee (from janitor to CEO) has access to valuable information. Whether the competitor commits an offense when it encourages or pays an employee of a competitor for information is a moral and ethical matter. In nearly all instances, identification of the employee offender remains rare. That factor encourages this type of embezzlement because, even if caught, the worst that can happen will be the loss of a job. Most often, the company asks the employee to resign instead of firing him or her. A liability problem can evolve from firing a person, and the corporation will prefer to avoid negative publicity.

Knowing who in your company might participate in information embezzlement for money helps to create effective awareness and preventive solutions. Determining who the offenders are stems from your company's configuration and business role. However, certain aspects apply to any business situation. Eight tips for identifying potential problem areas and those vulnerable to become embezzlers of information follow.

■ EIGHT TIPS FOR IDENTIFYING PROBLEM AREAS AND OFFENDERS

(1) Employees who have access to a broad range of corporate information can see sensitive information easily without anyone giving it a second thought.

(2) Employees who work in marketing departments and have knowledge of new products or services are prime targets. Because a marketing program may take several months to formulate, these employees and their staff have access to sensitive information and plans.

(3) Employees participating in research and development activities for the company, plus those who work with them (conducting surveys, polls, and maybe product or service sampling) may embezzle information.

(4) Employees accessing corporate computer databases may become involved. Although most companies have coded databases that require specific codes and procedures for entry, you cannot limit your scope to just those persons. Any employee having computer literacy might accidentally or deliberately discover codes and procedures that can enable access to the most sensitive databases.

(5) Employees working in purchasing divisions and those in accounts payable both have positions that will first identify the normal status of the company and immediately detect a shift in directions. For example, information they access can show a reduction in purchasing that is corroborated by accounts payable clerks.

(6) Security officers, especially those who have access to a building or offices containing sensitive files or other information such as that stored on computer disks, are at risk. Normally, the night shift will supply the greatest uninterrupted, unnoticed threat as well as those working on weekends and holidays.

(7) Accountants, auditors, and others with access to company financial information, including budgets and planned income, may embezzle information.

(8) Others within your company who have access to specific and general areas, such as cleaning crews, contractors, certain vendors, consultants, and more, may engage in information embezzling. If you believe that all employees in your company have a potential for embezzling information and selling it for a profit, you're probably right.

■ WHAT INFORMATION IS EMBEZZLED?

A key factor of information embezzlement stems from its demand on a continuing basis. A competitor might need a specific item of information and be willing to pay an employee of your company for that item. However, that type of information theft is not embezzlement. The embezzlement of information, like money or commodities, must be a well-developed scheme to supply continuing data (long range) to a buyer. Understanding that important aspect also helps you identify what information in your company falls into that category. The information sought might not stem from purely a competitive motive, but instead may involve leveraged buyouts, hostile takeovers, or an environment for corporate espionage. Collectively, these activities require precise timing. That timing depends on detailed, continuing sources of information from inside the targeted corporation. Other factors that determine the threat of information embezzlement in your company include the scope and scale of materials and documents that your competitors might want; your type of business; the size and success of your business; and the level of competition in your market. Some of the information categories that might be lucrative in your company for employee embezzlement include the following:

- New product plans, pricing, and sales information
- Research and Development projects and budgets
- Corporate planning, budgets, income, investment, and other financial information
- Employee personnel files, including executives and salary information
- Manufacturing costs, expansion projects
- Shipping and receiving information
- Audit information
- Mailing lists and customer lists and profiles
- Company manuals, policies and procedures, directives and letters
- Various other information and internal documents, such as interdepartmental memorandums.

■ SOLUTIONS FOR INFORMATION EMBEZZLEMENT

Dealing with the embezzlement of information from your company necessitates a somewhat different tack from other white collar crimes because of its intangible nature. However, contrary to popular belief, stealing information systematically does leave an audit trail, although it's not the traditional audit concept but instead your investigative audit. One of the key elements in ending the embezzlement of information is to treat your company information like money—because it *is* money, but in a different sense. Corporate information is money not yet tangible, and losing information to a competitor creates a loss of that money.

Protect the Corporation's Proprietary Rights

You need to create the proper framework first, which is often an effective deterrent for employees inclined to embezzle and sell company information. This action also serves to supply basic legal grounds when you detect an information embezzler. Often, embezzlement of company information begins (1) as part of planned retirement and opening of a subsequent and competing business; (2) as part of planned career moves to a competing company; (3) before a foreseen layoff or abolishment of a position within a company; (4) as part of a revenge scheme for perceived discriminating treatment; or (5) for a variety of other rationalizations. However, in reality, the motive always stems from some form of personal gain or perceived personal gain (See Exhibit 4-3.) The following action list should be your first steps in solving this problem.

Create a Covenant Not to Compete

Stealing or embezzling information serves no personal purpose unless the embezzlers can sell the information directly or indirectly to a competitor, either existing or planned, that is owned by others or owned totally or in part by the employee. The only legal protection you might have in your company against employees stealing information created in the company involves a covenant not to compete. Although creating this covenant is the task of your corporate attorneys in cooperation with human resource specialists and your Board of Directors, guidelines provided in Exhibit 9-1 help you understand the advantages, benefits, and parameters of this step. An employment covenant of this type traditionally applies to executives and upper management; however, you should ensure that it surpasses those categories and extends to any employee who has or might have access to any type of valuable company information. Deciding value follows a simple formula: If the information is valuable to your company, it surely will have as much or more value to a competing company. Your covenant must also consider the laws of the state(s) where the employee works and resides. The checklist shown in Exhibit 9-1 supplies corporate policy matters and procedural points that you need to consider in this step.

Exhibit 9-1
Checklist for Covenant Not to Compete

(1) Which employees should you cover?
- ☐ Corporate executives
- ☐ Management employees
- ☐ Professional staff, technicians, and specialists
- ☐ All employees who have access to company information
- ☐ Include consultants, vendors, maintenance persons, and others contracted who have access to company information, either openly or surreptitiously.

(2) When is the covenant made official?
- ☐ When it has been signed by every employee covered in the company policy
- ☐ When an employee is hired (if within the decided categories) or when promoted

(3) What type of format to use?
- ☐ This agreement can become an addendum to a written employment contract.
- ☐ This agreement can become a separate written agreement.

(4) What activities are barred?
- ☐ Actual service to the company's clients in own or another company
- ☐ Solicitation of clients personally, or by any company receiving information supplied by your company's employee
- ☐ Interference with the relationship between the company and its client
- ☐ Disclosure of any company information not approved by the Board of Directors
- ☐ Inducement of other employees to leave the company

(5) Which clients will be covered?
- ☐ Previous and existing clients
  - —Clients existing when employment ends
  - —Clients existing anytime during the employee's association with the company
  - —Clients the employees had professional contact with while working for your company
  - —Former clients who were clients anytime during the last year of employment
- ☐ Prospective clients
  - —With whom the employee had contact during employment in your company
  - —As listed by your company in writing and shown to the employee before or when ending employment
  - —Those the company has submitted a proposal for professional services to, whether at any time during the employment of the employee, during the last year of employment, or during some other specific time

(6) Are time and space limitations included?
- ☐ None
- ☐ Within a specific number of years after ending employment
- ☐ Within a specific geographical area of any company facility
- ☐ Within the city, county, or state where the employee worked

(7) Which state laws must you consider?
- ☐ State(s) where the employee works and resides
- ☐ State where your company has its principal office or facility
- ☐ Other state(s) where your company has offices or facilities

(8) Are sanctions specified?
- ☐ Money damages
  - —Actual damages
  - —Liquidated or fixed damages
  - —Sharing between company and employee of billings and profits
- ☐ Forfeiture of rights and benefits
- ☐ Arbitration
- ☐ Legal action

—Injunction

—Declaratory judgment

(9) Other Important Factors

☐ Difficulties of enforcing the provisions of the agreement, including

—Noncompetition agreements conflict with a social and economic policy favoring competition.

—Courts are reluctant to put people out of work or to deny them an income.

—Enforcement of an agreement is by injunction that places a heavy burden of proof on the employer.

—Unless restrictive covenants are reasonable (i.e., carefully limited in time and geographic reach), courts will strike them down as unenforceable or as contrary to public policy.

☐ Revision or waiver if the employee shows special hardship that makes it difficult for the employee to practice a highly specialized profession outside the company

☐ Reformation of covenant by the court to make it enforceable

☐ Separate compensation to the employee for compliance

☐ Assignability of covenant by the company but not by the employee

---

■ EMPLOYMENT AGREEMENT TO PROTECT TRADE SECRETS

When your company's employees have access to or knowledge of trade secrets or other confidential information, it's to your benefit to have them sign an agreement not to disclose that information either while they are employed by your company or after their employment ends. This agreement requires their signature and must be placed in personnel files. Your corporate attorneys, human resource specialists, and Board of Directors need cooperative development of this agreement. First, however, you must understand that this type of agreement serves both manufacturing and service industries. For example, the landmark court case deciding this issue said that a trade secret includes a formula, pattern, device, or compilation of information that is used in a business and that gives the company an opportunity to obtain advantage over competitors who do not know or use it (*Rimes v. Club Corporation of America*, Tex. Civ. App., 542 S.W.2d 909, 913). In addition, it includes a plan or process, tool, mechanism, or compound known only to its owner and those employees to whom it is necessary to confide it, or teach about it. Finally, a trade secret is secret formula or process not patented, but known only to certain persons using it in compounding some article of trade. Exhibit 9-2 shows a checklist for a trade secret agreement.

Exhibit 9-2
Checklist for Trade Secret Agreement

☐ Date

☐ Name and address of the employee

☐ Agreement that the employee will keep confidential the following information unless otherwise directed by your company's Board of Directors:

—Customer lists or confidential data concerning customers

—Confidential mechanical data, such as notes or memorandums and letters

—Confidential research and development data, such as drawings or plans

—Manufacturing processes, chemical formulas, and the composition of the company's product

—Any discussion from the recollection of these factors, or those over-heard

☐ Disclosure and assignment to the company by the employee of any rights to all improvements, discoveries, and inventions whether they were

—Made on company time or during off-duty hours or

—Patentable, conceived, devised, made, developed, or perfected during employment with the company

☐ Requirement that the employee helps the company in obtaining any domestic or foreign patents it is willing or able to get

☐ Continuation of the agreement after ending employment

☐ Requirement that the employee return any confidential material upon ending employment

☐ Stipulation that the agreement is enforceable by the company, its subsidiaries, affiliates, successors, and assigns

☐ Signatures of employee, representative of the corporation, and witness

---

■ FIVE STEPS TO PROTECT TRADE SECRETS

An important test for determining whether information or a special process is a trade secret stems from the steps you have taken to protect the security of the information. Courts have found that the following factors will tend to indicate the existence of a trade secret:

   1. Barring the public generally from the production area (if your company conducts tours, using screens and partitions around any machines used in the secret process)

   2. Not publicly exhibiting the machines, describing them in any publication, or selling them to other persons or companies

   3. Forbidding access to the area to employees who do not work on the machines

   4. Giving employees access only to those parts of drawings and specifications that directly concern their work so that only a few employees know all the details of the process

   5. Calling for employees to sign written agreements informing them of the confidentiality of the process and containing their promise not to disclose any information about the process that they may acquire during employment. Exhibit 9-3 shows a checklist for trade secret security.

Exhibit 9-3
Checklist for Trade Secret Security Program

The following checklist supplies you with 23 key points to help you to create an effective trade secret security program. You need to

   1. Establish basic determination of sensitive and nonsensitive information according to function, project, and other aspects specific to your company.

   2. Develop standards for assessment of specific dangers of prospective violations of information security.

   3. Prepare effective corporate policies and procedures and an addendum to your security manual.

   4. Ensure that each employee signs a trade secret confidentiality agreement at the time of hiring.

   5. Include corporate statements of position on this issue in new-employee orientation manuals.

   6. Establish sign-out procedures for departing employees.

   7. Inform future employers of the agreement when they contact your company for references.

8. Display bulletin board reminder materials regarding the employee's responsibilities.

9. Place occasional articles in company newsletters dealing with trade secret security.

10. Include awareness and cautions as a regular part of the corporate training program.

11. Establish procedures for transferred, reassigned, reclassified, or promoted employees.

12. Ensure that trade secret agreements extend to consultants and others with access.

13. Establish procedures and forms for invention disclosure to employees, consultants, and others.

14. Develop a clearance program for external communications.

15. Provide adequate security for corporate books and records.

16. Document ownership and blueprint legends, usually by a rubber stamp.

17. Place legends on passes for the public, salespersons, repeated visitors, casual labor (company hired or otherwise), plant-tour members, and other persons as needed.

18. Establish procedures for dealing with governmental inspectors.

19. Establish procedures for dealing with outside personnel such as insurance underwriters, contractors and their work force, in-plant caterers, industrial cleaning, and maintenance staff.

20. Make agreements indicated by government contracts when applicable.

21. Supply instructions to personnel about requirements of the government, military, space agencies, or outside companies that your company has a relationship for security in regard to their confidential materials.

22. Make detailed reports about internal breaches of security regarding trade secrets.

23. Establish procedures for reporting and handling trade secret thefts, especially to various law enforcement agencies.

■ HOW TO PREVENT INFORMATION EMBEZZLEMENT: THE INVESTIGATIVE AUDIT

With increasing competition worldwide and higher operating costs, corporations can no longer make guesstimates about markets and competitors. After you have established a solid company policy dealing with information security, you need to create an effective way to deter and detect any information embezzlement activities. You do that with tailored investigative audit techniques and criminal investigations. Information security cannot become 100 percent because what human ingenuity can devise, other human ingenuity can penetrate. Your goal must be to make the penetration of your information security system quickly recognized or detected, a high risk, and unprofitable to the offender. Information is a powerful business commodity, and keeping it where it belongs requires your systematic, routine, and decisive management action.

■ ESTABLISHING INVESTIGATIVE AUDIT PRIORITIES

The key to tailoring your investigative audit priorities is to assess the information within your company while asking an important question: "If I were a corporation, what information would I want to have about my competitors or potential competitors?" You also need to consider that competitors will not always pose the greatest threat—other problems involve corporate raiders and corporate acquisition or hostile takeover specialists, who have an insatiable appetite for information so they can assess the victim company's vulnerability. In the following sections, I discuss the most common priority business areas, how offenders can embezzle information from them, and how to curtail the problem and create strong preventive techniques.

Obtaining Competitive Intelligence

According to surveys conducted by the University of Pittsburgh (one of the foremost academic centers on business competitive intelligence activities), most major American companies spend about $250,000 each year getting information about their competition. Other companies, normally smaller, spend less but get heavily involved; and many foreign corporations surpass that amount. While most companies obtain competitive intelligence ethically, many others do not follow ethical standards, and some overzealous executives or employees step over the line. Brokers of competitive information also pose a problem—while most have legitimate and legal sources, others have less selective standards.

Controlling The Infamous Fax Machine

Besides the computer, facsimile machines have probably had the greatest effect on business communications. The phrase "fax it to me" is common in offices throughout the world. The fax machine has also become one of the major tools for the corporate information embezzler. For example, formerly information embezzlers had to copy or photograph documents, which subjected them to notice by other employees or internal surveillance equipment and security personnel. Next, embezzlers had to carry the documents from the workplace in a briefcase, handbag, or on their person. Today, however, information embezzlers can simply fax the document or documents (including writing, pictures, drawings, and notes) to their blackmarket purchasers. In many companies, sophisticated fax machines have a preset number capability designed to fax a document automatically to multiple locations simultaneously. A skilled information embezzler might program in the telephone number of the competitor or broker buying the information, and each item faxed out to corporate offices and facilities throughout the country or around the world automatically will go to a competitor.

Another technique is for embezzlers to send the fax themselves. Many companies have fax machines in every department, in copier rooms, and even on a desktop to speed business communications. In many companies it's easier for an employee to fax documents than to use a copy machine. Computers also have fax capabilities as well as traditional upload and download capabilities through a modem. With the proliferation of desktop computers in modern companies (even when those computers are not equipped for faxing or are equipped with a modem), any employee with minimal computer literacy can convert his or her desktop computer to fax capability. In doing this, information embezzlers can appear to be hard at work on a project and be faxing entire databases to their competitor buyer. Using a modem, the employee can download your company's data into the competitor's computer in seconds or a few minutes without any trace of having stolen the information.

Other fax problems stem from mobile fax machines and cellular telephones. Salespeople or other company representatives who travel can transmit their orders, memorandums, or other materials by fax from their car. They can also fax the information to a competitor, who buys it from them. For example, a salesperson can fax the same information to the buyer, who would have an interest in who the customer is, what they're buying, the pricing, and other information. That competitor can immediately develop a scheme to steal the customer by giving them a better deal.

This problem also extends to buyers, auditors, supervisors, and others who fax information to their company from their car or a motel room. They can easily fax it to their information buyer simultaneously without fear of detection within an office environment.

■ FIVE INVESTIGATIVE AUDIT TECHNIQUES

The best audit trail that supplies a beginning point in the fax problem is the company telephone bills. Start with the bills that list toll calls from the fax machine number. To perform this task, you should use a computer because the procedure should become a routine investigative audit technique. When the audit involves an employee who travels, using a fax in his or her motel room or in a vehicle, the telephone bill might supply valuable information. For example, traveling employees will either have a company cellular phone or their own, with the company reimbursing them for its use. Either way, the company must receive the call record and bill, even when in an expense account claim. Motel bills submitted with the expense account also show toll calls, and if there's no number shown, you can obtain that information from employees who submitted the bills.

1. Audit the Company's Telephone Bills

Audit the company's telephone bills, especially those numbers assigned to the fax machines and computers equipped with outgoing modems first. Although nontoll calls won't show on the listing of outgoing calls during the past month, you might find some not readily identified as legitimate, and this supplies you with a valid a starting point. Your corporate computer center, marketing and sales department, accounting and purchasing department, and others (depending on the configuration of your company) can supply you with all the names and telephone numbers of legitimate numbers often called.

2. Compare Unknown Numbers

When you find unidentified telephone numbers called from within your company on fax and computer system lines, compare them first with known competitors. For numbers of competitors unlisted in telephone books or other records, you can determine the location and telephone subscriber through a variety of database services available through legitimate information services, or through a criss-cross telephone number directory available commercially.

3. Determine Quantity of Information Outgoing

After screening and identifying numbers from the company's telephone service bills for fax and computer service lines, if you find any calls to a competitor, there's little doubt that your company has an information embezzler within. You can often determine the quantity of information outgoing to the competitor on that date by noting the seconds or minutes the call lasted.

4. Compare Employee Work Logs

When you have determined the date and length of the fax or computer time on the line, compare that with work logs throughout the company for that day. For example, you need to identify what the embezzler transmitted to your competitor, when possible. Begin with one department and work through each. Although you might find one work project that fits, continue your search because you need to ensure that no others exist.

5. Identify Each Employee with Opportunity

When you identify the probable information transmitted to a competitor, you will have narrowed the suspect to a specific department unless the document was circulated and others had access to it. When that happens, you will need to identify each employee who could have sent out the information. Frequently, you will find loose controls and have a long list of possible offenders.

■ SEVEN COUNTERMEASURES TO INFORMATION EMBEZZLEMENT

Although your investigative audit must be a routine preventive procedure, its purpose is to identify offender opportunities and employees that might be embezzling company information. When detecting these opportunities, you must immediately establish countermeasures, which may include the following:

1. Create a strict security policy for use of fax machines or computers with fax capability and for communicating with other computers using a modem.

2. Appoint a responsible employee (with alternates) as custodians or fax supervisors. These employees should be the only ones allowed to transmit or operate the machines.

3. Limit and tightly control all computers that have the capability of faxing or communicating with other computers using a modem.

4. Ensure the routine use of a fax cover or transmittal sheet, and make sure that it is kept on file by the fax supervisor. The fax operator or supervisor should also note on the cover sheet that he or she inspected the documents faxed and that they contained no restrictive classification.

5. Obtain written consent when sensitive information must be authorized by a CEO or designated representative. That authorization should be in writing and stapled to the cover sheet when it is placed on file.

6. Maintain a log of all materials faxed either by computer or machine. Exhibit 9-4 shows this type log or register.

7. Routinely monitor and verify all telephone toll calls for fax machines and computers.

Exhibit 9-4
Model Fax or Computer Data Transmittal Log

(File Maintained by Fax and Computer Data Supervisor)

ABC Corporation
Any City

Facsimile and Computer Transmittal Log

Person Sending Fax or Data
_____

Department or Division
_____

Time and Date
_____

Category and Classification of Document or Data
_____

Transmission of Document Authorized By:
_____

I have examined the document/data and believe it to be as represented. Authorization is verified.
_____

Signature of Fax or Data Supervisor

■ DOCUMENT AND INFORMATION CONTROLS

You need to create a comprehensive system of information control that generally denies access to any employee or other person who does not have a legitimate need to know. You also need to establish your information control program so it remains effective but does not impede operational efficiency. Although no program can guarantee that information embezzlers will not take high risks, a sound classification system for corporate information will generally curtail activities for even the most enthusiastic embezzlers. In the following guidelines, I'll show you one program to consider. However, you might need more stringent or less stringent controls depending on your situation and the threat of loss resulting from information embezzlement. The guidelines presented enable you to increase or decrease the controls anytime according to your corporate needs.

■ CREATING A "NEED TO KNOW" SYSTEM

Many aspects of corporate document and information control systems appear mechanical, but these appearances are misleading. Security must be an alert, live process to establish an effective company defense again information embezzlement or protect against careless disclosure of sensitive information (resulting in profit-damaging losses and gains to competitors). Creating your information control system must begin with a viable, effective information clearance program.

This phase of information security involves deciding who in your company has a need to know certain types and amounts of information. For example, a general knowledge among employees about a research and development program and its budget will lead to helping, instead of preempting, your competition. Access to the documents and other information involved in that program can lead quickly to embezzlement opportunities. If your company spends $2 million on a research and development program, a competitor might pay handsomely for that information because it not only profits from your company's costs, but can also put a similar, may be improved product on the market simultaneously or earlier. Your clearance program development begins by first classifying your company's documents and information.

▪ DOCUMENT AND INFORMATION CLASSIFICATION PROGRAM

A corporate document and information classification program should include the following four categories. However, you might need more or less depending on your specific needs.

Category A Classification would include all the most sensitive company information, such as R&D, budgets, marketing programs, sales information, customer lists, expansion plans, and other data that would clearly supply a competitor with preempting information and create long-term losses for your company.

Category B Classification would include sensitive information, but data more employees might need access to. This category normally includes certain personnel records, because when a competitor can learn specific qualifications of key personnel, it might be able to determine what your company plans to do in the marketplace. For example, a research and development engineer who specializes in a specific type of research that might be revealed in his records.

Category C Classification might include information such as procedural manuals and certain company policies, some personnel records, and other data that you do not want disseminated outside the company. A set of procedural manuals, for example, would save a competitor significant amounts of money, because it could copy yours and avoid the cost of preparing its own. In so doing, the competitor also gets into the market quickly and can mimic your company's success.

Category D Classification would include most routine company information. Although it might not have any real value to a competitor, the classification is necessary to establish an effective control program.

▪ ESTABLISHING EFFECTIVE DISSEMINATION CONTROL SYSTEMS

When you have decided the guidelines for continuing, routine classification criteria for your company's information, you need to supply each employee with an access code (for example, which employees can access Category A information, and so on). That access code must be noted on employees' personnel files and on a general company roster that each employee receives. Each change—such as new employees, those retiring and leaving the company, or those fired or resigning—can go to each employee as a supplement, and the entire roster can be consolidated and published each year.

Coupled with the roster, you should have an awareness training session to inform employees why the system is important. Tell them that they must all help ensure that the systems works (by reporting any suspected violation and adhering to the classification rules) so that the company is successful and they keep their jobs. Companies that experience heavy information embezzlement might suffer losses that lead to cuts and layoffs. However, with a clear, effective, and routine information classification program in place and a strong employee awareness of how it works and why it's important, information embezzlement can be prevented or stopped.

How to Control the "Need to Know" Factor

Another phase in your control system includes assigning prefixes, suffixes, or both to the employee access classification according to your needs. For a good information control system to have the best and maximum effect, you must further restrict access on a "need to know" principle. For example, research and development employees with a Category A clearance do not need access to all the company's Category A information. They should not have access to other research and development projects that have no effect on their project. This process further reduces the opportunity to become an information embezzler, or inadvertently supply company information to a competitor (such as an employee bragging about company expansion, or telling a family member or friend about a new product line in development).

Prefix and Suffix Principles

Your prefix can help control access by making it clear to employees who has a need to know within the information categories. You must develop this phase according to the configuration of your company. For example, you can assign blocks of prefixes or suffixes to various departments in the company, and those numbers could allow authorized access to information of other departments but also restrict information from other departments. An employee in the Marketing Division might have a Category B classification and be authorized to view foreign sales information that has the numbers 1 through 10 access suffixes. The manager of the Marketing Division might decide that certain foreign sales personnel need to see certain information, but not all. He or she classifies the data as B-1, B-2, B-3, and so forth. For instance, the category B-1 might be available only when the Marketing

Division manager can show that an employee has a B classification, plus a strong need to know, designated by the suffix 1. Whatever method you adopt, the key element to remember is to make your company information unaccessible as a whole and prevent those inclined to embezzle company information from doing so. You also protect your company's sensitive and routine information from unintentional harm, such as gossip over lunch or at cocktail parties, remarks to friends and relatives, and other possible information leaks.

■ GUIDELINES FOR IDENTIFYING COMPANY DOCUMENTS AND INFORMATION

With your category and classification system controlling your company information and documents, it's time to consider how you're going to identify which document is which. The following guidelines supply you with techniques to consider or modify to satisfy your needs.

1. Each document should have a stamp showing the category applicable to it, coupled with applicable notations that might show when the document will no longer remain in that category. For example, "This Category A document will become a Category C document on April 21, 0000."

2. Develop distinctive cover sheets for documents and staple them to the document when feasible. It's hard to remove and replace a staple exactly, and if the cover is folded back for copying, you will be able to detect it. See Exhibit 9-5 for an example of a sensitive document or file cover sheet. Also see Exhibit 9-6 for examples of how you can mark and identify your classified company information documents and files.

■ DOCUMENT AND INFORMATION STORAGE

Another necessity for your company information is secure storage (files). It does no good to categorize information and classify it on a need to know basis but leave it open to access by anyone. Your filing must have a double lock system for at least categories A and B information. Two people must be involved in this system. One person knows the combination or has the key to one lock while the other can access the second lock. Neither can access both locks. Alternative file custodians can access the storage only with combinations or keys locked in a sealed envelope maintained in the CEO's safe and used only when the primary custodians cannot both be present at the workplace. Files and storage should only be accessed during normal business hours and not during nonbusiness hours. Also, a file or document container

Exhibit 9-5
Model Restricted Use Document Cover

ABC Corporation
Any City

RESTRICTED DOCUMENT

WARNING

THIS DOCUMENT IS THE PROPERTY OF THE ABC CORPORATION.

UNAUTHORIZED USE OR DISCLOSURE IS PROHIBITED BY

COMPANY POLICY AND STATE CIVIL AND CRIMINAL STATUTES.

Category _____

Exhibit 9-6
Model Marking and Identifying Categories and Classification
of Sensitive Company Documents

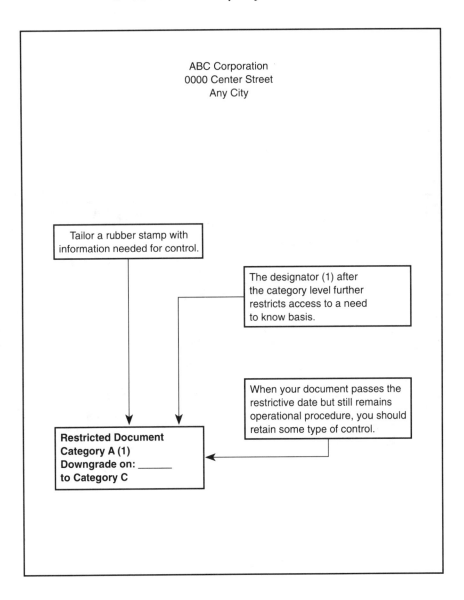

should contain only one classification category. Depending on how extensive your sensitive information files are, you might assign one drawer per category as opposed to the entire cabinet. However, you should not mix the categories within a single drawer. You can properly store sensitive and classified company information in heavy file-safes, or convert existing or standard files to increased security containers.

■ SIGN-OUT AND SIGN-IN LOGS FOR SENSITIVE INFORMATION

You should have the same custodians who are responsible for the double lock system keep a sign-out and sign-in log that's also maintained in the files. When an authorized employee needs a file, he or she signs the custodian's log, and when the file returns the custodian inspects it for completeness, logs it in, and files it. It's important that the documents and files signed out be described well, including how many documents are within a file. Exhibit 9-7 shows guidelines for creating an effective sign-out and sign-in log.

■ CONDUCTING YOUR INVESTIGATIVE AUDIT

Your investigative audit determines compliance with the company's information control systems, including related policies and procedures. Your audit must include the following steps as a minimum:

- Make audits to determine compliance by employees.
- Ensure that information receives proper categorization and classification procedures.
- Determine whether the information has proper storage and safeguards.
- Ensure that documents have clear markings showing their category.
- Ensure that there's a master access roster with supplements.
- Determine that employees know and understand the company policies.
- Ensure that information has restrictive, preventive controls such as sign-out and sign-in logs.
- Ensure employees' compliance with controls of fax and computer transmissions.

Exhibit 9-7
Model Sign-Out and Sign-In Document or File Control Log

Department/Division

_____

Description of Document or File—Category and Classification

_____

Sign-Out

Person Receiving Document or File

_____

I certify the accuracy of the description above and acknowledge receipt and
accept responsibility of the file or documents.

Signature

_____

Document or File Custodian releasing document or file

_____

Sign-In

I certify that the document or file described above was returned intact with no
differences noted unless otherwise shown below.

Signature of custodian receiving document or file

_____

Date _____   Time _____

Discrepancies:

■ THREE EFFECTIVE TYPES OF INVESTIGATIVE AUDITS

Because securing and controlling corporate information has different ramifications and security breaches can rarely be prosecuted, your investigative

audit techniques must be tailored to your situation. Depending on the situation you need to decide which audit technique to use: (1) announced audits, (2) unannounced audits, or (3) penetration-type audits.

1. Announced Investigative Audits

Announced investigative audits involve notice to department heads, which enable them to ensure that their area of responsibility is in order. This announcement often acts as a deterrent, and areas that are not meeting company standards or are dragging their feet in compliance will come in line with desired standards. Remember, your investigative audit serves as a preventive measure.

2. Unannounced Investigative Audits

Certain selected persons, such as the head of a division or department, might know in advance about an unannounced investigative audit, but they will have strict instructions not to notify other employees about it. The purpose of your audit is to correct deficiencies; and an unannounced audit is best when you suspect information embezzlement. It's a good idea to conduct an unannounced audit soon after an announced audit. This gives embezzlers enough time to return to their acts, believing that you will not conduct another audit for quite some time.

3. Penetration Investigative Audits

A penetration investigative audit also is useful when you suspect complacency in a specific area of the company about information control systems. This type of audit normally calls for bringing a new undercover employee into the division or department without notifying anyone (including the department manager) and having him or her test the system. When the undercover employee reports discrepancies or noncompliance, an unannounced audit using that information will often expose embezzlement or opportunities for embezzlement or information leaks.

The following checklist Exhibit 9-8 serves as a guide for conducting investigative audits of your company's document and information control systems. After answering all questions, you can better assess your company's vulnerability and compliance with company policies and procedures, and develop viable solutions to correct weaknesses in the systems.

Exhibit 9-8
Checklist for Investigative Audits of Information Control Systems

1. Storage Files
   - ☐ How is the most sensitive information stored?
   - ☐ Describe the containers, including size, weight, type of locking devices, and approximate entry delay time.
   - ☐ Do the storage files require two persons present to open the container?
   - ☐ Are storage files secured during nonbusiness hours, thereby denying access?
   - ☐ Do sensitive information Category A files have a log of file contents inside folder?
   - ☐ Are sign-out and sign-in logs kept in the files, filled out by the custodian, and signed by the employee checking out the file?
   - ☐ Are the files checked and audited by the custodian when returned by an employee?
   - ☐ Are file documents stamped with category and classification?
   - ☐ Are cover sheets used for single documents when taken from the file and stapled?
   - ☐ Are combinations to files written on calendars or other places where they could be accessed by unauthorized employees (or keys kept in a desk drawer)?
   - ☐ Do sensitive information file containers (cabinets) have a log inside that shows each time and date a file is opened and closed and is signed by both designated custodians?
   - ☐ Is the file storage container checked each day even when not opened?
   - ☐ Are separate file cabinets or containers used to store different categories of sensitive information?

2. Logs and Registers
   - ☐ Are logs or registers kept in containers and filled out for time and date each time the cabinet is opened or closed, including the signatures of the designated custodians performing the task? (See Exhibit 9-9 for an example of this log sheet.)

☐ Do sensitive information files have a log of file folder contents inside folder? (See Exhibit 9-10 for an example of the file log or register.)

☐ Are sign-out and sign-in logs kept in the files, filled out by the custodian, and signed by the employee checking out the file?

☐ Do entries in sign-out logs fully identify the file documents?

☐ Is a file inventory card left in place of the file before it is released to an employee?

☐ Are the files checked and audited for content by the custodian when returned by an employee?

☐ Are file documents stamped with category and classification?

☐ Are cover sheets used for single documents when taken from the file and stapled?

☐ Are files shredded when no longer needed and not placed in permanent storage?

☐ Are duplicate files shredded when not needed?

☐ Are signatures and writing on logs and registers consistent with designated file custodians?

3. Distribution and Use of Sensitive Company Information

☐ Are documents and files sent to other company facilities or offices sent as registered mail or registered through couriers or express services?

☐ Are receipt forms used?

☐ When documents are mailed or sent by courier service, do employees use a double envelope?

☐ Is a file of post office or courier service receipts maintained?

☐ Do employees requesting sensitive company information have the proper clearance and authorization?

☐ Are cover sheets used to cover sensitive information out of files and not in use?

☐ Do sensitive information custodians allow files to be used during nonduty hours?

4. Reproduction of Sensitive Company Information

☐ Are company employees or others reproducing sensitive information?

☐ If so, who authorizes the reproduction?

☐ Are documents and information files categorized and classified according to their own content?

☐ When printing sensitive information, do employees properly safeguard printer and typewriter ribbons?

☐ If a printing process is used for reproducing sensitive information (i.e., manuals and long reports necessary for wide use within the company), how are matrices, copies, excess copies, waste, etc. protected from unauthorized disclosure?

☐ If carbon paper is used, do employees shred it immediately?

☐ Are drafts of documents containing sensitive information properly protected?

5. Categories, Classification, and Marking Procedures

☐ Do files or groups of physically connected documents bear the overall classification of the highest classified components? (That is, when a file has ten documents in Category C and one document in Category A, the file classification must be Category A. When a manual has Category C and D classification, but has one page or section in Category A, the entire manual must be classified as Category A.)

☐ Are extracts or parts of sensitive information documents properly marked with the security classification?

☐ Are documents and paragraphs containing restricted data or formerly restricted data properly marked?

☐ How are photographs, films, recordings, charts, maps, and drawings containing sensitive information marked?

☐ How is the classification indicated on materials, products, or their containers?

☐ How is material for training purposes marked?

6. Regrading and Declassification

☐ What procedure is used for prompt review and regrading of all sensitive company information?

☐ Are regrading instructions understood by department managers, file custodians, and employees?

☐ Are regrading instructions placed on documents?

☐ Have documents and files been properly regraded according to company policy?

☐ How is authority obtained for regrading documents improperly classified?

7. Destruction Procedures
☐ Who is the person or persons authorized to destroy sensitive and classified company information?
☐ Are shredders used?
☐ Is the destruction of sensitive documents and files witnessed by an executive or board member?
☐ Are proper records of destruction maintained? Who keeps them? Is the authority for destruction shown?

Exhibit 9-9
Model Document and File Container Control and Accountability Log

Document Container _____   Department _____

Designated Custodian(s)

_____

_____

	Open		Closed
Time	_____	Time	_____
Date	_____	Date	_____
By	_____	By	_____
Time	_____	Time	_____
Date	_____	Date	_____
By	_____	By	_____

Exhibit 9-10
Model File Folder Contents Register

(Placed inside File Jacket for Accountability, Control, and Audit Purposes)

File Control Level

Category _____   Classification _____

File Contents

Description of Document	Category and Classification

Chapter Ten
Embezzlement of Corporate Assets by Organized Crime Syndicates

When we hear the term *organized crime*, we immediately imagine crude men with crooked noses wearing blue pin-striped suits and white neckties and driving black sedans. Much of this learned image stems from scores of movies and television shows and has nothing to do with organized crime's systematic effort to infiltrate and often take over important aspects of corporations. In this chapter, I'll show you how subtle the threat of organized crime can be in your company, how to identify such threats, and how to detect and prevent the problem and take the right actions when you encounter it. This chapter deals with organized crime syndicates that target legitimate corporations using embezzlement schemes and not involving violence, extortion, or other illicit activities.

The information and guidance in this chapter encompasses a broad range of entities and all corporate environments. The Investigative Audit Action section for each item discussed shows the corporate environment in which organized crime embezzlement activity will prevail:

- Parent corporation
- Subsidiary company
- Corporate division or group
- Corporate industrial plant
- Corporation owning more than 50 percent of the equity stock in another company
- Corporation having ownership control of another company but not having operating control

- Corporation having a joint venture interest with another corporation
- Corporation owning less than 50 percent of the equity stock in another company.

When your investigative audits detect organized crime, or when you're creating preventive countermeasures, consider focusing your attention on key divisions in the targeted company: accounting, sales, production, personnel, research and development, purchasing, or others according to the business conducted and scope of the company. Each of these divisions poses lucrative infiltration points for organized crime syndicates. Focus on the accounting division for problems regarding taxes, payroll, fraud, SEC problems or compliance reporting; focus on the sales division for FTC problems, price fixing, price discrimination, bribes, FCPA issues, contracts, or kickbacks.

■ INSIGHTS INTO THE ORGANIZED CRIME THREAT

Organized crime is a conspiratorial crime that has certain characteristics of formal organizations and sometimes involves the hierarchical coordination of several persons in the planning and execution of illegal acts, or in the pursuit of a legitimate objective by unlawful means. Organized crime involves continuous commitment by key members, although some persons with specialized skills may participate only briefly in the ongoing conspiracies. It's primary goal is economic gain, though some of the participants in the conspiracy may aspire to power or status. Organized crime is not entirely synonymous with the Mafia or La Cosa Nostra, although those traditional concepts of organized crime also target corporations as their victims. Often, the organized crime syndicate or group hierarchy stays within an ethnic framework as a safeguard, believing that "one's own kind" offers the most reliability and loyalty and lacks the natural prejudice of the human race. However, as the syndicates expand, they recruit underlings of all types, especially those who have purely mercenary motives and do not aspire to lead or make strategic decisions on behalf of the organized crime syndicate.

Organized criminals have regularly and increasingly attached themselves to legitimate business enterprises. Today, many organized syndicates spring from a group of people who, years ago, might have chosen instead to create a shoplifting ring, been conpeople, or sold swampland to unsuspecting victims. Now, however, they focus on bilking corporations. This category of white collar crime syndicates (as opposed to the Mafia, etc.) has found it much easier and more profitable to prey on corporations. The risk factor is almost

nonexistent because corporations, even when they know a major embezzlement of their assets occurred, will be reluctant to bring it to the attention of
law enforcement and the public.

■ THE BUSINESS-LIKE STRUCTURE OF ORGANIZED CRIME SYNDICATES

Organized crime features the characteristics of a formal business organization, including a division of labor, coordination of activities through rules and
codes, and an allocation of tasks to various roles to achieve certain goals. The
organization seeks profit from crime (although today the acts often do not
appear to be crimes) and tries to preserve itself in the face of external and
internal threats.

Although in years past organized crime focused primarily on overtly
illegal activities such as illicit gambling, narcotics, loansharking, extortion,
and others, today these pursuits are used mostly as a source of steady cash
flow. Organized crime elements have found that as much (if not more) money
can generate from seemingly legitimate and respectable businesses and aggressive white collar crime operations. Involvement in the business community calls for structuring much like that of a contemporary corporation, with
a chairperson of the board, a board of directors, president, chief executive
officer (CEO), vice-presidents (each in charge of a division), and an organizational chart similar to that of any conglomerate.

One question about the structure of organized crime in the United States
is whether it is organized at the national level or only at the local level. This
issue has been hotly debated for years. The answer becomes apparent when
you understand the concept of organized crime syndicates and switch from
a traditional perception of overtly illegal activities to those involving white
collar crime that victimizes the business world. The overt illegal activities
normally are localized while the illicit business enterprises extend nationally
(however, they are regularly veiled even from other organized crime syndicates).

Motives of organized crime syndicates in the business world also
play a role in the structuring (for example, whether the infiltration of
legitimate businesses is designed to support other illegal activities, such
as laundering money and supplying a cover for traditional criminal activities, or whether the business stands alone to produce added income for
the syndicate). A third motive often involves siphoning corporate assets,
thereby creating justification for insurance bonding claims, and moving
the company into bankruptcy. To protect your company from becoming a

victim of organized crime, you need to consider these three primary motives as well as others.

One of the glaring examples of organized crime involvement in business is the recent savings and loan scandal. Traditional thinking blames the collapse on management. However, if we look further we find clearly that management did not operate alone in this scheme. As you read this chapter, you will see some remarkable correlations with the S&L scandal (especially in later sections outlining categories that signal corporate distress and identifying internal organized crime activity). Keep in mind that organized crime syndicates can involve any group of people who conspire to embezzle, and the term must not always be linked to the Godfather image we have come to associate with organized crime. Exhibit 10-1 shows the typical structure of a Mafia-type organized crime syndicate. Exhibit 10-2 shows a non-Mafia-type organized crime syndicate.

■ HOW SYNDICATES CHOOSE THEIR VICTIM CORPORATIONS

Organized crime syndicates consider various aspects of potential embezzlement targets. Their scrutiny includes the form and value of property (including money, securities, information, or materials) and the vulnerability of the intended victim company. Some companies or entities will prove more prone to victimization than others because they have characteristics or situations that make them especially vulnerable.

■ HOW SYNDICATES INFILTRATE CORPORATIONS

Surprisingly, corporations rarely recognize that an organized crime syndicate has selected them to become their victim. The crime of embezzlement, especially when engineered by an organized syndicate targeting a corporation, will normally have a long-term goal of siphoning money or materials that convert to money, as opposed to short-term objectives.

Most organized crime syndicates will try to recruit established employees to take part in the scheme because the person already has a salary (and so does not require up-front money) and has intimate knowledge of the internal mechanics of the targeted corporation. When no existing employee is available for the organized crime syndicate's embezzlement schemes, the syndicate will often recruit someone from another company or a person looking for a job and try to place him or her in the targeted company's employ.

Exhibit 10-1
Structure of a Typical Mafia-Type Organized Crime Group

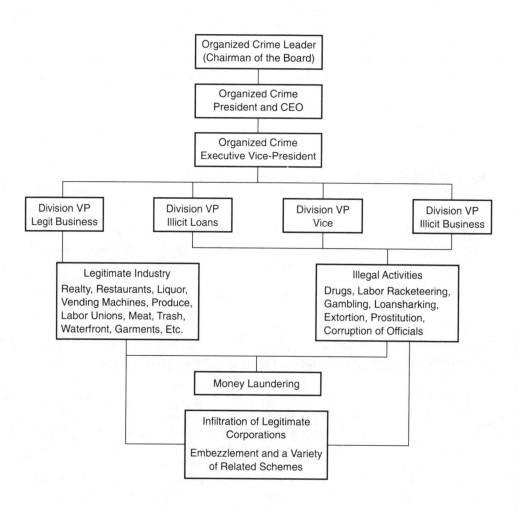

Exhibit 10-2
Structure of a Typical Non-Mafia Organized Crime Group

Leader(s):
Often two or three persons
skilled in fraud, embezzlement,
and other types of white collar crimes.
Normally one of these persons will become
the dominant leader: however, often they
share responsibilities according to expertise
and criminal activity experience.

VP for Administrative Activities:
Supervises a staff of accountants,
computer operators, clerks, and
others. Often, many of these
employees don't know of their
employer's involvement in
organized criminal activity.

VP for Targeting:
This person supervises a staff of con
artists who research and choose the
best corporate "marks" and conduct
research and recruiting activities.
Devises the best schemes for
corporate embezzlement.

VP in Charge of Cover Businesses:
This person supervises a group of
small businesses. Some are
legitimate, and others are "paper"
companies to create an appearance of
legitimacy and serve the efforts of the
group's fraud and embezzlement.

VP in Charge of Corporate
Embezzlement Activities within a
variety of companies:
Often the money will be channeled
through the series of companies set up
by this criminal group, with breakout
companies established to break the
audit trail if discovered.

■ EMPLOYEES WHO MAKE THE BEST EMBEZZLEMENT CANDIDATES FOR ORGANIZED CRIME

Organized crime syndicates look for several types of employees as possible candidates for collusion in embezzlement schemes. Likely participants normally include those employees who have gambling or other costly vices, or who are disgruntled or can easily become disgruntled with persuasive nudging by organized crime.

One of the organized crime's favorite techniques for recruiting corporate employees with costly vices, credit problems, and a taste for living beyond their means involves an organized crime member who "helps" such employees into deeply compromising positions and then offer to bail them out *if* the employees agree to take part in illicit activities. Normally, the well-crafted scheme creates a compromising position for the often unwitting employee. This deflects attention from the syndicate and ensures that the employee will make a firm commitment to the syndicate.

Employees not inclined to expensive lifestyles or vices, but who languish in dead-end jobs or have large families to support, college tuition to pay, and so forth may succumb when an organized crime staffer approaches them with a better offer. Normally, the employee needs to earn more money just to make ends meet and does not see any real future with the company. This can result from lack of sufficient formal education or training, age, past problems, or some other situation that precludes a higher income.

Organized crime groups looking for an opportunity to infiltrate a corporate entity also seek out respectable employees who have legitimate pressing financial problems that they perceive as nonsharable. It is not so much the objective severity of the problem that is crucial, but how the person defines his or her situation. For example, a situation that one person sees as highly disturbing and that he or she is unable to communicate to others may be handled with ease by someone else.

However, organized crime groups may develop information about such corporate employees through "moles" in banks and other creditor institutions and offer to help surreptitiously through a seemingly legitimate enterprise. Some of these enterprises include loan companies that might operate legitimately but also serve organized crime. For example, such organizations may send people advertisements that tell them that the loan company has preapproved a loan, and all they have to do is ask for the money by signing and returning the papers, and check will return to them quickly. The person in need of immediate money follows up on the advertisement and fills out a sheaf of personal information and gets the loan. The organized crime group knows that the loan solves the person's immediate problem; however, the debt must be repaid. The syndicate sends a representative to contact the person directly but confidentially, normally at work. The representative will act as a sympathetic person; the person is amazed because the representative knows all about his or her personal problems. The next step is to recruit the person with promises of increased income for helping with some simple task, which will compromise the person and put him or her in the organized crime group's pocket.

Although regularly an organized crime syndicate will have multiple employees within a company working for it, rarely will the employees themselves know that this is the case. People will tend to remain most loyal to the scheme when they believe that no other employees are involved. When they believe that other employees also have become involved in a scheme, they suspect that the organized crime group has somehow double-crossed them.

■ HOW SYNDICATES EMBEZZLE FROM CORPORATIONS

Although organized crime syndicates directly embezzle money, materials, and information from corporations, their objectives and goals are often subtle. The recruited corporate employees, for example, might influence company decisions such as expansions that require construction of new buildings, facilities, and plants. The organized crime syndicate might own or have schemes operating inside the construction companies "selected" to do the work. The company might buy certain pieces of property owned by the syndicate.

A common organized crime syndicate scheme involves embezzling information from moles inside a corporation about where a company plans to expand. For example, a company might instruct its real estate buyers to find an appropriate piece of property suitable for building a new manufacturing plant. When the organized crime syndicate receives that information well before the real estate buyers have had time to scout locations, it finds all the property that is suitable, makes generous offers to the owners, and backs the deal with a large deposit of "good faith" cash that's nonrefundable. Once the syndicate has "optioned" the real estate, the owners cannot sell it to the company. Instead, the company must come to the organized crime syndicate, which poses as a legitimate development or investment company. Because the syndicate knows all about the company's plans and how much the company is willing to spend for the land, the syndicate can tell the company that although there are other plans for the property (specifically, a plant construction project for another company), it is in the best interest of the community for the company to have the land. The price is set at the maximum that the company budgeted, and everyone is happy. The organized crime syndicate makes a heavy profit for "releasing" their option or continues with the sale and sells it directly to the company, whichever scheme nets the most money.

Often, depending on the syndicate's knowledge of how badly the company wants the property and plant (from moles inside the corporation), the land deal includes an acquisition agreement with the company that specifies use of the construction company, landscaping contractor, equipment supplier, maintenance contractor, and others owned or otherwise associated with the organized crime syndicate. Although on the surface these suppliers might appear legitimate, they all have some direct or indirect connection to the organized crime syndicate. Through this often intricate maze of dealings, the organized crime syndicate siphons off your corporation's money, regularly through a variety of seemingly unrelated but linked transactions. This happens because of well-placed corporate employees who work for the syndicate and receive added salaries, bonuses, and a variety of other promises.

Other similar activities include advertising contracts, marketing deals, supplier arrangements, and other activities that can come from both inside information and from key employees who can influence decisions and ensure that the company's activities move in conformance with the organized crime syndicate's direction.

■ SEVEN CATEGORIES SIGNALING CORPORATE DISTRESS

Your investigative audit activity can often detect distress signals involving corporations, their subsidiaries, or diversified plants and facilities that have been infiltrated and are surreptitiously controlled by organized crime syndicates. The following checklist supplies you with common indicators signaling distress within specific categories as well as the investigative audit action to be taken.

1. Business Activities

- Inventory increasing out of proportion to the sales increase or, even worse, inventory increasing when sales are declining.

Look for overbuying of materials or products from a specific company. Organized crime might have infiltrated sufficiently to control buying and have the purchases directed to a syndicate company. You might find that buyers have received erroneous information or requests for materials or products from another department. Find out why the buyers have increased inventory, and if you are satisfied that they have acted on requests from elsewhere in the company, trace the requests and compare with justifications and authorizations.

- Perception that the company is not responding to changes in the marketplace, to the demands of personnel, or to new ways of doing things.

First look at personnel changes in key positions and in marketing. Always remember that leadership might have acted on misleading information supplied by someone else in the company. Investigate where guidance from the head office went and if it reached management or became conveniently "lost" or "held back" by an underling. For example, a secretary or even a mail clerk on the organized crime rolls might screen incoming mail and information and simply trash it or replace it with misinformation.

- Actual performance that is largely different from projections.

Check to see who was responsible for the projections and what information and reasoning was used to create the data.

- Business plans based on highly optimistic sales levels.

Take a serious look at the sales department and look for links to outside influences such as organized crime connections. Often, a high forecast will depend on pledged business from another company. If so, find out background information about that company and if the order pledge has merit or if the company is only on paper and is a creation of organized crime.

- Major new equipment purchases.

First, investigate the source of the equipment and determine if the supplying company is legitimate or was formed recently. Also, check prices paid for the equipment (looking for competitive figures), and survey the equipment quality against industry standards. Determine if your company or subsidiary has bought equipment, parts, or maintenance from the company before. Organized crime might have influenced purchasing decisions to benefit a syndicate company, or a company it will receive kickbacks from.

2. Financial Activities

■ Frequent check account overdrafts.

Look at the cancelled checks and their endorsements, and match invoices to checks. Find out who received the checks and why, and then investigate the payee to ensure that it's a legitimate transaction. You might find a check that's disguised as a legitimate transaction to persons or companies linked to some organized crime syndicate.

■ Any debtor having over 29 percent of receivables or 15 percent of sales.

Whenever you find this situation, there's clear collusion. Organized crime may have significant influence in purchasing decisions. Develop a detailed background investigation on the company and its owners.

■ Large loans to the subsidiary or company.

First, determine who the loans come from and if there's any connection between that financial institution and organized crime. There might be a scheme to lend excessive amounts of money and then offer a cheap buyout for the amount owed as opposed to the real value.

■ Creditors' pressure on company to sell stock.

This situation is linked to the loan action noted earlier, in that company controlled stock might be demanded as payment or as collateral. If the loan is called, the financial institution might have also discreetly bought large blocks of public stock and gained control or taken over the company.

■ Liens put on assets by creditors or the IRS.

You need to determine why the bills weren't paid, and you will probably trace the problem to some form of embezzlement.

■ Inability to provide timely financial statements.

This is a clear indication that leadership or those responsible for creating the financial statements are dragging their feet to cover something unfavorable, like embezzlement loss. You need to find those responsible for the statements and determine why they're not timely. That action will probably lead you to the cause and persons involved in some type of embezzlement.

■ If a loan is secured, inability to provide timely accounts receivable and accounts payable aging.

Look for embezzlement activity and who granted the loan. Determine if the activity involves a takeover attempt (by putting the company in default and then negotiating a settlement or extension based on agreement to place employees of an organized crime syndicate in key positions in the company and on the board of directors). The company or subsidiary can accept the deal and become a puppet to the syndicate, or declare bankruptcy and have the syndicate as a primary creditor who siphons off more money from the scheme.

3. Communications with Lenders

- Failure to respond promptly to telephone calls.

You might find this information by talking to secretaries or others in the company who receive telephone calls. Many of these employees maintain a telephone log or copies of the memorandum of calls received and call-back requests for the person a lender tries to reach. When you have a list, contact the caller and ascertain the problem.

- Increased amount of calls from vendors.

Use the same techniques discussed earlier. You might also detect a dramatic drop in business given to traditional vendors with no apparent reason or complaint. When this is the case, and in the case of late payment or nonpayment, go to invoices and determine the vendor(s) now receiving that business and check them for possible links to an organized crime syndicate.

- Too busy to agree to prompt appointments.

Avoiding appointments also indicates pressure and control from an outside source. This source slowly tightens the grip on a business, including approving and disapproving who management will talk to.

- Frequent requests for new loans.

Acquiring capital to stay operational or postpone bankruptcy indicates organized crime involvement, especially when the syndicate's purpose is solely to siphon off money and materials convertible to money. The longer the business remains operational, through legitimate loans, the more assets can go to the syndicate. Talk to the lending institution and review the reasons stated for the loans, review the financial statement submitted, and compare that information to the company records.

- Request to restructure a loan.

Follow the same course of action as for frequent loan requests.

4. Communications Concerning the Business

- Announcements regarding technical problems with products.

This action can create a seemingly legitimate problem to justify bankruptcy. It can also show an effort to create legitimacy by using substandard materials in products making them defective. Keep in mind, however, that there can be legitimate errors causing the problem. But if there are technical problems as well as other problems with manufacturing or products, you probably have discovered another element of the organized crime scheme.

- Announcements of computer problems as a reason for failure to provide information.

This might serve the same purposes as technical problems with products.

- Announcements of major new investments.

Investigate fully what the new investments encompass, and you might uncover a scheme to siphon assets through an investment that appears legitimate but involves an organized crime scheme. Examples include real estate, equipment, or some other move to transfer corporate funds in a seemingly legitimate way.

- Announcements of major new products that may mean going into production too early.

Examine the marketability of the new product and the reasons for rushing it to the marketplace. This might be part of an effort to legitimize a planned business failure by blaming poor judgment and management instead of the real reason—embezzlement.

5. Accounts Payable and Receivable

- Increase in over-sixty-days accounts payable as a percentage of payables over the previous level.

This is a clear sign of a movement toward a declaration of bankruptcy, and a clear sign that embezzlement within the company has occurred and continues to take place.

■   Over 5 percent of the total accounts receivable exceeds 90 days.

One type of organized crime involvement and embezzlement includes large and steady purchases of materials or products that the syndicate has no intention of paying for. Instead, the syndicate will sell off the purchased items cheaply, and it makes the money—not the selling company.

■   Sixty-days accounts receivable is over 15 percent of the total.

Examine the problem in light of the same probable causes noted for the preceding two items.

6. Financial Reports

■   Company growing over 40 percent a year in net sales.

Excessive growth might occur in a small company; however, growth rate will stay consistent with the market, the products, and (most importantly) the size of the company in the previous year. For example, when a company has a high-demand product and in the previous year did little business, it's possible that there will be a high growth jump. However, for a company that does not fall into that category, if there is a sudden jump in growth, two factors will become apparent. First, the books are cooked or inflated with false figures; or second, some element has made huge purchases as part of a scheme to defraud the company, with no intention of paying for the items.

■   Decreasing sales.

An organized crime syndicate might have a takeover in mind, but it needs to place the company in severe financial strife. Investigate why sales have dropped, especially when the staff and method remain consistent, the products remain in demand, and there's no new competition that would cause this. The decrease might have internal reasons. For example, employees recruited by an organized crime group may have been told to slow the sales to devalue the company and put it in financial trouble. The syndicate would then make an offer to take over the company, or would present a bailout opportunity that involves making a loan, stipulating placement of syndicate people on the board and in key leadership roles, and a variety of other moves that put the syndicate in control.

■   Decreasing pretax profits.

This is another indicator with the same motivations as for decreasing sales.

- New intangibles, such as goodwill, appearing on the balance sheet.

This activity will surely indicate "puffing" the company value. However, in addition to poor management, it might also show a means of concealing embezzlement activity and prolonging outside knowledge that the company is moving to bankruptcy declaration.

- Any abrupt change in key areas of the balance sheet.

This element can signal a plan for selling or declaring bankruptcy, and normally indicates that embezzlement activities have become commonplace.

- Meaningful shifts in key profit and loss categories as a percentage of net sales.

This is similar to the preceding items.

7. Personnel

- Key employees leaving the company.

When key employees leave the company, talk to them and find out why. Often, when an organized crime syndicate gains enough control over a company, those who are loyal to operating a legitimate business and who have unbendable integrity must go.

- Several newly hired executives.

This is related to the departure of key employees. Determine who the new executives are, their background, and other qualifications. When an organized crime takeover begins, the old executives must leave, especially when they do not want to be corrupted and new executives who are puppets of the syndicate enter the key management positions.

- Significant changes in the board of directors.

Investigate this carefully, especially when there's no apparent reason for the changes and when new executives are hired and those in place previously are leaving suddenly. Keep in mind that this could be linked to a necessary reorganization with legitimate reasons. However, you can normally trace the backgrounds of the new board members easily, and this will tell you what you need to know.

■   Several new promotions.

This might be linked to the aforementioned personnel changes. Keep in mind that organized crime syndicates do not announce their takeover or control. Instead, they gradually infiltrate and keep outward appearances normal. However, their success in these schemes depends on loyalty to them, employee greed, and having loyal employees in controlling positions (because each operational part of a company links to another). The scheme cannot work if only some key positions are in syndicate control.

■   Significant restructuring with promotions and higher salaries.

This activity is related to the aforementioned items.

■   Key employees taking extraordinary salaries and "perks."

Buying loyalty, or rewarding cooperation from the inside, always depends on the greed of the persons that organized crime syndicates corrupt or recruit to install in a company. Although seemingly legitimate and often blamed on poor management, excessive salaries and perks become a part of the embezzlement scheme. In a large operation, large salaries and perks might be one of many or the only embezzlement scheme, with the syndicate receiving a significant payoff percentage of the salaries. For example, an executive normally earning $150,000 receives an increase to $250,000 and pays 50 percent of the increase to the syndicate. When multiplied by the number of executives and down through the other key positions (adding some bonuses as perks), both the syndicate and the corrupted employees profit.

■   Chief executive officer often absent or appearing bored.

Investigate this problem, especially when there's no clear personal problems and no apparent lack of interest, because you will probably find that the CEO has become a puppet of an organized crime syndicate who keeps him or her in place as a figurehead to legitimize the scheme. That person will undoubtedly become the "fall guy" when and if the company collapses from the excessive embezzlement activities. (Remember the S&L scandals.)

■   Labor union strife.

With a growing white collar unionization movement (discussed earlier in this book), as well as the traditional labor unions, labor union strife can become a tool of the organized crime syndicate. It's no secret that organized crime groups infiltrate and control many elements of labor unions. They do that in much the same way as they infiltrate businesses. When the organized crime scheme needs the cooperation of a company that has unions throughout or in key parts of the business, the unions can exert a great persuasive pressure to bring about this cooperation. Although the strife might have legitimate grounds, investigate it carefully to determine the linkage, if any, to an organized crime effort.

- Relatives added to the payroll.

Include as part of your investigative audit a search for relatives on a company payroll. Examine carefully their positions. When you find a steady hiring of relatives, an organized embezzlement scheme might be developing or already in place.

- Disputes among top management.

This could signal a conflict between the corrupt and noncorruptable in top management positions. Examine this carefully.

■ EIGHT-POINT INVESTIGATIVE AUDIT FOR IDENTIFYING INTERNAL ORGANIZED CRIME ACTIVITY

Your aggressive investigative audit program can often detect the presence of an organized crime syndicate operating within your company through employees the syndicate recruited. You must be aware of the conditions and events that signal the existence of these schemes. Normally, they fall within one of the eight following areas of activities: management behavior, business conditions, deterioration of earnings, internal accounting control, operating performance, personnel policy, relations with outside parties, and audit field work. Remember that the organized crime elements might choose only one division, department, subsidiary, or other internal operation instead of the entire company. Much of their targeting scheme depends on the size and type of company. The investigative audit action following each point below shows the most prevalent corporate environment for the applicable indicator of organized crime syndicate embezzlement activity:

Type of Corporation:

(1) Parent corporation
(2) Subsidiary corporation
(3) Corporate division or group

(4) Corporate industrial plant

(5) Corporation owning more than 50 percent of the equity stock in another company

(6) Corporation having ownership control of another company but not having operating control

(7) Corporation having a joint venture interest with another corporation

(8) Corporation owning less than 50 percent of the equity stock in another company.

Point 1. Management Behavior Checklist

The following conditions and events relating to management behavior may signal the presence of an organized crime syndicate's fraudulent and embezzlement schemes:

■ A senior management executive who dominates specific or all operating decisions within his or her area of responsibility. This characteristic becomes apparent when the executive demands that he or she personally approves or disapproves each detail and micromanages his or her department, division, or subsidiary. This executive may also go through the motions of listening to advice but will not heed it even when it's obvious that the suggestion would improve operations.

This situation normally involves types 1 through 8 in the preceding list. Although some people become stricken with their ego and position, most senior executives have sufficient age and experience to know that they alone cannot run a company. When executives want to run the show alone, you will normally find that they are in a position far beyond their capability and they fear failure, or they think that this type of management will scare off any questions. Often, this behavior also indicates organized crime involvement. The only way the person can ensure that nothing goes wrong and that things go in the direction that the syndicate wants is to demand total personal control. When you suspect organized crime involvement, recommend a transfer or a sizeable period away from the position (two or three months) to attend school or manage some other company project. The absence and stand-in replacement might reveal the truth of the situation, especially when no other information develops from other sources.

■ An ineffective board of directors and/or audit committee. When an organized crime syndicate manages to have a solid grip on the targeted corporation, the board of directors and audit committee might also become a hand-picked figurehead hierarchy. Normally, this happens most often in a subsidiary company established or acquired by a major corporation as part of its conglomerate.

This action clearly signals that some organized crime group has moved to gain surreptitious control of the company. It is primarily found in types 4 through 7.

- Indications that management is overriding significant integral account-ing controls. This indicator becomes apparent during your investiga-tive audit, which looks for compliance standards according to corporate policies and procedures. For example, managers with a certain amount of autonomy clearly do things "their way" as opposed to following headquarter's desires and instructions.

This effort to "cook the books" also signals that some significant embez-zlement scheme has begun or is developing. Your effort here must focus on documenting clear evidence of repeated and deliberate noncompliance, de-livering it to the corporate hierarchy, and suggesting immediate management restructuring. You might also find proof of embezzlement that already has begun. This situation involves types 1 and 3 through 7.

- Compensation or meaningful stock options tied to reported perfor-mance or to specific transactions over which senior management has actual or implied control.

Look for policies that restrict award of compensation or stock options to key employees based on their performance and ratings that do not coincide with company records reflecting the same performance levels. For example, the director of production receives laudatory performance ratings from top management when company records show flawed or decreased production levels. Compensation (bonuses) and stock options are among the favorite forms of organized embezzlement activities that can lead to control of a company and further embezzlement schemes. This situation involves types 4 through 7.

- Indications of personal financial difficulties of senior management.

Your investigative audit must review the financial status of senior management when looking for the probability of organized crime involve-ment. Executives in financial trouble will try to conceal their difficulty and turn to unconventional sources of money to bail them out. Often, these unconventional sources include organized crime loan sharks, who charge large amounts of interest. The person in trouble gets immediate relief, but greater problems ensue that becomes oppressive to a person, giving them immediate relief but greater problems ensue later because of the high interest. Organized crime groups might be willing to forgive a debt or put it on hold in return for the executive diverting company money or commodities in the ways noted earlier, which enables the group to begin a systematic infiltration of the company. This situation involves types 1 through 7.

- Proxy contents involving control of the company or senior management's continuance, compensation, or status. This element often targets subsidiaries or distant operating facilities of a major corporation.

Gaining control of the company by organized crime schemes often involves gaining control of the stock and proxy voting power. You must watch for these indications, which might signal a hostile organized crime takeover or enable control of the company sufficiently to divert assets and stifle competition of vendors by diverting business to organized crime companies or those they control. This situation involves types 1 and 4 through 7.

Point 2. Business Conditions Checklist

Certain business conditions can exert unusual pressures. You must consider the presence of an organized crime syndicate fraud and embezzlement scheme when your investigative audit detects the following conditions:

- Inadequate working capital.

When company performance and records show you that working capital should be present but is inadequate, search for where it went. Siphoning off capital will never be readily apparent, but might include investments such as real estate, hiring more employees than needed, buying new and needless equipment, expansions, hiring obscure consultants at high fees, hiring outside marketing assistance when not relevant, and a variety of other possibilities. Trace the origins and control of these areas, and you will probably find links to organized crime. When you do find links or suspect organized crime's involvement, determine any links between employees and any control by organized crime groups. This situation involves types 2 and 4 through 8.

- Minimal flexibility in debt restriction, such as working capital ratios and limits on more borrowing.

Your investigative audit relating to this links to inadequate working capital.

- Rapid expansion of a product or business line more than industry averages.

When a business decision makes no sense and puts the company in jeopardy, you can expect that it has something to do with an organized crime embezzlement scheme. This situation involves types 5 through 8.

- A major investment of the company's resources in an industry noted for rapid change, such as a high-technology industry.

This problem calls for the same general investigative action as noted earlier. Look for some subtle embezzlement scheme and remember that embezzlement can take many forms. This situation involves types 5 through 8.

- Unfavorable economic conditions within the geographic area of operations, distribution, and marketing.

Look for signs that organized crime has influenced the creation of conditions either to stifle competition or to force the company to submit to organized crime's scheme. This situation involves types 2 and 5 through 8.

- Unusually heavy competition.

Your action must be the same as noted above.

- Significant litigation.

Look at the reasons for this litigation. You might find that it is a subtle way of embezzling money from the company. This might become especially important when your examination finds that a law firm not traditionally used by the company is hired at high fees to handle the problem. For example, an organized crime syndicate (operating through "cover" companies or persons who do not have any traditional links to criminal activities) brings a stream of lawsuits against the company. The company knows that in a court situation it stands a good chance of winning. However, instead of using in-house or regular law firms, top management goes to a new law firm and hires it to defend the company's position. Since civil lawsuits can continue for years, the company pays huge sums of money to the law firm, while organized crime owns or controls that firm. This is one of those created forms of subtle embezzlement that does not look like embezzlement in the records of the company. It involves types 2 and 5 through 8.

- Pressures to sell the company or merge with another enterprise.

This is a move by the organized crime group after applying a variety of ways to "soften" up the company. Most often the syndicate will want to buy the company cheaply to strip it of assets and declare bankruptcy, or merge it with one of the other companies it owns or controls (to increase the capability of embezzling larger amounts of money or products). This involves types 5 through 8.

- Dependence on a limited number of products or services.

This can tip you to an organized crime scheme that first ensures that organized crime gets all the company's business through their own suppliers. As time passes they gradually increase prices to siphon off company money. Look for these and other indicators and link them to organized crime syndicates. This involves types 2 and 5 through 8.

Point 3. Deterioration of Earnings

The quality of earnings may deteriorate, and that may signal fraud and embezzlement. Such a deterioration may appear with the following conditions:

- A decline in the volume of quality of sales (e.g., increased credit risk or sales at or below cost).

This might lead you to find key employees in the pocket of organized crime who have been directed to slow down company sales. Several motives might surface, including stifling the company as a competitor to another company that organized crime owns or controls, softening the company for a takeover either openly through a cover or surreptitiously by infiltration, or forcing the company to hire one of the syndicate's "consulting or marketing firms" for high fees that will "get the company back on track." This involves types 1 and 4 through 7.

- Significant changes in business practices.

When there's no particular reason for the change and there is not a new head officer, there may be an outside influence of organized crime. Search for the stated reason, and then you probably can link it to the organized crime source. This involves types 4 through 7.

Point 4. Internal Accounting Control

The failure to correct known material weaknesses in internal accounting control that could be corrected on a practical basis may signal the possibility of fraud and embezzlement. This includes the following:

■   Access to computer equipment or electronic data entry devices that is
    not adequately controlled.

When you find little or no controls for access to computer equipment
and all data (including a lack of coded entry restrictions), look for reasons
beyond an ignorance of security measures. With the proliferation of computer
dependence within corporations, all executives or those who advise them
understand the clear need for security of data. When they ignore that action,
there's a reason beyond ignorance and it's often a form of embezzlement. This
allows organized crime syndicates access to the data files of the company and
enables a person from a remote location to alter company records, transfer
funds, divert property, and pay invoices from bogus "paper" companies. This
involves types 1 through 7.

Point 5. Operating Performance

During operations, certain conditions and events may signal the possibility
of fraud and embezzlement. These include the following:

■   Severe losses from major investments.

Determine the credibility of investments and who authorized and controlled them, as well as their standing when the investment occurred. If it's
clear that the investment was at best uncertain at the beginning, identify the
true reason it occurred (such as a means of siphoning off corporate money in
ways that appear legitimate or as poor management decision making). This
involves types 1 and 4 through 7.

■   Excess idle capacity.

When there's an unexplained and unwarranted slowdown in company
operations, you can probably ascertain that it's deliberate and why it has
happened. You probably will link it to some organized crime syndicate
scheme that is making a move on the company through its infiltrated or
recruited employees. This involves types 1 through 7.

■   Severe obsolescence of inventories.

A company that retains a large inventory of obsolete products may be
padding its value. You will want to check the current products and compare
your count and calculation against the balance sheet to determine its accuracy.
If you find that the company books have been padded with unrealistic values
based on obsolete inventory, an organized crime scheme might be in progress,

especially when a variety of other indicators have attracted your attention. This involves types 1 through 7.

- Excessive increases in inventory.

Trace the reasons and sources of the excessive inventory increases. You need to search for the source and compare it first with traditional sources. If the purchases occurred at traditional suppliers, check the purchase orders for authorization, and determine the status of the supplier (who might have experienced a clandestine takeover recently, or been infiltrated and controlled by an organized crime group). If the orders were placed at a new group of suppliers, determine why and who controls that company or companies. This involves types 1 through 7.

- A complex corporate structure that is unwarranted by the company's operations or size.

An unjustifiably complex structure in the company will probably make it difficult for you to focus on who's responsible for specific decisions or who's in charge. This technique of confusing the lines of communication in a company often signals the surreptitious control of organized crime, and probably serves as a means of embezzling funds or materials. This involves types 4 through 7.

- Widely dispersed business locations accompanied by a highly decentralized management with an inadequate responsibility reporting system.

This type situation, coupled with weak performance and a decline (either apparent or hidden) within inflated balance sheets and other company financial information, signals the presence of widespread embezzlement activities. It involves types 4 through 7.

Point 6. Personnel Policy

The existence of fraud and embezzlement may appear through certain characteristics of personnel policies and related transactions, such as the following:

- Certain company employees working unusual hours, forgoing vacation, or working substantial overtime without valid justification.

This symptom clearly indicates organized crime infiltration and probable embezzlement activities controlled by certain employees. Look for this situation, and normally you will find hidden declines in the same operations. Overtime hours often serve as another form of cloaked embezzlement and point to organized siphoning of corporate money (when the overtime is widespread, significant, and consistent). This involves types 1 through 7.

- High turnover rate in key financial positions such as treasurer or controller.

This situation can easily point to employees who would not go along with covering up embezzlement activities or who the organized crime bosses did not want in the picture. It involves types 1 through 7.

- Inadequate screening practices and procedures when hiring key personnel.

Look at procedures in hiring, such as verifying application information. This should uncover additional data, including credit, financial status, civil or criminal problems, and other pertinent information according to organized crime's control and influence within the company. This involves types 1 through 8.

- Material transactions with related parties when such transactions may involve conflicts of interest.

Whenever you find evidence of clear conflict of interest action by executives or others, you might also find indicators of embezzlement and organized crime involvement (for example, purchasing from a company that has a reputation for poor products, taking action that might help a competitor, and other management activity that appears out of the ordinary and for which there is no reasonable strategy or reason). This involves types 1 through 8.

Point 7. Relations with Outside Parties

Evidence of organized crime fraud and embezzlement may surface through a review of the company's relations with outside parties. Your investigative audit must be attentive to the following:

- Frequent changes of independent auditors and legal counsel.

This action can reveal people who are uncooperative with organized crime embezzlement schemes or an effort to limit the knowledge of illegal activities to one person. Research such people and interview them about their knowledge of the situation and reasons given for their dismissal. This involves types 1 through 7.

- Unusually large payments to services supplied in the ordinary course of business by lawyers, consultants, agents, and others (including employees).

Investigate the legitimacy of those supplying services, their normal rates, credentials, and affiliations. Try to obtain a list of other clients they work for and how much charged, and identify the other clients and their business standing. Other companies might also be targeted and worked by the organized crime group simultaneously. This involves types 1 through 7.

- Use of several different banks beyond normal requirements.

Examine this activity carefully because it might show you a regular transfer of company money from one account to another in addition to excessive expenditures. This activity will often serve the organized crime embezzlement scheme by concealing transactions within a maze of accounts and account activity that becomes confusing and difficult to verify. It can also show the presence of "kiting," which makes the company's liquid assets appear greater than they are and normally leads to a disclosure of embezzlement.

Point 8. Audit Field work

The conditions and events described earlier will generally be noted during the actual field work of an operations or financial audit. However, certain tests and procedures done during a particular audit may signal the possibility of fraud and embezzlement.

- Analytical review procedures disclosing important unexplained fluctuations, such as the following:

  Material account balances

  Financial or operational interrelationships

  Physical inventory variances

  Inventory turnover rates.
- Difficulty in obtaining audit evidence about the following:

  Unusual or unexplained entries

  Incomplete or missing documentation and authorization

  Changes in documentations or accounts.
- Unreasonable or evasive responses of management to audit inquiries.

■ HOW SYNDICATES SYSTEMATICALLY DRAIN CORPORATE ASSETS

When companies fail because of organized crime involvement, the failure is normally sudden because companies cover their embezzlement activities, as noted in the preceding checklists. Most corporate failures presided over by organized crime syndicates are not predictable, and the blame regularly falls on a variety of other influences such as the economy or political climate, bad management or bad luck. Actually, corporate failures resulting from organized crime schemes rarely occur suddenly. Instead, they are caused by a long path of managerial, financial, operational, and strategic activities that manifest themselves through symptoms that are rarely detected or are ignored by management.

Exhibit 10-3 shows common techniques that organized crime syndicates use to siphon off company assets and lead companies into bankruptcy, which is masked as mismanagement. Your investigative audit based on earlier indicators can create preventive countermeasures against this type of systematic takeover and destruction. Using the checklist in Exhibit 10-3, you can find solutions to the organized crime threat and bring the company back to solvency. This checklist supplies you with the tools to prevent this type of clandestine takeover. Include them in your work list during investigative audits.

Exhibit 10-3
Common Techniques That Lead to Bankruptcy

Poor Management—by Chance or Design?
- ☐ Gradual autocratic rule by a chief executive officer (CEO)
    - (1) Does the CEO have a normal desire to achieve, or is there no apparent reason for this attitude?
    - (2) Has the corporation become too large to be managed safely by one person?
- ☐ Lack of participation by board of directors, and interest only in the areas of specialty instead of in the corporation as a whole
- ☐ Imbalance in skills and specialties of officers and boards (i.e., too many marketing experts and not enough financial experts)
- ☐ Inadequate level of management below board of directors
- ☐ No one above the chief executive, who becomes accountable only to him or herself

Defective Information System

- ☐ Budgetary control inadequate or absent
- ☐ Cash flow forecasts out of date or absent
- ☐ Costing system is inaccurate, does not take the various types of cost into account, is misleading or absent
- ☐ Valuation of assets incorrect
    - (1) Nonassets treated as assets
    - (2) Overvaluation
    - (3) Failure to isolate true appreciation from inflation

Inadequate Response to Change

- ☐ Competitive trends or events
    - (1) Competitor's introduction of new products
    - (2) Opening of a new company in same industry
    - (3) Emergence of foreign low-cost producers
    - (4) Merger of two competitors
- ☐ Political change—local, national, and international
    - (1) Imposition of quotas, taxes, and duties
    - (2) New legislation
    - (3) Changes in attitudes of the government and consumers to business generally and certain industries specifically
- ☐ Economic change
    - (1) Major changes in values of foreign currencies
    - (2) Domestic economy—inflation, interest rates, etc.
    - (3) International monetary crisis
- ☐ Sociological changes
    - (1) Changes in attitudes of workers
    - (2) Changes in composition, life styles, needs, and tastes of consuming public
    - (3) Attitudes to pollution, consumer protection, employees' rights, and other issues
- ☐ Technological changes

Large projects beyond a Corporation's Resources and Abilities

- ☐ Error or design decisions that lead to underestimating costs and overestimating revenues, that magnify in a large project

☐ Corporations run by autocrats have a stronger tendency to enter obligations they may not be able to meet if things go wrong.

Overtrading

☐ A corporation expanding faster than its cash flow expands must borrow

☐ Turnover increasing faster than profits will lead to the loss of confidence of banks, which eventually will cut off a corporation's line of credit.

Amount of Leverage (Debt/Equity) beyond a Prudent Level

☐ An optimum level of leverage depends on interest rates for loan instruments, the corporation's prospects for growth, and its vulnerability to extreme downswings in profits.

☐ Too high a level of leverage makes a corporation vulnerable to normal business hazards, including severe or unforeseeable hazards.

Creative Accounting

☐ This involves inaccurate reporting of a corporation's adverse economic developments, motivated by either ignorance, optimism, or design as a means to impress lenders and commit fraud and embezzlement. It signals impending failure.

☐ Delayed accounts of bad news (subject to legal limits)

☐ Capitalization of research costs, training costs, and advance payments

☐ Continuation of dividend payments, even when needing new equity or loans for this

☐ Postponement of routine repairs until plan calls for major renovation (treated as capital)

☐ Accounts department instructed to treat extraordinary income as ordinary and ordinary costs as extraordinary whenever possible

☐ Significant overvaluation of assets

Symptoms of Declining Liquidity

☐ Decline of sales orders

☐ Sales below break-even level

☐ Raw materials more difficult to acquire

☐ Increasing difficulty in controlling expenses

☐ Increasing costs that cannot be passed on

- ☐ Decline in daily cash inflows
- ☐ Cash balances lower than normal
- ☐ Decline in working capital
- ☐ Increase in accounts receivable
- ☐ Decline in receivables turnover
- ☐ Decline in inventory turnover
- ☐ Inventories built up
- ☐ Increase in debt ration
- ☐ Funds from primary source of financing becoming limited
- ☐ Some corporate short-term debt not eligible for conversion into long-term funds
- ☐ Increase in accounts payable
- ☐ All or most assets pledged to secure existing debt

■ TIPS FOR RESTORING AN ORGANIZED CRIME INFILTRATED CORPORATION

Whenever your investigative audits reveal that organized crime has infiltrated a company, you must take immediate and drastic steps to salvage the business operations and credibility. Companies in this type of trouble can be saved if all restoration alternatives are studied, including the following:

- ■ Get organized and, if necessary, hire known legitimate outside consultants, such as lawyers, investment bankers, industry specialists, and accountants who have a proven track record working with troubled companies.

- ■ Attempt to restructure the company without formal bankruptcy proceedings, keeping in mind that creditors often force companies into bankruptcy (so prepare for that contingency). In certain cases, bankruptcy proceedings can serve effectively to restructure and rehabilitate a company.

- ■ Create internal teams to complete the needed tasks. Someone must work on the problem full time, and someone must run the business.

- ■ Designate new key company executives and personnel, a CEO, board of directors, controller, company counsel, and others to manage the company's response to the problem. Screen each person carefully to ensure that there is no organized crime involvement.

- Screen (and change as necessary) suppliers and other business affiliations.

- Screen other employees to the extent that is possible.

- Change all computer system access codes, and limit access to need to know.

- Change all bank accounts, consolidate funds, and limit access.

- Call in investments and reorganize the company investment policies with known brokers.

- When the company is in default on its debts, try to stay on the offensive and control the financial restructuring.

- Try to build cash to maintain flexibility by cutting any needless expenses and any expenses that organized crime used to siphon company assets.

- Stay realistic with projections. When explaining the company's troubles to creditors, unrealistic projections and the resulting loss of credibility can be devastating.

- Do not wait until the last minute to consider developing a final restructuring plan, because at that point there will be fewer options.

- If the company is privately owned, with principal shareholders whose financial affairs are intertwined with corporate affairs, be sure to address that relationship.

- When there are convincing reasons to put new money into the corporation or to convert debt to non-interest-bearing equity, attempt to borrow more money from creditors whose loans cannot be repaid. Often, the corporation's creditors represent the cheapest and most readily available capital source.

Exhibit 10-4 provides you with guideleines and procedures for preventing organized crime embezzlement activities in your corporation.

Exhibit 10-4
Guidelines for Preventing Organized Crime Embezzlement Activities

(1) Screen all employees of the corporation, including the CEO and board of directors, as much as necessary to ensure that there is no organized crime group affiliation in the past or present. Also ensure that employees have no apparent weaknesses that make them compromised easily, such as excessive personal debt and vices.

(2) Screen all companies, consultants, and others the company deals with to ensure that they have proven legitimacy and there's good reason to do business with them.

(3) Establish effective controls so that one person does not have the authority to make decisions that can lead to financial trouble or conflicts. Key decisions should also be approved by the parent company. Although this takes time, it decreases the probability that the company will become a target of organized crime. The fewer executives involved in decision making, the greater the probability.

(4) Conduct both traditional and investigative audits regularly and with a carefully designed plan. However, do not fall into a pattern. Whenever possible, keep audits and inventories unannounced (such as informing the company of scheduled audits happening on a timetable for the year, but not telling the company what section, division, or operation will be the target of the audit). It's best to decide this immediately before the audit, and it's wise to choose at random.

(5) Create an investigative audit work program tailored to the company that enables you systematically to detect the presence of embezzlement and organized crime involvement. The following checklist outlines the minimum audit steps to consider in creating your program (a manufacturing company or plant is used as the basis for these steps). You may alter this checklist as necessary, depending on your situation.

In General

- ☐ Obtain location balance sheet, exhibits, and vouchers for the month to be audited.
- ☐ Prepare or obtain a balance sheet for work papers and trace it to the plant or company ledger.
- ☐ Review entries to accounts as given in plant exhibits for several months and question all unusual entries to accounts.
- ☐ Prepare summary of approval authorizations.
- ☐ Consult the company's accounting manual and determine the company's adherence to record-retention periods.

Receivables

- ☐ Verify the account balance to detailed records.
- ☐ Investigate old items in the balance.
- ☐ Determine the types of transactions handled in the account.
- ☐ Review procedures for handling miscellaneous sales.
- ☐ Investigate noncash credits.

☐ Determine the sources of charges to the account.

☐ Obtain order cost schedules and test balances.

☐ Review sources of charges to the orders. Note expense allocations and pricing issues.

☐ Investigate order clearances to expenses.

☐ Review credit approvals.

☐ Determine whether proper controls are in effect regarding posting receivable registers.

☐ Consult the company accounting manual and determine adherence to record-retention periods.

Inventories (Including product in process)

☐ Verify the balance of each inventory account to detailed records by making a test check of the tape of electronic data processing (EDP) scrolls.

☐ Review material distributions.

☐ Examine the balance of the company records for

—Proper account classification of materials.

—Application of freight and other costs charged to account.

—Calculation of cost per unit. When standard values apply, note variations from current prices and trace the variance to the cost of shipments.

—Pricing of issues.

—Distribution of separate items.

■ Review work papers supporting calculation of usage of bulk materials.

■ Check normal usage data with production engineering or another group that supplies the data.

■ Test company issues for approval signatures and for information regarding the type of material used.

☐ Examine physical inventories.

—Check adherence to inventory schedules.

—Review physical inventory sheets. Test check calculations when engineering surveys are made.

—Trace the disposition of adjustments.

—Review the procedures involved in taking, reconciling, and adjusting inventories (noting proper division of responsibility).

☐ Review the balance of the company's records for slow-moving items. (Compare this with the plant's obsolescence review. Investigate significant items. All appropriate materials should be listed on the "recommended obsolescence" report.)

☐ Review last-in, first-out (LIFO).

—Verify entries on the LIFO receipts and production and inventory reports.

—Review the recosting procedures for product in process, worked materials, and finished goods.

  ■ Note the elimination of employees' plans expenses from the inventory value.

  ■ On a sampling basis, choose receipts that involved materials in transit (MIT) at year-end; ensure that they do not include MIT items as receipts in January–March.

  ■ In the costing of crude mixtures of other materials in product in process, see that there are LIFO value unit pers for December to January inventories per the company accounting procedures manual.

  ■ Review the balance of the company's records to check the addition of unloading charges and freight to items received from other plants.

  ■ Investigate any writedowns for market depreciation and any inventory revaluation adjustments.

☐ Review the cost-accounting system. Determine the reason for making clearances from product in process to accounts other than worked materials or finished goods inventories. Review the following:

—Allocation of expense to product

—Major expense items other than clearances from deferred charge orders

—Procedure for calculating material usage and determining ending inventories

—Handling of variances

—Valuation of material in process.

☐ Review the procedures for determining interdivision profit elimination. Verify amounts reported under the following captions:

—Direct cost reserves

—Unearned interdivision profits in inventory.

☐ Review the gross fixed-investment allocation procedure.

☐ Consult the company accounting manual and determine adherence to record-retention periods.

Special Orders

☐ Obtain a copy of all special order summaries and trace totals to the plant ledger.

☐ Obtain a copy of the description of the orders in those special order accounts that do not have summaries.

☐ Review authorizations. Check expenditures against the amount authorized.

☐ Obtain cost schedules for active orders during the period included in your investigative audit and for any closed orders of material amounts during the past year.

☐ Verify the trial balance or balance tape.

☐ Review sources of charges, particularly those clearing through the unclassified account.

☐ Review the method of expense allocation.

☐ Review the methods and bases of clearances from orders.

☐ Review the year-end analysis of special orders.

☐ Investigate major repair or arrangement jobs that were authorized because of a cost saving. Review the calculation of cost savings compared with discounted cash flow procedures. Determine the type of follow-up used to compare actual savings with the estimate.

☐ Consult the company accounting manual and determine whether record-retention periods are adhered to.

Special Manufacturing Orders

☐ Determine that the account is authorized in the locations chart of accounts.

☐ Review and determine whether approvals and instructions for each type of transaction have been followed.

Materials-in-Transit Accounts

☐ Reconcile the month-end balance of the account to the date of your investigative audit.

☐ Examine invoices held pending receipt of the receiving report.

☐ Investigate items that have been outstanding for thirty days or more.

☐ Review supplementary invoice payable registers clearing items from materials-in-transit accounts.

☐ Examine year-end receipts for items that should appear on the annual statement of MIT.

Accrued Liabilities

☐ Examine all receiving reports held pending receipt of an invoice.

☐ Review all accrual registers and trace totals to the plant ledger.

☐ Investigate old items.

☐ Examine separate accrual registers for MIT items.

Accrued Vacation and Shutdown Expenses

☐ Verify the accuracy of estimated expenses.

☐ Review accrual calculations and contract charges.

Home Office Entries

☐ Check monthly reconciliations.

☐ Review entries. Investigate unusual items. Trace unusual items through the general books.

Chapter Eleven
Recovery of Losses and Prosecution of Embezzlers Under RICO

This chapter examines one of the most powerful criminal and civil statutes in the federal and *most* state government arsenals. Although the statute was enacted primarily to diminish organized crime infiltration of legitimate businesses, it has served to convict business persons who are not the classic racketeers.

Throughout Part Two, I have discussed a variety of serious white collar crimes that victimize companies, as well as how to detect, investigate, prevent, and take positive corrective action. However, as we prepare to move into a new category of white collar crime that targets companies, I discuss some added solutions and remedies using the RICO statutes to recover your losses and prosecute perpetrators. I examine the acts prohibited by RICO, statutory construction problems engendered by its complex provisions, and its criminal and civil sanctions, including the powerful punitive measure called "forfeiture."

■ THE RACKETEER INFLUENCED AND CORRUPT ORGANIZATIONS ACT

The Racketeer Influenced and Corrupt Organizations Act (RICO) (18 United States Code §§ 1961–1968), effective October 15, 1970, originated in Congress to control organized crime but has become the federal government's major weapon in the fight against white collar crime. The concept of RICO stems from the perpetrator committing two acts classified as racketeering within a ten-year period. If convicted, the racketeer could receive imprisonment for twenty years (or for life, if the violation is based on a racketeering activity for which the penalty is life imprisonment). Through a rigid surgical procedure of "forfeiture," RICO not only poses an awesome potential for imprisonment to the racketeers who fall under its statutory sanctions, but it also permits the forfeiture of:

1. Any interest the racketeer acquired or maintained in violation of RICO
2. Any interest, security, claim, property, or contractual right that afforded him or her a source of influence over any enterprise he or she established, operated, controlled, conducted, or participated in the conduct of, in violation of RICO.

Simply put, RICO's unusual forfeiture provisions remove the illicit economic base from the hands of the racketeer, while its traditional provisions permit lengthy periods of incarceration. RICO immediately strikes both at the racketeers and at their illicit coffers.

RICO's language is complex and its provisions not readily understood by a simple reading of the statute. I will try to explain the mechanics of this law in comprehensive terms. I believe that you can use it effectively within your company as a strong tool to recover losses and prosecute those who prey on your corporate assets.

To fall within the coverage of RICO, the prohibited activities must concern an enterprise that engages in or affects interstate or foreign commerce. This includes all significant business enterprises, since they all have some effect on interstate commerce. The term *enterprise* includes not only persons, partnerships, corporations, and unions, but also any other legal entity or any group of persons associated with them, e.g., organized crime groups, groups of employees, and others).

Title IX of the Organized Crime Control Act of 1970 (Public Law No. 91-452) occurred in response to what Congress perceived as a threat to the American economy from the unchecked growth of organized crime groups. The Act's intention includes ways to remedy:

"defects in the evidence-gathering process of the law inhibiting the development of the admissible evidence necessary to bring criminal and other sanctions or remedies to bear on the unlawful activities of those engaged in organized crime and because the sanctions and remedies available to the Government are unnecessarily limited in scope and impact." (1970 U.S. Code Cong. & Ad. News at 1073)

The Racketeer Influenced and Corrupt Organizations Act was added to Title IX, U.S. Code to enable, first, punishment of individuals and second, separation of the defendants' corrupted enterprise from the criminal organization. The ambition of Congress was that RICO would permit prosecutors to revitalize corrupted interstate enterprises into legitimate businesses, instead of merely imposing a "compulsory retirement and promotion systems (within those enterprises) as new people intervene to replace those convicted."

RICO focuses on certain types of racketeering activities. When a person engages in two or more racketeering activities, the person is considered as engaging in a pattern of racketeering activity. A person engaged in racketeering activity commits a crime under RICO if he or she engages in any of four specified activities:

1. Use of income derived from a pattern of racketeering activity to acquire an enterprise or an interest in an enterprise (e.g., Chapter 10).

2. Acquisition of an interest in or control of an enterprise through a pattern of racketeering activity (e.g., Chapter 10).

3. Conduct of an enterprise's affairs through a pattern of racketeering activity.

4. Conspiracy to commit any of the first three acts.

■ ACTIVITIES PROHIBITED BY RICO

Section 1962, entitled "Prohibited Activities," is RICO's substantive offense section. Briefly stated, this statute is directed toward

1. The prevention of investment of illicit funds in legitimate enterprises engaged in or whose activities affect interstate or foreign commerce (18 U.S.C. § 1962 (a).

2. Preventing the acquisition, maintenance or control of an enterprise, engaged in or whose activities affect interstate or foreign commerce, through racketeering activity (18 U.S.C. § 1962 (b).

3. Elimination of carrying on or participating the affairs of an enterprise through racketeering activity (18 U.S.C. § 1962 (c).

Also, it is an offense to conspire to commit any of these (18 U.S.C. § 1962 (d).

■ "PREDICATE" ACTS DEFINED: STATE AND FEDERAL OFFENSES

To violate RICO, a person must commit any two of the enumerated state or federal crimes listed in 18 U.S.C. § 1961 (1) at least twice. These crimes are perceived by Congress as "racketeering" activities and characterized as "predicate offenses" by the courts. Subparagraph (a) and (b), immediately following, set forth the state and federal crimes enumerated in § 1961 (1):

1. Predicate State offenses include any chargeable felonious act or threat involving:

- Murder
- Kidnapping
- Gambling
- Arson
- Robbery
- Bribery
- Extortion
- Narcotics or other dangerous drugs

To constitute a state predicate offense, the act must be punishable by a prison term of more than one year. Furthermore, "State" includes any of the fifty states, the District of Columbia, the Commonwealth of Puerto Rico, any territory or possession of the United States, any political subdivision, or any department, agency or instrumentality of it (§ 1961 (2).

2. Predicate Federal Offenses (Generic Offense Description) Under Title 18

- Bribery
- Sports bribery
- Counterfeiting
- Felonious theft from interstate shipment
- Embezzlement from pension and welfare funds
- Extortionate credit transactions
- Fraud and related activity connected with access devices

- Transmission of gambling information
- Mail fraud
- Wire fraud
- Obstruction of justice
- Obstruction of criminal investigations
- Obstruction of state or local law enforcement
- Tampering with a witness, victim, or an informant
- Retaliating against a witness, victim, or an informant
- Interference with commerce, robbery or extortion (Hobbs Act)
- Racketeering (Travel Act)
- Interstate transportation of wagering paraphernalia
- Unlawful welfare fund payments
- Illegal gambling business
- Laundering of monetary instruments
- Monetary transactions in property derived from specified unlawful activity
- Use of interstate commerce facilities in the commission of murder-for-hire
- Sexual exploitation of children
- Interstate transportation of stolen motor vehicles
- Interstate transportation of stolen property
- Trafficking in certain motor vehicles or motor vehicle parts
- Trafficking in contraband cigarettes
- White slave traffic

Under Title 29

- Restrictions on payments and loans to labor organizations
- Embezzlement from union funds

Under Title 11

- Any offense involving fraud connected with a case under Title 11 (11 U.S.C. § 1 et seq.), in the sale of securities, or felonious manufacture, importation, receiving, concealment, buying, selling, or otherwise dealing in narcotics or other dangerous drugs.

Under the Bank Secrecy Act

The Comprehensive Crime Control Act made violations of Title II of the Bank Secrecy Act predicate acts for RICO liability.

Under the Bank Bribery Act

The Comprehensive Crime Control Act (1984) also adds violations of the federal bank bribery statute as predicate acts for RICO liability.

3. Descriptions of Federal Offenses are Generic in Nature

The preceding descriptions of federal crimes are generic. The courts have decided that these should be mere aids in identifying the content of a statute and should not limit the kinds of activities prosecutable under RICO (*United States v. Herring, 602 F.2d 1220 (5th Cir. 1979)*).

An indictment shows a predicate offense that the defendant violated an existing statute, although the description of the predicate offense in the indictment differs from *Herring*. The United States charged two persons with a RICO violation supported by the predicate substantive offenses of converting or fraudulently taking securities (violating 18 U.S.C. § 2314). The defendants, relying on the parenthetical language following the listing of 18 U.S.C. 2314 in section 1961 (1) relating to interstate transportation of stolen property, argued that the indictment did not charge a RICO violation since the charged § 2314 offense stems from activities different from those set forth in the parenthetical language. The Court rejected this contention, writing that this "overly restrictive reading of the statute would undermine the remedial purposes that Congress intended." The Court reasoned that since in one instance (18 U.S.C. § 659), Congress limited a predicate offense to felonious acts, it would have supplied limiting or more specific language to the other crimes listed in § 1961 (1) if it also wanted to limit RICO prosecutions to the descriptions of those offenses in the statute. Without the type of limiting language that appears in the parenthetical description of 18 U.S.C. § 659, RICO prosecutions are not limited to the literal parenthetical descriptions of the crimes.

The liberal interpretations of the predicate provisions are further underscored by the Seventh Circuit's construction of § 1961 (C). Section 1961 (1) (C) defines racketeering activity as "any act that is indictable under Title 29, United States Code, section 186."

In *United States v. Kaye*, 556 F.2d 855 (7th Cir. 1977), the defendant contended that since 29 U.S.C. § 186 offenses were misdemeanors, they were not "indictable" within the meaning of § 1961 (1) (C). The Seventh Circuit court held that since Fed. R. Crim. P. § 7 (a) permits prosecution of a § 186 offense (and all misdemeanors) by either indictment or information, § 186 misdemeanors are susceptible to prosecution by indictment.

■ DESCRIPTIONS OF STATE OFFENSES ARE DEFINITIONAL ONLY

United States v. Salinas, 564 F.2d 688 (5th Cir. 1977) dealt with a question of statutory construction: whether 18 U.S.C. § 1961 (6) (defining an unlawful debt as one incurred violating state laws against gambling) applies in a state forbidding gambling, but has no specific statutory proscription against the business of gambling. The court held, however that § 1961 (6) did apply to such conduct.

For purposes of 18 U.S.C. § 1962 (c), "unlawful debt means a debt:

1. Incurred or contracted in gambling activity that was violating the law of a State
2. That was incurred on the business of gambling violating State law.

The expansive application of the state predicate charges is highlighted by the fact of including a state offense as a predicate charge even if a defendant was acquitted in state court for the same conduct. Further, the expiration of a state statute of limitations on the state predicate offenses does not diminish the validity of a RICO indictment that recites as a predicate an otherwise indictable offense. As the Third Circuit wrote in *United States v. Forsythe*, 560 F.2d 1127 (3rd Cir. 1977):

> "RICO was not designed to punish state law violations; it was designed to punish the impact on commerce caused by conduct that meets the state's definition of racketeering activity. To interpret state law offenses to have more than a definitional purpose would be contrary to the legislative intent of Congress and existing state law."

This position is reaffirmed in *United States v. Malatesta*, 583 F.2d 748 (5th Cir. 1978) where the Fifth Circuit held that there was no requirement to obtain a state conviction where a state offense is part of the charged racketeering activity. Nor is the United States collaterally estoppel from proving facts in a federal trial that the state could not prove. Further, the federal court overseeing the RICO trial need not charge the jury on the various provisions of state law that would apply in the state where the predicate offense(s) were committed. An example is the state statute of limitations or a state requirement that the testimony of an accomplice must be corroborated; see *United States v. Brown*, 555 F.2d 467, 418, n. 22 (5th Cir. 1977).

■ THE MEANING OF ENTERPRISE

A recurring issue in RICO cases is the meaning of the word *enterprise*. The focus of debate is whether *enterprise* includes illegitimate and legitimate businesses. The underlying issue is whether the statute becomes redundant if a RICO "enterprise" may also be an "illegal enterprise."

Section 1961 (4) of Title 18 defines *enterprise* to include: "…any person, partnership, corporation, association, or other legal entity, and any union or group of individuals associated although not a legal entity."

United States v. Rone, 598 F.2d 564 (9th Cir. 1979), held that the existing association of two persons who engaged in a wide range of unlawful activity was an *enterprise* for RICO purposes. The Ninth Circuit held that there are broad and unrestricted uses of the term *enterprise* throughout the Act. The specific wording, "any enterprise," in the "Prohibited Activity" section was all encompassing and, so, included illegitimate and legitimate operations. The *Rone Court* noted that although Congress's primary concern was to eradicate the infiltration of legitimate business by organized crime, the prohibition of illicit enterprises advanced this congressional purpose by retarding "the infiltration of normal business in the first instance by denying racketeers the source of their investment funds."

The Seventh Circuit court, when faced with a similar challenge in *United States v. Cappetto*, acknowledged that the target of Congress in enacting RICO was the "infiltration of legitimate organizations by any pattern of racketeering activity affecting commerce." In United States v. Winstead, 421 F.Supp. 295 (E.D. Ill. 1976), the court declined to limit Cappetto to an illegal operation connected to a legitimate business.

The Sixth Circuit, in *United States v. Sutton*, 605 F.2d 260 (6th Cir. 1979), ended the unanimity of its sister circuits on the question of enterprise. It held that a narcotics distribution and fencing operation was not an "enterprise" for RICO purposes. The *Sutton Court* reasoned that if the "enterprise" element of RICO could be satisfied by an illegal enterprise, the "enterprise" would become:

> "wholly redundant and transform the statute into a simple proscription against "patterns of racketeering activity."

According to the Sixth Circuit court, every "pattern of racketeering activity" becomes an enterprise" whose affairs happen through the "pattern of racketeering activity." This, the *Sutton Court* held was not the statute Congress had written.

There is legislative history to support the *Sutton Court's* conclusion, that the statute was enacted in response to organized crime's growing subversion of legitimate labor and business institution. As Senator McClellan stated during the floor debates on the Act, RICO aimed at those who "operate illegitimately in legitimate channels."

Public and Private Enterprise

With one exception, the courts are uniform in applying RICO to both public and private "enterprises." In *United States v. Brown*, 555 F.2d 407 (5th Cir. 1977), the defendants contended that the definitional language in § 1961 (4) could not be construed to include a municipal police department, since the statute on its face limits an *enterprise* to entities of a private commercial nature and to those less formal groups "associated in fact." The Brown Court rejected this analysis, holding the actual language of § 1961 (4) defines *enterprise* as any "legal entity" or "group of individuals associated although not a legal entity." From this broad language *Brown* concluded that a police department may be, at the least, a "group of individuals associated," if not a "legal entity." Further scrutinizing the pertinent legislative history, the court recognized that Congress enacted the Organized Crime Control Act of 1970, of which RICO was a part, to reduce the flow of illegal activities into organizations that corrupt "democratic processes" and "threaten domestic security." A police department is surely such an organization. Lastly, *Brown* held that Congress intended that RICO be liberally construed to fulfill its remedial purposes. This objective could lead to no other conclusion but that the public sector (not only private commercial entities) receives protection by the Act. There is no foundation in the statute for the distinction between public and private sectors. In the statutory definition, individuals and corporations both receive consideration as legal entities and enterprises. A person may as easily be a public official as a businessperson. Similarly, a corporation may be either a private concern or a public or quasi-public entity, such as a municipality or utility.

Association in Fact

There is little doubt that an "enterprise" may have informal, loosely bound persons. In *United States v. Elliot*, 571 F.2d 880 (5th Cir. 1978), the Fifth Circuit court held that an "enterprise" may include an informal existing association. In *Elliot*, the association included at least five persons informally associated and involved in more than twenty criminal endeavors. In effect, their venture became an association to commit crime. The Court reasoned that in defining *enterprise*, Congress made clear that the statute extended beyond conventional business organizations to reach "any group of persons whose association, however loose or informal, furnishes a vehicle for the commission of two or more predicate crimes." RICO calls for only a need for an association "in fact" where it cannot be implied in law. Further, the Court held that there was no distinction, for "enterprise" purposes, between a duly formed corporation that elects officers and holds annual meetings and an "amoeba-like-infrastructure that controls a secret criminal network." Briefly, an "enterprise" under RICO calls for no particular structure nor "badge of recognizability." All that's needed is that the persons be "associated in fact." A RICO "enterprise," decided by the courts, includes, for example, a group of persons associated with various corporations to operate a pornography business, three persons running rigged card games in a Nevada hotel, a group of corporations, and a foreign corporation.

■ THE MEANING OF "CONDUCT OR PARTICIPATE THROUGH"

The courts remain unresolved over the degree whereto the government must allege and prove a nexus between the defendant's illegal conduct and the enterprise in question. However, the constitutionality of this requirement has been upheld in the courts.

18 U.S.C. § 1962 (c) provides that

It shall be unlawful for any person employed by or associated with any enterprise engaged in, or the activities of which affect, interstate or foreign commerce, to conduct or participate, directly or indirectly, in the conduct of such enterprises's affairs through a pattern of racketeering activity or collection of unlawful debt.

In *United States v. Stofsky*, 409 F.Supp. 609 (S.D.N.Y. 1973), the defendants contended that while RICO's definitional section (18 U.S.C. § 1961) adequately defines "person," "enterprise," "racketeering activity," and "pattern of racketeering activity," it never defines the phrase "conduct or participate…in the conduct of such enterprise's affairs through a pattern of racketeering activity…" as used in § 1961 (c). The defendants argued that RICO does not set forth the degree and intensity of the relationship between the racketeering activity and the usual operation of the enterprise and that without such definition the prospective defendant cannot predict with any certainty the conduct sought as unlawful behavior. Further, the defendants urged that the constitutional requirement of definiteness in criminal statures would call for the statute to state whether the alleged racketeering activity (1) must be in furtherance of the enterprise or (2) if it need be merely not harmful to the enterprise, or even contrary to the goals of the enterprise, or (3) whether it must be an important and constant part of the usual operation of the enterprise. The *Stofsky Court* considered at length this constitutional vagueness argument and rejected it. The Court concluded that the absence of explanatory language regarding the requisite nexus between the unlawful acts of a person and the enterprise was not fatal because there's no requirement for a particular degree of interrelationship. As the Court wrote:

> "......§ 1962 (c) sufficiently places persons of reasonable intelligence on notice that persons employed by the type of enterprise in it cannot resort to a pattern of specified criminal acts in the conduct of the affairs of that enterprise. Set forth then, on the face of the statute, is a necessary connection between the person who would commit the enumerated predicate acts and that person's participation in the operations of the enterprise."

In *United States v. Field*, 432 F.Supp.55 (S.D.N.Y. 1977), the defendant, an alleged union organizer, moved to dismiss the RICO counts in his indictment on the ground that it did not specify in what manner he was alleged to have conducted or participated in the conduct of the union's affairs through a pattern of racketeering activity, as distinct from simply engaging in corrupt activities on his own behalf. *Field* contended that RICO did not aim at individuals who merely happen to be union employees who took advantage of their position for personal gain, but at unions whose activities are conducted in an illegal fashion. According to *Field*, a valid RICO indictment must necessarily allege that the union (or other enterprise) was itself corrupt. It is simply not enough, *Field* contended, to allege corrupt behavior by the union employee. The *Field Court* disagreed, holding that the reasoning of Stofsky was dispositive of Field's contention:

> "Section 1962 (c) nowhere calls for proof regarding the advancement of the union's affairs by the defendant's activities or proof that the union itself is corrupt, or proof that the union authorized the defendant to do whatever acts form the basis for the charge. It needs only that the government establish that the defendant's acts were committed in conduct of the union's affairs."

In *United States v. Dennis*, 458 F.Supp. 197 (E.D. Mo. 1978), the Eastern District of Missouri confronted the question of whether the collection of unlawful debts by an employee from co-employees on the premises of an enterprise (affecting interstate commerce) constitutes participation in the enterprise's affairs through the collection of unlawful debts. The Court held that the mere fact that the defendant was hired by the enterprise and collected unlawful debts on the enterprise's premises did not establish that he participated in the conduct of the enterprise's affairs through the collection of the unlawful debts. Although the Court conceded that RICO needs neither (1) proof regarding the advancement of the enterprise's affairs by the defendant's activities, nor (2) proof that the enterprise is corrupt, nor (3) proof that the enterprise authorized the defendant to do the acts that formed the basis for the charge, it however held that RICO calls for a "nexus between the prohibited activity and the conduct of the enterprise's affairs."

■ PATTERN OF RACKETEERING ACTIVITY

18 U.S.C. § 1961 (5) defines "pattern of racketeering activity" to require "at least two acts of racketeering activity, one of which happened after the effective date of (the Act) and the last of which occurred within ten years (excluding any period of imprisonment) after the commission of a prior act of racketeering activity." Racketeering activity is defined in 18 U.S.C. § 1961 (1).

Although this definition appears at a glance to be simple enough to comprehend, federal courts have disagreed about whether the acts of racketeering need share a certain relatedness. A corollary contention has been that the term is unconstitutionally vague.

In *United States v. Stofsky*, 409 F.Supp. 609 (S.D.N.Y. 1973), a case that involved payments to union officers and agents for permitting illegal subcontracting to non-union shops, the court expressed concern that § 1962, without a limiting construction, might be unfairly used to punish isolated or unrelated criminal acts. The court construed "pattern" to include: "a requirement that the racketeering acts must have had a connection with each other by some common scheme, plan or motive...."

Sharing this view, a Wisconsin District Court, in *United States v. White*, 386 F.Supp. 882 (E.D. Wis. 1974), held that the term *pattern* was applicable to a combined matrix of qualities or acts forming a characteristic arrangement. Congress's use of the word *pattern* associated with two racketeering acts committed by the same person evokes the suggestion that the two acts must have a greater degree of interrelationship than simply commission by the same perpetrator. The *White* case showed that the prosecution must prove such an interrelatedness beyond a reasonable doubt to obtain a § 1962 (c) conviction.

Directly colliding with the *Stofsky* and *White* cases and court view, several other courts have heralded the position that does not need "interrelatedness" between the acts of racketeering under RICO. (E.g., *United States v. Elliot*, 571 F.2d 880 (5th Cir. 1978); *United States v. DePalma*, 461 F.Supp. 778 (S.D.N.Y. 1978).)

In *United States v. DePalma*, a defendant, relying heavily on the *Stofsky* case, asserted that an alleged bankruptcy fraud bore no relationship to the second charged racketeering act of securities fraud. The Court roundly rejected that notion, holding that the statutory definition of "pattern of racketeering activity" was unambiguous and contained no requirement of "relatedness." Further, "a review of the legislative history," the *DePalma Court* wrote, "establishes that Congress was concerned with proscribing illegal activities of legitimate business, and that the only relation it thought necessary for the two predicate acts are that they both be in the conduct of the affairs of the same enterprise."

"The term pattern," the Court continued, "applies to the relationship of the acts to the enterprise, and no more."

The emphasis in *DePalma*, as opposed to the *Stofsky* and *White* line of cases, was on the enterprise, not merely the persons committing the criminal acts. This emphasis was a result of *DePalma's* appreciation that protection of enterprises was the primary Congressional concern in enacting RICO. The enterprise is the anchor typing the acts of racketeering into a "pattern." DePalma agreed with the Court in *United States v. White* that the two racketeering acts "must have a greater interrelationship than simply commission by a common perpetrator… satisfies the other element through showing the predicate acts were both committed in the conduct of the affairs of the same enterprise or business."

In *United States v. Elliot*, the Fifth Circuit court accepted this line of reasoning and noted that the Organized Crime Control Act:

> "does not criminalize either associating with an enterprise or engaging in a pattern of racketeering activity standing alone. The gravamen of the offense described in 18 U.S.C. § 1962 (c) is the conduct of an enterprise's affairs through a pattern of racketeering activity. The Act does need a type of relatedness: the two or more predicate crimes must be related to the affairs of the enterprise but need not otherwise be related to each other."

Although the *DePalma* through *Elliot* line of cases seems to be on sounder footing than the *Stofsky* through *White* line of cases, since clearly

Congress enacted RICO to purge all enterprises of racketeering, both sides of the argument neglected consideration of a basic issue: the intent of the so-called racketeers. Congress's purpose in enacting RICO was to ensure that "organized crime's activities were forcefully circumscribed." Clearly isolated, unrelated acts by persons in an illegitimate enterprise would fall into a pattern under RICO since Congress sought to identify and dismantle such organizations entirely. However, in legitimate organizations that have been tainted by so-called racketeering activity, a different test will sometimes be necessary. The fact that a person within a ten year period may commit two predicate offenses may or may not constitute a "pattern of racketeering." If the perpetrator merely was seeking to advance his or her own career at corporate expense, a RICO prosecution clearly should not happen. Prosecutors on RICO charges must consider before filing such indictments whether the defendant designed to pervert the corporate purposes. Similarly, in defending such prosecutions, their counsel should lay a record at each step of the trial, from opening statement to summation, to establish that each act was isolated and that the accused did not seek to corrupt, taint or corruptly use essential organs of the enterprise. The linkage between the enterprise and the two acts of racketeering provides a rich area for further development in the courts.

■ MEANS OF VIOLATING RICO

1. Investment of Illicit Funds in Legitimate Enterprises: (18 U.S.C. § 1962)

Section 1962 (a) prohibits funds received through a "pattern of racketeering" from investment in an "enterprise" engaged in or affecting interstate or foreign commerce. The design of this section intended on keeping so-called dirty money out of the streams of interstate commerce. The linchpin of any analysis of the elements of a 1962 (a) offense is proof that the invested funds stemmed from a "pattern of racketeering activity."

There is strong counterargument to the position there must be some "intent" to create a "pattern." It is that Congress recognized how difficult it is to determine such "intent." Instead of advance complex rules or tests to determine intent, Congress simplified matters by deciding that the commission of two predicate acts within a ten-year period is a pattern of racketeering for RICO purposes.

2. Acquiring, Maintaining or Controlling an Enterprise through Racketeering Activity: (18 U.S.C. § 1962)

This section forbids the direct or indirect acquisition or maintenance of any interest in or control of any enterprise affecting interstate or foreign commerce, by a pattern of racketeering activity or through the collection of an unlawful debt. Here, the focus is not on the source of the funds used to acquire an interest in an enterprise (as in § 1962 (a)), but on the racketeering means used to acquire or maintain control of an enterprise. Unlike subsection (a), in a § 1962 (b) offense, monies used to acquire or maintain an interest or control in an enterprise may have a legitimate source; and like subsection (a) the means used to acquire or maintain an enterprise must result from the same "pattern of racketeering activity." This pattern is the common denominator for RICO offenses.

3. Conducting or Participating in an Enterprise's Affairs through Racketeering Activity: (18 U.S.C. § 1962)

Section 1962 (c) prohibits persons hired by or associated with any enterprise engaged in or affecting interstate or foreign commerce to "conduct or take part" in the conduct of the enterprise's affairs through a "pattern of racketeering activity." The unique aspect of this RICO violation is the utilization of the enterprise in racketeering activities.

4. Conspiracy to Violate RICO: (18 U.S.C. § 1962)

Section 1962 (d) contains the language for a RICO conspiracy. It provides that: "it shall be unlawful for any person to conspire to violate any of the provisions of subsection (a) (b) or (c) of this section."

It differs from the general federal conspiracy statute in several respects. Under the general federal conspiracy statute (18 U.S.C. § 371):

"The precise nature and extent of the conspiracy must be determined by reference to the agreement that embraces and defines its objects. Whether the object of a simple agreement is to commit one of many crimes, it is therefore that agreement that constitutes the conspiracy that the statute punishes." (*Braverman v. United States*, 317 U.S. 49, 53)

The prosecutors often view the general conspiracy statute as ineffective when dealing with organized crime groups because a "single agreement" or "common objective" cannot generally be inferred from their highly diverse activities often perpetrated by apparently unrelated persons. Section 1962 (d) of RICO ended this problem by creating a substantive offense that tied together these diverse parties and crimes. The RICO conspiracy calls for as its object the violation of a substantive RICO provision, either § 1962 (a) (b) or (c).

In *United States v. Elliot*, a group of persons informally associated which enabled them to profit from criminal activity, was charged with substantive and conspiracy violations of RICO. The evidence at trial implicated six defendants and thirty-seven unindicted co-conspirators in more than twenty different criminal endeavors. These acts included arson, counterfeiting titles for stolen cars, stealing 33,000 pounds of meat, efforts to influence the result of a stolen meat prosecution, stealing a truck, and other diverse crimes. Although the government did not have a viable prosecution against these persons under the general conspiracy statue, it successfully prosecuted them under RICO § 1962 (c) as having agreed to take part, directly or indirectly, in the affairs of this enterprise (group associated to commit crime) by committing two or more predicate crimes. Under RICO it is irrelevant that each defendant participated in their enterprise's affairs through different, even unrelated crimes, since the government proves the intention of each crime had an aim to further the affairs of the enterprise. The requirement to prove the RICO conspiracy in the *Elliot* case included an agreement on a general objective to commit crime.

A RICO conspirator, like a conspirator under the general federal provisions, need not have full knowledge of all the details of the conspiracy. He or she must merely have acquired knowledge of the essential nature of the plan. For example, in the *Elliot* case, the essential nature of the plan (the "pattern of racketeering") was to associate for making money from repeated criminal activity. The fact that one conspirator may be unaware of the crimes committed by another member of the conspiracy is irrelevant to their liability under the Act, since RICO charges each conspirator with agreeing, not to commit each of the crimes through which the affairs of the enterprise were conducted, but agreeing to take part in the enterprise through his or her own criminal conduct. (This applies to those examples shown in Chapter 10 and other chapters involving corporate employees agreeing to participate in the organized crime group's enterprise.)

■ PENALTIES AND APPLICATION OF RICO

RICO provides for both criminal and civil liabilities (the latter often enables a company to recover losses). The criminal punishment can include a maximum fine of $25,000; imprisonment for a maximum of 20 years; or both (each count). Also, an offender requirement can include forfeiture of any interest he or she has acquired in the legitimate enterprise, and any interest in the enterprise that gave him or her the source of influence or the legitimate enterprise (e.g., another company or business, including money).

An examination of RICO shows that its coverage is very broad. RICO not only forbids the acquisition of a business enterprise through illegal methods or with money obtained by illegal methods, but it also prohibits the use of legal business enterprises to commit illegal activities (e.g. those discussed in earlier chapters, plus those to follow in Part Three).

Most states now have a RICO statute and you will probably apply state statutes more often than the federal RICO statutes. However, there are provisions for assimilating the state RICO laws into the federal prosecution and civil remedies when the case spreads out of the state jurisdiction.

Since recovery of losses will normally become your first priority, I will focus on civil RICO in the remainder of this Chapter. The two actions (criminal and civil) remain separate, so one or the other or both apply according to the situation you confront.

Civil Remedies and Recovery of Losses

Civil RICO contains several civil remedies, including injunctive relief, divestiture and dissolution of an enterprise and treble damages. (Treble damages are given by statute in certain cases, consisting of the single damages found by the jury, actually tripled in amount) Until recently, few corporate litigants availed themselves of the remedies under the RICO statute (federal and state). However, the number of civil RICO claims has increased dramatically during past years, and recent Supreme Court decisions have lightened the pleading burden of civil plaintiffs which signal yet greater expansion of this form of loss recovery. Courts deciding civil RICO actions have struggled to determine the scope of the application of the civil remedies. They are mindful that while in enacting RICO, Congress was primarily concerned with the infiltration of legitimate businesses by organized crime groups, it also sought to separate those racketeers from their profits. This latter goal required sweeping legislative measures.

■ QUICK REFERENCE OVERVIEW: FEDERAL STATUTORY REFERENCES—CIVIL REMEDIES

§ 1964 RICO (Federal)

(a)   The district courts of the United States shall have jurisdiction to prevent and restrain violations of section 1962 of this chapter (law) by issuing appropriate orders, including, but not limited to:

- Ordering any person to divest him or herself of any interest, direct or indirect, in any enterprise.

- Imposing reasonable restrictions on the future activities or investments of any person, including, but not limited to, prohibiting any person from engaging in the same type of endeavor as the enterprise engaged in the activities of which affect interstate or foreign commerce.

- Ordering dissolution or reorganization of any enterprise, making due provision for the rights of innocent persons.

(b) The Attorney General (or representative) may start proceedings under this section. In any action brought by the United States under this section, the court shall proceed when practicable to the hearing and determination thereof.

(c) Any person injured in their business or property because of a violation of section 1962 of this chapter (law) may sue therefor in any proper United States district court and shall recover threefold the damages he or she sustains and the cost of the suit, including a reasonable attorney's fee.

(d) A final judgment or decrees given for the United States in any criminal proceeding brought by the United States under this chapter shall estop the defendant from denying the essential allegations of the criminal offense in any later civil proceeding brought by the United States.

§ 1965. Venue and process

(a) Any civil action or proceeding under this chapter against any person may originate in the district court of the United States for any district in which such person resides, is found, has an agent, or transacts their affairs.

(b) In any action under section 1964 of this chapter in any district court of the United States in which shown that the ends of justice call for that other parties residing in any other district come before the court, the court may cause such parties to be summoned, and process for that purpose may serve in any judicial district of the United States by the marshal thereof.

(c) In any civil or criminal action or proceeding begun by the United States under this chapter in the district court of the United States for any judicial district, subpoenas issued by such court to compel the attendance of witnesses may be served in any other judicial district, except in any civil action or in any other judicial district, except in any civil action or proceeding no such subpoena shall be issued for service upon any person who resides in another district at a place more than one hundred miles from the place at which such court is held without approval given by a judge of such court upon a showing of good cause.

(d)   Other process in any action or proceeding under this chapter may be served on any person in any judicial district in which such person resides, is found, has an agent, or transacts their affairs.

§ 1966. Expedition of actions

In any civil action started under this chapter by the United States in any district court of the United States, the Attorney General may file with the clerk of such court a certificate stating that in his or her opinion the case is of general public importance. A copy of that certificate shall be furnished immediately by such clerk to the chief judge or in his or her absence to the presiding district judge of the district in which such action is pending. Upon receipt of such copy, such judge shall designate immediately a judge of that district to hear and determine action.

§ 1967. Evidence

In any proceeding ancillary to or in any civil action instituted by the United States under this chapter the proceedings may be open or closed to the public at the discretion of the court after consideration of the rights of affected persons.

§ 1968. Civil investigative demand

(a)   Whenever the Attorney General has reason to believe that any person or enterprise may be in possession, custody, or control of any documentary materials relevant to a racketeering investigation, he or she may, before beginning a civil or criminal proceeding thereon, issue in writing, and cause to be served upon such person, a civil investigative demand calling for such person to produce such material for examination.

(b)   Each such demand shall:

(1) State the nature of the conduct constituting the alleged racketeering violation which is under investigation and the provision of law applicable thereto;

(2) Describe the class or classes of documentary material produced thereunder with such definiteness and certainty permitting fair identification of such material;

(3) State the demand is returnable forthwith or prescribe a return date which will provide a reasonable time within which the material so demanded may be assembled and made available for inspection and copying or reproduction; and

(4) Identify the custodian to whom such material shall be made available.

(c) No such demand shall:

(1) Contain any requirement which would have a judicial view as unreasonable if in a subpoena duces tecum issued by a court of the United States in aid of a grand jury investigation of such alleged racketeering violation; or

(2) Require the production of any documentary evidence that would be privileged from disclosure if demanded by a subpoena duces tecum issued by a court of the United States in aid of a grand jury investigation of such alleged racketeering violation.

(d) Service of any such demand or any petition filed under this section may be made upon a person by:

(1) Delivering a duly executed copy of it to any partner, executive officer, managing agent, or general agent of it, or to any agent of it authorized by appointment or by law to receive service of process for such person, or upon any person;

(2) Delivering a duly executed copy of it to the principal office or place of business of the person to be served; or

(3) Depositing such copy in the United States mail, by registered or certified mail duly addressed to such person at its principal office or place of business.

(e) A verified return by the person serving any such demand or petition setting forth the manner of such service shall be prima facie proof of such service. In service by registered or certified mail, such return shall be accompanied by a return post office receipt of delivery of such demand.

(f) (1) The Attorney General shall designate a racketeering investigator to serve as racketeer document custodian, and such added racketeering investigators as he shall determine from time to time to be necessary to serve as deputies to such officer.

(2) Any person upon whom any demand issued under this section has been duly served shall make such material available for inspection

and copying or reproduction to the custodian designated in it at the principal place of business of such person, or at such other place the custodian and such person after that may agree and prescribe in writing or as the court may direct, under this section on the return date specified in such demand, or on such later date the custodian may prescribe in writing. Such person may upon written agreement between such person and the custodian substitute four copies of all or any part of such material originals of it.

(3) The custodian to whom any documentary material is so delivered shall take physical possession of it, and shall be responsible for the use made of it and for the return of it under this chapter. The custodian may cause the preparation of such copies of such documentary material as needed for official use under regulations that shall be promulgated by the Attorney General. While in the possession of the custodian, no material so produced shall be available for examination, without the consent of the person who produced such material, by any person other than the Attorney General. Under such reasonable terms and conditions as the Attorney General shall prescribe, documentary material while in the possession of the custodian shall be available for examination by the person who produced such material or any duly authorized representative of such person.

(4) Whenever any attorney has been designated to appear for the United States before any court or grand jury in any case or proceeding involving any alleged violation of this chapter, the custodian may deliver to such attorney such documentary material in the possession of the custodian as the attorney determines to be necessary for use in the presentation of such case or proceeding for the United States. Upon the conclusion of any such case or proceeding, such attorney shall return to the custodian any documentary material so withdrawn which has not passed into the control of such court or grand jury through the introduction of it into the record of such case or proceeding.

(5) Upon the completion of:

- (i) the racketeering investigation for which any documentary material was produced under this chapter, and
- (ii) any case or proceeding arising from such investigation, the custodian shall return to the person who produced such material all such material other than copies of it made by the Attorney General under this subsection that has not passed into the control of any court or grand jury through the introduction of it into the record of such case or proceeding.

(6) When any documentary material produced by any person under this section for use in any racketeering investigation and no such case of proceeding arising from it has started within a reasonable time after completion of the examination and analysis of all evidence assembled during such investigation, such person shall be entitled, upon written demand made upon the Attorney General, to the return of all documentary material other than copies of it made under this subsection so produced by such person.

(7) In the event of the death, disability, or separation from the service of the custodian of any documentary material produced under any demand issued under this section or the official relief of such custodian from responsibility for the custody and control of such material, the Attorney General shall promptly:

- (i) designate another racketeering investigator to serve as custodian of it, and

- (ii) transmit notice in writing to the person who produced such material about the identity and address of the successor so designated.

Any successor so designated shall have regarding such materials all duties and responsibilities imposed by this section upon his predecessor in office with regard thereto, except he or she shall not have responsibility for any default or dereliction that happened before their designation as custodian.

(g) Whenever any person does not comply with any civil investigative demand duly served upon him or her under this section or whenever satisfactory copying or reproduction of any such material cannot happen and such person refuses to surrender such material, the Attorney General may file, in the district court of the United States for any judicial district in which such person resides, is found, or transacts business, and serve upon such person a petition for an order of such court for the enforcement of this section, except if such person transacts business in more than one such district such petition shall be filed in the district in which such person maintains his or her principal place of business, or in such other district in which such person transacts business as may be agreed upon by the parties to such petition.

(h) Within twenty days after the service of any such demand upon any person, or at any time before the return date specified in the demand, whichever period is shorter, such person may file, in the district court of the United States for judicial district within which such person resides, is found, or transacts business, and serve upon such custodian a petition for an order of such court modifying or setting aside such demand. The time allowed in compliance with the demand in whole or in part as thought proper and ordered by the court shall not run during the tendency of such petition in the court. Such petition shall specify each ground upon which the petitioner relies in seeking such relief and may be based upon any failure of such demand to follow the provisions of this section or upon any constitutional or other legal right or privilege of such person.

(i) At any time when any custodian is in custody or control of any documentary material delivered by any person in compliance with any such demand, such person may file, in the district court of the United States for the judicial district within which the office of such custodian is situated, and serve upon such custodian a petition for an order of such court calling for the performance by such custodian of any duty imposed upon him or her by this section.

(j) Whenever any petition is filed in any district court of the United States under this section, such court shall have jurisdiction to hear and determine the matter so presented, and to enter such order or orders as needed to carry into effect the provisions of this section.

While the statute's provisions have the potential for an extension of federal remedies into areas of state law, such as common business fraud and against non-organized crime defendants, a general agreement exists that such a result is warranted by the broad sweep of the section's language. Addressing the concern that Congress, endeavoring to deal a serious blow to organized crime groups, created overly expansive corrective measures, the seventh Circuit Court observed:

"We agree that the civil actions provided under RICO are dramatic, and will have a vast impact upon the federal-state division of substantive responsibility for redressing illegal conduct, but, like most courts who have considered this issue, we believe that such dramatic consequences are necessary incidents of the deliberately broad swath Congress chose to cut to reach the evil it sought; we are therefore without authority to restrict the application of this statute." (*Schact v. Brown*, 771 F.2d 1343, 1352 (7th Cir. 1983) and *U.S. v. Turkette*, 452 U.S. 576, 587, 101 S.Ct. 2524, 69 L.Ed. 2d 246 (1981)).

"The availability of more specific state causes of action does not preclude a plaintiff from bringing a civil RICO action." (*Slattery v. Costello*, 586 F. Supp. 162, 168 (D.D.C. 1984).)

■ CONSTITUTIONAL ISSUES UPHELD

The constitutionality of section 1964 (civil RICO) was upheld by the Seventh Circuit in *United States v. Cappetto* (502 F.2d 1351–1974). In *Cappetto*, the federal government sued a group of several persons, seeking injunctive relief against alleged gambling activities. The defendants challenged the statue as unconstitutionally vague and as an improper exercise of authority under the Commerce Clause. The court roundly rejected both arguments. Regarding vagueness, the court held that the section "is merely a specific grant of jurisdiction to enforce the substantive provisions of the statute by injunction." Since these substantive provisions are sufficiently particular to withstand a vagueness challenge, the grant of jurisdiction under section 1964 (of the federal RICO) also passes constitutional muster.

The court had more difficulty with the Commerce Clause challenge. Clearly Congress may provide alternate civil and criminal remedies in an area that is subject to federal regulation (for example, there are such alternate remedies in the tax, antitrust, and food and drug areas). It is equally clear that RICO is a valid exercise of congressional authority. However, the civil remedies provided are very close in nature to the criminal remedies, but the standard of proof in a civil action is largely lower than in a criminal proceeding. Defendants argue that prosecutors could seek the same relief in cases where there is insufficient evidence to seek a criminal remedy. The court rejected this argument on the ground that the remedies are not that close, particularly since forfeiture would not be available in a civil action, and instead issued a judgment under the statute for recovery (*Moss v. Morgan Stanley, Inc.*, 719 F.2d 5, 17 (2d Cir. 1983)).

Standing to Sue: "Any Person"

Section 1964(c) provides a private cause of action for "any person injured [suffering loss] in their business or property because of a violation of section 1962 [federal RICO]." A "person" under definitional section 1961 (federal RICO) includes "any person or entity capable of holding a legal or beneficial interest in property." A corporation, in a legal sense, is a "person."

The question of whether a person may sue on his or her own behalf when the corporation with which he or she is associated sustains a loss received a judicial decision in *Warren v. Manufacturer's National Bank of Detroit*, 759 F.2d 542 (6th Cir. 1985). The plaintiff brought a section 1964(c) action in his personal capacity as sole share holder and chairperson of the board of a corporation allegedly defrauded by the defendant in several loan transactions. The district court dismissed the complaint, holding that in his personal capacity, the plaintiff (Warren) was sustained by the corporation (Manufacturer's National Bank of Detroit). The Sixth Circuit Court agreed, finding that any injury (loss) incurred by the plaintiff was sustained by the corporation. Redress (recovery of loss) for the separate share holder must be had through a derivative suit; any damage to the corporation must be redressed by a suit brought in RICO under the corporation's name. (Also see *Gallagher v. Canon, USA, Inc.*, 588 F. Supp. 108, 110 [N.D. Ill 1984]; when a corporation does not act on its own behalf, the share holder must bring derivative action since he or she does not have a standing as a "person injured.") Equally unavailing was the plaintiff's contention that as a corporation employee left jobless when the situation forced bankruptcy on the corporation, he was entitled to maintain an independent cause of action. The court ruled that since the alleged acts of fraud were directed at the corporate entity and not at the plaintiff, any injury (loss) suffered by the plaintiff was "merely incidental" to those of the corporation. The "any person" right to sue is limited to those persons whose loss arises "by reason of" the challenged conduct, and while the plaintiff's injury could be called a result of the defendant's actions, it could hardly be said to have been directly "caused" by the asserted conduct.

Injury (Loss) to a "Business or Property"

The Second Circuit Court (federal) has described the "business or property" injury (loss) language of section 1964(c) of RICO as the "proprietary" loss: "For example, a person physically injured in a fire whose origin was arson does not have a right to recover for his personal injuries; damage to his or her business; or their building the type of injury for which § 1964(c) permits suit." (*Bankers Trust Company v. Rhoades*, 741 F.2d 511 [2d Cir. 1984]) Civil RICO damages for personal injury were disallowed in *Morrison v. Syntex Laboratories, Inc.* (101 F.R.D. 743–D.D.C. 1984), a products liability case in which the plaintiff, injured by the defendant's infant formula, brought a civil RICO action based on the defendant's use of the mails for fraudulent advertising. The court wrote,

> "The limitation of injury to being injured in one's business or property cautions extending this provision to personal injury arising out of a tort in a products liability case. Had Congress intended to create a federal treble damage remedy for cases involving bodily injury, injury to reputation, mental or emotional anguish or the like, all which will cause some financial loss, it could have enacted a statue about injury generally,

without any restrictive language. If RICO applied here, it would most probably apply in every products liability case involving alleged false representations, and use of the mails or the channels of interstate commerce."

Causation

Considerable debate has been generated by the "by reason of" causation language of section 1964(c). Much of the controversy concerns the potential reach of the section as it relates to the congressional purposes underlying the statute as a whole. Seeking to align their decisions with congressional intent to attack organized crime groups, some courts reasoned that the "by reason of" language limited standing to those parties suffering a "RICO-type" injury—that is, one "different in kind from that happening because of the predicate acts themselves." (*Sedima, S.P.R.L. v. Imrec Co.*, 741 F.2d 482, 496 [2d Cir. 1984]) The parties in Sedima had entered a joint venture to export aviation parts when the plaintiff, believing that the defendant was cheating it out of its profits, brought suit on a theory of unjust enrichment and other common law claims, and under section 1964(c), based on predicate acts of mail and wire fraud. The district court dismissed the RICO counts for failure to state a claim, finding no allegation of injury except for that resulting directly from the mail and wire fraud. The Second Circuit affirmed the dismissal after a consideration of the legislative history of the statute and a conclusion that the "by reason of" language expressed an intent to impose standing barriers similar to those in the antitrust laws that call for a showing of "competitive injury." The court held that the section requires "that plaintiffs allege injury caused by an activity which RICO was designed to deter, which, whatever it may be, is different from that caused simply by such predicate acts as are alleged here." (The court did not offer any clear definition of the "racketeering injury" whereto it refers. And although it expressed concern that legitimate businesses often become caught in a web originally designed for organized crime groups, it did not go so far as calling for an organized crime nexus.)

The U.S. Supreme Court reversed in a 5–4 decision. Noting first that "racketeering activity" as set out in definitional section 1961(1) has no more than the commission of a predicate act, the court expressed doubt about the need for an injury (loss) except for the harm of the predicate acts. The plain language of the statute suggests that if the plaintiff shows that the defendant engages in a pattern of racketeering activity in a manner forbidden by section 1962, and those activities injure the plaintiff in his or her business or property, a claim under section 1964(c) is stated. The "essences of the violation is the commission of [the predicate] acts on the enterprise," and the plaintiff need show no more.

The Supreme Court found support for its interpretation of the statute in the congressional directive that RICO be "liberally construed to make its remedial purposes." A narrow reading of the private action section would rob it of its potential for aggressively supplementing existing remedies and developing new methods for fighting crime. The Second Circuit's effort to restrict the reach of the statute to the activities of mobsters, by a narrow reading of its provisions, would contravene express congressional intent. If, as alleged by the Second Circuit court, civil RICO suits have largely been improperly brought almost exclusively against legitimate businesses, it is left to Congress, the court concluded, to restrict the application of the statue.

The Seventh Circuit court, in *Haroco, Inc. v. American National Bank & Trust Company of Chicago*, 747 F.2d 384 (7th Cir. 1984), interpreted the "by reason of" language to impose a proximate cause requirement on plaintiffs; a plaintiff can only recover to the extent that he or she has been injured in his or her business or property. "A defendant who violates section 1962 is not liable for treble damages to everyone he or she might have injured by other conduct, nor is the defendant liable to those who have not been injured." For example, in *Cenco, Inc. v. Seidman & Seidman*, 686 F.2d 449 (7th Cir. 1982), share holders brought a class action against Cenco, Inc. alleging that many members of the company's top management took part in the inflation of the price of its stock through fraudulent activities. Seidman & Seidman, Cenco's accounting firm, was also named as a defendant for its failure to prevent Cenco's fraud. Seidman cross-claimed against Cenco, alleging that it was a victim of Cenco's fraud and seeking damages under RICO and principles of indemnity. The district court dismissed Seidman's claim on the ground that Seidman lacked standing, and on appeal the Seventh Circuit addressed the question of whether treble damages were available to a party injured "as a consequence of being used as a tool of the criminal enterprise." Finding no answer in the language of section 1964(c), analogies to section 4 of the Clayton Act, or the legislative history of the section, the court considered the "compensatory and deterrent objectives of RICO." Given the congressional concern with the infiltration of legitimate businesses, the court reasoned, it was for the owners, customers, and competitors of such businesses that the civil damages remedy was created, and not for those "who supply office equipment or financial or legal services to criminal enterprises that may be violating RICO." Affirming the dismissal of the complaint, the court observed, "It is unlikely that Congress if it had referred to the issue would have chosen to create in the wake of every RICO violation waves of treble-damage suits by all who might have suffered indirectly from the violation, especially when many of these would inevitably be, as here the witting or unwitting tools of the violator."

"Violation of Section 1962"

In *Sedima S.P.R.L. v. Imrex Company*, 741 F.2d 482 (2d Cir. 1984), the Second Circuit court held that a private RICO action would not lie where the defendant had not earlier been convicted of the predicate acts underlying the RICO violation (mail and wire fraud in this case) or of a RICO violation. The requirement was inferred, the court found, from section 1964(c)'s reference to a "violation" of section 1962 and supported by constitutional and practical considerations about the burden of proof and the stigmatization of perpetrators of "garden-variety" fraud or securities violations as "racketeers."

Reversing the Second Circuit court, the Supreme Court held that no prior criminal conviction requirement could be read into the statute. Such a requirement, the court observed, cannot be found in the language of the statute, the word *conviction* appearing nowhere in the relevant parts of it. The predicate acts described in section 1961(1) involve conduct that is "chargeable" or "indictable" or "punishable" under various statutes. The term *violation* refers only to "a failure to adhere to legal requirements" and does not imply a criminal conviction. Had Congress intended to impose the criminal conviction requirement here, it would have spelled it out as it did in the criminal forfeiture section 1963. And in the legislative history of the statute, the statute was to be read according to its terms.

The Supreme Court rejected the Second Circuit court's finding that without a prior criminal conviction, proof of the predicate acts would have to be beyond a reasonable doubt, necessitating confusing instructions about different standards of proof for different aspects of the case. In some situations, conduct that can be punished as criminal will support civil actions on the lesser "preponderance" standard. However, the court chose not to decide whether this was one of those situations, noting that the logistical difficulties in multiple burdens of proof cases were not so great as to call for invention of the "prior conviction" solution proposed by the circuit court.

Addressing the circuit court's concern for constitutional protection of the civil defendant, the Supreme Court held that the court below also feared that any other construction would raise severe constitutional questions, as it

> would provide civil remedies for offenses criminal in nature, stigmatize defendants with the appellation "racketeer," authorize the award of damages clearly punitive, including attorney's fees, and constitute a civil remedy aimed in part to avoid the constitutional protections of the criminal law. We do not view the statute as being so close to the constitutional edge. As noted above, the fact that conduct can lead to both criminal liability and treble damages does not mean there is not a bona fide civil action. The

familiar provisions for both criminal liability and treble damages under the anti-trust laws show as much. Nor are attorney's fees "clearly punitive." On stigma, a civil RICO proceeding leaves no greater stain than do many other civil proceedings. Furthermore, calling for conviction of the predicate acts would not protect against an unfair imposition of the "racketeer" label. If there is a problem with stigmatizing a garden variety defrauder through a civil action, it is not reduced by making certain that the defendant is guilty of fraud beyond a reasonable doubt. Lastly, to the extent an action under § 1964(c) might be considered quasi-criminal, requiring protections normally applicable only to criminal proceedings, the solution is to provide those protections, not to ensure that they were earlier afforded by calling for prior convictions.

Lastly, we note that a prior conviction requirement would be inconsistent with Congress' underlying policy concerns. Such a rule would severely handicap potential plaintiffs. A guilty party may escape conviction for any number of reasons, not least among them the possibility that the Government itself may choose to pursue only civil remedies. Private attorney general provisions such as § 1964(c) are in part designed to fill prosecutorial gaps. This purpose would be largely defeated, and the need for treble damages as an incentive to litigate unjustified, if private suits could be maintained only against those already brought to justice.

An example

In *Alexander Grant & Company v. Tiffany Industries*, 742 F.3d 408 (8th Cir. 1984), the Eighth Circuit court rejected the *Cenco* reasoning, which supplied a different result in a suit filed by an accounting firm against its client. In the *Alexander Grant* case, plaintiffs alleged that the defendants committed wire and mail fraud to obtain a favorable audit to mask financial instability. Relying on the *Cenco* case, the district court dismissed the complaint and the circuit court reversed. Here, the court reasoned, the plaintiffs did not seek indemnification but the amounts instead spent in legal fees during an SEC investigation and the amount representing loss of business reputation. These were direct injuries, distinguishable from a claim for indemnification "which, by its very nature, is secondary and indirect." Also, the court held, *Cenco*'s reliance on the purpose and objectives of section 1964(c) was misplaced. The language of the section providing damages to "any person injured in their business or property" is unambiguous and the legislative history nowhere denied merely because the injuries are "indirect."

■ QUICK REFERENCE GUIDE TO RICO

RICO does not create a new type of substantive crime but instead prohibits "racketeering activities" that are defined by the incorporated federal and state crimes.

- This statute takes these various state and federal crimes and declares that if a person commits two of these offenses, the person is guilty of racketeering activity and subject to harsh penalties.
- 18 United States Code (U.S.C.) § 1961 includes definitions of several words or phrases used in the Racketeer Influenced and Corrupt Organizations Act (RICO).
- 18 U.S.C. § 1962 defines the "prohibited activities" whereto Title IX is directed.
  - —§ 1962(a) prohibits the use of proceeds derived from a pattern of racketeering activity or through collection of an unlawful debt to acquire an interest in an enterprise engaging in or affecting interstate commerce.
  - —§ 1962(b) proscribes the acquisition of an interest in such an enterprise through a pattern of racketeering or loansharking.
  - —§ 1962(c) focuses on the method of operating the enterprise once it is acquired and prohibits the use of racketeering or loansharking in the conduct of the business.
  - —§ 1962(d) provides that it is unlawful for any person to conspire to violate any of the substantive provisions of subsections (a), (b), and (c).
- Under § 1963, those convicted of violating § 1962 may be fined a maximum of $25,000 and imprisoned a maximum of twenty years, or both (each count), and shall forfeit any interest acquired or maintained violating § 1962 or any property, interest, right, or claim affording a source of influence over any enterprise established, controlled, or operated violating § 1962. (The Comprehensive Crime Control Act of 1984, Public Law No. 98-473, has greatly expanded the scope of forfeiture under 18 U.S.C. § 1963.)
- § 1964 provides for a variety of civil remedies—including divestiture, dissolution, restraints against violations, restrictions on the future activities of violators, and, in suits brought by injured private parties, triple damages and costs, including reasonable attorney's fees.
- Added to normal discovery, § 1968 provides for a "civil investigative demand" under which the attorney general (or underling), before the institution of criminal or civil proceedings, may call for any person or

enterprise to produce "any documentary materials relevant to a rack-eteering investigation."

■ Civil remedies include
—Injunctive relief
—Acceptance of performance bonds
—Restraining orders
—Dissolution
—Treble (triple) damages
—Cost of the suit, including a reasonable attorney's fee
—Venue
—Weight of contacts test.

■ *Glossary of RICO terms and phrases*: This glossary defines those words and phrases uniquely characteristic of the RICO applications, both criminal and civil.

—*Enterprise*: Any person, partnership, corporation, association, or other legal entity and any union or group of persons associated although not a legal entity.

—*Pattern of racketeering activity*: Two acts of racketeering activity, one of which happened after RICO's effective date (October 15, 1970) and the last of which happened within ten years (excluding any period of imprisonment) after the commission of a prior act of racketeering activity.

—*Person*: Any person or entity capable of holding a legal or beneficial interest in property.

—*Racketeering activity*: Any one of the acts enumerated in 18 U.S.C. § 1961.

—*State*: Any state of the United States, the District of Columbia, the Commonwealth of Puerto Rico, any territory or possession of the United States, any political subdivision, or any department, agency, or instrumentality of it.

Part Three
How to Avoid Becoming a Victim of White Collar Crime Committed by Another Company Doing Business with You

▓ INTRODUCTION

The old maxim "caveat emptor (buyer beware)" applies with the same weight to corporations as it does to personal business. During the next two decades, white collar crimes targeting business will continue to experience unprecedented growth, and much of that criminal activity comes from doing business with seemingly legitimate companies.

In recent years, crimes against businesses by other businesses have become a growing force in the United States, costing billions of dollars annually. White collar criminal enterprises have come to recognize that businesses, especially complex corporations, supply fertile ground for a variety of their fraudulent activities (such as bankruptcy schemes, counterfeit and substandard supplies and products, phoney invoices, unfair competition, advertising fraud, and a variety of other ways to siphon off your company's profits with fraudulent, but seemingly legitimate, business activities).

Once reason why this segment of white collar crime continues to grow is the level within corporations that these schemes deal with regularly. For example, top management executives and even middle management employees don't become involved in day-to-day, routine business matters and the businesses targeting your company know that. Instead, much of the hands-on company business management comes from assistants and lower-level employees who aspire to climb the corporate ladder and want to impress their bosses. Criminal enterprise businesses also knows that and create a variety of lucrative schemes to persuade the employee they're dealing with that doing business with them will impress the boss. The end result does leave an impression, but not the one the employee anticipates at the onset. Instead, it will often cost the employee his or her job.

Normally, businesses who prey economically on other businesses fall into two primary categories:

1. White collar crimes incidental to, and in furtherance of business operations, but not the central purpose of the business
2. Crime as a business or as the central activity of a business. This might include supplier fraud, counterfeiting products, substandard supplies and products, bankruptcy schemes, and many others.

Corporations and businesses suffer from white collar crime in three ways:

1. As the direct victims of fraud
2. By being placed at a competitive disadvantage
3. As indirect victims through public loss of trust in the corporation or business.

■ BUSINESSES AS DIRECT VICTIMS

Business enterprises suffer consequences from white collar crime that range from relatively minor financial losses, to massive financial hemorrhaging that often causes their insolvency and destruction or forces dramatic cutbacks, layoffs, mergers, and other efforts to save the business. The most serious of these consequences stem from the activities of employees or other insiders who wittingly or unwittingly act in concert with outside confederates.

A common white collar crime against corporations and businesses is embezzlement (discussed in Parts One and Two). Embezzlement amounts may be large enough to collapse an otherwise healthy business, especially those involving commercial bribery (when business employees or officers take bribes from those who sell goods or services to their employers, or bankers make loans to those who give them bribes or other incentives). Insider dealings will also involve conflicts of interest (for example, when a corporate officer or employee causes the company to enter into contractual relationships with outside firms in which he or she has an ownership interest, or when a banker causes his or her bank to lend money to an enterprise in which he or she has an ownership interest). These and similar insider operations are, in essence, ways in which the assets of a company can be looted. Pension funds, which are enterprises set up to manage beneficiaries' funds on a business-like basis, can also be similarly looted through the device of making risky investments in return for special kickbacks and participations in potential profits.

Companies also become direct victims of a host of white collar thefts by outsiders, who probably rob our economy of countless billions of dollars each year. Common examples include fake insurance claims, credit card frauds, and the occasional gigantic swindle involving may tens of millions of dollars (such as the Equity Funding case, in which several of major U.S. insurance companies were sold fraudulently concocted insurance contracts). With the onset of electronic transfers of funds, both nationally and internationally, the way has been opened to massive thefts. One New York bank, for example, avoided losses in the millions through such an electronic transfer only by the accident of an unclear transmission, which triggered a routine and nonsuspicious request for a repeat of the original message. Many business frauds also happen frequently, often unreported, on a smaller scale. Ripoffs such as advanced fee schemes, false directory advertising bills, and many others cumulatively cost the business community vast sums of money.

The increasing dominance of computers in the business world has greatly increased the potential impact of fraud that victimizes companies. It is now possible for white collar thieves to stage and keep records of vast numbers of fraudulent transactions almost instantaneously. Computer reprogramming techniques have given thieves the capability simultaneously to generate both fraudulent book entries and backup concealment systems. Few computer frauds of any magnitude have been discovered by routine internal audits; most have been discovered by accident, revealed by nervous scheme participants, or came to light when the scheme developed to a scale beyond a participant's capacity to control it.

Such direct losses to the business community do not come only out of business profits. In many instances, they have caused the destruction of businesses and contributed to multimillion-dollar insolvencies and reorganizations. In all cases these white collar thefts represent costs of doing business (both the thefts themselves and the costs of guarding against and detecting them).

Finally, the increasing sophistication of organized criminal syndicates makes businesses vulnerable to mixed white collar crimes. Organized criminal groups have demonstrated the ability to get their hooks into legitimate businesses or employees of such businesses through such avenues as loansharking, enforced collection of gambling debts, and purchases of businesses. They have used that control to execute traditional white collar schemes such as bankruptcy frauds (scams) and the marketing of stolen securities through the device of using them as loan collateral at banks.

■ BUSINESS VICTIMIZATION THROUGH RESTRICTION OF COMPETITION

Antitrust violations, price fixing, and restraint of trade represent a major area in which damage is inflicted on the business community and, as a consequence, on the public who are the customers of the business community. When suppliers of goods and services are able to control their markets, many will be placed at a competitive disadvantage because they will be unable to seek new business in the marketplace by offering better services or lower prices. Retailers and wholesalers will be unable to shop for lower prices and will be at a competitive disadvantage if their suppliers give lower prices to favored customers through such devices as kickbacks, rebates, and phony advertising or promotional allowances. In many instances, such practices can become subject to criminal sanctions; in all cases they are unlawful, and the overall dollar costs of these violations may well equal that of all other white collar crimes and related abuses combined.

In most instances, the consequences of such unlawful activities are strictly economic (confined to rising costs, elimination or hobbling of business competitors, and retarding innovation and development of new and efficient services). In other cases, when organized criminal syndicates combine white collar crimes with strong-arm tactics, actual physical harm to people and physical damage to property (such as arson) will occur.

■ DAMAGE TO THE REPUTATION OF THE BUSINESS

The business community's reputation is important on four levels:

1. Within the separate companies
2. Among the company's customers
3. In relationships with other companies

4. In the general community (politically).

The existence of white collar criminal activity, even on a petty level, tends to undercut the overall integrity of an enterprise and to encourage other illegal activity (such as commercial bribery or pilferage) and will substantially contribute to poor administration of the businesses affected. There is no way to measure the impact of white collar crime, but it is clearly a significant cost. Internal corruption, as well as negligence in dealing with it, have led to increases in the frequency of large-scale stock holder suits against directors and officers of corporations who are charged with conflict of interest or incompetence. Such litigation may make it difficult to acquire the services of well-qualified corporate directors, geometrically increase premiums for liability insurance to protect officers and directors, and erode stock holder confidence in officers and directors generally.

Many white collar crimes and related abuses (such as commercial bribery and misrepresentations concerning the quality and utility of merchandise or products, the true costs of installment payments, or the serviceability of products) result in cynicism about business ethics. This cynicism reflects on and harms not only those who engage in wrongful practices but also their honest competitors who are not guilty of such practices. These honest competitors must suffer the costs of anticipating and responding to the suspicions of the marketplace.

Disclosures of past abusive practice may also seriously affect the future of a business trying to "go straight." For example, a company that manufactures jets and is exposed for payment of bribes to airline executives will have a special and costly burden in making subsequent sales, because prospective purchasing agents will not want to be labeled as bribe takers.

Business enterprises operate in relationship not only to their customers, but also in relationship to suppliers and organizations (e.g., bankers, underwriters, factors) who provide financing and credit. Any activity that indicates lack of integrity and control, such as substantial commercial bribery or a large-scale internal computer fraud, must undercut the confidence of others in such an enterprise and obligate the firm to added expenses related to auditing, internal investigation, and management changes to meet such problems.

Many of the greatest costs of white collar crime that victimize business are the costs that the business suffers in the community at large. The perception of wide-scale consumer fraud in ghetto areas, for example, is believed to have been a significant factor in the urban riots of the 1960s. Concerns about business credit practices led to the development of "truth-in-lending" legislation and undercutting of the "holder in due course" doctrine (so important to financing of legitimate commercial transactions). Other disclosures have led to state legislative and congressional investigations and to ever more stringent restriction and control of business financing, through detailed state and federal regulatory steps that were the natural consequence of white collar crime and related abuses. The costly consequences to legitimate business operations (and to the business customers) reflect both past abuses and the fear of such abuses and law violations in the future.

In Part Three, I'll show you the pitfalls of doing business with other companies that target your company for illicit profits and, through their dishonest dealings, create a difficult business environment. I'll show you how to prevent and effectively deal with white collar crimes that victimize your company through awareness and aggressive prevention and recovery programs.

Chapter Twelve
White Collar Crimes Committed by Another Business Incidental To and In Furtherance of Its Own Business

Businesses use many deceptive practices and anticompetitive illegalities to target those in business and the professions. Often, a company your corporation has done business with for years suddenly or systematically begins victimizing your company through a variety of schemes that increase their profits and cash flow, although they continue to do business legitimately. One of the reasons for this source of loss to your company is that management delegates dealing with an established supplier of products or services to lower level and less experienced employees.

■ THE PERVASIVE GRAY MARKET

The gray market isn't product counterfeiting, because your company *did* manufacture the product. It isn't black market, because your company's products are sold on the counters and displayed in legitimate retail or wholesale outlets. Often, the gray market doesn't create illegal activity. It does, however, create a subtle perversion of conveyance channels from a United States corporation to a United States commercial operation or consumer. The gray market, in its most common sense, involves the merchandising or selling domestically of goods that a United States firm has produced and exported to a foreign country and that unethical entrepreneurs have then sold back into the United States.

Many U.S. corporations, large to small, produce a subgroup of their normal product line for export purposes. This type of production often involves the following and more:

- Cosmetics Film   Automobiles   Electronic Crystal
                                                   equipment
- Watches   Cameras   Automobile parts Soaps   A variety of consumables.

Because the marketplace regulations of many foreign countries have less stringent standards than those in the United States, these exported products may not meet U. S. standards of quality, packaging, safety, purity, or other parameters set by regulatory and compliance agencies of the government. The products might also be obsolete, have no warranties, or involve discontinued models or items. Because of the relaxed standards, a company can produce the export version of the product more cheaply, which can lead to significantly lower prices abroad than counterparts of higher quality in the United States. Often, unscrupulous distributors, often those you might do business with regularly and believe legitimate, can reap windfall profits by selling you the export quality items, but representing them as meeting U. S. standards. These types of distributors (or manufacturers) can create large profits by purchasing the goods for export to a company in a foreign country that they also own or in which they have a significant interest. Their scheme involves shipping the lower standard products to the foreign company (sometimes only on paper) and then having the foreign company export the products back to them in the United States. They might have them repackaged by the foreign company (or do it in the U.S. to make it appear as done in a foreign country), to make the product appear to meet U.S. import standards. Exhibit 12-1 shows an example of how this gray market can be operated by an otherwise legitimate company.

In the gray market scheme, a legitimate company, shown in Exhibit 12-1 as Legitimate Authorized Distributor, sells your foreign distribution product to its own export company, ABC, Inc., who sells it to British and Mexican companies, which it also owns and operates. Its subsidiary companies export the product, sometimes with the same or similar packaging to ABC, Inc., who then sells it to the distribution company to sell to retail and wholesale markets in the United States. This activity often only involves "paper" export and import activity while in reality the product never leaves the distributor's warehouses or, if necessary, it makes the round trip.

Exhibit 12-1
Example of a Typical Gray Market Operation

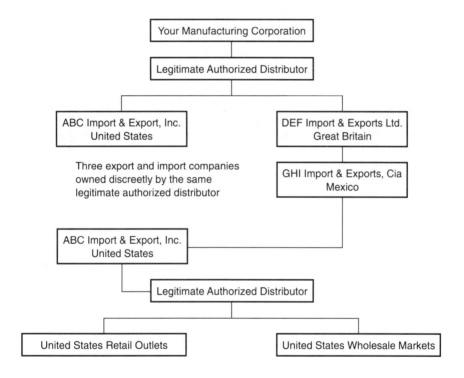

The Losses Sustained in Gray Market Operations

Your company sustains losses in two ways by gray market operations involving your manufactured products. The other company's cost for purchasing, exporting, importing, and then distributing your product is low enough so the product's ultimate shelf price stays below your normal domestic price. With some creative paperwork, the product may never leave the United States; instead the paperwork makes the trip and it appears that the product moved through the process. The technique that the other company uses to create its gray market depends on your product and the varieties of legal requirements the other company must fulfill.

Remember, the company engaging in gray market activities has a legitimacy and perceived integrity in the business community and, outside the gray market, remains honest in most of its dealings. The end result of the gray marketed product may be selling in one store at a price 20 percent or more below the price of your similar product in the store across the street. What you intended for consumption abroad without any adverse effect on your domestic sales is now cutting into your U.S. sales and creating often heavy financial losses to your company.

The second major problem from gray market sales stems from increasingly adverse customer relations. The consumer, wholesaler, or other company that buys your product and believes that it's getting a bargain might find the product unsatisfactory because you never intended it for domestic use. Your company might experience a bombardment of complaints, including the following:

Packaging: Often the outside wrappings show damage or signs of tampering. Sometimes the fine print on the package shows that the product was "imported" from a foreign country while still showing that it was manufactured in the United States by your company.

Ingredients: Gray market items might lack elements that enable a product to perform under U.S. regulatory standards. Further, because you intended the product for a foreign market, it might contain prohibited ingredients or have substandard characteristics.

Labeling and instructions: An ingredient listing, including the importer's name, in the form of a stick-on label over your company's printed information leaves a question of authenticity and credibility. It may further hide this gray market scheme with a foreign language set of instructions or if the ingredients of the product are in another language. The latter disguise of ingredients might conceal the use of prohibited ingredients which makes the item substandard in the U.S.

Shipping and warranties: Your international warranty does not apply in the domestic market, since your authorized distributor (who is technically responsible for the gray market) will not honor the warranty and will act innocent in this entire matter. Your distributor might even voice a complaint to the manufacturing company for allowing this type of gray marketeering (and in so doing the distributor gives itself a cloak of integrity). Your company will often have to issue recalls, make significant refunds, and try to convince customers that this wasn't your company's fault (however, few would accept that excuse).

How to Combat Gray Market Products

Some gray market practices might violate laws; however, often there are no existing laws covering them. However, you do have remedies, especially in the manufacturing process. Ensure that a deep imprint is placed on the product that it is manufactured only for export and is not intended or authorized for sale in the United States. The exact language of your imprint can develop from consultation with your company's legal counsel. It may cost more to create the stamping process, but it is well worth the cost compared with the potential losses. You should also include this information on sales agreements and invoices. It might not eliminate the gray marketeering problem entirely, but it serves as a strong deterrent and protects your company's integrity and bank account.

■ DOUBLE OR TRIPLE BILLING SCHEMES

The larger the company, the easier this scheme works. Established trade accounts are the greatest culprit. This "cash flow enhancement" often is initiated by an otherwise legitimate company needing money or headed by a person or management team that sees a lucrative way to increase company profits, perhaps to supply pay raises and perks.

In this scheme, the other company, regularly a supplier, sells your company 10,000 widgets a week as it has for twelve years. When the billing arrives, it's paid without question because there's no reason to doubt this familiar business name. The scheme can involve a "test" double billing to determine how easily or difficult it will be to defraud the victim company. However, because most companies verify billings with invoices and receipt of shipment by others, the scheme often requires a more complex system to confuse the issue.

For example, the supplier might ship your company 10,500 widgets and send you a bill for 10,000. The next shipment may 9538. The shipments received by your company over a three-month period vary in quantity to confuse the inventory process. The supplier will always ensure that your inventory is sufficient to meet production demands, however the varied quantities establish a basis for the next phase of their billing scheme. After several shipments, an adjusted billing arrives, showing the errors and adjusted amounts plus credits for payments. When the scheme is complicated enough, normally your company will pay the "adjusted" amount without spending long hours auditing the account and taking inventories. This can amount to significant losses that are probably never detected.

However, if a sharp internal auditor catches the overbilling, it's assumed to be an error. Your company will send a letter to the supplier and receive an apology. The supplier will state that its books are now being audited and that when the audit is complete the supplier will get back to you. The supplier tells your company that if its auditors agree with your auditors, a credit will be issued promptly. Meanwhile, the shipments continue and the billings remain accurate. After a couple more months, you send the supplier another letter about the difference, and the supplier replies that its auditors found a slight error much less than your auditor reported, but they will continue to search for the problem. Meanwhile, the supplier grants a small, insignificant credit on the next shipment. This scheme can continue for months, and be cause of the size of your company and daily business, the matter will eventually fade. Meanwhile, the supplier has worked the same scheme with its lengthy list of major customers, and later it will be your turn again (may be a year or two hence). This might sound trivial and like a lot of work, but depending on the account, this scheme can produce several million dollars across the board if the supplier has a sizable number of large accounts.

How to Combat Double or Triple Billing

You need to create agreements or contracts with your primary suppliers that describe their performance and that of your company. In the agreement (developed by your company attorneys and controller), you need to address the problem of error on the part of either company.

Next, establish a policy of handling billing from your suppliers that calls for an exact count by employees receiving the goods and a signed copy of the invoice and verification count provided to the accounting department. Upon receipt of the supplier's invoice, pay only for what you receive instead of relying on the supplier's billing or balancing the payment later (you make the adjustments, not the supplier). When the supplier implements a scheme similar to the one just discussed and learns that you pay for what your company receives (as should be stipulated in the agreement), your problem will end.

■ OFFICE SUPPLY SCHEMES

These schemes will often follow a sales representative calling on your company from a new local (legitimate) company. The sales rep will tell you that his or her company has recently opened and wants to supply your company with all its office supply needs. He or she persuades you to give the company a chance by placing small orders at first and then comparing the quality and service with your current supplier. Normally, the salesperson will leave with a small "test" order. When the order arrives, you are impressed because the items are of the best quality and cost considerably less than the supplier you've been using charges. In addition, the service was unequaled. The person delivering the order, accompanied by the same salesperson, insists that part of the service includes helping you store the order, not just dropping off heavy cartons and leaving the rest to you.

This scheme allows the representative and delivery person to view your supply closet and get an idea about what you use, your needs, and the quality level you're buying. Having impressed you, the salesperson will probably leave with another order, maybe suggesting a few items that he or she viewed in your supply room. Again, the quality and service continue. The sales representative tells you that his or her company can do all this with the lowest prices because the owners buy in vast quantities and will open stores across the country soon.

If your company has branch offices or subsidiaries, they might also buy from the new company based on your recommendation. After a few months (and maybe after a few bonuses to you personally, like an expensive pen and other courtesy and appreciation gifts), things begin to change. The company's prices increase slowly, as quality decreases. At first, the changes are so subtle that they escape notice. If you do notice and call the supplier, a special representative appears and replaces the poor quality product, offering a profound apology and explaining that the company received the wrong order and the shipping room did not recognize the error until after orders went to customers. You receive another appreciation or promotional gift, and place another order.

Eventually and gradually the quality erodes further. When you threaten dropping the account, a representative reminds you of the costly gifts you received and discreetly advises you that if your company drops the account, a complaint will go to your company's board of directors with a full accounting of the gifts. You may protest that such activity is illegal, but the company will protect itself with carefully written letters explaining changes in policy resulting from the economy or some other excuse, and you have the burden of facing top management to explain the gifts you received (which management will undoubtedly perceive as a bribe). You need the job, and although your company pays premium prices for low-quality supplies, the scheme will probably continue. It's a no-win situation that victimizes more companies across the country than most would ever admit.

How to Combat Office Supply Schemes

Your first step must include a clear purchasing policy as well as removing decision-making responsibility from naive employees and moving it to middle management or higher. When the persuasive salesperson comes calling and learns that he or she has to convince and gain approval of an executive, the scheme will usually end. The employee in charge of office supplies should take part in the purchasing discussion, but the decision must remain at a higher level.

You also need a firm company policy about accepting gifts of any type from suppliers, as noted earlier in this book. The most innocent of gifts must be recorded and reported, and the decision to allow keeping the item or returning it must be left to policy and executive decision. Your company policy for buying any product or service should include use of a purchase order to specify exactly what quality and quantity you order and thus to ensure that there's no question about your company's expectations. The purchase order also creates a legal document that helps settle any dispute and establish an effective deterrent against companies that believe they can siphon your profits using an office supply scheme.

There's strong merit for your company supporting a local entrepreneur. However, when you do, ensure that you have a clear written agreement about quality, service, and other important guidelines before placing an order. If the new company is well intentioned and opposed to a scheme, it will be happy to enter this agreement with your company. The agreement must permit your company to get out of the deal when the supplier's products or performance do not meet your standards.

■ UNFAIR METHODS OF COMPETITION

The various practices that create massive losses for companies and are inflicted by other companies include a variety of unfair methods of competition. The cases ruled on by the courts are too numerous and diverse to list in detail. The ones most likely to injure competitors (create losses) include the following:

- Using false or deceptive advertising
- Making unusually restrictive agreements, both horizontal and vertical

- Entering into conspiracies to fix prices
- Allocating markets, or preventing others from procuring goods
- Selling below cost to injure competitors (create losses)
- Mislabeling products
- Conducting gray and black market activities.

Deceptive Advertising Losses

There's an ever-present question concerning the enforcement of laws in the advertising of products or services by companies and advertising companies. Identification of deceptions is sometimes easy, but it is often difficult because even well-intentioned advertisers regularly engage in puffery. Puffery exaggerates the praise for a product or service and is not actionable under common law. We often use puffery in our everyday speech. "That was a great movie," we might say. Do we mean to say that it was one of the best movies of all time or merely that we enjoyed the movie? In a similar way, a company might say that its manufactured pens "write smoother." Smoother than what? This is just puffery. Read any print ad, listen to any radio commercial, watch any television commercial, and you will find clear examples of puffery. Another example includes the familiar line, "50 percent off while supplies last!" The question becomes, 50 percent off what? It is often difficult to draw a line between what is meant only as puffery and what is meant to be deceptive.

In one area of advertising, however, the use of puffery is strictly regulated. The Securities and Exchange Commission (SEC) has established strict regulations against puffery in the advertising of securities. The "tombstone ads" in the financial sections of newspapers are closely watched by the SEC to ensure that the advertisings confine themselves to basic statistical information about any forthcoming stock issue. No discussion of a stock's merits is permitted.

Years ago, the priority of the Federal Trade Commission (FTC) was to take action against fictitious price ads, misuse of words like *guarantee*, and bait-and-switch advertising. (In bait-and-switch advertising, a company would advertise one product at a low price as bait to lure customers. However, the advertisement would tell the customer that the advertised product had sold out and persuade the customer to switch to a more expensive product.) Today, the FTC's objectives are much broader. Of particular interest is its advertising substantiation program. Under this program, many advertisers in widely varied fields must prove the claims made in their advertising.

Although regulatory agencies serve as watchdogs, publicize their findings, and impose penalties that include corrective advertising, the victimization of your company by another company through deceptive advertising can occur. A favorite legal trick in court involves a shrewd lawyer who makes a clear and damaging statement that he or she knows the opponent will object to. The lawyer knows the judge will sustain the objection and order the statement struck from the record. The problem, however, is that the jury heard the statement, and although technically the jurists must not consider the statement in their decision, the idea is planted and stays in the back of their minds. They wonder about the truth of the lawyer's revealing statement and often perceive it as fact despite the court's instructions to ignore it.

The same damage is done to your company by deceptive advertising. No matter what, the public and other companies have heard it clearly and perceive it as true. For example, in a case brought before the court by the FTC in September 1978, an FTC administrative law judge ordered that American Home Products, then manufacturing Anacin,™ correct its future advertising because it earlier said that taking Anacin relieved tension. Although the company had stopped making the claim in its advertising by December 1973, evidence showed that consumers continued to believe that tension relief was an important attribute of Anacin. The judge said the image was likely to persist for some time, so he ordered a corrective message in a $24 million ad campaign that included recanting the original claim. The judge also barred the company from future advertising that stated that the Arthritis Pain Formula™ had special or unusual ingredients, because such ingredients are also available in other products.

After years of litigation, the FTC also acted in commercials advertising Listerine.™ A judge ordered the manufacturer, Warner-Lambert Corporation, to disclaim in its next $10 million worth of advertising that the product would not help prevent colds or sore throats or lessen their severity, as the company claimed earlier.

Additional legislation has enlarged the capacity and scope of the FTC in the years since the passage of the Wheeler-Lea Act. The creation of the Wool Products Labeling Act of 1939, administered and enforced by the FTC, protects manufacturers and consumers from the deliberate mislabeling of wool products. The Textile Fiber Products Identification Act of 1958 requires that clothing, rugs, and household textiles carry a generic or chemical description of their fiber content. The Fair Packaging and Labeling Act of 1962 regulates packaging and labeling of food, drug, and cosmetic products under the jurisdiction of other agencies such as the Food and Drug Administration (FDA).

How to Combat Deceptive Advertising

Often, the best you can do involves putting an end to the deceptive advertising and trying to obtain corrective future advertising. You can also bring damage suits, although these are hard to prove. However, the most viable action includes bringing the advertising to the attention of an appropriate government regulatory agency, including the FTC.

The FTC has a parallel agency, the Food and Drug Administration (FDA), that polices the labeling of foods, drugs, and cosmetics and stems from a 1938 law passed by Congress. The federal Food, Drug, and Cosmetic Act divided regulation duties between the FTC and the FDA. The FTC is responsible for advertising in promotional media, and the FDA has power over claims that appear on the label or package. Added legislation in 1962 gave the FDA unlimited authority over prescription drugs. While the FDA's jurisdiction is confined to the label, its role is broader than that. If it finds that any claim in an advertisement is not supported by the information on the label, it can proceed with a mislabeling action. The agency's interest in advertisements is deeper than it may seem from the enabling legislation. However, the FDA has not been merely a police agency. It has cooperated with the food industry in the development of standardized nutritional labeling systems for foods.

Closely allied to the FTC and FDA in regulatory activities is the fraud staff of the U.S. Postal Service. Since 1872, U.S. Postal fraud laws have supplied effective criminal and civil remedies against companies using the mail to deceive or defraud recipients. Because fraud, from a legal standpoint, involves "intent to deceive," postal service cases ordinarily involve misrepresentation that surpasses the false advertising handled by the FTC. Most problems have been in the food and drug fields. The postal inspectors refer the most serious cases of postal fraud to the Department of Justice, but the majority of the postal service's cases are resolved through administrative civil procedure hearings similar to those used by the FTC.

In broadcasting, the Federal Communications Commission (FCC) enforces rules regarding the types of products allowed in legal advertisements on broadcast media, the number and frequency of commercials allowed within a certain time, and what broadcast programs and commercials may or may not state or show. Under the Communications Act of 1934, the FCC received authority to regulate the U.S. communications system in "the public interest, convenience, and necessity." Through its control over licensing, the Commission wields indirect control over broadcast advertising. Specific problem areas that the FCC has emphasized include misleading demonstrations, physiological commercials (such as nudity) that are considered in poor taste, and excessively long commercials.

In addition to the FTC, FDA, the U.S. Postal Service, and the FCC, there are many other federal agencies with specialized roles related to advertising. Among these agencies are the following:

The Department of Agriculture, under the Packers and Stockyards Act, plays a role similar to the FDA in regulating the labeling of meat products.

The Environmental Protection Agency (EPA) regulates pesticide labels just as the FDA regulates food labels.

The Consumer Product Safety Agency asks advertisers to avoid any themes that may promote unsafe use of products.

The Federal Deposit Insurance Corporation and the Federal Home Bank Board both exercise close supervision over the advertising practices of banks and similar financial institutions.

The Truth in Lending Law, enforced by the Federal Reserve Board, regulates installment credit advertising by banks.

The Treasury Department's alcohol bureau enforces a rigid advertising code on the advertising of alcoholic beverages that precludes many advertising techniques used by other products. These regulations specifically ban any attempt to impute therapeutic benefits to alcoholic beverages. They also ban any brand names that might imply that a product originated in another country. For example, American manufacturers of vodka may not name their products "St. Petersburg Vodka" or a similar label that implies Russian production of the vodka. To avoid such problems, American vodka producers have been content to use Russian-sounding names with labels adorned with images that may look like the imperial crest of the czars.

The Civil Aeronautics Board monitors the advertising of airlines and travel agents.

■ ANTITRUST

The area known as antitrust was born in 1890 when Congress enacted the Sherman Antitrust Act (15 United States Code §§ 1 et seq.). *Trust* in this context means a combination of producers or sellers of a product, the purpose of which is to control prices and suppress competition. The Sherman Act intention involves the effort to preserve competition in the marketplace and to prevent further concentration of the vast wealth accumulated by a few corporations and persons.

Space limitations do not permit me to explain the myriad of complexities and inner workings of antitrust law, a subject that would take a book in itself. Instead, I examine the major violations that include (1) the Sherman Act, (2) the Clayton Act, and (3) the Robinson-Patman Act. I focus on the more frequent types of antitrust violations that might affect your company profits and losses, as well as some remedies or solutions available when you find your company falling victim to the categories within antitrust.

Antitrust law is both complex and controversial. It seeks to balance conflicting interests. On the one hand, there is the consideration of protecting the public against the power exercisable by vast corporations (yours and competitors' alike). On the other hand, there is the question of to what extent the capitalistic system of free enterprise will be permitted to operate. Antitrust legislation is intentionally broad, general, and vague. Phrases such as *restraint of trade, monopolization, unfair methods of competition,* and *conduct that tends substantially to lessen competition* abound. This language has only definite meaning when courts interpret the statutes and apply them to the facts of particular cases.

Due to expanding judicial construction of antitrust laws, a continuously increasing number of antitrust cases have been filed by public and private litigants. There has been a tendency to expand the role of antitrust law from one of maintaining commercial competition and a free market to one of monitoring business activities and producing social reform. Your company must develop attentive awareness of possible antitrust consequences of activities, especially when your company becomes a victim through another company participating in this activity.

Restraint of Trade

Section 1 of the Sherman Act (15 U.S.C. § 1) provides that "every contract, combination in the form of trust or otherwise, or conspiracy, in restraint of trade or commerce among the several states, or with foreign nations" is illegal. For there to be a violation of § 1 there must be some combination or common action by two or more persons or companies.

In interpreting the statute, the courts have equated "restraint of trade" with "restraint of competition." The interstate commerce requirement ("commerce among the several states") originally was interpreted as meaning that the mere manufacture or production of goods was not interstate commerce even if the goods were destined for shipment from one state to another. Today, however, satisfying the commerce requirement stems from a clear showing that the business or activity in question, even when purely intrastate, has a "substantial economic effect" on other states.

The Rule of Reason and the Per Se Doctrine

In a sense, every company or business contract restrains trade since it sets terms that at least one commercial transaction will happen and removes that transaction from the field of competition. This was obviously not what Congress intended to prevent. Accordingly, the United States Supreme Court held that the Sherman Act intention remains within parameters of forbidding only "unreasonable" restraints of trade and that it did not weaken freedom to enter ordinary business contracts. (*Standard Oil Company v. United States,* 221 U.S. 1, 55 L.Ed. 619, 31 S.Ct. 502 [1911]) Certain types of business conduct, however, according to the courts, establish the condition of "unreasonable per se." This means that the conduct is unreasonable alone; proof that the conduct happened is enough to establish a violation of the Sherman Act. Examples of conduct that is unreasonable per se include (1) price fixing and (2) dividing market territories among competitors.

Price Fixing

Price fixing means any combination or agreement between or among competing companies formed for the purpose of fixing prices, and it has the effect of raising, depressing, fixing, pegging, or stabilizing the price of goods in interstate commerce. For example, if several corporations form a trade association that fixes prices of the corporations' products and limits sales to a select list of jobbers, the corporations are guilty of illegal price fixing. There is no defense or recognized justification for price fixing (e.g., the price fixing was meant to end "ruinous competition" in the marketplace, or the price fixing served to eliminate unstable prices that plagued both producers and consumers).

The courts have been expansive in determining what creates price fixing. Even agreements among competitors fixing minimum prices create illegal price fixing. For example, the courts decided that a state bar association's establishment of minimum-fee schedules for legal services creates price fixing (*Goldfarb v. Virginia State Bar,* 421 U.S. 773, 44 L.Ed. 2d 572, 95 S.Ct. 2004, United States Supreme Court, 1975)

Division of Market Territories among Competitors

Any agreement among businesses performing similar services or dealing in similar products, so that the available market is divided and each company is given a share, is illegal per se. Similar to the preceding price-fixing discussion, no justifications or defenses receive legal recognition by the courts. The rationale for this rule is that an agreement among competitors to divide the market for a particular product gives each an effective monopoly in its share of the market, allowing each company to set prices in its region.

■ MONOPOLIES

Section 2 of the Sherman Act (15 U.S.C. § 2) makes it a criminal offense to monopolize, attempt to monopolize, or combine or conspire to monopolize any part of interstate or foreign commerce. The courts have defined *monopolize* as acquiring or exercising the power to exclude competitors from a market or to control prices within relevant markets. By using that term, instead of *monopoly*, the state contemplates action instead of merely defining a status. For example, Newspaper Company B distributes thousands of free copies of its newspaper in a geographical area in which Newspaper Company A operates. Company B's free distribution happens during a four-month period, and most of it occurs on Wednesdays, the heavy grocery-advertising day. Advertising creates 80 percent of Company A's revenue, and an important part of that revenue comes from grocery advertising. Company B has engaged in an illegal attempt to monopolize, because if Company B succeeds in driving Company A out of business, a dangerous probability exists that Company B will achieve a monopolistic position in the daily newspaper market and be able to exploit that position to the disadvantage of the people and businesses in the area.

Relevant Market

At some point, the subject of much antitrust litigation (market power) becomes monopoly power—the power to control prices and to exclude competitors. To determine whether a company has monopoly power, it is necessary to define the relevant market, based on what creates (1) the relevant geographic market (for example, California, the West, or the nation) and (2) the relevant product markets (for example, the market for cellophane wrapping material, or the inclusive market for flexible wrapping material). An antitrust defendant (a company charged with a violation of the antitrust laws) will argue that it has a large market that will make its share of the market small, while the company alleging the violation will argue that the defendant's company market is small, making its market share large.

The general definition of a geographic includes the area in which the defendant and competing sellers market the product. If the product sells nationwide, the market is viewed as a national market. There may be regional submarkets where several local sellers compete with nationwide sellers (e.g., the market for beer). The courts might view the submarket as the relevant market. Transportation cost is the principal factor limiting the size of a geographic market.

The determination of a product market often stems from consumer preferences and the extent that physically similar products can fulfill the same consumer need. In *United States v. E.I.DuPont De Nemours and Company* (351 U.S. 377, 100 L.Ed. 1264, 76 S.Ct. 994 [1956]), the so-called Cellophane Case, the United States Supreme Court announced the rule that goods found interchangeable by consumers for the same purposes creates that part of the trade or commerce, monopolization of which may be illegal. In the Cellophane Case, the court decided the relevant market to be all flexible wrapping material, not merely cellophane wrapping material. The court stressed the functional interchangeability of those products. The viewpoints under this rule include perceiving photocopiers, for example, as interchangeable for antitrust purposes, even among brands using different mechanical processes.

Market Share

Courts often take the share of the market that an alleged monopolist has presently captured as the principal indicator of monopoly power. Depending on the circumstances, 90 percent (or even 75 percent) is sufficient to create monopoly power. A legal argument contends that market share creates an imperfect measure of market power, since it does not consider the availability of close substitutes for the product in question and reduces the ease with which new entrants, not presently selling in the market, can enter the market.

Tying Agreements

A tying agreement is an agreement by which a person or corporation agrees to sell a product (the tying product) only if the buyer also purchases a different product (the tied product). For example, a cement company might agree to sell its premixed cement (the tying product) to a building contractor only if the contractor also buys cement mixers (the tied product) from the cement company.

The tying doctrine originated under § 3 of the Clayton Act (15 U.S.C. § 14). Section 3 makes it illegal to sell or lease goods in interstate commerce if the purchaser or lessee does not use or deal in the goods of a competitor of the seller or lessor, if the effect may be largely to lessen competition or tend to create a monopoly in any line of commerce. There are two basic requirements for an illegal tie: (1) There must be separate tying and tied products, and (2) the seller must have enough economic power to restrain competition appreciable in the tied amount of commerce. Although the seller offers the two products as a unit at a single price, there is no tie if the buyer is free to take either product alone.

The tying product and the tied product can be related in a variety of ways. For example, they can be products for which the use of both involves fixed proportions (e.g., nuts and bolts); the tied product might have a use design with the tying product (e.g., data processing programs used with a computer); or the tied and tying products might include use either together or separately (e.g., seed and fertilizer).

Franchise Tying Agreements

The illegality of certain types of tying agreements has particular importance to the franchising industry. The so-called business format franchises are characterized by the franchisee's being granted the right to use, within a designated area, a franchisor's service mark, trade name, distinctive building, structure, or style of decor, and techniques of doing business. This type of franchising largely depends on linking the distinctive image to a standardized operation, hoping for high-quality control. Because the commercial success of the franchising usually depends on a nationwide, uniform image, the courts tend to allow the franchisor to call for the business format franchisee to use particular products to maintain high quality. However, whenever a franchisor insists that the franchisee buys all services, equipment, or supplies from the franchise, a potential tying problem exists.

Mergers and Acquisitions

A merger is one company's acquisition of the stock or assets of another company in such a manner that the latter company will fall under the control by the former. Because mergers can lead to concentration of power in a few companies in an industry, it's an area closely regulated by antitrust laws. Section 7 of the Clayton Act, later amended (15 U.S.C. § 18), provides that a corporation cannot acquire the stock or assets of another corporation engaged in interstate commerce if, in any line of commerce in any section of the country, the effect of the acquisition may be largely to lessen competition or tend to create a monopoly. The issues in merger cases usually relate to definitions of the product market (the "line of commerce") and the geographic market (the "section of the country") and to determination of the market shares of the corporations involved, the status of the corporations as actual or potential competitors in the market or markets involved, and the probable effect of the merger.

A merger that violates § 7 of the Clayton Act might also violate the Sherman Act. However, the showing of anticompetitive impact needed for a successful prosecution is much less rigorous under § 7 than under the Sherman Act provisions. So the trying of most merger cases in court stems from § 7 of the Clayton Act instead of the Sherman Act provisions.

Interlocking Directorates

Section 8 of the Clayton Act (15 U.S.C. § 19) prohibits a person from being on the boards of directors of any two or more corporations if two conditions exist. The first condition is that any of the corporations has capital, surplus, and undivided profits aggregating more than $1 million and is engaged in commerce (the Act excludes banks, banking associations, and common carriers subject to the Interstate Commerce Act). The second condition is that the corporations are or were competitors, so that the elimination of competition by agreement between them would create a violation of any provision of any antitrust law. Section 8 has been construed to forbid corporations from having the same director if an agreement between the corporations to fix prices or divide territories would violate § 1 of the Sherman Act. By forbidding "interlocking directorates," § 8 seeks to prevent violation of the antitrust laws by removing the opportunity or temptation to enter illegal arrangements.

■ PRICE DISCRIMINATION

The Robinson-Patman Act (15 U.S.C. § 13) makes it unlawful to discriminate, directly or indirectly, in price among different purchases of goods of like grade and quality under certain conditions. Those conditions are that (1) any of the transactions is in commerce and (2) the effect of the discrimination may be largely to (a) lessen competition, (b) tend to create a monopoly, or (c) injure, destroy, or prevent competition with any person who grants or knowingly receives the benefit of such a discrimination, or the customers of either. The courts have decided many types of conduct amounting to price discrimination as illegal under the Act. For example, the ABC Corporation is a large national company with a milk-processing plant in Louisville. ABC Corporation sells milk in surrounding areas at lower prices than in Louisville, where it has a large share of the market. Several local companies serve the surrounding areas, and ABC Corporation is trying to get a share of that market. ABC Corporation's policy is price discrimination, violating the Robinson-Patman Act.

Both the seller who offers and the preferred buyer who knowingly receives discriminatory prices are guilty of violating the act.

Like Grade or Quality

Generally, physical differences in two products that affect their acceptability to buyers will prevent the products from being of like grade or quality.

However, differences in the selling brand name or label of the product alone do not create enough reason to justify price discrimination.

Defenses

The Robinson-Patman Act expressly provides that nothing in it shall prevent price differentials that make only "due allowance for difference in the cost of manufacture, sale, or delivery" resulting from the differing quantities, selling, or delivery methods or quantities. This defense will rarely have the legal weight necessary for a defendant, however. For one thing, it is costly to compile the necessary proof. For another, according to the Federal Trade Commission's interpretation of the defense, quantity discounts must have a basis stemming from actual cost savings because of the quantity sold, not merely on a generalized policy that larger deliveries are automatically more economical. A seller can also rebut a presumption of price discrimination by showing that its lower price originated in good faith to meet a competitor's equally low price, but this defense is hard to prove.

■ REMEDIES AND ENFORCEMENT

The variety of lawsuits through which antitrust legislation is enforced is nearly as broad as the scope of the laws themselves, and each type of lawsuit has its own characteristics. The government can begin either a civil damages action or a criminal prosecution against a suspected violator. Private persons can also seek damages through a lawsuit.

Civil Actions

The Antitrust Division of the United States Department of Justice has primary responsibility for enforcing the Sherman and Clayton Acts. The Antitrust Division investigates alleged antitrust law violations stemming from complaints received, often from businesses that believe they are injured by a particular practice.

The Department of Justice has authority to begin a civil action to recover damages to the United States Government resulting from violations of antitrust laws. One such violation would be a price-fixing conspiracy that raised prices on goods sold to the government. In cases other than those in which damages are sought, the object of a civil antitrust proceeding by the Department of Justice is a decree to enforce the Sherman Act or Clayton Act by stopping or remedying violations. Antitrust decrees can enjoin whole categories of conduct and permit the Antitrust Division to investigate subsequent business activities of the defendant.

Consent Decrees

Often, the government and an antitrust defendant agree to settle a government antitrust case by a consent decree. This type of decree stems from a stipulation by both parties for what remedy or relief the court should order, without the defendant acknowledging any guilt. The ultimate responsibility in fashioning an antitrust decree lies with the court, however. The court must determine what is or is not in the public interest, and is not relieved of this responsibility simply because all parties to the proceeding (including the government) agree on or request a particular form of relief.

Private Antitrust Actions

Section 4 of the Clayton Act (15 U.S.C. § 15) allows a private person who has or will sustain loss in his or her business or property because of anything forbidden in the antitrust laws (either the Sherman Act or the Clayton Act) to sue in a federal district court. A plaintiff who proves the violation of an antitrust law and resulting injury can recover treble damages (three times the proven damages) plus the costs of the action, including a reasonable attorney's fee. A plaintiff who shows only threatened injury is entitled to injunctive relief, such as the issuance of an injunction prohibiting the illegal conduct.

In recent years, private antitrust lawsuits have increased and are normally brought as class actions, meaning that all persons similarly injured by the antitrust defendant's conduct have joined as plaintiffs in the same action. Sometimes even very small actual damages attributed to each of many transactions (such as sales of a common but cheap consumer product), when multiplied by many plaintiffs in the class and further multiplied by three under the treble damages provision of the Clayton Act, will become a large sum.

Criminal Prosecutions

The Department of Justice can begin a criminal prosecution if (1) the case involves a per se violation of the Sherman Act and (2) there is proof of a knowing and willful violation of the law (i.e., there has been a planned program of concealment). Most criminal antitrust prosecutions involve price fixing. Antitrust criminal cases normally stem from an investigation by grand jury conducted, as in other areas of criminal law, through grand-jury subpoenas commanding either the testimony of witnesses, the production of documents, or both.

Administrative Enforcement

The authority to enforce the Clayton Act on business firms subject to regulation by particular federal regulatory agencies is vested in those agencies. For example, the Interstate Commerce Commission can enforce the Clayton Act on railroads and motor carriers, while the Civil Aeronautics Board can enforce the act on airlines.

■ AN INVESTIGATIVE AUDIT OF DEALING WITH OTHER COMPANIES

Our business society continues to move into more complex relationships. Often, the relation of one business to another is complicated by less than honorable business intentions. There's an erroneous view that the recognition of incipient white collar crime is obvious. Some believe that the mark of a good executive is that he or she can instinctively recognize such problems, and thus efforts to assist management in identifying incipient problems are not necessary. Perhaps there are some legal problems for which recognition is obvious (e.g., those types that are characterized in jurisprudence as *mala in se*, or morally wrong in themselves), but in large part the legal structure within which a company operates and relies on can be described as *mala prohibita* (acts made illegal by law).

As I've noted throughout this book, your best approach to identifying existing and potential problems is an investigative audit of policies and procedures of internal and external dealings of your company at every level involving money, goods that turn into money, and the several other aspects that can create potential financial loss to your company. (See Chapter 17.) The adage that "opportunity encourages white collar crime while the lack of opportunity negates the potential for crime" applies just as strongly when your company does business with another legitimate company.

This chapter could not cover every conceivable type of white collar crime that exists in legitimate company-to-company business. However, I have pointed out common occurrences and how they can affect your business, and have suggested remedies to end the threat and recover your losses, if possible.

Key Concepts and Terms in Chapter 12

(1) The Sherman Antitrust Act is the foundation of antitrust law. Section 1 prohibits contracts, combinations, or conspiracies in restraint of trade. Only unreasonable restraints of trade are prohibited, but certain practices, such as price fixing, are unreasonable per se.

(2) Section 2 of the Sherman Act makes illegal monopolizing, attempts to monopolize, or combining or conspiring to monopolize any part of interstate commerce. Monopoly power is the power to control prices or exclude competition in the relevant market.

(3) Section 4 of the Clayton Act allows private persons injured in their business or property by any violation of the Sherman or Clayton Act to sue in federal court. A winning plaintiff can recover three times the damages sustained. Section 7 prohibits certain corporate mergers, § 3 prohibits tying agreements, and § 8 prohibits certain interlocking directorates of competing corporations.

(4) The Robinson-Patman Act prohibits illegal price discrimination if the effect may be substantially to lessen competition or tend to create a monopoly. Both the seller who offers and the preferred buyer who knowingly receives discriminatory prices are guilty of violating this Act.

(5) Antitrust legislation enforcement stems from a wide variety of lawsuits, including civil or criminal proceedings by the Antitrust Division of the United States Department of Justice, private antitrust actions by individuals or classes of individuals, and suits by federal administrative agencies.

The following list reviews the laws and terms pertaining to business crimes against other businesses covered in Chapter 12.

- Antitrust
- Class action
- Clayton Act
- Consent decree
- Interlocking directorates
- Market share
- Monopoly
- Per se doctrine
- Price discrimination

- Price fixing
- Relevant market
- Restraint of trade
- Robinson-Patman Act
- Sherman Antitrust Act
- Treble damages
- Trust
- Tying agreement

Chapter Thirteen
White Collar Crime As the Other Company's Primary Business

Scam artists swindle homeowners and the average person out of their life's savings, their homes, and more with phony "get rich quick" or "I've come to help you" schemes. In recent years, this type of criminal enterprise has moved into new schemes that are more lucrative and respectable and carry less risk or none at all. Scam artists set up shell corporations and target legitimate businesses, reaping billions of dollars each year. These white collar crime experts have come of age, and many become respected pillars of the community (until they're found out). Their business has white collar crime as its central activity, and their customer list might have your company's name on it. Their schemes have few limits and a myriad of techniques. In this chapter, I'll show you the most common styles of operations and how to prevent your company from becoming a victim of this new breed of crook.

■ BANKRUPTCY FRAUD

Corporate victims of bankruptcy frauds normally include creditors, suppliers, and banks of the failed or failing business, although silent partners and stock holders can also be victimized. There are two major types of bankruptcy fraud:

1. The scam or planned bankruptcy, in which the assets, credit, and viability of a business are purposely and systematically milked.

2. Fraudulent concealment or diversion of assets in expectation of insol-
    vency to prevent selling by bankruptcy court for the benefit of creditors.

Solutions

You can regularly detect a bankruptcy fraud scheme by watching for the
following:

- A sudden change in a company's business management, particularly a
  change without a public notice
- A company that lists only a post office box as its contact point
- A business that uses an answering service
- A company you sell to that has a dramatic increase in its credit balance
- A new corporation that involves persons from a distant state
- A new corporation that gives vague answers about ownership or the
  business it is in
- A company that has credit references you cannot verify or references
  that seem too eager.

See the descriptive example of these schemes later in this chapter.

■ SECURITIES AND COMMODITIES FRAUD

Securities fraud involves fraudulent activities including the sale, transfer, or
purchase of securities or of money interests in the business activities of others.
Victims are generally securities investors, such as corporate fiduciaries and
others in the company making investments with corporate money. The fraud
occurs when these corporate representatives are not fully aware of the facts
regarding transactions they enter. Abuses cover a broad range and can include
the following:

- Businesses or promoters seek to raise capital unlawfully or without
  proper registration and oversight.
- Securities of no value are sold, or are misrepresented to be worth more
  than their actual value.
- Purchasers are not informed of all facts regarding securities, and there
  is a failure to file proper disclosures with federal and state regulatory
  agencies.

- Insiders use special knowledge to trade in securities to the disadvantage of the company representative that lacks such knowledge.
- Broker-dealers and investment advisers act for their own benefit instead of for the benefit of their corporate clients.
- False information is supplied to the security holder and the investing corporation in financial statements published or filed with securities regulatory agencies, or by payments to financial writers or publications.
- Manipulation of the price of securities by purchases and sales occurs in stock exchange or over-the-counter markets.
- There is a failure to file registration or other reports with federal and state regulatory agencies.

Securities fraud is subjected to vigorous federal enforcement by the U.S. Securities and Exchange Commission and state regulatory agencies.

Boiler Room Operations

The boiler room technique is used to promote fraudulent sales of securities, charitable solicitations, and similar frauds. It involves the use of telephone sales that might operate locally or use long distance lines. Salespersons call lists of prospective victims, normally corporate executives or fiduciaries (especially those involved in managing pension and retirement funds in a company). The salespersons in boiler room operations work on high commissions using pre-planned sales pitches. Their services, in addition to securities, often involve charitable solicitations that might be legitimate but are not authorized by the operation. Sometimes seemingly legitimate service companies operating boiler rooms sell their services to a legitimate but naive charity that sees little or none of the money gathered by the operators.

■ DIRECTORY AND OTHER ADVERTISING FRAUDS

These frauds stem from the selling of printed mass advertising services and often involve two basic types and techniques:

(1) Impersonation schemes in which white collar crime perpetrators send bills to companies that look like those usually received (e.g., from the telephone company for yellow page advertising), with directions to make checks payable to companies that look like legitimate payees of such bills.

(2) Schemes in which it is promised that advertising will appear in a publication distributed to trade customers but in which distribution goes only to the advertisers themselves. However, often the defrauders don't even print the directory.

These types of cases often become federally prosecuted offenses under the mail fraud statute and can also fall under state general fraud laws, larceny, and false pretenses statutes.

■ CHARITY AND RELIGIOUS FRAUDS

American businesses regularly receive requests for donations to worthy causes. According to the American Association of Fund Raising Counsel, about $4.8 billion in money and merchandise is contributed to charitable causes by American corporations each year, and the amount increases annually (it is up from $3.8 billion ten years ago). Although many of these causes are legitimate, their success has drawn the white collar criminal to mimic them and even use their names without any affiliation. Deceptive charity pleas defraud businesses and injure legitimate, cost-effective, and responsible charitable groups by undermining their efforts to raise funds for truly worthy causes. Keep in mind the following important points:

(1) Frauds generally stem from organizations representing themselves as fund-raising representatives of legitimate charitable and religious groups, or using names and titles that sound legitimate to create a false perception of legitimacy.

(2) Such schemes enjoy success because almost any company has an interest in creating the best possible public relations.

(3) Bogus charity or religious groups include those that solicit money for a nonexistent organization or cause, or for a charitable front created for the sole purpose of soliciting funds that end up in the collectors' pockets.

(4) Misrepresentation of association with a charity or religious group is common. Money appears to be solicited for a legitimate organization or cause (such as environmental interests) by individuals with no ties to the organization or cause they claim to represent. They have no intention of giving the money to the organization or cause.

(5) Misrepresentation of the benefits or uses of contributions is common. In this situation, those companies solicited for donations to a legitimate charity or religious organizations are unaware that most of the money collected reverts not to the charitable cause but instead is used to cover the cost of professional fund raisers and administrative overhead expenses. (This is a gray area since professional fund raisers perform a legitimate service for which they may properly and legitimately be compensated.)

(6) Sometimes charitable organizations themselves are the victims of con persons who use them as a front and keep the lion's share of the collections (such as in boiler room operations). In other instances the falsification falls into a gray area where otherwise legitimate charities and causes will cover up that most of the monies collected from corporations go to their salaries, fund raisers, and the like.

Solution

Appoint a charitable contribution manager. Normally the best choice will be an employee under the management of the company controller. Next, create a corporate policy that supplies guidelines for company donations and requires validation of the request as legitimate and worthy. Ensure that your company charitable contribution manager asks for a report from the requesting agency that includes

- The full name and address of the organization represented as a legitimate charity
- A complete description of the organization's purpose for the donation
- Descriptions of the organization's programs (i.e., What is the money used for?)
- A list of accomplishments and bona fide references
- Details about how much of the donated money goes to meet overhead expenses
- A financial statement that you can verify
- IRS verification that the organization has nonprofit status and qualifies as a tax-deductible charity
- Any added information that your best judgment tells you to obtain.

This might seem to be too much time-consuming work for the money donated. However, if companies do not begin this practice, honest charities suffer and companies subsidize white collar crime.

■ COLLATERAL FRAUDS

These frauds involve the holding, taking, or offering of collateral pursuant to a financial transaction. Often, these frauds will be banking transactions. Beyond this, however, such frauds may be encountered with any transaction that provides bogus security, such as nonexistent accounts receivable sold or pledged to companies. Sometimes collateral used as security may not belong to the person offering it. It could be stolen (e.g., stolen securities), borrowed, or already subject to an undisclosed lien or other encumbrance. There can also be some gross misrepresentation about its value.

■ COMPETITIVE PROCUREMENT FRAUD

This entails unlawful manipulation of the public or private contracting process. Victims normally involve competitor companies not participating in the fraud; the public or private company soliciting bids (believed to be competitive); and customers or stock holders of those companies who do not realize benefits that stem from a truly competitive procurement process. The three primary types of competitive procurement fraud include the following:

Bid Rigging:

This is a form of illegal anticompetitive conduct in which bidders in a competitive procurement collusively set their bids to deprive the corporate bid solicitor of a competitive process. The effect is an administered bidding process in which the terms and prices of the goods and services involved in the procurement are set by the conspirators instead of by the competitive process. Parties to the conspiracy can divide among themselves a relevant set of procurement contracts and fix prices for goods and services simultaneously.

Bid Fixing:

This is a form of illegal manipulation of the corporate procurement process in which one bidding party receives inside information (by the corporate solicitor or an agent of the company) that enables the bidder to gain an unfair advantage over other bidders.

Bribery and Kickbacks:

In this fraud, procurement contracts are awarded based on payment of bribes and kickbacks to a corporate procurement official instead of legitimate competitive procurement guidelines.

Competitive procurement frauds are prosecuted under federal and state criminal laws proscribing mail fraud, criminal conspiracy, bribery, kickbacks, and others. Proof in these cases involves

(1) The most painstaking analysis of bidding patterns

(2) Examination of relationships between bids to the corporation whose defrauding injures, and bids by the same bidders to other corporations for possible broader patterns of tradeoffs

(3) Close scrutiny of performance on the jobs done pursuant to contracts.

■ INSURANCE FRAUDS

Insurance frauds include frauds directed at corporations by or against insurance companies. The victims might include the client company or stock holders of insurance companies or the insurer itself. Insurance fraud divides into the following categories and subclasses:

(1) Frauds perpetrated by insurers against client companies or stock holders include the following deliberate and intentional practices:

—Failure to provide coverage promised and paid when a company or employee files a legitimate claim

—Failure to compensate or reimburse properly on claims

—Manipulation of risk classes and high-risk policy-holder categories

—Embezzlement or abuse of trust in management of premium funds and other assets of insurance companies

—Twisting—the illegal sales practice where the insurer persuades client companies to cancel current policies and purchase new ones from them

(2) Types of frauds perpetrated by insureds against insurance providers include

—Filing of bogus claims for compensation or reimbursement; multiple claims for same loss from different insurers

—Inflating reimbursable costs on claim statements

—Payment of bribes or kickbacks to local agents to retain coverage or coverage in improper risk category

—Failure to disclose information or provide false statements in application for insurance.

Cases of fraud will often involve insurance company investigators or state insurance departments and be referred to investigative and prosecutive agencies. Federal prosecutions generally fall under the mail fraud statue; state and local prosecutions fall under general fraud laws, larceny statutes and others.

◼ COUPON REDEMPTION FRAUDS

These frauds involve cheating manufacturers or merchandisers who promotes sales of their products by offering coupons that return part of the purchase price of the products bought.

Many manufacturers, primarily in the food business, place coupons in newspaper and magazine advertising media offering, for example, "50¢ Off" if the product is purchased. The grocery store redeems the coupon and will usually receive a service charge of about 5 cents for handling the transaction. Frauds committed against the manufacturers occur when a party amasses large numbers of coupons and submits them to the manufacturers without any bona fide purchases of the products. These frauds probably amount to many tens of millions of dollars annually.

The method of operation (modus operandi) of this type white collar crime involves two basic steps:

(1) *Collecting coupons*: Collecting coupons may involve searching through large numbers of old newspapers and magazines; sometimes trash collection or waste disposal companies do this as a side venture.

(2) *Processing for redemption*: Processing for collection involves the collaboration of retail merchants and is most efficiently done with the cooperation of officials of food retail chains, often without the knowledge of their companies.

Prosecution of these white collar crimes normally falls under federal mail fraud statutes, although they could be prosecuted under numerous state fraud statutes.

◼ INSIDER SELF-DEALING

Insider self-dealing involves benefiting oneself or others in whom one has an interest by trading on privileged information or position. It victimizes banks and corporations. According to government statistics, insider self-dealing has been responsible for about half the bank failures in the United States since 1960.

Typical violative situations include those in which a corporate officer or director trades the stock of his or her company because of inside information about prospective profits or losses; bank officers lending money to themselves or businesses in which they have an interest; and corporate executives or purchasing officials setting up suppliers of goods and services to contract with their companies.

■ REAL ESTATE FRAUDS

Commonly called "land fraud," this is a type of investment fraud that includes the sale of land to investing corporations based on extensive misrepresentations about the land's value, quality, facilities, or state of development (e.g., industrial park). Victim companies normally include those investing or purchasing land for later expansion or diversification ventures. Land frauds normally involve the sale of land or of interest in land

- When the seller has no present title or claim of right (i.e., seller cannot properly transfer title or interest to buyer as represented at the time of the sale)
- About which there is a misrepresentation or failure to disclose a material fact to the purchasing company
- At inflated or unjustified prices based on misrepresentations to the purchasing company
- On the promise of future performance or development that the seller neither intends to provide nor can reasonably expect to happen
- Through misrepresentations, such as the presence of utilities, water, roads, credit terms, and other important aspects.

Such frauds have been perpetrated for decades and have resulted in many successful prosecutions on both federal and local prosecutive levels, and in extensive civil court actions by regulatory agencies that have brought restitution to victim companies and options to cancel improvident purchases. There is substantial federal, state, and local cooperation in this enforcement area.

■ INVESTMENT FRAUDS

These frauds create losses to investing corporations induced by the prospect of capital growth and high rates of return. The victimization occurs when the corporations invest money in imprudent, illusory, or bogus projects or other companies or businesses.

Hallmarks of these frauds generally include the following:

- Higher than average promised rates of return
- Developmental nature of investment (i.e., project or business is not a mature entity)
- Sales made by strangers (i.e., through boiler room operations)
- Generalized definition of the nature and scope of project or business, lacking detailed plans that permit observation of real progress
- Object or site of investment geographically remote or a distance from the investing company
- Failure to disclose fully facts to the investor before company money is committed
- Nonregistration with U.S. Securities and Exchange Commission and comparable state regulatory agencies
- Promise of special advantages.

Examples of such frauds are too numerous to include here. They are generally violations of special statutes such as the federal Securities Acts enforced by the U.S. Securities and Exchange Commission, state securities regulatory laws enforced by state agencies, the mail fraud statute, and state general fraud, larceny, and false pretenses statutes.

■ THE PLANNED BUSINESS BANKRUPTCY SCHEME

This popular scam has bilked countless companies and banks, large to small, out of their profits because such scams are hard to detect (according to government statistics, the losses are about a billion dollars a year). Normally, the planned bankruptcy scam begins as a two- or three-year project with the first year of operations strictly legitimate. The central scheme will include developing an unquestioned credibility and a comfortable line of credit with as many companies as possible. The objective will include obtaining as much merchandise as possible through the established credit, then selling it off at low prices, and claiming business bankruptcy before leaving town to create a new enterprise elsewhere.

There's a strong trend for formerly honest business persons to turn to this type of white collar crime, probably because they know how to work the banks and corporations (based on their former experience inside such organizations). A 1979 change to the federal bankruptcy code eased the filing of bankruptcy but also created an environment that encourages bankruptcy fraud.

Business Bankruptcy Scam One: Forming a New "Sham" Corporation

A new corporation is formed and managed by a front person, or "pencil," who has no criminal or personal bankruptcy record or adverse personal credit information. This person often will come from a distant state and offer a legitimate reason for coming to the area, (e.g., he or she visited the area on vacation once and it offered exactly what he or she always looked for in a place to live and work). Another common theme includes visiting the area over the years to visit a great aunt who passed away some years back. The old newspaper files will give them enough information about the contrived "loved one" to make the story credible. The "staff" this person brings in creates the real brains of the operation. Normally, the new corporate president will also try to find some local workers to serve as secretaries, sales personnel, and other low-level employees. The hiring of respectable locals enables the new corporation to gain credibility and supplies important startup information about other companies, areas, and people. A local attorney is hired by the new corporation as its corporate counsel; however, accountants will normally be part of the traveling team.

Normally, depending on the startup capital available for the scam, the corporation will select two to four local banks and make initial large cash deposits (known as the "nut" or "carrot") to create an image of wealth. It will later approach the bank for a line of credit. Having two or more sizable bank accounts will also help the company obtain a favorable Dun & Bradstreet rating later.

Small operators often work out of a store; however, the real pros normally will not waste capital on this method, choosing instead to pose as a supplier and rent one or more warehouses to supply their mostly out-of-state customers and those they can develop locally or in state. These operators will regularly have connections to others across the country who market the goods purchased at a low price, thus maintaining an impressive cash flow during the first few months. It's essential for the company to pay its bills punctually, meet payroll, and keep the appearance of growth and solvency. Selling merchandise to "customers" (others running scams elsewhere) who fax or call in orders creates a credible paper trail, and the local employees hired as sales representatives create a customer base in the area. The corporate executives live well but not conspicuously, and do nothing that might tip off the banks or the business community that they're setting them up for a huge fall. All appearances show creditors that the people running this company have what it takes. Eventually, the creditors will do all possible to help them meet their goals.

The next step involves approaching manufacturers (across the country and locally), acting interested in their products (items easily sold elsewhere quickly at cost), but maintaining a rigid attitude that makes the company appear to be a "hard sell" group. Company representatives negotiate for the best possible deal, the best terms, and bait the suppliers into bending over backward to sell their products to their corporation.

The new corporation also approaches the banks and asks for short-term loans to make payroll (or some other excuse) using their large deposits as the incentive to persuade the bank that it cannot lose. The loans, just like the commercial accounts, always stay current and soon the corporation has the credibility it needs to make its move.

After a year or so of operations, with a strong credit rating, a record of perceived growth, and a credible excuse for expansion, the corporation rents another warehouse and begins to place huge orders and obtain large loans. Within a month or two it has millions of dollars in merchandise flowing in and moving out its warehouses to parts unknown. The loans go into the company's bank accounts, and checks in large sums begin going to other "shell corporations" across the country and into accounts established there. Checks from the shell companies go to other companies and finally disappear into "services" companies and personal bank accounts and transferred to off-shore banks. Some operators establish twenty or more shell or paper corporations to confuse the paper trail.

When the company obtains all the loans, merchandise, and other advantages and the money and products are moved out, the corporate counsel receives word that the company has become irreversibly insolvent and counsel must file bankruptcy for the corporation. As this process begins, the company team goes on vacation and waits for a reasonable time (in a place like the Cayman Islands, probably where their money was consolidated), and when the time is right everyone disappears. The bankruptcy court finds no assets, and the creditors (including your company or bank) have lined the pockets of these white collar criminals to the tune of many millions of dollars. The huge orders received and not paid for, plus the large bank loans, supply the corporate officers' take.

Business Bankruptcy Scam Two: Buying an Established Corporation

This business bankruptcy scam has become popular. In this scam, the operators, using a "front" person, buy an established and successful local business that has excellent community and business standing plus a strong credit rating. No notice of the change in ownership and management is reported to

Dun and Bradstreet or other credit agencies, so the scam artists can begin trading on the previous owner's good credit and reputation.

Manufacturers are approached at their companies or trade shows to arrange for the purchase of merchandise. Since the orders placed are usually of a large quantity, suppliers who did not sell to the acquired company earlier are politely informed by the scam operator that if they do not sell to him or her on an open account, some other companies will be glad to do so. This technique is commonly called the "sketch." Large orders are then placed, including orders for many items not bought by the former owners. However, orders are limited to items that can be trucked out and sold easily through the black market network of professional fences.

After receiving the orders and the merchandise or goods are moved out to sell, and the money is siphoned into a labyrinth of accounts, the acquired company files bankruptcy and the operators leave town.

Business Bankruptcy Scam Three: The Same Name Scam

This technique is a variation of the others and operates as follows: A company is formed with a name that is deceptively similar, and often almost identical, to a successful company known in a widespread area (normally as far away as a distant state). The idea is that name recognition is perceived as an expansion of the well-known company. Large orders are placed with suppliers, who, assuming the company is legitimate because of the similarity in names, fill the orders.

The merchandise is sold in the same fashion as with other types of scam operators, with a systematic siphoning of the money from the business. As with other types of scams, the company files bankruptcy, leaving the creditors to take the loss.

■ MAIL AND WIRE FRAUDS

Most frauds that victimize corporations develop or are carried out using the mail or wire (telephone, facsimile machines, and computer-to-computer links). Although a personal visit or conference might begin a fraudulent transaction, at some point mail or wire becomes the means of contact or culmination. This works to your advantage in all or almost all cases when your company becomes a victim of another business, because it supplies effective legal remedies (either criminal or civil or both). On the following pages, I supply an overview of the possibilities using the federal statute on mail and wire frauds to focus on definitions and remedial action you can take when victimized. You can use this guide for training your management staff and employees and creating an effective group of company policies and procedures to eliminate the opportunities that make your corporation vulnerable.

The following glossary defines those words and phrases uniquely characteristic to or applied to this type of white collar crime and that have acquired specialized meaning in statutes:

- *Artifice*: An ingenious contrivance or device such as a trick or fraud
- *Fiduciary*: A person holding the character similar to a trustee
- *Kickback*: Secret payments made for secret consideration
- *Lulling*: Letters designed to occasion delay in the detection of a scheme to defraud
- *Stopgap device*: A phrase used by the Supreme Court about Section 1341 (Mail and Wire Fraud) as a statute serving to prosecute fraudulent schemes when no specific legislation yet exists
- *Wire communication*: Communication by television, radio, telegraph, telephone, or any other form of radio signal, including microwave signal.

■ FRAUDS AND SWINDLES UNDER UNITED STATES CODE, TITLE 18, CHAPTER 63

Section 1341: Frauds and Swindles

This section reads as follows:

Whoever, having devised or intending to devise any scheme or artifice to defraud, or for obtaining money or property through false or fraudulent pretenses, representations, or promises, or to sell, dispose of, loan, exchange, alter, give away, distribute, supply, or furnish or procure for unlawful use any counterfeit or spurious coin, obligation, security, or other article, or anything represented to be or intimated or held out to as such counterfeit or spurious article, for the purpose of executing such scheme or artifice or attempting to do so, places in any post office or authorized depository for mail matter, any matter or thing whatever sent or delivered by the Postal Service, or takes or receives therefrom, any such matter or thing, or knowingly causes to be delivered by mail according to the direction thereon, or at the place at which it is directed to be delivered by the person to whom it is addressed, any such matter or thing shall be fined not more than $1,000 or imprisoned not more than five years, or both.

Section 1343: Fraud by Wire, Radio or Television

This section reads as follows:

Whoever, having devised or intending to devise any scheme or artifice to defraud, or for obtaining money or property by means of false or fraudulent pretenses, representations, or promises, transmits or causes to be transmitted by means of wire, radio, or television communication in interstate or foreign commerce, any writings, signs, signals, pictures, or sounds for the purpose of executing such scheme or artifice, shall be fined not more than $1,000 or imprisoned not more than five years, or both.

Section 1346: Definition of "Scheme or Artifice to Defraud"

For this chapter (U.S. Code, Chapter 63), the phrase *scheme or artifice to defraud* includes a scheme or artifice to deprive another of the intangible right of honest services.

■ APPLICATION OF MAIL AND WIRE FRAUD STATUTES: ELEMENTS OF THE STATUTES

The Scheme to Defraud

There is no rule of thumb to determine what creates a company or consumer fraud prohibited by the mail or wire fraud statutes. The courts have long held that what creates a scheme to defraud is not subject to a precise definition (for example, *Blachly v. United States*, 380 F.2d 665 [5th Cir. 1987]). What has made these statues (mail and wire fraud) so useful in fraud cases is that the phrase *scheme to defraud* has been broadly defined as including all the many and varied ways that human ingenuity can devise and be resorted to by any persons to gain an unfair advantage over another by false representation, half truths, or concealment of material facts. (Decided by *Weiss v. United States*,

122 F.2d 675, 681 [5th Cir.]) Put more succinctly, a scheme to defraud defined by this case and court included any plan to obtain something of value by trick or deceit.

To prove a fraudulent scheme, it is unnecessary to show that the scheme was successful in the sense that some person or corporation was cheated or swindled; however, it must have the capacity to defraud to be within the purview of these statutes. Deceitful conduct alone is insufficient to create a scheme to defraud. Your company must also establish that the company or person at least planned some actual injury (loss) or harm to your company or persons within it.

Use of the Mails

The broad reach of the mail fraud statute becomes clear when we consider that almost every business uses the mails. If a business becomes engaged in fraudulent conduct, the activity is within the reach of the mail fraud statute, even when the mailings are entirely intrastate. It is also unnecessary that the people defrauding you or your company physically mail anything. It is enough if they make use of the mail to further a fraudulent scheme. For example, if your company mails a check in payment for something the defrauder induced you to purchase or donate, that will serve within the statute as a mailing in furtherance of the scheme to defraud.

Use of Interstate or Foreign Wire Facilities

Unlike the mail fraud statute, the wire fraud statute calls for the wire communication in furtherance of the scheme to be an interstate or foreign communication. The defrauder need not personally make the wire communication. The interstate or foreign wire communication can originate from the victim (your company) of the fraud, or even a third party, if the communication in some way furthers the scheme. The wire fraud statute has been particularly useful in prosecuting defrauders using a boiler room operation to solicit customers by phone from across the country. It has also served when defrauders use radio and television to advertise falsely their product or service.

Mailing and Wire Communication in Furtherance of the Scheme

Not every mailing or interstate or foreign wire communication is, *ipso facto* (by the fact itself), fraudulent. A jurisdictional basis for a mail or wire fraud violation stipulates that the mailing or wire communication must have some nexus to the scheme and must in some way further the scheme. If the mailing or wire communication happens after the scheme to defraud reaches completion, it cannot remain within the definition of "furtherance of the scheme" and cannot become the basis for a mail or wire fraud prosecution unless it happened to conceal the fraudulent scheme. (For an example of this reasoning, see *United States v. Decker*, 411 F.2d 306 [4th Cir. 1969] or *United States v. Sampson*, 371 U.S. 75, 83 S.Ct. 173, 9 L.Ed. 2d 136 [1962]).

■ WHAT CASES ARE PROSECUTED UNDER THESE STATUTES

Schemes involving only a few isolated transactions with minor losses to companies or persons will probably become a matter for criminal or civil litigation in the state courts. If, however, a scheme is of sufficient magnitude and involves a substantial pattern of conduct that uses the mails or interstate or foreign wire facilities, then the chance of federal prosecution increases.

Criminal Liability of Corporations, Officers, and Employees

A corporation acts through its officers, employees, and agents. Further, a corporation has responsibility for the criminal acts of its officers, employees, and agents if the acts happen within the scope of employment and with intent to benefit the corporation or further the corporate business. This reasoning of the courts stems from key cases such as *Boise Dodge, Inc. v. United States*, 406 F.2d 771 (9th Cir. 1969); *United States v. Carter*, 311 F.2d 934, 941–43 (6th Cir. 1963); *Magnolia Motor & Logging Co. v. United States*, 264 F.2d 950, 954 (9th Cir. 1959); *American Medical Association v. United States*, 130 F.2d 233 (D.C. Cir. 1943).

Participation by a corporation in a scheme to defraud does not automatically make its officers criminally liable (for example, *United States v. Amrep Corporation*, 560 F.2d 539 [2d Cir. 1977]). Instead, it is necessary for the prosecution to establish that the corporate officers were "conscious promoters" of the scheme as decided by *United States v. Dilliard*, 101 F.2d 829, 834 (2d Cir. 1938). However, under the mail and wire fraud statutes, as in a conspiracy case, it is unnecessary for each of the schemers to have knowledge of all facets of the scheme. Nor is the guilt of the corporate person governed by the extent of his or her participation. Even if the corporate person participated in the scheme to a lesser degree than others, he or she has equal culpability if he or she joined the scheme with knowledge of its general scope and purpose (for example, *United States v. Amrep Corporation*).

If corporate employees and salespeople take part in what they know to be a fraudulent scheme, they become criminally liable. The courts have defined "participating" in a scheme as associating with it with a view and intent to make it succeed. However, a mere onlooker is not a participant in a scheme to defraud. For a salesperson to be criminally liable, he or she must know the fraudulent nature of the scheme and share in the requisite criminal intent (for example, *United States v. Pearlstein*, 576 F.2d 531 [3d Cir. 1978]).

■ PROVING YOUR CASE AGAINST A DEFRAUDING COMPANY

Investigation

The United States Postal Inspection service is the federal law enforcement agency primarily responsible for investigating violations of the mail fraud statute, while the Federal Bureau of Investigation has primary responsibility for investigating violations of the wire fraud statute. Both agencies work closely with the prosecutor when investigating this type of fraudulent activity. A fraud perpetrated against a company or person normally begins after your complaint or other information received by the government about the fraudulent activity.

Proving the Scheme to Defraud

Proof of the fraudulent scheme against your company normally stems from recounting the representations that induced your corporation or its representative to accept the defrauder's offer. Proof that those representations were false or misleading often follows. However, it is unnecessary to prove that an actual misrepresentation happened, since a statement figuratively true may nonetheless remain entirely misleading (for example, *Durland v. United States*, 161 U.S. 306, 314, 16 S.Ct. 508, 40 L.Ed. 709 [1986]). Moreover, "the deception need not be premised on the verbalized words alone." "The arrangement of the words, or the circumstances in which used may convey the false and deceptive appearance" (for example, decided by *Gusow v. United States*, 347 F.2d 755, 756 [10th Cir. 1965]; and *United States v. Sheiner*, 273 F. Supp. 977, 983 [S.D.N.Y. 1967]). A statement may also become misleading because material facts were omitted or concealed (for example, *Lustiger v. United States*, 386 F.2d 132 [9th Cir. 1967]). Further, representations couched as opinion may also become criminally actionable. An opinion—such as that something is a "good investment"—must remain honestly held by the speaker, who must have a good-faith basis for it. Otherwise, he or she may become subject to prosecution for false representation (for example, *United States v. Grayson*, 166 F.2d 863, 866 [2d Cir. 1948]).

It is necessary that only the most gullible would have been deceived (for example, *Lemon v. United States*, 278 F.2d 369, 373 [9th Cir. 1960] or *Deaver v. United States*, 155 F.2d 740, 745 [D.C. Cir 1946]). Caveat emptor (let the buyer beware) can no longer serve as a shield to criminal prosecution. The courts have decided in key cases that "the lack of guile by those generally solicited may itself point with persuasion to the fraudulent character of the artifice." (For example, see *Norman v. United States*, 100 F.2d 905, 907 [6th Cir. 1939] and *Blue v. United States*, 138 F.2d 351, 358 [6th Cir. 1943]).

When establishing the fraudulent nature of the scheme against your company or its representatives, proof of high-pressure selling techniques and "hard sell" is permissible (for example, *United States v. Uhrig*, 443 F.2d 239, 242 [7th Cir. 1971]). High-pressure sales tactics are not per se fraudulent. Yet evidence of the use of this type of undesirable commercial conduct is relevant on the issues of a scheme to defraud and intent to defraud.

Maybe the most powerful proof of the fraudulent nature of a scheme will come from the testimony of the victims themselves. It is well settled that victims of a scheme to defraud may testify about the impressions they received from the defrauder's representations, how and why they became deceived, and why they relied on the representations (for example, *United States v. Blachly*, 380 F.2d 665, 673 [5th Cir. 1967], *Phillips v. United States*, 356 F.2d 297, 307 [9th Cir. 1965], *United States v. Baren*, 305 F.2d 527 [2d Cir. 1962], *Linden v. United States*, 254 F.2d 560 [4th Cir. 1958], or *Rice v. United States*, 35 F.2d 689, 695 [2d Cir. 1929]). Your company can also testify that had your corporate representative not been misled in the manner stated, he or she would not have committed your company and entered the transaction involved.

Finally, to establish the scheme to defraud, the government does not need to prove every misrepresentation alleged in an indictment. It is sufficient if there is overall proof that a scheme to defraud existed (for example, *United States v. Amrep Corporation*, 560 F.2d 539, 546 [2d Cir. 1977]).

How to Gain Knowledge of the Accused Defrauder and the Sales Presentation

Most schemes directed at businesses involve carefully orchestrated sales presentations that often include scripts that sales representatives must follow exactly. Moreover, it is not unusual for a defrauder to be intimately involved in preparing and reviewing the sales presentations and advertisements or even training sales personnel. When the sales presentation is standardized by the defrauding company and used consistently, the knowledge of a high-level company officer will often be inferred even without direct evidence (for example, *United States v. Andreadis*, 366 F.2d 423, 430 [2d Cir. 1966] and *Reistroffer v. United States*, 258 F.2d 379, 387 [8th Cir. 1958]).

Since the selling effort is usually at the center of a company's business, it is difficult, if not impossible, for a high-level corporate officer to deny having knowledge of the claims made concerning the corporate promotional literature. But a company and its high-level officers cannot be held criminally responsible for unauthorized statements made by sales representatives in their employ (for example, *United States v. Interstate Engineering Corporation*, 288 F.Supp. 402, 408 [D.N.H. 1967] or *New England Enterprises, Incorporated v. United States*, 400 F.2d 58 [1st Cir. 1968]).

The Fraudulent Nature of the Scheme

Proving that an accused defrauder knew the fraudulent nature of the scheme normally evolves from circumstantial evidence. Such knowledge generally will become inferred from a pattern of conduct or from a series of acts "aptly designated as badges of fraud" (for example, *United States v. Amrep Corporation*, noted earlier). For example, proof that salespeople were specifically trained by the accused defrauder to use high-pressure selling techniques and to make the complaint of representation concerning the product or service can supply proof that the defrauder knew of the fraudulent nature of the scheme. The evidence of the defrauder's knowledge about the fraudulent nature of the scheme can come from proof of your company's complaints to the defrauder. This is relevant not only on the issue of the defrauder's bad faith and fraudulent intent, but also to show the defrauder's knowledge about methods used by people making the sale. So the courts have decided that failure to give refunds is probative of a defrauder fraudulent intent. (These important issues stem from the cases cited earlier.)

Another fertile area of proof about a defrauder's knowledge of the fraudulent nature of the scheme comes from depositions, affidavits, and interrogatories submitted with parallel civil litigation. Corporate officers often supply depositions or submit affidavits or interrogatories on some issues relevant in the criminal case. Often, these documents will contain admissions by a person about his or her familiarity with the sales practices of the company, and the complaints received by the company from other companies it has done business with. This circumstance is strong reason for counsel for the corporation or its officers to cast a wary eye toward the possibility of criminal prosecution. Civil complaints of fraud, be they private or regulatory, should alert counsel to consider whether the company representatives will testify or answer interrogatories. An assertion of privilege early on may be in the company's best interest and should be weighed carefully.

■ HOW TO AVOID BECOMING A CORPORATE VICTIM: COLLECTIVE PREVENTIVE ACTION

Whether organized along national, regional, or local lines or structured to focus on specific industrial and corporate problems, collective action by business and professions goes far to becoming a key ingredient in an informed response to white collar crime. A company acting on an individual basis may lack financial resources, expertise, perspective, and other aspects, but the clout to deal with white collar crime could form through a coalition or organization to which all legitimate companies belong and support. Through such a collective effort to curb the victimization of corporations and industry from white collar crime enterprises, each member benefits and results that could not be attained alone are achieved jointly.

A cooperative effort between legitimate companies can become highly effective when

(1) It involves a large and professional staff to apply the necessary time coupled with the expertise to the problem at hand.

(2) It is supported on an equitable basis by all legitimate companies and creates an inexpensive contribution that's clearly cost effective.

(3) It analyzes each member company's problems and threats and develops a comprehensive perspective coupled with viable solutions.

(4) It promotes unified action and shields each member company from the problems that would result if there were not a joint action.

Objectives of collective preventive action by corporations include the following:

■ Funnel criminal intelligence to law enforcement agencies and to participating companies.

■ Conduct investigations and compile evidence that involves expertise, time, and personnel not regularly available to hard-pressed police and prosecutors.

■ Upgrade the ethical codes of companies and professions.

- Serve as a central source of information that was fragmented, scattered, and difficult to obtain.
- Begin and support protective legislation.
- Help law enforcement agencies who normally must begin at the bottom of a corporation and work up by identifying the problems at the top.
- Serve as a coordinating factor between the companies and law enforcement and thus save time.

■ ORGANIZATIONS SUPPLYING SUPPORT SERVICES TO CORPORATIONS

A variety of separate support services can help you solve your company's problems when you believe another company (normally a nonlegitimate company operating under the guise of a legitimate company) has targeted your company for white collar crime.

The Fraud Prevention Department of the National Association of Credit Management: This organization supplies an early warning service and conducts investigations to obtain information necessary for indictments and convictions in scam cases. For example, this department can add to the scope of a bankruptcy fraud investigation by collecting pertinent information from every part of the nation. It spreads the cost of the investigations to develop evidence of fraud among subscribing member companies.

American Bankers Association: This organization supplies free white collar crime investigative services to member banks. For example, the investigations include swindles such as stolen or fraudulent credit cards and forgery of checks. It also publishes a protective bulletin alerting readers to various frauds and criminals.

Insurance Crime Prevention Institute: This organization seeks to deter insurance fraud through the investigation of key cases and presentation of evidence to prosecution authorities.

Joint Industry Committee: The principal goal of this New York City-based organization is to reduce securities theft and fraud and increase recoveries. Members of the JIC include representatives of banks, stock exchanges, securities dealers, and brokerage houses. It serves as a liaison between law enforcement and the financial community.

Other Important Sources of Assistance

The following list is not all inclusive but notes some of the sources that can provide information or assistance and can supply you with other current sources.

- District or prosecuting attorney
- Police or sheriff departments
- Local or state law enforcement or regulatory agencies specializing in white collar crime
- State attorney general
- U.S. attorney for your area
- State insurance commissioner
- Antitrust division, U.S. Department of Justice
- Criminal division, U.S. Department of Justice
- FBI office in your area
- Federal Trade Commission and nearest regional FTC office
- Intelligence division, Internal Revenue Service in your IRS district
- Office of Interstate Land Sales Registration, U.S. Department of Housing and Urban Development
- Office of Labor, Management and Welfare, Pension Reports, U.S. Department of Labor
- Postal inspector or postmaster nearest to your location
- Securities and Exchange Commission
- U.S. Secret Service, Department of the Treasury

Part Four
The Corporate White Collar Crime Management Unit

■ **INTRODUCTION**

Too few people in the corporate and industrial business world squarely face the problem of white collar crime. This is also true of most law enforcement agencies, although heightened attention to such offenses seems to have become a growing trend. A principal reason why corporations and law enforcement alike seem to deal with white collar crime offenses delicately stems from an insufficient understanding of what it is, what its consequences are, and why the traditional response to the problem is inappropriate.

The problem of white collar crime and how it affects corporate and industrial security of assets surpasses lines of geography, types of businesses, and variety of threats. It creates massive profit losses each year totaling billions of dollars. As this problem continues to grow, it's apparent that only when corporations tackle it as a management function will the trend reverse. However, managing white collar crime cannot fall within traditional business management concepts; instead it must become a specialized internal function equal in importance to any other department within your company. It must also become a function that operates from the highest levels yet integrates its activities into a cooperative working relationship with all the company operational functions. It must not become a "witch-hunt" activity but instead a unit that protects the company assets fairly, efficiently, and effectively.

This type of white collar crime management unit should form independent from other duties and become an administrative and investigative arm of your company's security division. For corporations that contract security or do not have a security force, a white collar crime management unit should work autonomously for the company president or the level close to that position. White collar crime investigators must remain impartial and fair, and have the unquestioned authority to conduct investigative audits and other investigative and intelligence activities to protect the company.

In Part Four, I supply you with guidelines for creating this important management unit using existing security forces or creating it as a separate company activity. I also discuss white collar crime intelligence collection and management, coordination with law enforcement and other agencies, ways of finding experts to help when necessary, and a variety of subjects that enable you to get control and management of this formidable threat. In addition, I present guidelines for selecting and training white collar crime management specialists and how to create effective, comprehensive cases for civil and criminal actions. Throughout the book I've discussed a myriad of problems, solutions, techniques, and legal aspects of white collar crime. I devote the remainder of the book to discussing creation of the unit to carry out these functions.

Chapter Fourteen
How to Create a White Collar Crime Management Unit

Even the most competent white collar crime investigative specialists will not be effective unless they can work within the proper organizational structure. The ways in which investigators share responsibilities, communicate, cooperate, and supervise can have a strong influence on how well they do, separately and together.

If your white collar crime management unit is focused on detection (investigative audits for internal problems, subsidiaries, and other company affiliations), prevention solutions, and protecting the company from external threats such as organized crime enterprises, other businesses and the spectrum of threats they present become a priority. What would satisfy the needs of an industrial complex might differ importantly from those of an urban corporate headquarters, a bank or other financial institution, or some other company operation. Different approaches to the types of white collar crime and a focus on criminal or civil remedies play an important role in how extensive your investigative unit needs to be. However, the basic organizational concept remains the same despite the type of corporate operation. I will outline that universal structuring and procedural process in this chapter. You can adapt it to your company, either increasing or decreasing its size and capacity as your needs and threat levels dictate.

■ PLAN THE WCC UNIT'S GOALS AND OBJECTIVES

The security director or white collar crime management unit manager must first plan the white collar crime (WCC) management unit's goals and objectives. Organization for detection, prevention, and investigation of white collar criminal activity and related abuses will depend on resources available and require explicit goals and priorities. There are a variety of possible goals for the unit, and the standards each company may set to achieve those goals can be equally numerous. Some of the goals to consider include maximizing, but not limiting them to, the following categories:

- The number of investigative audits performed
- Creating solutions, policies, and procedures supplied to top management
- Setting priorities for the investigation of white collar crime activities found or reported
- Recovering company assets
- Preparing necessary civil actions and prosecutions
- Increasing the deterrent aspects throughout the company for external threats
- Increasing the deterrent aspects throughout the company for internal threats.

General statements of goals and objectives such as "fighting white collar crime" or "protecting corporate assets" will give people the idea that no true direction will come of them. Enunciated goals, priorities, and policies may not always be compatible with each other. Sometimes approaching one objective will prevent achieving another. For example, concentrating all resources on a recovery effort or investigation of an obvious major problem might prevent criminal prosecution or investigation of minor but growing problems that might have a greater effect later.

Confronting the problem of white collar crime within your company has some unique dimensions that make it difficult to determine goals and objectives. To begin with, the term *white collar crime* represents a complex and extremely varied range of conduct, as described in earlier chapters. You cannot merely set the goal of "reducing white collar crime in the company" because that would be meaningless. Instead, it is necessary to settle on what white collar crime activities or specific types of conduct your corporation plans to reduce (this decision often stems from the balance sheet and working papers that show where unexplained losses or operating costs exceed normal ranges). Furthermore, white collar crimes generally will not come and find you; instead you will have to find them through systematic investigative audits and intelligence collection. To approach white collar crime generally as a corporate problem in hopes of reducing it leads to difficulty in assessing the performance toward reaching that goal.

Setting goals and related objectives in the white collar crime area must be largely a process of specifying and limiting the focus of an investigative effort to some manageable part of this crime area. You must recognize that the investigative unit cannot do everything; there must be some determination of what best serves the corporation and what you can do effectively with the staff, resources, and time available.

What you can do effectively is largely a function of staff characteristics and resources. What you can do to serve the corporation best must relate primarily to an assessment of what is happening in your corporate environment. Your assessment should seek to answer the following questions:

- What abuses are happening and with what frequency? (Much of this will be revealed through effective investigative audits that identify the abuses and then create policies and procedures that eliminate the opportunity for such abuses.)
- Are these abuses being responded to effectively?

You should regularly review the major abuses affecting your company against the current responses to them. For example, if a major WCC abuse does not receive an effective preventive response from your unit, or is ineffectively handled by staff investigators, you should determine if your white collar crime management unit is capable of appropriately and effectively providing the needed response in all areas. A good planning and continuing assessment tool is a matrix similar to the one shown in Exhibit 14-1.

Three Techniques for Setting Effective Unit Goals

The following techniques can be used in creating effective goals and objectives for your corporate white collar crime management unit. These are only examples; you need to develop techniques that best serve your company needs.

1. Set Goals for Identified Victim Components of the Corporation

In most corporations (including industrial complexes), assessment of white collar crime problems well reveal that some components of the company are more vulnerable, especially to specific kinds of fraud abuses. For example, a company that has an intensive R & D division may experience more problems of proprietory information embezzlement than a company that contracts R & D projects. Other examples include manufacturing companies that ship large

Exhibit 14-1
Model Matrix for Determining Your Goals in White Collar Crime Investigation and Prevention

Major or Frequent Abuses	Responses to Abuses		
	Quality of Response		
	Poor	Adequate	Good

amounts of cargo, or a corporation that is heavily computerized and sells services. Each corporation has its own structuring and with that come problems that another company may not experience.

Setting WCC management unit goals based on the variety of identified victim components of the company (such as a section within a department or division) has several advantages. First, it gives your effort a clear focus. Second, because the component selected to benefit from your effort has a history of experiencing a high level of victimization, the prospect for progress also is high. This factor serves not only to motivate your investigative staff but also supplies them with satisfaction in their achievements. Third, by focusing specifically on the victimization of particular corporate components, your effort limits the range and type of cases the unit deals with. This is particularly advantageous as the WCC management unit begins operations. It allows staff members to develop expertise in a limited number of areas that will give them the confidence to go onward into less familiar investigative territory.

This technique carries with it some requirements that may prove troublesome for some corporations. First, a focus on victim components within the company normally obligates the commitment of resources and time to an important education effort, both to enhance your communications with targeted components of the company and to encourage a strong policy, procedure, and preventive effort to change current operating methods. While some degree of the education will be a part of any white collar crime management effort, the obligations of the victim-component-oriented effort are greater than usual.

The targeting of corporate victim components, however, provides a method of setting goals that can contribute a specific focus and agenda to the white collar crime prevention and response effort. However, this technique demands a commitment from the company management to a range of activities and roles that can contribute greatly to the investigative role but lie outside it. Companies unprepared to recognize, plan for, and respond to these added functions might need another method for setting goals.

After weighing the advantages and disadvantages and choosing a victim-component-oriented focus for the white collar crime management effort, your unit and company management must formally enunciate its goals and define objectives that will aid in attaining those goals. An example of a victim-component-oriented goal and accompanying objectives is as follows:

Goal: To reduce and prevent expense and travel account fraud.

Objectives:
- To conduct complete investigative audits of the expense accounts and travel claims.

- To conduct complete investigative audits of the expense account and travel claim procedures now in use and determine how best to create better policies and procedures.
- To coordinate with the internal audit section, the corporate controller, the corporate counsel, and top management staff to create recommended changes for this company component.
- To develop an employee and component education program and administer it.
- To monitor the changes and preventive benefits routinely and work with the component to ensure implementation and any modifications needed.

2. Select Your Goals by Focusing on Specific Abuses

Another technique of setting goals for your white collar crime management effort involves targeting specific white collar crime abuses within or against your company for special attention. Again, singling out specific abuses should be based on some assessment of the offenses committed in your corporation. It would be meaningless, for example, to choose land fraud as a focus of attention when there's no evidence that your company experiences losses from investing in land.

Similarly, your choice of abuses to focus on should reflect the resources available to you and the constraints under which your white collar crime management unit will operate. For example, when a white collar crime victimization appears to have staggering proportions and your unit has neither the resources, expertise, nor the authority to intervene appropriately, singling out that type fraud is ill advised.

Setting goals on the basis of selected offenses relies heavily on two key factors:

(1) The presence of adequate information so you can make intelligent choices

(2) The planning of a later effort to include supplying the resources necessary to address the offense you select.

In the absence of either of these factors, using this technique for goal determination becomes a hollow exercise that will provide little guidance or sense of mission for the corporate white collar crime management unit.

3. Set Goals to Develop Staff Expertise

A third technique for goal selection involves setting objectives related to developing the expertise of the white collar crime management unit staff in responding to a spectrum of white collar crime activities affecting or threatening your corporation. Often, this goal merges with other more specific goals such as those described earlier. This goal can become particularly important for your new white collar crime management unit, since it logically creates a first-phase goal designed to enhance the achievement of your unit staff and later will enhance achievement of more specific, offense-related goals.

One important advantage of making skill development an object of your unit's achievement is that it encourages the unit to undertake cases of greater significance and effect on protecting corporate assets. Often, these cases or investigative audits will have greater complexity and difficulty, and be more time consuming and demanding of investigative resources. Enhanced staff skills are likely to encourage the corporate white collar crime management unit staff to exercise these skills in combating white collar crime (in familiar and new forms) that threatens your company. The capacity to deal with white collar crimes often facilitates their recognition as prosecutable or civil recovery offenses.

The disadvantage of this approach is that no clear focus is provided to your corporate white collar crime management unit. Thus, your unit may drift from one investigative area to another with little sense of a coherent set of priorities. Unless you craft this goal-setting technique and carefully guide it with more substantive emphasis, the white collar crime management effort could fail.

An example of an expertise-development goal and accompanying objectives follows:

Goal: To substantially improve the capacity of the corporation's white collar crime management unit staff capacity to respond successfully to problems of white collar crime that threaten or victimize the company.

Objectives:
- To take advantage of special training programs designed to enhance or impart white collar crime investigative skills.
- To improve the quality of investigative and case preparation materials.
- To undertake investigation in novel and complex cases and bring them to satisfactory conclusions.
- To complete complex investigative tasks in cooperation with other components of the corporation and with proper criminal justice or civil litigation agencies.
- To improve the satisfactory delivery of white collar crime prevention and response services to the company.

■ CREATE PERFORMANCE CRITERIA FOR THE UNIT

When you have selected your goals and objectives for the corporate white collar crime management unit, your next step is to create acceptable criteria with which to measure your staff and unit's performance related to those goals. The term *acceptable criteria* should not imply that some standards serve better than others; instead it suggests the process through which standards become established. Performance criteria must be agreed on, accepted, and understood by all those concerned if your evaluative effort is to be useful and valid. The performance criteria, like goals and objectives, supply the best results before implementation of the WCC management effort and should involve maximum participation of the unit staff and appropriate corporate management personnel.

Obviously, acceptable criteria must relate to the goals and objectives established. If the major objective of your WCC management unit is to secure criminal penalties and parallel civil remedies for particular abuses, then an acceptable criterion of performance should relate to cases accepted by a prosecutor instead of those for which civil or mediation outcomes suffice. Sound performance criteria should measure not only outcomes, but also the consistency and rigor of the processes through which your unit achieved the outcomes.

This is why the mere counting of numbers of investigations and convictions or tallying the dollar total of restitutive settlements do not serve as sound evaluative measures. Instead, such measures must combine with other criteria for proper interpretation. The raw number of investigations must have a ground in some framework that adjusts for the quality and significance of investigations so you can distinguish quality, time-consuming investigative efforts from the mere spinning of investigative wheels to drive up the tally. Sound performance criteria can provide managerial guidance to you and contribute to the unit's evaluation for corporate management.

Performance criteria relate specifically to objectives instead of to goals. Although your unit goals generally create the anticipated results of an effort, your WCC unit objectives represent clear incremental statements and steps that your unit proposes to take to reach a particular result. It's more practical to gauge successes in meeting your objectives than to measure ultimate or anticipated consequences to safeguarding corporation assets. I don't suggest that performance criteria do not contribute to an evaluation of the extent to which you achieve your goals. Inasmuch as stated objectives are logical, positive, and related to the achievement of goals, successful performance criteria involving your unit's objectives leads to satisfactory progress in reaching your goals.

Develop a Data Collection and Analysis Plan

An important step in your planning involves choosing what types of information you will need to determine if your WCC management unit meets its performance criteria, who will gather that information, when it will be gathered, and who will become responsible for organizing and presenting it. This may sound like a massive and arduous task, but if the evaluation plan has been sound to this point, it will be as difficult as you imagine. The information needed for the evaluative effort is largely the same as the information required for running a well-organized and supervised WCC management unit.

Your files and records will supply you with the major sources of self-evaluation. Good management of a corporate white collar crime management unit dictates that investigators keep separate records of their activities for your review. Good evaluation requires the same documentation of aggregate staff activity. Maintenance of information received by the unit can permit you to observe changes in the pattern of abuses and make decisions concerning the allocation of resources. Maintenance of information also serves as a valuable source of evaluative data.

A sound self-evaluation plan gives you a framework with which to interpret the information you receive—not in the sense of its being good or bad, but in the sense that it indicates if the unit's effort is where it should be. Having this framework allows you to supply feedback to the unit staff, and congratulate them for a job well done, and make suggestions or redirect activities that appear unproductive.

A data collection plan for evaluation will provide you with information needed to manage your unit, since your need for information will be parallel in both cases. You should have a WCC unit clerk or analyst who prepares monthly summaries of evaluative data. These summaries amount to a synopsis of unit activities during a specific reporting period. The unit staff and corporate management should have access to these summaries. On a less frequent basis (quarterly, for example) you should prepare cumulative summaries to use as a formal technique of presentation to the unit's staff and corporate management. These cumulative summaries should clearly measure your WCC unit's milestones and progress.

The information needed to satisfy a particular evaluation and management plan will depend on the goals, objectives, and criteria you adopt for your corporate white collar crime management unit and the results the corporation expects. Exhibit 14-2 shows an example of an effective matrix for a data-gathering plan.

Exhibit 14-2
Model Matrix for Data-Gathering Plan

Criteria	Information Needed	Source of Information

Develop a Statement of Expectations

A final step necessary for developing your corporate white collar crime management unit evaluation system design is to prepare a formal statement of expectations in both short- and long-range terms. Both you and corporate management should consider carefully and formally state what you collectively see as the course your efforts will take. For example, what does the corporate management expect will happen in the first three months as opposed to the last six? What activities will likely become most prominent at one stage and not at another? Why?

Your statement of expectations is especially important for corporate management, whom you will probably not apprise of your unit's day-to-day operations and who may see only monthly or quarterly activity summaries. In light of this, corporate management might have unreasonable expectations for your WCC unit. A statement of expectations can prepare corporate management not to expect, for example, an immediate solution for large numbers of white collar crime offenders within and outside the company that threaten corporate assets. Similarly, you can use a statement of operations effectively to prepare your unit staff for the kinds of painstaking drudgery or growing pains you'll probably encounter. When you have an existing unit, the statement of expectations can document what the unit knows from experience. Finally, the statement of expectations, by stressing the relationships and differences between the short and long terms, helps your unit and company avoid situations in which an effort is unjustifiably condemned or lauded prematurely. By creating a steady, defined course, your statement prevents the type of recrimination or self-adulation that can prove fatal to the general success of the WCC unit.

Information to be Included In a Statement of Expectation

An example of the type information you could include follows. Suppose, for example, that

(1) Your goal for the white collar crime management unit is to reduce and eliminate, if possible, the victimization of corporate assets by targeting a specific component of company operations (e.g., a widget manufacturing plant).

(2) You propose that the unit will attain that goal through an employee and management education effort and through investigative audits of the operations.

After a period of time, you might find that the number of abuses reported by concerned employees has substantially increased, a result somewhat contradicting the ultimate goal. In this situation, the statement of expectations should explain that increases in the aggregate abuses stem from an effective employee education and awareness program conducted by your WCC unit. Instead of confounding the ultimate goal, your unit has successfully met its objectives and created a sense of employee responsibility. Abuses that were once concealed and difficult to determine now are in the open and can become manageable. You can show that through the unit's education program employees have seen that concealing white collar crime by a few not only injures the corporation, but the drain on profits easily creates a need for company cutbacks, layoffs and often prevents the company from supplying the employees with more benefits. Showing employees that it's everyone's responsibility to protect corporate assets has prompted the honest majority to report what they perceive might involve white collar crime. To the extent that your white collar crime management unit can show a stable, new, and higher reporting level for the targeted component, then you and the company can expect that the unit's ability to respond to abuses and reach the ultimate goal will be enhanced through awareness programs.

Your continuing self-evaluation of the WCC unit's performance might lead you or company management to believe that this effort is a burdensome and unproductive activity. I hope that the design for self-evaluation presented here will provide you with a positive perspective about this important management tool. The steps that make up a sound evaluation are clear (i.e., collectively creating goals and objectives, establishing performance criteria, developing a data collection plan, and stating your expectations). These are precisely the steps needed for a sound organization and management plan. No mystery need be attached to the evaluation process. Most of it is just common sense. The best way to get somewhere includes first, to knowing where you want to go; second, deciding how you plan to get there; and, finally, honestly stating how far you expect to get over a given time. A good evaluation will assist your corporate white collar crime management effort not only in attaining its goals, but also in clarifying the process and documenting the milestones that create the substance and tokens of that achievement.

Exhibit 14-3 shows you the general guidelines to consider in your planning stage. These principles will help you get the unit operational effectively and efficiently and allow refinement as needed later.

■ DEVELOP OPERATIONAL STANDARDS

You must develop general operational and performance standards for your corporate white collar crime management unit and staff. In addition to those mentioned earlier in this chapter, I discuss others that you need to consider in the following pages. These standards should not be perceived as unvarying directives, but rather should be considered as guidelines.

Exhibit 14-3
Model Planning Process for Investigative Management Unit

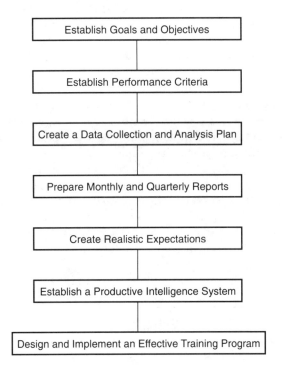

Coordinate Activities of Investigative and Legal Staffs

This standard may appear obvious, but you must bring to bear both investigative and legal skills on each possible lead or case your unit staff deals with. Any corporate WCC management unit that moves forward with great investigative skill but without understanding what information is needed to make a legal case, or without considering the legal admissibility of evidence gathered, will not only be ineffective but will also, in the long term, become demoralized by the failure to coordinate skills successfully. Prosecutors and attorneys who do not concern themselves with the imagination, skill, and difficulty of investigative work will not be able to marshal effectively the capabilities of investigators and thus secure the evidence needed for criminal or civil suits. Investigators and lawyers sometimes ignore this elementary point. They may recognize, but not sufficiently appreciate, the problems that WCC unit staffers face and the ways in which they must conduct their business. They may delay dealing with WCC unit staffers' concerns until evidence is overlooked, lost, missed, or becomes legally useless.

You should ensure that your planning and organizational standards call for a close working relationship with local, state, and federal prosecutors as well as your corporate attorneys. Remember, their time has great demands on it, just as does yours. When you prepare a case for them or need advice, ensure that you can present the facts clearly, comprehensively, and concisely. When attorneys learn your professional approach, cooperation will become commonplace and of great benefit and advantage to both sides.

Exhibit 14-4 provides guidelines for preparing an investigative report that satisfies most criminal prosecutions. Since civil litigation calls for much less information, the checklist will serve for that effort as well.

Exhibit 14-4
Guidelines for Preparing a Comprehensive Report Involving White Collar Crime for Corporate Counsel, Attorneys, and Prosecutors

1. Introductory Summary—A brief narrative that explains
   - ☐ The type of white collar scheme
   - ☐ How it came to the attention of the corporate white collar crime management unit
   - ☐ Period of operation involving the white collar scheme
   - ☐ Names, fictitious names, company names, and so on used by the perpetrators
   - ☐ Evidence of prior criminal activity

☐ Whether the person or persons received any previous warnings or counseling

☐ Type and total amount of loss

☐ Number and type of victims

☐ Possible statutes (criminal, civil, administrative) that were violated

2. Description of Suspects or Proposed Defendants—A standard identification record that contains as least the following information:

☐ Name

☐ Alias

☐ Addresses (home and business)

☐ Physical description

☐ Place and date of birth

☐ Criminal identification number (FBI or state)

☐ Occupation and employers

☐ Associates and accomplices

☐ Prior record

☐ Identification of persons who have cooperated or might cooperate with the attorneys

3. Description of Offenses—A detailed exposition of all pertinent data about the who, what, when, where, why, and how of the white collar scheme from its conception through its perpetration. For example, for each event (to the extent possible) describe the following:

☐ How was the white collar scheme conceived?

☐ Who executed it? Who played what parts?

☐ Where was it put into operation?

☐ How long was it in operation?

☐ What was the scheme; what were the types of funds, goods, services, or concealed trickery involved?

☐ What was the specific loss to the corporation?

☐ Any information that will provide the attorney with a firm comprehension of the magnitude, nature, and characteristics of the scheme

4. Results of Investigation—A narrative description containing the evidence that might serve for development of proof of misrepresentations, fraudulent intent, or other essential elements of proof showing violation of the statutes.

☐ Any occurrences that might lead to a conclusion of criminal intent. To this should be attached any diagrammatic outlines of the white collar crime operation that the investigator prepared.

☐ When applicable, each major misrepresentation, false pretense, or false promise that the suspect used in obtaining money or property from the corporation should be included.

5. Possible Evidence

☐ List of witnesses (including cooperating persons) addresses, and telephone numbers

☐ Oral, documentary, and physical evidence associated with each witness

☐ How evidence was obtained—interview, surveillance, survey questionnaire, investigative audit, or criminal investigation

6. Other Agencies Involved—a brief description of the involvement or interest of government, law enforcement, or private agencies and organizations

---

■ SUSTAIN THE MOTIVATION OF THE INVESTIGATORS

Investigative work involving white collar crimes often becomes frustrating and tedious. Cases take a long time to develop. New difficulties arise as offenders invent new schemes or variations of those in progress. There must be painstaking attention to detail, and most investigations involve a myriad of aspects such as analysis of financial matters, and corporate policies and procedures. In short, investigation of white collar crimes takes persistence and imagination. Imagination and persistence often become difficult to sustain if an investigator is simply told that he or she is expected to exhibit such qualities. These qualities are so difficult to define concretely in any specific case that you simply can't instruct a person to give that extra measure of imagination, that extra push that can make a case. You need to remain strongly motivated to attain the unit's goals. Further, the unit's goals and the corporate investigators' own goals must coincide to a high degree.

As suggested earlier, the clearer the unit's goals, the easier it becomes for each investigator to mesh his or her personal goals with those of your

WCC management unit. When the goals coincide, the corporate investigator can measure his or her progress appropriately and can make decisions in a personally satisfying way.

To maintain high motivation among corporate investigators, there must be clear standards that signal achievement of goals (including signs that attainment of enunciated goals is possible and has occurred). Whatever the goal of the unit, investigators need to see at least some progress resulting from their efforts. Not all goals need to be attained every time, but investigators must have a genuine sense that there's a clear potential for success.

■ MAINTAIN APPROPRIATE EMPHASIS ON CORPORATE POLICY

A corporate white collar crime management unit has many options for resolution of its investigations, including civil remedies and criminal prosecutions. Each corporation has its own policies, and each WCC management unit will have an organization and management quite different from others, depending on which of these alternatives are exercised. Most corporations choose the civil litigation or mediation route even when criminal prosecution is clearly possible. The favored civil or mediation approach is frequently selected because corporate investigators often don't have the experience or training necessary to become involved in white collar crime criminal cases. However, a better balance of emphasis among alternatives must become part of your WCC efforts so that your corporation can take advantage of the most appropriate action.

In addition to the legal reasons for choosing between civil and criminal action, motivational and organizational issues also need consideration. Even when civil or mediation remedies appear to be the best choice, investigators must be familiar with recourses involving criminal prosecutions when appropriate. Without this knowledge, investigators' motivation may drop to the point that both the quantity and quality of investigations may deteriorate. You, your staff, and the corporation should always clearly understand (even in WCC units least oriented to the criminal remedy) that where there's prima facie evidence of a violation of a criminal statute, you not only have the right but often the obligation to supply investigative results to prosecuting attorneys for enforcement consideration. Some state laws, for example, make it a crime to withhold knowledge of a crime from authorities, especially when the investigator has physical or other evidence in possession. (Check with your prosecutor and corporate legal counsel).

■ SUSTAINING THE FLEXIBILITY OF INVESTIGATIVE APPROACHES

One of the most dangerous characteristics of white collar criminals is their great ingenuity in fleecing the corporation in what appear to be brand-new ways. The ways are usually variations of old and traditional schemes, but the number of variations is almost limitless.

If your corporate white collar crime management unit specialized so much that only certain types of schemes are responded to effectively, this specialization invites the sophisticated crook to move in the unit's areas of nonspecialization. In a process of Darwinian competition, only those crooks may survive who specialize in the areas that the WCC management unit overlooks. Some sophisticated operators may sense the limits of your unit and capitalize on them. This problem does not demand that your WCC unit maintain a full staff of investigators who are expert in every variety of white collar scheme. Instead, your unit must focus on analyzing and detecting new scheme variations and on developing the resources (either in house or from outside contract experts) to combat such schemes. For example, an imaginative investigator might specialize in analyzing and coping with unusual and seemingly new fraud situations.

■ RESISTING THE PRESSURE TO WEAKEN INVESTIGATIVE THRUSTS

Often, especially when white collar crimes happen at high corporate levels or in a subsidiary or other interest of your company, your corporate white collar crime management unit might have some direct or indirect pressures to modify its operations. Such pressures will normally come in subtle forms but might become strong, especially if the scheme has significant magnitude. You need to ensure that your unit remains organized and managed with the support of the highest level of corporate leadership. Even a small shift in your efforts resulting from this type of pressure can undermine the credibility of the entire unit efforts and the morale of your staff.

Pressures against a specific investigation might be concealed within general policy positions. For example, new priorities may develop that shift white collar crime investigators and resources to some other area of investigation, or a decision might come down that some other corporate entity, such as a conventional audit team, can best handle the situation. Alternatively, your unit might become distracted from its work by a barrage of "fire-fighting" requests that effectively undermine a probe.

If your corporate leadership allows your unit to succumb to such pressures, you will soon find that the cooperation you receive from employees and others will be severely undermined. You need a clear understanding and unshakeable mandate and commitment from the highest level in your corporation, or your efforts will become a drill in futility.

■ TASK ASSIGNMENT: EXPERTISE AND MOTIVATION

In small corporate white collar crime management units, such as those with two or three investigators, the issue of specialization hardly exists. Instead, your staff members will have to become generalists. However, in larger units, you have a choice: Your investigators can be generalists, taking on all sorts of corporate investigations, or they can specialize. There are advantages to well-conceived and well-organized specialization of investigators' assignments in large corporate white collar crime management units that serve large companies or conglomerates. The obvious advantage is that the development of expertise increases the breadth and depth of an investigator's knowledge of a type of crime. Specialists become walking repositories of great volumes of information and ideas about investigations. Second, individual investigators may often possess specialized information about a particular line of business because of previous experience. When forming your corporate white collar crime management unit, you should recruit investigators who possess specialized information as one basis for staffing your unit. Third, individual investigators will often have a particularly negative feeling about certain types of white collar criminals, sometimes because of the investigator's identification with a special class of corporate victims. Finally, investigator-experts will be recognized by their fellow investigators for their special capabilities, and the respect they gain can raise their motivation even more.

The professional pride that investigators can develop in their expertise and the other satisfactions they find in their work have many added benefits beyond those conferred on particular investigative efforts. Investigators can gain a great deal of intrinsic satisfaction from their own work. They can gain satisfaction from the sheer exercise of their skills, such as personal contact with white collar criminals that lead to success in making a case; from the satisfaction of doing justice for the corporate victim; and from handling undercover work and realizing that they are well able to cope with criminals whose stock-in-trade is their cleverness. You need to recognize the importance of these factors when assigning cases to your staff investigators.

Specialization can also become a characteristic of subunits. You might create a subunit of specialized groups of investigators in very large corporate white collar crime management units. However, it is important that specialization does not become so great that the unit loses it capacity to respond to new types of schemes. If specialization becomes well known throughout the corporation, white collar criminals may simply move into the areas of non-specialization.

Accordingly, your unit must stay flexible enough to respond to new scheme investigations. Whenever possible, investigators who are particularly oriented to take on new challenges should be assigned to a type of special assignments role—to take on new and different types of white collar crime schemes. Such special assignment investigators should not, however, be exempt from taking on cases in one of the more "routine" areas when the backlog in one of these areas is excessive. Sometimes you might find it necessary to shift specialist investigators into new areas because of the magnitude or complexity of the new schemes.

■ LEADERSHIP AND MANAGEMENT OF THE UNIT

One major implication of respecting the professionalism of your staff investigators is that managers and supervisors with the unit remain supportive and helpful rather than overly dominating or micro managing in their approach. You should ensure that investigators are held accountable for their performance, but not for the details of their day-to-day work. When and if your staff investigators encounter problem situations that they find difficult to handle, they should feel free to turn to you for help or guidance. However, for the most part the decision to ask for help should be left to them.

■ PHYSICAL ARRANGEMENTS FOR THE UNIT

The physical arrangement for your corporate white collar crime management unit is important. First, your staff investigators need quiet, comfortable, and private areas in which to work and concentrate on the complex cases they will become involved in. Often, investigative audits can take place primarily in investigators' offices after completing field research at the specific department or division. Second, your staff investigators and the entire unit need a physical arrangement that protects the confidentiality of information and results inherent in white collar crime investigative work, as well as a secure facility to store evidence and ensure its integrity.

Once the investigation ends, the process of analyzing the data, organizing it, and writing a comprehensive report also demand privacy and an environment that permits concentration. You also need a common area where information exchange, discussions, training, and briefing can occur regularly or as needed (such as a conference room or classroom). Avoid the traditional open areas found commonly in departments within companies. This type of physical arrangement creates an environment that will be distracting and uncomfortable for staff white collar crime investigators. It also creates a lack of security of information. Any curious visitor who wants to browse through the area may overhear confidential information. Telephone calls and conversations conducted in the investigative effort demand privacy. Exhibit 14-5 provides an example of an adequate working environment for a corporate white collar crime management unit.

■ RELATIONSHIPS WITH OTHER COMPONENTS OF THE CORPORATION

Your corporate white collar crime management unit will have to develop a working rapport with other components of the company, and that's not always easy. Do not assume that your investigative effort will receive a welcome reception from the rest of the corporate staff and employees. The first problem you'll have to overcome is that others in the company may perceive your unit members as threats or rivals (members of the accounting and auditing staff may feel especially threatened). Internal auditors, for example, will rarely understand that an investigative audit differs greatly from theirs. People who have created policies and procedures often don't take your suggestions of change lightly—instead they view your suggestions as a personal affront.

Your second problem stems from the perception that the WCC management unit is a type of witch hunt or Gestapo that has investigators sneaking around looking for any employee indiscretion or looking for reasons to get employees in trouble. You and your staff investigators can often overcome this misconception at the onset by explaining to groups of employees the true purpose of your unit and asking them to help you find ways of making the corporate assets more secure. Tell them that doing so will benefit everyone working for the company. You will probably never achieve total harmony throughout the company, but the more your investigators and you try to get opinions and assistance from employees the greater your chance of success in that area.

Exhibit 14-5
Corporate WCC Management Unit Offices

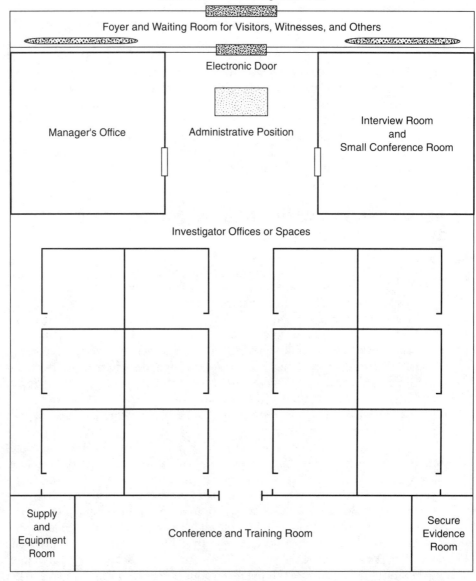

Entrance to WCC Management Unit

Foyer and Waiting Room for Visitors, Witnesses, and Others

Electronic Door

Manager's Office

Administrative Position

Interview Room
and
Small Conference Room

Investigator Offices or Spaces

Supply
and
Equipment
Room

Conference and Training Room

Secure
Evidence
Room

Other positive relationships may grow out of developing joint orientations and educational programs with internal auditors, security officers, and others that have a direct interest in protecting corporate assets and developing preventive policies and procedures. Often, your investigators might need to call on auditors for their support, expertise, and records of past activities. The best rule of thumb for fostering good internal relations with others in the company is to make a strong effort to include them in your investigations to some degree. However, keep in mind that you or your staff should not take such individuals into total confidence about the investigation. Explain only what you absolutely have to. Often you need only ask for general advice without disclosing that you're conducting an investigation. Keep all corporate white collar crime management information confidential, and create policy guidelines that ensure that the release of unit activity information stays on a "need to know" basis.

■ HOW TO CREATE YOUR INVESTIGATIVE AUDIT POLICY

Investigative audits and criminal investigations must follow a pattern of explicit guidelines and policies. Always ensure that corporate investigators remain focused on prevention by eliminating opportunity and that they move their audit to the procedures and evidence collection techniques when their investigative audit discloses clear white collar crime offenders. In the following discussion, I provide you with guidelines from which you may create your own guidelines and policies.

Policy and Procedure Guidelines

An investigative audit of a specific component or facility of the corporation should stem from the approval of the board of directors or high-level executives to whom the board has delegated authority. Normally, the approving authority will ask you to submit a list of corporate components or facilities recommended coupled with a proposed schedule of activities.

In theory, almost every facility, activity, area, and component of a corporation could benefit from an investigative audit, especially when they control company assets. However, because of the limited investigative resources that are probably available to your corporate white collar crime management unit, it's essential that you set priorities to determine how you'll use those resources to the best company advantage. One important decision you'll make as the manager of the WCC unit is to establish realistic priorities for investigative audits.

Six Steps for Planning the Audit

Any investigative audit calls for effective planning, thorough research, and appropriate technical advice from experts, when applicable, as well as the following steps:

1. Determine the scope of the audit. Depending on the situation, you might find it advantageous to audit specific functions of a company activity and make each function the subject of a separate audit and report. Spot audits often serve your objectives for large-scale activities and monitoring progress of implemented changes in policy and procedure. A decision during your early planning stages will dictate the intended audit scope.

2. Determine the availability and technical qualifications of your investigative staff and select assignments of investigative audits to achieve the best results.

3. Collect and review previous information, if available, such as internal audit reports and others. Obtain and review all applicable references on the activity intended for audit. This invaluable information provides much of the necessary information needed to formulate specific plans for the audit.

4. Determine the need for outside technical assistance. You should anticipate problems that will call for special skills, such as accounting and engineering, that might not be readily available among investigators in your WCC unit.

5. Determine covert requirements. The covert part of an investigative audit must have sufficient coordination before starting. Normal investigative techniques should accompany the covert stage of the audit. The covert part might include placing a "new employee" in the activity to observe and hear discussions when the investigator is not present.

6. Prepare an investigation plan (outline) to cover the various phases of the audit. The outline must remain flexible to bring the investigative audit to the proper conclusion.

Use an Entrance Briefing to Gain Advantage

At the onset of the overt phase of every investigative audit, you should conduct an entrance briefing with the person in charge of the activity. At a minimum, your briefing should outline the scope of the audit and the general techniques you intend to use. The person briefed should understand that the intention of the audit is to help him or her in the operation of a crime-free activity. The cooperation of the person responsible for the activity will simplify the completion of your audit and enhance the possibility of achieving positive results.

Five Important Steps to Follow During the Audit

1. You should apply normal investigative techniques during the conduct of an investigative audit. The investigative audit is best described as an investigation with the objective of identifying criminal acts, crime-conducive conditions, persons engaging in criminal activity, and preventive solutions.

2. Specific criminal acts that you detect during your audit will normally lead to a conversion of the audit to a criminal investigation.

3. The use of informants before and during the audit will provide advantageous information about the operation of the facility. You need to create a continuous effort to develop reliable sources of information within those facilities targeted for audits.

4. During your audit, criminal intelligence not suitable for inclusion in your audit may develop. In this case, you should immediately prepare a criminal intelligence report.

5. Specific guidance presented in earlier chapters (see Chapters 5, 6, and 7) explains the conduct and techniques to apply during your investigative audit.

Conclude the Audit with an Exit Interview

At the conclusion of your investigative audit, after you have thoroughly reviewed the findings, conduct an exit interview with the person responsible for the activity audited. The person receiving your briefing should be given a verbal report of your audit of his or her department's activity and the expected completion date of your audit report.

Encourage the executive management to create a policy that calls for department or division heads to submit an "action taken report" to them and to your unit within ninety days following receipt of your final report. This enables you to monitor corrective processes (when you find discrepancies and white collar crime indicators in a company activity) and the prevention measures the department head has implemented (based on your suggestions) to eliminate opportunities for white collar crime.

■ POLICY AND PROCEDURE GUIDELINES FOR CRIMINAL INVESTIGATIONS

Criminal investigations evolve when an element or possible element of a specific crime or offense creates the basis for an investigation. These cases might stem from your investigative audit activity or from other reports. For example, the corporate controller asks for the investigation of an embezzlement scheme he or she discovered.

A criminal investigation of white collar crime within or against your corporation must stay extremely specific in intent and limited in objective. For example, you cannot allow yourself to become involved in expanding that specific case or going on a "witch hunt." Instead, isolate a clear offense and develop it to the fullest. Then move on to other offenses if you determine their presence. Your criminal investigation must always be based on an allegation of the violation of a law when it threatens corporate assets or the reputation of the company.

The criminal activity information (most commonly developed from your investigative activities) or allegations (such as those from the company controller or internal audit teams) may also point to an employee or other person (e.g., a vendor, contractor, etc.) as either probably or possibly responsible for the commission of the alleged offense. The object of your criminal investigation is to establish whether a crime has been committed, to determine the identity of the person or persons responsible for its commission, and to collect relevant evidence for prosecution or civil litigation.

Remember that although you conduct a criminal investigation and collect relevant evidence in a way that would enable a successful prosecution, this does not mean the corporation must prosecute. However, when you supply the company management and counsel with sufficient evidence enabling prosecution, they will clearly have the options and the tools needed to make a decision that is in the best interests of the corporation.

For example, the board might prosecute with a parallel civil litigation, only a civil lawsuit, an administrative mediation remedy; or the board may only warn or fire the person or persons responsible. Your objective in a criminal investigation conducted by your corporate white collar crime management unit is to supply the company management with the broadest range of choices possible. Corporate management will generally rely heavily on your expertise and advice. When the case falls within the criminal or civil jurisdiction of outside agencies, you might suggest that the company refers the case to a local, state, or federal agency that specializes in the findings, especially when the scheme involves an outside threat that your company may have no control over. You might also recommend that the company hires the services of a well-known expert in the field to evaluate and recommend the best remedial action under the specific circumstances of the case.

■ IN SUMMARY

In this chapter, I've supplied you with the general guidelines necessary to create or organize your corporate white collar crime management unit. You can use them as the foundation to create your specific policies and procedures according to the type of corporation you safeguard and its specific needs. This chapter establishes the groundwork for Chapter 15, which discusses the collection of white collar crime intelligence. Such collection should be an important, time-saving, cost-effective, and efficient way of protecting your company's assets from the constant threat of internal and external white collar crime enterprises. Each chapter in Part Four builds on the information and techniques I've supplied here.

Chapter Fifteen
The Important Role of a White Collar Crime Intelligence System

Aggressive collection and application of corporate white collar crime information and intelligence on subject categories, known offenders, and suspects—whether through formal or informal processes—should become an integral part of your corporate white collar crime management unit's investigative effort. Essentially, white collar crime (WCC) intelligence develops from a process through which new information adds to information already possessed and is made available to operational corporate investigators when and where they need it. The information is used to educate and train investigators, to detect white collar crime inside and targeting your corporation from the outside, to trigger investigations, and to affect positively the course and outcome of your corporate white collar crime management unit investigations. The intelligence process may be limited to the store of knowledge retained and accumulated in the minds of separate investigators about suspects and their activities.

Alternatively, you can formalize and structure the process into an intelligence system in which accumulated knowledge of investigators is molded into a usable, advantage-oriented system. Their knowledge is placed in report form, enabling a pooling and sharing of the collective data. The latter is by far the more useful model and the subject of this chapter. In this chapter, I'll lead you through the creation and maintenance of a WCC intelligence system.

The purpose and advantage of a WCC intelligence system is to provide your corporate investigators with the best source of accumulated information about specific schemes, offenders, suspects, and their activities. I must emphasize the words *single* and *best source*. Too often, the intelligence process creates little more than an accumulation of information—a formal dumping ground for disparate bits of data concerning corporate problems or corporate gossip. No matter how formalized, that type of process does not represent a bona fide intelligence system. Your white collar crime intelligence system must be more than an accumulation of information. It must also be the best available source of accurate information. To achieve this, your intelligence system must have three basic characteristics.

1. It must establish criteria by which information offered can be evaluated for inclusion. This effort prevents the inclusion of specious and unreliable information that would affect the reliability of the system.

2. Your intelligence system must have a basic organization and analytic structure into which information can fit and be interpreted accurately. New information should not merely add to your system; instead it should be related to existing information and serve to augment, supersede, or invalidate previous knowledge.

3. Your white collar crime intelligence system must have a well-defined protocol by which conflicting information is reconciled and outdated or invalid information is purged. Maintenance and upkeep of your intelligence system must be continuous to assure that it remains the most reliable and accurate information source available.

■ THE THREE ESSENTIAL FUNCTIONS OF AN EFFECTIVE WCC INTELLIGENCE SYSTEM

Corporate white collar crime intelligence system creation and maintenance begins with three important functions: identification, detection, and education.

1. The Identification Function: Identifying Schemes and Offenses

Probably the most frequent use of white collar crime intelligence involves identifying known and active offenders as well as schemes targeting and victimizing corporations. Knowing about an offender does not always enable positive action. For example, an investigative audit plus conventional audits clearly shows an embezzlement scheme and a suspect, but the person has destroyed relevant evidence and without evidence there's no proof sufficient for any type action. Another example involves collecting information about schemes outside the company such as fraudulent charities, land frauds, organized crime track records of infiltration, and others. With an effective intelligence identification system in place, a scheme and probable offenders can easily be matched with a developing situation, and your investigators can avoid delays associated with trying to determine these crucial factors. It's much like beginning a race when you have the advantage of beginning at the halfway point instead of at the starting point.

In white collar crime, as opposed to conventional crime, you will rarely have to ask "Whodunit?". The perpetrator is generally clear. Instead, you must ask bigger questions: What did the offender do (i.e., was a crime committed, or a civil wrong inflicted, or was there merely the exercise of poor judgment by a suspect or the victim company)? Who becomes the real victim because of the offender's activities (i.e., how many victims are there)? How did the offender commit the act (i.e., what specific acts, in what character and style did the events happen)? Where did it happen (the jurisdictional issue)? Each of these questions is interrelated to the others. For example, where a white collar abuse happens (i.e., whether in the province of federal or local authorities) may make the difference between its being a crime or a civil wrong.

The identification function of intelligence has important advantages and benefits to your white collar crime management unit and its investigative role within your corporation.

2. The Detection Function: Documenting the Method and Means

Closely related to the identification is the detection function of intelligence. Normally, this function occurs as the result of structured observation, awareness, and surveillance efforts that record the important role of investigative and conventional audits. This function also enables you to anticipate emerging criminal activities, head them off, or provide a basis for going forward in an investigative audit or criminal investigation when expected events occur.

Because the white collar offender's activities are not readily anticipated in detail, there is a tendency to overlook the value of the detection function of intelligence. This specialized information, combined with a more generalized investigative effort, plays a major role in economic and business environments that you must safeguard. Signals of a scheme in progress that might target your company can be as simple as a newspaper advertisement or article that when combined with other intelligence has meaning otherwise overlooked.

Another benefit of your corporate white collar intelligence system involves documenting the methods and means of white collar schemes and offenders, which allows your staff investigators to interpret seemingly unrelated or trivial events and put them in a proper perspective. This investigative importance of your intelligence system adds an important advantage to your efforts. A factor of substantial importance in the white collar crime category is that criminals frequently operate through corporate or other business fronts. Your investigators can receive invaluable help in determining when proper acts, such as the rental of office space, may signal preparatory steps in the perpetration of a white collar crime fraud against your company. Most importantly, the detection function can focus the investigator's gut feelings of suspicion into a well-focused interpretation and then enable positive and productive action.

3. The Education Function: Providing Continuity and Analytic Power

The education function of white collar crime intelligence has two dimensions: continuity and analytic power. Of the two, the continuity dimension is probably best recognized and understood. It is clear, for example, that a well-developed intelligence system supplies a continuity to your corporate white collar crime management unit's functioning that would not exist otherwise. WCC units that keep corporate intelligence systems do not experience major information losses on the departure of active investigators. Instead, their knowledge, expertise, and experience are preserved for the use and benefit of those who follow. Similarly, new investigators do not have to start at square one in confronting white collar crime and offenders that threaten your company's assets. Instead, they begin with solid information bases supplied by those who preceded them.

The manner in which your education function provides analytic power also has advantages. As I have noted throughout this book, the victimization of corporations by white collar crime enterprises is extremely complex. The type of white collar crime diversification you will have to deal with regularly rarely stays within a discrete set of easily described acts. Instead, these acts are conducted in a vital and dynamic process through a subtly perpetrated theft of company assets (including reputations and competitive spirit). Your intelligence objective, then, is to capture the process of WC schemes in progress and those persons known or able to perpetrate white collar crime because the opportunity to do so is available to them. It also helps you preempt WC crime by detection while still in planning stages. If you achieve this objective, you should be able to anticipate the course of current activities and reconstruct events that have already taken place. Without a composite source of information, your white collar crime management effort is poorly equipped to face the white collar offender or to interpret the widely varied schemes he or she perpetrates.

■ DESIGNING YOUR INTELLIGENCE SYSTEM

The basic rule that should guide your design of a white collar crime intelligence system is to arrange it for maximum use by your WCC unit. Two features of a white collar crime intelligence system will probably affect its use and its ultimate value to your efforts. The first of these is your system's design. The simpler the basic design of your white collar intelligence system, the easier you can develop and maintain it and the more likely it will become a valued tool in constant use. Unnecessarily complex systems discourage use and take more time to access properly than most corporate investigators have available to them or too much time relative to the perceived benefits.

The second feature connected to your use of the white collar crime intelligence system is the extent that it is directly and easily accessible to the investigative effort it's designed to enhance. No matter how well you design an intelligence system, if it is divorced from the investigative function benefiting from it, it soon becomes little more than a repository for dust instead of a source of vital information. Utilization will positively increase when your intelligence system is operated and maintained by the corporate white collar crime management unit that has investigative responsibility for the areas about which it is concerned. A white collar intelligence effort must be a functional responsibility of your unit instead of being integrated as part of a general intelligence function.

Four-Stage Basic Design

Your corporate investigative staff members are best qualified to make decisions about the design of your WCC unit intelligence system because they become its ultimate users. In this sense, textbook blueprints for intelligence files can only provide ideas, not precise designs that will serve everyone best. Still, there are some basic decisions that you must make when developing a system that will affect its ultimate design.

1. Investigative Versus Intelligence Files

Clearly, there is a difference between investigative and intelligence files. Your investigative files represent focused efforts linked to a specific crime known or believed to have been committed or the search for weaknesses in the procedural systems that create opportunities for white collar crime. Intelligence files, however, reflect general investigative efforts associated with an offender, offender groups, enterprises, or entity involving illegal activities known or suspected over time. Obviously, investigative and intelligence efforts have a close relationship to each other, but rarely should you file them together. Generally, your investigative unit must maintain separate investigation files both for the entire WCC unit and for each investigator. Also, the investigative work of your WCC management unit should have a filing system that uses historical design with separate places for investigations that have passed and have been completed, those that have closed, and those that are ongoing. You should also maintain your intelligence files separately, generally using an alpha arrangement by name or scheme but not subject to a historical separation through filing. Instead, your intelligence files must remain intact and subject to updating and purging procedures that ensure their maximum use.

Investigative and intelligence functions cannot be independent of each other. The strength of your intelligence system relies on the practical relationship it has to investigative efforts and the extent to which you continuously update intelligence functions to reflect new investigative efforts that concern file subjects. Your intelligence system divorced from the operational reality of a corporate WCC management unit may appear beautiful on file but have little value. The point to remember is that while the two efforts are intertwined, rarely will the two files be joined into one. The unit that decides to develop an intelligence system must expect to have, at minimum, two sets of files.

2. Deciding the Offender Factors of Your Intelligence Files

This important decision will affect the design of your intelligence system, including the determination of who will and who will not be regarded as an intelligence offenders or suspects. This determination is critical from both a policy and utilization standpoint. With respect to policy, the criteria for entry to an intelligence file may determine the legal permissiveness of the activity and the degree of privacy to be accorded the files. From a utilization perspective, the size of the intelligence system, determined by the number of diversified files, affects its value to both staff investigators and your corporate asset safeguard program. Too many listings may transform the intelligence files into a garbage file or telephone book rather than a useful investigative tool, while too few supply little reference or investigative value.

You must consider several questions when developing and deciding the scope of your corporate white collar crime management unit intelligence system in this area:

- Will you include all persons identified as offenders in your WCC unit intelligence system?

- Will you include all persons who have been a subject of a complaint or unsubstantiated information in your WCC unit intelligence system?
- Will you include persons who have not been the subject of official action by the corporation or the unit in your WCC unit intelligence system?
- If the answer to any or all of the preceding questions is yes, what criteria will you use for deciding whether to include or identify persons in your intelligence file?

There are no pat answers to these questions. Some corporate WCC units may decide to make all investigative subjects a part of their intelligence file and later exclude them if the situation did not lead to investigations or was otherwise resolved and substantiated. Others may call for more substantiation regarding information or complaints against a person before inclusion in their intelligence system. Still others may make a qualitative decision to include persons because of the scheme alleged and harm done to their company or other companies despite official disposition of a case. The major point you must consider in your decision-making process is to think through and anticipate white collar crime threats to your company with clear intelligence system guidelines established. Your corporate legal counsel should be consulted about these issues.

My recommendation includes using great care in putting names into intelligence files. Despite the tightness of your security, people within the unit might inadvertently discuss a situation or name and imply that the person is guilty of a white collar crime. You could also easily create a massive liability for your company and yourself by carelessly implying that an employee or other person is a crook. I favor intelligence files that use numbers and veiled terms such as *confidential source* and *suspect* or a combination of both. For example, an intelligence report and file could offer an explanation such as the following: "A confidential company source (24) reported that Suspect (32) consistently pads his expense and travel claims."

In a corporation with 200 employees filing weekly travel and expense claims, even if the information is leaked that fraud is taking place, it would mean little because the description doesn't clearly identify any person. The investigator receiving the information should record the names of suspects and informants on a master list keyed to the numbers shown in the intelligence report. To protect privacy of informants and suspects, you should maintain that list in a sealed envelope in your office safe and attach a strict "need to know restriction" to the names associated with the intelligence report numbers. If you prepare the list on a computer system, it should remain only on floppy disks that are kept in your safe or in another secure place. Your intelligence reports must also have attentive scrutiny to ensure that they are complete but do not pinpoint either sources of information or suspects.

After an investigative audit of a suspect's travel and expense claims, you might find that the allegation is either founded or unfounded. That information, coupled with the case number for the audit, should become an entry in your intelligence report addendum. Once or twice a year, the intelligence files should be reviewed. If a report of information is unfounded, you should shred the entire file. An intelligence file should stay active until there's clearly no further reason to have it. When shredding outdated intelligence files, ensure that you delete the code numbers and names from the master list. When deletions occur, prepare a new list with only current information, shred the old list, and secure the new master list.

Do not allow your intelligence program or system to become a collection point for gossip, and do not let anyone in the corporation outside the corporate counsel know that you have an intelligence program. The fewer people who know increase security and prevent the misinterpretation of it by employees who are not members of the white collar management unit. While all your unit information must be well secured and revealed on a need to know basis only, your intelligence files need even greater security and discretion about who outside your unit sees them or knows the information they contain. These files could become a powerful weapon in the politics of the corporate environment, just as your investigative reports have the same effect and no one except at the highest level should have access to them. A rule of thumb dictates that if you are pressured to release an investigative file that should not be handed around, it's better to shred the file. Otherwise you may suffer an irreversible detriment to your anti-WCC effort.

3. Creating a Simple System Design

Once you have made the aforementioned important decisions, it's time to begin designing your system. Remember that once designed, your intelligence system will and should go through a period of evolution as investigative staff members begin to build the information and learn how to use it effectively. With that in mind, ensure that you build flexibility into your initial system design.

The intelligence system described in this chapter supplies the basics so that you can create a manual system as I describe or, better yet, develop the same basic principles into your computers. This system is designed to be well within the capacity of even the smallest of WCC management units and does not focus on implementation within any specific corporate WCC unit structure. I have based it on the assumption that your unit will need at least three sets of files:

- Investigation files, including past, closed, and ongoing
- A complaint or information received file, past, closed, and ongoing
- A central intelligence file.

This system does, however, allow the situation in which supplementary aliases, business names, photographs, or other files can add to it as part of an integrated intelligence system. Since you might expect that both investigations and complaint or information files will have a predetermined format, the following discussion focuses on the intelligence file itself and the intersection of this file with other types of files. The design presented here uses a mastercard as the cover sheet for the central intelligence file and is discussed as the mastercard file. The idea behind the mastercard is that it provides summary offender information to a user of the system without requiring him or her to wade through an entire file. It also allows, as I will discuss, for arrangement options of the central file. Most of the following discussion involves information necessary to the mastercard itself. The kinds of information shown on the mastercard also reflect the major content of its accompanying file.

4. Informational Inputs of a System

White collar offenders and their schemes present great potential as intelligence subjects, but that does not make development of an intelligence system regarding them and their activities an easy task. This because although the white collar offender has a well-developed and defined manner of operating, his or her basic scheme is subject to innumerable variations. This makes WCC offenders' activities far more challenging to probe than those of an average thief. For example, there may be only a limited number of ways to gain entry to premises or to open a safe, but the ways in which an embezzlement scheme may happen will normally be limited only by the imagination and ingenuity of the perpetrator. Because white collar offenders are capable of a large number of variations on a theme, the compilation and analysis of information regarding them can be complex.

Nonetheless, there is a simplicity to the activities of the white collar thief that derives primarily from the fact that the offenders themselves are an important component of their modus operandi. Whether it be the studied glibness of the swindler, the unrelenting persuasiveness of the con person, or the manipulative influence peddling of the corrupt public official, the personal characteristics of white collar offenders play an important role in advancing their activities. They become distinct and unmistakable hallmarks of their activities despite how many variations on a theme they perpetrate. They are the composite of what might be called their style.

Because style is somewhat an indefinable quality, it is easy to complicate it. However, to do so is to miss the realization that the white collar thief's style is his or her least changing feature and the one quality easiest to learn about him or her. The simplicity of style for many such offenders is often their most marked characteristic and the one by which their enterprise or handiwork is best recognized.

But how do you communicate style, particularly for intelligence purposes? Your first step includes understanding what style really is. It is nothing more than the personal application of available tools to effect a particular fraud or deception. Knowing the tools of the white collar offender, then, when combined with a knowledge of how and to or against what corporate entity the white collar offender uses, creates a good, substantive definition of his or her style.

Even a simple intelligence system relevant to white collar offenders must consider both the complexities of their activities and the simplicity of their style. The design of the mastercard file system suggested will do this. It includes a front sheet with a summary profile of the offender or offenders in question (the mastercard) and shows other files in which more detailed information is available. You should include the specific items discussed later in the summary form on the mastercard and treated more extensively in the master file itself. At minimum, the mastercard and its accompanying file should contain the following types of inputs:

- Information bearing on usual or primary fraudulent activity
- Information bearing on personal background and characteristics
- Information bearing on style of operation.

Fraudulent Activity of the Offender: A key item in your mastercard intelligence system is an indication of the dominant fraudulent scheme or activity that a white collar offender or offender group engages in. Generally, this item will have a broad categorization of the type of crime that the white collar thief prefers. It might, for example, have a notation about the scheme. Under that heading, you need to include information about known variations of a general scheme that the offender uses. You also need to include a notation showing the source of information and where to find added information. Exhibit 15-1 shows an example of this application for repeated business bankruptcy fraud involving a principal and others.

Exhibit 15-1
Mastercard for Dominant Scheme

Dominant Scheme: Business Bankruptcy Fraud Supplier/Wholesaler—George Stickler et al.		
Known Variations	Source of Information	Added Information Available
Business Bankruptcy New Jersey	Prior investigation R. Smith—FBI	File No. 6587
Business Backruptcy New York	John O'Hara N.Y. Attorney General	File No. 87A45B
Business Backruptcy Florida	Samuel Johnson States Attorney Miami	File No. 3005

In the example shown in Exhibit 15-1, the offender's variations of business bankruptcy fraud schemes are characterized by a consistent pattern of operation. Despite repeated investigations, the principal person involved continues.

Personal Characteristics and Background of the Offender: A second item integral to a white collar offender mastercard file relates to the personal characteristics and background of the offender. This becomes especially important for nonemployees or former employees who have targeted corporations with their schemes (such as planned business bankruptcy or any other fraud). It can also include organized crime enterprise principals known to operate front businesses or have a history of infiltrating and taking control of legitimate companies. Keep in mind that your intelligence file purpose is to create a record of complaints, information, and investigative findings that will be important for new investigators, for you while you are investigating, and for your successors perhaps years from now. Although you and your staff might have considerable personal knowledge about threats, schemes, and the personal characteristics and background of persons involved, those who come later probably will not—unless you've left them a complete record.

Generally, white collar offenders do not attempt to disguise themselves. While their types of activities may change, their basic appearance will normally remain constant. Ensure that notations about minor changes in personal appearance (such as a mustache, beard, or glasses) are noted and added to the card as needed.

The background of the white collar offender can also provide useful information to your staff investigators. For example, a person known to have operated in planned bankruptcy schemes might have roots in some part of the country, or characteristics that became apparent during any of the past investigations noted on the mastercard entries. That could become important in determining his or her whereabouts, especially when you believe the person might have moved into a new scheme nearby and might target your company. The characteristics and background information might help you when the suspect owns a business (either in part legitimate or not legitimate) by suggesting added remedies against the offender, such as seeking an injunction against his or her pursuit of specific business practices as well as information about his or her business affiliations.

When a suspect is a collusive member of a white collar crime or the perpetrator, personal characteristics and background information might help you identify persons who may be interviewed during your investigation.

Even if white collar offenders are not rooted in one place, they might have a background of employment that contributes to their skill as an offender. Experience as an insurance salesperson, for example, may equip a white collar thief engaged in investment swindling.

When you know the specific skills of the offender (which he or she may have legitimately received), such knowledge may explain not only the schemes in which the person will probably engage but also the tactics that he or she may use in perpetrating them. Legitimately acquired skills, then, may create an important element of the white collar thief's style, supplying him or her with the language and mien of a reputable profession or occupation.

Master file card information about the personal characteristics and background of the white collar offender should include entries shown in Exhibit 15-2.

Collecting Intelligence about the Offender's Style: A final component important for inclusion in your mastercard file for a white collar intelligence system concerns the style of the offender. I said earlier that style is really nothing more than the personalized application of a particular scheme or fraud. Style can, however, be a difficult offender characteristic for your intelligence system to verbalize and communicate. In characterizing the white collar offender's style, you might find it helpful to describe those modus operandi components contributing to it. I will describe four key elements as illustrative of the style of white collar criminal and enterprise activity. There are undoubtedly others that the experienced corporate investigator may add or find useful and revealing. The four style elements describe are (1) the legitimate tools that offenders use to initiate and consummate their schemes; (2) the illegitimate

---

Exhibit 15-2
Master File Card Relating to the Personal Characteristics
and Background

Changes in Appearance

Photograph

Personal Characteristics and Background

Date of Birth:_____

Race/Sex:_____

Height:_____ Weight:_____ Eye Color:_____

Hair Color:_____ Voice Tone:_____

Mannerisms:_____

Place of Birth:_____

Alias Names or Nicknames:_____

Permanent Address:_____

Business or Occupation:_____

Prior Employment History:_____

_____

Known Skills or Professional Competence:_____

_____

Known Associates: (Should include financial associations)

_____

tools that offenders use; (3) the characteristics of the victim corporations or others against whom the offenders act; and (4) the approach the offenders use to identify and contact the victim companies and others.

(1) Legitimate Tools

White collar offenders often develop astute abilities in the use of legitimate devices and tools to advance their schemes. Such a tactic produces two broad effects. First, the legitimacy of the tool or device itself often contributes to a false perception that the offender is a respectable person. Second, the uses of tools that by themselves are not illegal often complicate your investigation of and case building against the white collar thief. The stuff of offenders' crimes may create the illegal element, although the totality of their acts may be illegitimate. The summing up of a person's technically legal acts into an illegal whole is far more difficult for a corporate investigator than is the documentation of separate illegal acts for overt criminal activity.

The legitimate tools that WCC offenders use will vary widely with their access to specific devices. A corporate employee or business owner, for example, may have the capacity to use many trappings of his or her position (stationery, office space, computers, copiers, telephone, and other aspects) to exude a facade of legitimacy. The use of such tools may even create the impression that the person's acts are authorized in some manner by those with greater position and power.

Other white collar offenders may use the good reputation of various trade journals, newspapers, or other publications to advertise themselves, in this way relying on the potential victim's perception that the publication vouches for the advertisement's reputability. Dishonest franchise peddlers may hold conferences in the best hotels in an attempt to create similar impressions. The rental of office space replete with all the "right" furniture, for example, lends a legitimacy to a business that may not exist. The selection of an office suite itself may create an unassailable image of the operation found there. Having a prestigious or well-known business address can evoke an impression reputability, as can location adjacent to a well-respected law firm. The offender will often note in advertising, during personal calls, and on stationary or business cards that his or her office suite is next to a reputable, old-line company or professional service.

None of the aforementioned acts (i.e., the rental of office space, leasing of a hotel for a conference, or advertising in a publication) is itself unlawful. Yet each of the acts by an offender may signal a preparatory step in a white collar thief's scheme, much as the casing of premises for a burglar. Many of these acts, however, signal the initiation of a scheme by the white collar thief.

(2) Illegitimate Tools

Not all white collar offenders confine their activities to the use of legitimate tools. Often, the white collar thief uses unlawful tactics but the victim company or its representative might not understand them as illegal. For example, when a charity or contribution fraud is represented as legitimate but does not exist and the solicitor convinces your corporation that it will receive favorable community or national publicity from a generous contribution of money or goods, the company representative perceives the cause to be worthy. Many con games rely on a naivete of the victim or lack of such information about the activity to execute an illegal scheme.

Other white collar offenders may illegally use the mails or offer investment opportunities in direct violation of state and federal law. In such cases, they may rely on the already-secured investment (i.e., monetary commitment) of the victim company to avoid detection for the use of such tactics. Some victims may continue to hope against hope that their "investment" will eventually pay off and thus help offenders conceal their illegal acts. A style characteristic of many white collar thieves is to draft victims into becoming their "tools." A similar situation is the one in which the original victim becomes a coconspirator with the offender.

Itemizing the many tools, both lawful and unlawful, that WCC offenders use is essential to building a complete picture of their operating style. It can also help in anticipating how offenders will proceed in the perpetration of future schemes. Similarly, when there's an observation of an offender's characteristic preparatory step, his or her next move will often become predictable. Knowing that the offender's unmistakable style is often merely a patterned invocation of a finite set of legal and illegal tools robs the white collar thief of the "mystery" in which he or she likes to shroud illegal activities. It also tells you that, tedious and time consuming though it may be, an attentive cataloging of the thief's tools and tactics will stand you in good stead.

(3) The Corporate or Other Victim Profile

The white collar offender is a predator, and an important component of his or her style of operating is the type of victim company or person he or she targets. Building a profile of the characteristic victim of an offender becomes, then, an important element in your intelligence system. Often, the white collar thief's victims have a definable type based on their business or occupation instead of their personal attributes. For example, many white collar criminals involved in the business of investment frauds look for wealth and target physicians, corporate executives, and other professional persons seeking income tax shelters or high returns for their money. Other white collar crime schemes may focus on groups of corporations or executives and employees who share a common attribute or station in life. Choosing certain particular kinds of victims is part of the white collar thief's style. This is essential to the development of your intelligence profile.

(4) Approach to the Victim Company

Closely related to the choice of a victim company or member of a corporation in determining the white collar offender's operating style is the offender's manner of making an approach to his or her chosen victim. Often, the first overture is impersonal (businesslike) and uses some legal or illegal tools noted earlier. Such an overture may generate victim self-selection by calling for the victim company to perform an act that ensures further contact (sending back a request for information, for example) or results in a direct seeking of the offender by the victim (e.g., responding to an offer for extraordinary savings on office supplies). In cases of planned bankruptcy, the offender will create a perception of being a prime, sought-after customer of manufactured goods or services. In other instances, the offender may make a direct, personal overture to the victim using various tools in a sales-pitch technique. Offenders may show the victim company impressive-looking brochures and phony endorsements by prominent companies or persons. They may show copies of trade journal advertisements and fashion their visit as a follow-up contact that they believe the victim company has requested. Often, then, the style of offenders is a combination not only of the tools they use but also of the order in which they invoke their use in their approach to the victim.

Sometimes a victim company's anonymous participation in a public event can create a basis for future contact. Nominal fees for business seminars, for example, can provide the offender with the names of corporate employees and their companies, who can be contacted later. To draw the employees to the seminar, even at their own expense and on their own time, the white collar offender might tell them that the "seminar board selected them" to take part in a rare opportunity for self-improvement that will help them get promotions and higher salaries. The seminar might have an air of legitimacy, but the underlying motive is to create contacts and intelligence about the companies the seminar attendees work for, often through completion of well-crafted forms and personal interviews. The more complex the route, however, the more distinctive it will be as a stylistic trademark of the offender's mode of operating.

■ QUICK REFERENCE GUIDE TO THE MASTERCARD FILE

Intelligence mastercards containing summary information relating to an offender's dominant scheme (and variations), personal characteristics, and operating style should be attached as cover sheets to intelligence files and be arranged alphabetically according to subject name. When the subject of intelligence is a group or enterprise rather than an individual, the common group name should be used as the mastercard heading. Prominent persons in the group can also be listed separately but should be cross indexed with the group's mastercard file.

1. Although the suspect or offender's name represents the file card heading, information about the white collar offender's dominant scheme or activity should appear on mastercards before personal information. This will allow you to make an arrangement of files by types of fraud, with alphabetical filing within each type. For example, a file might contain a section labeled "Planned Business Bankruptcy Fraud" followed by an alpha card file of appropriate subjects. A later section of the file might have labels such as "Office Supply Fraud," or "Embezzlement—Internal," or "Organized Crime Threats" and be followed by a similar alpha listing. Some corporate WCC management units might prefer to handle types of frauds or crimes by a supplementary file and leave the mastercard file intact with one alpha arrangement of all subjects.

2. A mastercard file can include cross-reference sheets noting all aliases or business names used by white collar suspects and offenders. Alternatively, you can limit such added references by using supplemental alias and business name files. In the first instance, the mastercard file might contain an entry for the suspect under his or her true name; followed by AKA (also known as) showing all known aliases or business names; followed by an entry showing true name and referring the reader to that mastercard. In the second situation, you might file the mastercard under the true name and refer to the alias file which lists other known or suspected aliases. You should treat business names in a manner consistent with that used for aliases.

3. As I discussed earlier, you should note the sources of information on the offender's scheme or variations. This is particularly true when previous investigations involved such sources. When the person has been a suspect because of prior activities but an investigation was never started, it will help to include such information. Often, you can do this by referring to a complaint or information received file in which the suspect is noted.

4. Personal data are straightforward items for the mastercard file. In addition to the necessary information for the mastercard noted earlier, your

corporate white collar crime management unit might want to include summary criminal history information. However, that information is usually more appropriately contained in the file instead of on the mastercard.

5. Style characteristics related to legal and illegal tools used by the offender can be handled in several ways. Preprinted cards might list examples of the offender's tools that signal his or her operation, with an open-ended "other" listing. A more useful technique, however, is to allow ample space for listing tools and tactics. This will allow additions and space for supplemental notes when appropriate. Victim profiles and approaches should be similarly handled.

6. Exhibits 15-3 through 15-8 show sample mastercard file entries. All names and information remain fictitious. The entries shown in the exhibits reflect the most complex entry situation for such an intelligence file—one in which a group and individuals with aliases associated with that group are noted. You should cross-reference supplemental files with an asterisks or other coding.

■ SOURCES OF WHITE COLLAR CRIME INTELLIGENCE

Your company, when it's a victim of white collar offenders, is a major source of information for intelligence and investigative purposes. Most personal and style characteristics for a mastercard, for example, can be determined by careful interviewing of the company representative who was taken in by the offender. Other sources of information such as records in local, state, and federal systems are also helpful, and although criminal justice files might not be readily available to corporate white collar crime management unit investigators, you will often be given access if you disclose your crime prevention purposes. Also, court records supply excellent information, and they are public records. Similarly, once you have established a sound intelligence system, methods for obtaining inputs from other companies, government, and private agencies can become routine. Another valuable source of intelligence is corporate employees, especially those responsible for corporate asset accountability (such as internal audit teams, controllers, and others).

The white collar offender with roots in the community will be easier to track, as are company employees. If the offender is a member of a professional occupational group or some particular business operation, surprising amounts of information are available in local and national directories. Employers, employees, and business associates also supply good sources of general information on suspects and offenders. Offenders might volunteer

Exhibit 15-3
Mastercard for Offender Group

Mastercard No. 007

Subject: Anderson Enterprises   **AKA:** "Enterprise Associates" and
(See Bus. Name File #316)

   See Also: Anderson, Edward (MC #004) Martinson, Andrew (MC #142)

Dominant Scheme: Planned Business Bankruptcy Fraud

Known Variations	Info Source	Additional Info

Suspect via Complaints and Other Information

Complaint or Info	Offense	Disposition

Background and Characteristics

   Photographs: Include photographs available on all persons

   Business Address: List all business names and addresses or reference to
business name file

Style

   Legal Tools: Read local business directories;   **Illegal Tools:** False Ref.; Misrepresentation
ads in business publications, etc.   in brochures, letters, etc.

   Victim Profile: Discuss common types of businesses targeted,
such as manufacturing, services, etc.

   Victim Approach: Explain how offender commonly contacts
the companies or persons victimized

Exhibit 15-4
Mastercard for Offender in Group

Mastercard No. 004

Subject: Anderson, Edward   **AKA:** "Tex" or Alias File #2075
                                                              (MC #007)

   See Also: Anderson Enterprises

Dominant Scheme: Planned Business Bankruptcy Fraud

Known Variations	Info Source	Additional Info

Suspect via Complaints and Other Information

Complaint or Info	Offense	Disposition

Background and Characteristics

Date of Birth: 11/04/58   Place of Birth: Dallas, Texas
Race/Sex: White/Male   Hair: Brown   Eyes: Brown
Photo: (See File #005)   Appearance Changes: Glasses
Voice/Manner: Deep/Polite   Permanent Address: Unknown
LKA: 55 Elm, Miami, FL   Business Address: Acme, Inc., Box 5
                                             Clearwater, FL (see Bus. File)

Style

Legal Tools: Read local business directories;   **Illegal Tools:** False Ref.; Misrepresentation
             ads in business publications, etc.   in brochures, letters, etc.

Victim Profile: Discuss common types of businesses targeted,
             such as manufacturing, services, etc.

Victim Approach: Explain how offender commonly contacts
                the companies or persons victimized

Exhibit 15-5
Mastercard Offender—Alias

Mastercard No. 121

Subject: "Tex"

See: Anderson, Edward MC #009
Anderson Enterprises MC #007

Dominant Scheme: Planned Business Bankruptcy Fraud

Known Variations	Info Source	Additional Info

Suspect via Complaints and Other Information

Complaint or Info	Offense	Disposition

Background and Characteristics

Date of Birth: Place of Birth:
Race/Sex: Hair: Eyes:
Photo: Appearance Changes:
Voice/Manner: Permanent Address:
LKA: Business Address:

Employment Background:

Skills:

Known Associates:

Style

Legal Tools: **Illegal Tools:**

Victim Profile:

Victim Approach:

Exhibit 15-6
Mastercard—Business Name of Group

Mastercard No. 121

Subject: Enterprise Associates

See: Anderson Enterprises (MC #007)
Anderson, Edward (MC #004)
Business Name File (#316)

Dominant Scheme: Planned Business Bankruptcy Fraud

Known Variations	Info Source	Additional Info

Suspect via Complaints and Other Information

Complaint or Info	Offense	Disposition

Background and Characteristics

Photographs:

Business Address:

Style

Legal Tools: **Illegal Tools:**

Victim Profile:

Victim Approach:

Exhibit 15-7
Sample Cards—Supplementary Alias File

#2075

Anderson, Edward (MC File #007)

DOB: 11/04/59

Race: White   Sex: Male

Background:

Aliases:

"Tex" (best known)

Ted Anderson

Stewart Anders

#3016

"Tex" Alias of Anderson, Edward (MC #004)

DOB: 11/04/59

Race: White   Sex: Male

Background:

Other Aliases:

Ted Anderson

Stewart Anders

Exhibit 15-8
Sample Cards—Supplementary Business Name File

#316

Enterprise Associates
Box 5, Miami Florida

Front For Anderson, Edward (MC File #004)

Other Names Used:

Anderson and Associates

Martinson, Wilson and Sons

Ace Enterprises, Inc.

#402

Anderson Enterprises
Box 5, Miami, Florida

Front for Anderson, Edward (MC #004)

Other Names Used:

Enterprise Associates (Best Known)

Ace Enterprises, Inc.

Martinson, Wilson and Sons

information about themselves that has no apparent culpability implications but will give you clues about their modus operandi and style.

Once you have made an offender a subject of a white collar crime investigation, much of the information you need for the mastercard will develop quickly. Initial contacts made during your investigation can be valuable information sources for ongoing intelligence. The major value of the mastercard is that it isolates specific information that is considered important. This supplies you with a focus for inquiries made not only to the victim company and representative but also to other agencies. In this sense, the mastercard can serve as a checklist of basic information needed, helping you to structure both initial and ongoing intelligence efforts.

Initiation and Maintenance of an Intelligence System

Even a simple intelligence system such as the one I've described using a mastercard file can become a significant and time-consuming task. While much file production (including cross-indexing and referencing) is a clerical function, basic mastercard file information requires experienced investigative decisions and input. Getting such input can be an important management undertaking. In new corporate white collar crime management units, mastercard file development may serve as an organizational and orientation project in which relevant information can be tracked down, reviewed, and digested into the proper format. Corporate WCC management units that have some prior history of fraud investigation but are newly created might use the mastercard file development process as a general updating and housecleaning task, getting old files in some order for the new effort. Often, information known to the WCC unit but not appropriate for investigative files can find a home in the mastercard index. This gives the intelligence process an opportunity to provide some beneficial information from the beginning and establishes the level of use and upkeep to which the intelligence system will be subjected. Finally, working on mastercard development can also help train and orient new WCC unit investigators.

Despite the tedious tasks associated with early file development, the process is an important one. Effective and appropriate managerial stress on its importance, combined with the marshalling of adequate clerical resources, can remove the more arduous elements and ensure that the process is well initiated and completed. While you should have general responsibility for management of the system, your intelligence process is important enough that day-to-day responsibility for maintenance and upkeep should be specifically delegated. The ideal situation (if your unit has enough resources) would be one in which the staff of the unit includes an intelligence analyst who is expert in the design and upkeep of files and in the assessment of information supplied for file inclusion. Under such an arrangement, data provided by investigators, internal sources, and external sources would go to the analyst, who would maintain records of such communications and decide how and to what extent new information will modify existing files.

Keeping records of communications is important even when you are not using information from a singular source, for two reasons. First, it can permit the analyst to assess the reliability of multiple sources; and second, even if information received is redundant, other sources can be developed and encouraged to supply further information.

Major decisions about such an intelligence system should be a WCC management unit-wide responsibility and should not be left in the province of the analyst. The decision to start a file, for example, should begin with a staff investigator's request to you as the unit manager. You should review the investigator's rationale and consult with others in the unit who are knowledgeable about the subject. If you make a positive decision, the analyst should then gather the relevant materials from the investigator, briefly review the subject's significance, and determine the best formatting of the file in consultation with the investigator. It is then the analyst who prepares the mastercard and organizes the file. In a particular case, an analyst might identify a crime and trigger the opening of a file in consultation with you, the unit manager, or an investigator.

The decision to purge a file follows the reverse procedure. It is the intelligence analyst who is in the best position to identify the files that go unused. Periodic assessments by the analyst may lead to the pulling of unattended files for unit review. A staff meeting to review the continued necessity of maintaining the file(s) would then be in order. While the final decision will rest with you, the unit manager, the entire staff should become involved. When there is uncertainty about the value of a particular file, you should defer the decision until checking with specific sources.

If a company or unit budget cannot afford to have its own intelligence analyst, it would be wise to consider designating one staff investigator to take major responsibility for your unit intelligence system. While you cannot expect a staff investigator to be as expert in the design of files as an analyst would be, there may be some advantage to this model. First, an investigator may be more credible to outside contacts than an analyst would be and so could serve as the focal point for communication with local, state, and federal agencies.

It makes no sense to establish an intelligence system without delegating specific responsibility for its upkeep. The usefulness of a white collar crime intelligence system is inextricably tied to the quality of maintenance it receives. Initial development and ongoing maintenance cannot be divorced. If you make no commitment involving maintenance, there is little reason to initiate the system. A similar error, and one often as fatal, is the failure to provide adequate clerical assistance for the maintenance function. Even the best analyst can quickly get bogged down without sufficient clerical assistance. This situation will detract from the quality of the system and the use made of it.

Earlier I noted that the system suggested in this chapter is one of simple design. However, if you have access to a computer, you can obviously handle added information in more complex ways. Remember, however, that added complexity requires adequate staffing for optimum benefit. Computers do not confer automatic benefits; you can become snowed under by computer printouts. Also, remember some basic points. First, the simpler your file designs of the intelligence system, the easier upkeep becomes and the more useful the system will be. Because of this, the ultimate system users must be intimately involved in initial design and policy decisions.

Second, no matter how carefully you design and how ideal the staffing for an intelligence effort is, it should be subjected to a semiannual review. When doing this, you can consider when a thorough housecleaning should occur and decide when you need a reevaluation of your general policies about the system. Shortcomings of your system should be addressed and decisions for future improvement made at this time. While such decisions do not have to wait for a six-month review time, scheduling such a review will ensure that needed system assessment occurs.

Finally, resources in any white collar enforcement effort must be judiciously expended. Carefully weigh the justifications for such costs. Also, consider your constraints on the use of resources for specific purposes. Your intelligence effort holds great potential for supplying useful information obtained and organized in an optimal fashion. Legal restraints bearing on the permissibility of the form of intelligence activity adopted, however, may severely dilute its potential. Half-hearted attempts at an intelligence system will produce the same result. When your unit faces either of these situations, you might want to consider better placement of your resources elsewhere in the safeguarding of your corporation's assets. Remember, what your corporation and your unit get out of an intelligence system is directly related to the investment and continued commitment put into it.

Chapter Sixteen
Conducting Criminal Investigations of White Collar Crime

Investigation of white collar crime that victimizes your corporation calls for imagination, patience, and clear understanding and appreciation of the range of possible approaches that you can use in your investigative processes. All the skills required in more conventional investigations will be called for, as well as other skills, but you will also have to apply conventional techniques with a different emphasis.

It will not always be easy to focus on a specific criminal act and gather evidence bearing on it. You will probably need to observe a pattern of general criminal activity that will be subject to attack in several aspects. For example, a scheme might fall under federal mail or wire fraud charges or within the jurisdiction of state statutes dealing with larceny or false pretenses, local laws involving licenses to solicit, or a variety of other local, state, and federal laws. Further, even when a criminal investigatory focus is possible in the first stages of your investigation, for a variety of reasons the prosecutor may decline to prosecute criminally even when the company so wishes. I do not suggest that your time was misspent, because it may bear fruit through (1) civil or administrative litigation to stop the wrongful, fraudulent activity; (2) civil action to achieve restitution for white collar crimes committed against your company, (3) laying the groundwork for private action by your company, affiliates, or employees victimized; and (4) educating the company personnel and executives about the frauds you're investigating, thus contributing to white collar crime prevention and deterrence efforts.

Your investigative approach must focus on gathering information that will be useful in achieving remedies in addition to the primary goal of your corporate white collar crime management unit. The added remedy may prove either more or less severe than the primary remedy. For example, you are conducting a charity fraud investigation and are facing difficulties under a local larceny statute. However, such a case might progress under a local false pretenses statute, or under mail and wire fraud.

Your investigation of embezzlement of corporate assets might not yield proof that convinces the prosecutor that he or she can show guilt beyond a reasonable doubt. However, the attorneys or prosecutor may have enough evidence to meet a civil burden of proof and begin a civil action, or may refer the case to the state attorney general's office or other office for a civil action, or move for a fitting injunctive action.

Beyond this, you need to recognize that your investigation of the white collar crime may not have a clear beginning and end in the same way that conventional crime investigations do. White collar crimes normally involve schemes that operate over time. The evidence you gather may be the missing piece of the investigative jigsaw puzzle that another investigator confronts later. Your investigation may become a success even when no remedy is invoked. If you conduct your investigation thoroughly, expertly, and with proper regard for presentation, the evidence you have gathered might prove valuable for future legal action.

The techniques of investigation I discuss in this chapter cannot be viewed as a group of tools used only for investigating white collar crime. Instead the techniques are an inventory of perspectives that will (1) help you to identify what evidence to gather, (2) show the different ways you can enhance conventional investigatory tasks when investigating white collar crime cases, and (3) become a guide for the analysis and organization of evidence supplying maximum advantage to prosecutors or other litigators. How you use these techniques will vary depending on the type of offense; the manner in which the case came to your attention; and the character, mission, and resources of your corporate white collar crime management unit.

The special distinguishing features of white collar crime investigation stem from the fact that white collar crimes are generally hidden or disguised within the framework of apparently legitimate undertakings. From the onset, your investigation must determine whether a white collar crime happened and whether there might be legal evidence to support a prosecution or other remedy that your corporation decides on. The WCC management unit staff investigators must be adept at the application of general investigation techniques such as handling complaints and information, interviewing, interrogation, finding documents and public records, finding expert assistance for specialized technical areas, and preparing a package for the attorneys involved. Your investigators must also develop the techniques that enable them to identify and develop the proof that a white collar crime occurred.

In this chapter, I first discuss the importance of shaping your investigation to bring together proof of the elements of white collar crime. I then outline application methods for general investigative techniques and how you can best use them in white collar crime cases to develop proof related to these elements. The principles underlying these approaches should be generally valid despite the particular jurisdiction, statutes, or corporate action decisions. Remember, as I noted earlier in this book, conducting a criminal investigation supplies the corporate leadership with broader options of dealing effectively with the situation, including criminal prosecution.

The total proficiency of any corporate staff investigator includes avoiding wasting time and effort on a hopeless case, avoiding fruitless investigative steps, building a sense of professional confidence, conducting continual self-examination of what techniques succeed and what do not.

■ HOW TO PROVE THE FIVE COMMON ELEMENTS OF WHITE COLLAR CRIME

One of the characteristics that distinguishes the investigation of white collar crime from that of common crimes is that you must establish the intent and underlying motives of the offender by placing together jigsaw puzzle pieces of apparently legitimate activities to add up to a picture of illegitimacy, rather than by simply showing of one event that by itself flatly demonstrates wrongful intent. For the most part, the intent and motivation of offenders become obscure and confusing because they seem unlikely to commit white collar crimes.

It's helpful to have a thorough knowledge of every type of white collar crime perpetrated against companies and the ways in which they were investigated earlier, prosecuted, or otherwise handled. White collar crime that victimizes corporations is often so complex and varied that you should use reference resources such as books like this, earlier investigative cases and intelligence files, and advice from attorneys and others. Furthermore, you will not always find an obvious and definite legal theory to rely on when you start investigating the case. Definitions of specific white collar crimes will also vary from one jurisdiction to another.

The absence of such legal certainty should never be an excuse for inaction. Thorough knowledge of all technical points of law affecting white collar crime is not an essential prerequisite for successful white collar crime investigation. What *is* essential is a clear understanding of the basic elements that can show whether a white collar crime has happened. Once you understand the elements, you can focus on what wrongs happened and how they happened, instead of relying on statutory definitions of crimes.

You should not allow yourself to be locked into any rigid legal framework of definitions about white collar crime violations that victimize your company. You must, however, understand and remain aware of elements common to all white collar crime, as noted earlier in this book:

(1) *Intent* to commit a wrongful act to achieve a purpose inconsistent with law or public policy

(2) *Disguise of purpose*—falsities and misrepresentations used to accomplish the scheme

(3) *Reliance* by the offender on the ignorance or carelessness of the victim

(4) *Voluntary victim action*—an act or attitude that assists the offender and supplies them with an opportunity

(5) *Concealment* of the white collar crime.

The presence and right mix of these elements normally signals that a white collar crime exists as well as a parallel civil remedy. However, it is not necessary to have evidence for each of these elements to support a criminal or civil action. You should consider each element when deciding the scope and characteristics of your investigation.

The type of white collar crime, level of sophistication, and type of victim the case involves do not matter. The crimes can be as different as antitrust violations, bank embezzlements, or planned business bankruptcy schemes. When a set of circumstances can be reconstructed that strongly supports certain combinations of the aforementioned elements, there is likely a prosecutable violation. The following discussions examine each of the elements in greater detail.

Criminal Intent

There must be adequate proof that the offender or suspects intended to commit the wrongful acts. This will usually become apparent by gathering evidence from witnesses and documents that prove that the suspect knew of his or her involvement in a wrongful activity, or that the circumstances are such that any contrary conclusion lacks credibility.

There are several ways of doing this. The most common ways are to show that

(1) The suspect could have had no legitimate motive for his or her activities.

(2) The suspect repeatedly engaged in the same or a corresponding activity of an apparently wrongful nature.

(3) The suspect made conflicting statements.

(4) The suspect systematically organized the dissemination of misleading information.

(5) The suspect made admissions about the white collar crime.

(6) The suspect acted to hinder investigation of his or her offense.

(7) The suspect made statements about the situation that he or she clearly knew to be false.

(1) Activity Inconsistent with Legitimate Intent

Suspects of white collar crimes will often claim a defense that shows them as respectable, legitimate persons who acted in good faith and never intended to violate any laws. You should consider every possibility that the suspect's activities may have had some legitimate purpose; however, it's often clear from the onset that they did not (e.g., embezzling through consistently fraudulent travel and expense claims). When your investigation of a seeming white collar crime supplies sufficient persuasive evidence that there was a legitimate purpose, the suspect will have a defense that makes prosecution and conviction impossible or unjust. Conversely, if you can show that the suspect's activities demonstrated bad faith (i.e., with clear intent to defraud), a court or jury will seriously question any other defenses the suspect claims and the suspect will be less likely to risk cross examination by taking the witness stand in his or her own defense. Should your company decide only to discipline or terminate an employee, the employee will probably not bring any suit or action against the company. This latter action also creates a greater possibility that civil litigation may help your company recover embezzlement or other theft losses from the perpetrator(s).

White collar crime suspects will often make preparations to defend their activities by seizing on every possible argument that could show they operated in good faith (although foolishly, unwisely, sloppily, or incompetently), so you must continually consider in detail what explanations the suspects in your investigation will offer in defense of their questionable activities. Such an analysis will supply a guide to the search for evidence that will eliminate avenues of escape. Eliminating the possibility of a seemingly legitimate explanation that excuses the suspect's white collar crime activity will increase the probability of conviction or winning civil litigation and heighten the prosecutor's or other attorney's willingness to pursue the case.

In white collar crime cases, legitimacy or illegitimacy of a suspect's activity can often be determined by comparing the suspected activities to normal practices. Often, you will deal with normal and understandable business and personal transactions, or at least with transactions that experts can analyze to determine whether the suspect's explanations are consistent with legitimate ends.

For example, a wholesaler supplier buys manufactured merchandise from your company on credit at a cost of $200,000. He sells the merchandise to a person for $50,000 cash and takes a promissory note for the balance of $200,000. The supplier's buyer picks up the merchandise from your company and is never heard from again. The supplier goes bankrupt. When charged with bankruptcy fraud, he claims that he cannot locate the purchaser and that he lost the $50,000 at a legal gambling casino. This strange transaction (i.e., the alleged acceptance of a $200,000 note from a stranger who you can neither identify, verify, or locate) does not fall within acceptable or normal business terms and may, coupled with other evidence, contribute to successful prosecution of the supplier for bankruptcy fraud.

In this instance, the activity relates to the subject of misrepresentations, discussed later in this chapter. The distinction to keep in mind is that the unexplainable activity shows the criminal intention of the suspect, while the purchase from your company creates the misrepresentation.

Many cases become matters of degree. For example, if an executive for a manufacturer buys a supplier an expensive lunch or sends him a bottle of scotch at Christmas, it would be in line with common perceptions of normal business practices. Standards will differ based on time and place, customs of the industry, and other explainable factors.

Some test cases are straightforward and thus the techniques for determining legitimacy seem relatively simple. They are not. Your investigators must understand that all cases they encounter won't always be so clear cut. For example, if, in the preceding bankruptcy fraud example, the supplier is a wholesaler who bought the merchandise at a cost of $200,000 on credit, payable to your company at the rate of $25,000 per month, and then sold it for $250,000 payable to him at the rate of $55,000 per month, he would make $50,000 profit. For three or four months the supplier claims he receives no payment from the buyer, but does receive letters supposedly from the purchaser excusing nonpayment with a claim that the merchandise picked up at your company was defective, damaged, and generally unacceptable. Letters are exchanged, and over that period the supplier receives a total of $35,000 in payment, does not pay anything to his creditors (or at most makes a token payment), seems lethargic in taking action, and then goes bankrupt. These transactions raise questions. Your investigation must demonstrate that the situation is unexplainable in normal business terms, and to do so you must probe below the surface. You should be suspicious and follow up on the alleged claims. For example, the claim of allegedly damaged merchandise accepted by the purchaser at your company would surely have become an immediate issue between the purchaser, the supplier, and your company, but it did not.

An investigator may have to consult with experts depending on the particular type of business activity your WCC unit investigates. In cases involving intricate financial transactions, for example, an accountant could help you determine whether a particular transaction made sense in legitimate business terms. Similarly, a bank examiner can help you understand intricate banking transactions. Staff investigators should not dismiss the possibility that businesspersons may sometimes act incompetently or irrationally instead of with wrongful or criminal intent. Experts can help you in these areas, but you must consider motives when trying to determine the suspect's intentions.

Considerations of whether there are possible legitimate explanations for the questionable activities of suspects also become important because it is common in a white collar crime investigation to defer interrogation of the suspect until close to the conclusion of your work, and often to refrain totally from such interrogation.

In summary, you should analyze carefully possible motives for the transactions at the core of the alleged violations (as in any other criminal investigation) coupled with other transactions involving the suspect. In addition to countering potential defenses (white collar crime excuses), such consideration and related investigation will prevent misallocation of investigative and prosecutive resources or a highly publicized but later embarrassing indictment (because the activity turns out to be legitimate).

(2) Repetitious Wrongful Activity

As I emphasized in the previous discussion, you must continually consider what explanations a suspect in your investigation will offer in defense of his or her questionable activities. A common defense or explanation is that a false representation (e.g., a charge of embezzlement) stems from a mistake or unintentional slip of the tongue or the pen. Although the commission of a single wrongful act is enough in theory to bring a violator within the jurisdiction of a criminal statute, as a practical matter a single instance of wrongful behavior will not supply sufficient support to justify a finding of criminal intent. To counter such a claim by a suspect, you must develop proof that the suspect made the same, or similar, "mistakes" repeatedly. One of the principal means of establishing the needed element of intent is to demonstrate that misrepresentations, use of false pretenses, and promises made by the suspect surpassed a single instance.

You should seek evidence, through investigative audits, conventional audits, victim or witness statements, witness or nonvictim statements, or undercover operations of similar misrepresentations involving the suspect. You can use this evidence to support your conclusion that the same misrepresentations happened in other situations and that fraudulent activities exceeded this instance. By expanding the number of instances, you might find a possibility to charge a broader scheme.

Before a court or your company can infer fraudulent intent from the commission of an act, you must prove that the act happened. You must expect that the suspect will deny the testimony of others who will describe what he or she did or quote what the suspect said to them.

During a criminal investigation, you and your staff investigators cannot search every corner for evidence that proves that your suspect participated in a white collar fraud similar to the one under investigation. However, you should stay alert to gather proof of similar frauds if you learn of them. Routine searches into the background and activities of your suspect is a basic investigative technique (this includes systematic searches of your corporate white collar crime management unit's intelligence file). You might uncover evidence of earlier frauds in public and private agencies that have responsibility for or interest in the activity under investigation (this is especially true when your company is victimized by offenders outside the company).

(3) Conflicting Statements

Proof that a suspect in your investigation made conflicting statements to different persons will often help you prove his or her fraudulent intent. Your objective must remain focused on gathering relevant, admissible facts that will help attorneys convince a court or assure corporate management that the suspect shows a clear pattern of consistent disregard for truth. A legitimate employee or businessperson will generally make consistent statements. In contrast, a dishonest person will say whatever is necessary to consummate his or her fraudulent act or scheme. When conflicting statements involve highly subjective judgment questions, such as matters of value, it will be difficult for you to make a valid fraud case without supporting evidence of involvement of the suspect in other types of white collar crime.

You must try continually to eliminate opportunities for suspects to explain away their conflicting statements when a case comes to court or other action. The suspect's first line of defense might include denial of inconsistent representations. A second line of defense might include claiming that the activity was a mistake or claiming that the inconsistent statements were mere "puffing" or expressions of opinion. You may overcome each of these defense claims through gathering evidence showing that the suspect's acts were part of a deliberately executed pattern of white collar crime activity. To develop a pattern of conflicting statements that points to fraudulent intent, you need proof of repeated inconsistent statements. The method for establishing the repetitiousness of inconsistent statements is the same as discussed earlier. Proof of repeated inconsistencies refutes the claim that the misstatements were made innocently.

Although conflicting statements may not in themselves become enough proof of fraudulent intent, they do show a deliberate disregard for truth by the suspect and provide support for determining fraudulent intent. This consideration is important in persuading a court or jury that so-called inconsistent puffing was really part of a fraudulent scheme.

(4) Systematically Organized Dissemination of Misleading Information

Large-scale fraudulent schemes do not rely solely on the skills of separate persons. Most, if not all, large-scale white collar fraud schemes are based on carefully planned operations. For example, in schemes targeting your company that involve use of a sales force, the salespersons will normally attend intense sales training sessions. At these sessions sales representatives receive instruction on various techniques for successful sales, usually including the cautious dissemination of misleading information or methods to avoid supplying victim companies or company representatives with suitable information that would cause them to reject the deal offered to them. The systematic dissemination of misleading information will most likely stem from oral statements that are hard to prove. However, misinformation will often be disseminated by white collar criminals in written form through brochures, prospectuses, charts, graphs, and pictures accompanying their oral presentations. Collect copies of all brochures, prospectuses, and other written information supplied to your company or its representative. Similarly, during interviews of possible witnesses, you should always ask about the defrauder's use of such materials that might have persuaded them to act. The written material may include misleading information that supports claims of misleading statements and refutes the suspect's denial of having made them.

The following are two reliable techniques of collecting evidence of misleading information:

Development and uses of informants: This technique often involves using other employees or persons outside the company as information sources that supply you with valuable leads about a scheme discussed or one in progress. You must use caution in developing employees as informants so that you safeguard your image as fair and impartial and do not come across as a person who is out to get someone in trouble.

The best approach, and first technique, is a discreet but persuasive appeal privately to a person whom you believe is honest. Ask this person to supply you with his or her observations and knowledge in limited confidence. However, don't promise totally confidentiality because the success or failure of your case might make it necessary to reveal your source of information that prompted a criminal investigation. A public police officer does not have those options available. Police officers are also governed by laws and procedures that do not apply to a corporate investigator. For example, your actions based on an informant's information, and using that information as a lead, you can conduct an investigative audit or request an internal conventional audit. The results of either or both may lead to your basis for conducting a criminal investigation. Just make certain you know what the allegations from an informant mean and make no promises you cannot fulfill. Selling out an informant or appearing to do so will immediately end any further opportunities of developing these important sources. Also, before you approach a person for information, ensure that you have researched him or her sufficiently to be confident that the person is not involved in the same or another white collar crime scheme.

You may also "turn" one of the perpetrators in a white collar crime. Normally, this type of informant has two primary motives for becoming an informant that implicates others. First, the person recognizes the wrongful participation and wants out of the situation; and second, the person hopes that his or her cooperation might lead to forgiveness of his or her white collar crime acts or participation. You must exercise great care with informants of this type because they might be the key perpetrator, and once they have supplied you with their knowledge, they have created a strong defense for their own part in the scheme. In other words, the big fish supplies information that gets it off the hook in return for your efforts to catch several little fish that were often recruited by the informant.

Your best course of action when dealing with any informant is to consult with the applicable attorney, such as a prosecutor or corporate counsel. Any promises of immunity or confidentiality must come from them directly to the informant. Always ensure that any deal to offer immunity to an informant comes from the applicable authority. Only then can you proceed with an informant with confidence that later the situation will not be embarrassing or detrimental. Also, ensure that you have other staff members of the corporate white collar crime management unit present as witnesses to any deal offered to an informant.

Collection of Physical Evidence: The second technique involves collection of physical evidence in a criminal investigation of a white collar crime that targets your company. Physical evidence includes charts, graphs, photographs, illustrations, brochures, sales pitch scripts, recordings, videotapes, books and records, working papers, and nearly any tangible item that supports your conclusions. Since easy destruction or concealment of this type of evidence is a threat to your investigative result, your timing and collection techniques are crucial. If you are going to seize some items, make sure that you have competent legal counsel to guide your actions.

For example, if you have started a criminal investigation of a sales representative for your company for whom an investigative audit and an internal audit showed consistent padding of expense and travel accounts, you can collect physical documents safely that are within the company's control (e.g., the claims filed and other records not in control of the perpetrator). However, suppose you need to obtain documents that you believe are locked in the employee's desk at the office or in his or her personal car. Although the desk belongs to the company, as does the office space, the items inside the desk belong to the person under investigation. You might obtain voluntary permission from the suspect to search and seize any documents in his or her desk (such permission must be witnessed by a reliable and impartial person), but normally you cannot expect to receive that type of cooperation. If you ask and the suspect declines, he or she will certainly destroy or further conceal the evidence necessary to the successful result of your investigation.

The information that you need from the physical evidence in a suspect's desk, car, or home probably stems from an informant's first-hand knowledge. When you need to obtain such evidence, consult with and follow the instructions of the corporate legal counsel or prosecutor. You might need to involve the police or prosecutor in the case to obtain a search warrant, but before you take any independent action, consult with your corporate management and counsel to determine what action they want you to take.

(5) Admissions by the Suspect

During any criminal investigations, you must be alert for and prepared to handle any acts or statements made by suspects that clearly demonstrate that they know they have lied and have been deliberately perpetrating a fraud. These acts or statements may have been made to their associates or even to others in the company.

Emphasize trying to get a statement from the suspect whenever possible. Although a confession does not seem likely, white collar criminals will often tie themselves down to some story, particularly if they believe it to their advantage. They normally show confidence in their ability to convince others of the truth of their statements or the image they present. Remember, deception is their stock in trade. However, statements will often contain inconsistencies when compared with other evidence obtained from the victim company or its representative. Such inconsistencies might become tantamount to the suspect admitting that he or she lied. You should recognize, however, that most white collar criminals will have anticipated becoming the suspect of your criminal investigation or arrest and will not make any confessions. Instead, suspects might have sufficient legal knowledge to understand that it's in their best interest to say nothing.

Should that situation arise, consider the importance of "turning" lower-level functionaries in a white collar crime scheme. These schemes, particularly in large fraud cases that involve several people inside the company, outside the company, or a combination of the two, often involve people who lack assets and are thus unlikely defendants in civil actions. They have a defense of being poor as opposed to the image that white collar criminals gain great wealth. Also, many perpetrators in large white collar crime schemes insulate themselves from the scheme using underlings to take the fall if things go wrong. However, unless the underling has been isolated from information, he or she will often turn and thus allow you to reach the key member of a group. If you are successful at turning one or more underlings in a large scheme operation, they might open the floodgates of added evidence that brings down those in control of the scheme.

(6) Acts That Impede Your Criminal Investigation

Evidence that a suspect attempted to hinder or sidetrack your criminal investigation (or an investigative or conventional audit) may support criminal intent. It is perfectly reasonable for the guilty and innocent alike to attempt to prove their innocence. However, when the overall scheme includes such things as fabricated evidence, destroyed evidence, precontrived defenses, and preplanned payoffs to possible witnesses, you can often use these actions to support your conclusion of criminal intent in a white collar crime scheme.

Misrepresentation and Disguise of Purpose

A prominent characteristic of white collar crime that victimizes corporations is that offenders have misrepresented facts and disguised their true purpose, thus creating a deception. This happens in all the crimes discussed earlier in this book, and it includes altering records, taking bribes, embezzlement, and other acts. The offender(s) or suspect(s) attempts to create a situation that parts the victim company from its money or property by deliberate deception.

The detailed methods and specific types of misrepresentations will vary from case to case, scheme to scheme, and offender to offender. However, you need not know the specific profile of every possible scheme, but you must be alert to the general characteristics of misrepresentation. A good rule of thumb is that misrepresentations may stem from more than direct false statements (including false claims and alterations of records). Misrepresentation by a defrauder also encompasses creation of an appearance that later is shown as false and deceptive. This situation can occur in several ways (e.g., through a discreet arrangement of words, through the manner in which the words appear or are displayed, and through circumstances in which the offender uses the words). Any of the innumerable deceptive practices used by a suspect to steal from the victim company might create admissible and persuasive proof of fraud.

Four Key Steps in Proving Misrepresentation

In many cases you investigate, proving *misrepresentation* will be obvious. However, remember that you also have to prove *intent* to misrepresent as an element of the crime. The following four key steps will help you in the investigative task.

(1) The Suspect's Written Material

The variety of written material that evolves from most white collar crimes that victimize corporations is boundless. The following tips (at best a partial list) will supply you with a guide to collecting physical evidence.

- Correspondence from external offenders and internal information contained in memorandums, notes, claims, and requests
- Sales brochures that often accompany business-to-business frauds, including office supply schemes, bankruptcy, investment, and charity frauds, to name only a few
- Newspaper, magazine, or trade journal advertisements that offenders often use effectively when creating a perception of endorsement
- Prospectuses, especially those used by the offender when attempting to sell the company something, including land, buildings, products and materials, investments, or other items
- Securities discovered to be bogus, stolen, false, or forged
- Financial statements, especially when another company applies to your company for credit or other purpose for obtaining money or property
- Lists of prospective victim companies, often obtained from a turned informant (Ensure that you talk to your corporate counsel or prosecutor before you accept and use this type of proof, because you must make sure that the informant obtained the information legally and does not claim later that you promised an immunity deal or used coercion.)
- Lists of other corporate investors or endorsers of the scheme
  —Contracts
  —Receipts

—Warranties

—Guarantees

You should routinely collect these types of data and documentation during your criminal investigation of a white collar crime and analyze them carefully to determine if they separately or collectively support your investigative conclusion. They may also provide you with an added source of proving false representations.

(2) The Suspect's Books and Records

In certain types of fraud, corporate or private records will exist that may help you prove that misrepresentations happened. It's often difficult to determine from records exactly who is involved intentionally in a white collar scheme. Many business enterprises cannot operate without filing with some public agency. You might contact the persons who made the filing and persuade them to disclose the identity of those for whom they front. Such filings would include articles of incorporation, certificates to do business under a trade name, applications for licenses to solicit for charities or other types of sales, information filing to legalize sales of securities or real estate, and others. Attentive searches for such material may not only make it possible for you to identify and reach the principal perpetrators of schemes who wish to discourage pursuit of civil or criminal liability, but may also make it possible for your company to ask prosecutors to invoke criminal statutes that penalize false statements made in such filings or that provide penalties for failure to file.

(3) The Suspect's Oral Representations

When an offender makes an oral misrepresentation to your company, you might succeed in getting the person responsible to repeat it again to a corroborating representative of your company. Without such corroboration, the person can easily deny having made the statements. Another alternative is to develop proof that a suspect committed similar acts. This is usually done by gaining the cooperation of another company victimized by the same person. The cumulative effect of several witnesses attesting to the representation made to them by the suspect is persuasive in legal actions.

(4) Proving Falsity in Representations

False representations, false pretenses, and false promises can take an infinite variety of specific forms depending on the type of fraudulent scheme. They can develop as false statements, omissions of key facts, or a transaction between your company or within your company by the offender. The misrepresentation may concern the quantity, quality, value, nature, utility, status, or other characteristic of an article, service, or proposed transaction.

Your approach to collecting evidence about the falsity of representation might include the following:

- Collecting evidence from representatives of your company or other companies victimized that shows that the product or service was not as represented
- Testing the validity of the suspected misrepresentation (for example, trying out a product or service to an extent that will convincingly supply admissible evidence of the falsity of the representation)
- Accumulating documentation that disputes the suspected misrepresentation
- Obtaining expert testimony (when applicable) that is counter to the suspected misrepresentation

Examples and applications of investigative techniques

The following examples will help you consider the varieties of investigative approaches used to achieve the aforementioned requirements.

Example: A group of companies victimized by an advertising directory scheme does not know the offer doesn't come from a legitimate company. The offender entices them through advertising or representatives that make the following statements to obtain money from the victim companies:

- The fraudulent scheme, operating as a seemingly legitimate company, will publish a sample directory dated the year before using company listings in a distant city.
- The fraudulent company already has a list of local subscribers to show the victim companies that don't want other corporations to gain an advertising edge.
- The fraudulent company does not have to be licensed in the victim company's state because it is already licensed in another state.
- The fraudulent company shows documents that it has been in business for six years and claims that because of its success a decision to go into another state or nationwide prompted this offer.
- The fraudulent company offers a costly advertisement at a huge discount, claiming that it is an introductory offer.
- The fraudulent company will often make a promised discount for the next four years, resulting in a considerable saving to the victim com-

pany if the company agrees to advertise in their directory and pays the discounted price for the first two years now. The fraudulent company shows a list of competitors who have already signed up and shows their signed contracts.

■ As promised, the directory arrives six months later with an acceptable representation of the victim company. However, the victim company later learns that the directory went only to those who subscribed and was not mass distributed, as promised. Victim companies receive a directory that told them no more than they already knew, and no one else ever sees it. Although the victim companies learn of the misrepresentation and fraud months later, they learn that the shell company publishing the directories has folded and the perpetrators have gone, probably to operate under another shell company name in another part of the country.

Investigative Steps Leading to Recovery of Losses

The amount of payment made by your company will often determine how much effort your company will want to expend in recovering assets or taking legal action against the fraudulent directory company. However, it might be easier to do so than you think at the onset.

First, you need to obtain the incorporation papers from the state in which the fraudulent company formed. Even a shell corporation must have this filing, which supplies the name of the person who formed the company and his or her address. A few phone calls or letters will move your investigation forward to that point. You should also check that state to determine the other shell companies filed and obtain the articles of incorporation for them.

Second, once you have obtained the name of the company's owner, you can locate him or her in several ways. One contemporary technique involves reliable companies across the country that use computer networks to develop massive amounts of database information about companies and persons, including addresses and telephone numbers. Once you have identified where the defrauder maintains a residence, you can move to the third step.

Third, you can ask these information sources to perform a nationwide search for assets of a specific person or company. Should the person have enough assets that would satisfy your company's losses due to the fraudulent scheme, your corporate counsel or other attorney can file a civil action against the responsible defrauder's personal assets to recover your company's losses.

Fourth, you can refer the matter to the proper local, state, or federal agency, supplying it with your investigative information if it wants to file for indictment.

Reliance by the Offender and Voluntary Victim Action

Earlier, I discussed two essential elements of white collar crimes that victimize corporations: (1) reliance of the white collar offender on the carelessness or ignorance of the victim that supplies an opportunity; and (2) the voluntary victim action that assists the offender in carrying the scheme against your company.

Proving voluntary victim action by your company will not be difficult, but it is an essential element in your investigative process. For example, your company or its representative can supply this element. If he or she cooperated with the offender in any way and can testify to signing a contract, sending a letter with a check, or any other cooperative act, the voluntary action happened. Your investigative task includes obtaining certainty that your company, acting through an authorized officer or employee; accepted the offender claims in good faith and took some action based on that belief.

Information (evidence) on the steps taken by white collar criminals to make them confident that your company representative would respond in the way they wanted will generally involve proof of more subtle misrepresentations. Question company representatives carefully to determine what caused them to accept written or oral misrepresentations. What was there in the setting that persuaded them to supply their signatures or approvals or that made them act without doing much verifying? This should not suggest that the victim is obliged to check everything, but when you can show that the offender conned the victim into not verifying, you have a stronger case. In this way vague sales pitches are transformed into clear and obvious misrepresentations. The following are examples of evidence that help prove fraud to a court or jury (or to a prosecutor who is considering either civil or criminal action).

(1) False statements made to a regulatory agency that must clear securities or land sales will often be accepted, and the resulting prospectuses will carry the legend that the facts in them were filed with the state or federal agency as called for by law. The same legend will usually include a statement that acceptance for filing or registration does not create any form of government approval. However, the fact that there has been some appearance of governmental involvement, filing tends to increase victim confidence in the validity of the opportunity offered.

(2) In such cases, you or your staff investigators should concentrate on showing that misrepresentation happened in application to the government regulatory agency with the aim of getting the state agency to accept the suspect's filing and as part of the scheme to defraud the corporate victim. Possible lies made by the white collar criminal to the accountant who prepared a financial statement for filing should be targets of your inquiry.

(3) You must obtain details about the setting in which the fraudulent deals occur and answers about how the offender obtained the essential element of voluntary victim action. Misrepresentations or even vague statements become more deceptive with shills present to stampede victims into signing on the dotted line. The shills might be as simple as a list of competitors of your company.

(4) Seek evidence about the manner in which innocent third parties, or parties with lesser degrees of culpability, might encourage voluntary victim action. It is not uncommon for fraud operators to enhance their own credibility by using otherwise legitimate advisers, such as accountants and attorneys, to persuade clients to take advantage of the offender's offer. Often, these intermediaries will be lured into a conflict of interest situation through some type of gratuity. Their position is equivocal, since they helped to perpetrate the fraud but they are not particularly important subjects for prosecution or civil litigation. Under these circumstances they will frequently cooperate with you during your investigation and provide evidence about how the primary offender used them to lull others into acquiescence (particularly if they believe there's a chance of becoming subject to prosecution). You should not generally treat them as innocent victims if they received special compensation; if so treated they will become apprehensive about being sued by your company and will be lost as a source of evidence. Also, sometimes these intermediaries will have operated so closely with the principal scheme operators that they may be charged as unindicted co-conspirators so their own misrepresentations can serve as evidence against the principal scheme operators.

(5) One form of fraud against corporations is bid rigging, (i.e., collusion among bidders to present a facade of competitive bidding while ensuring that the colluding bidders determine the winner and the price of the goods or services). In addition to seeking evidence of an illegal agreement to act in concert among bidders, you should seek information on steps taken to enhance appearances of competition (i.e., half-hearted appeals following bid awards by your company, carefully contrived random-appearing bid disparities, and agreed-on winners). These actions were taken by contractors to entice the voluntary victim action by creating a facade of bona fide competition.

(6) Proof of activities designed to get voluntary victim action, such as those described earlier, can be extraordinarily important to the success of your case and to the attorneys or prosecutor agreeing to take the case. If you obtain evidence that misrepresentations occurred, and if your company relied on these misrepresentations and sustained losses from them, the evidence might be sufficient for a technical legal case. But the evidence of the many activities used to break down your company's resistance can spell the difference between a strong winning case and one lost because of weak circumstances.

Concealment of the Crime

The concealment element of white collar crime generates the most significant distinctions between the investigation of white collar crime and other crimes. In white collar crimes there are rarely any simple indicators or events that trigger reactions, as would be the case in a clear case of a large, one-time theft from one of your company's warehouses. In white collar crimes, victim corporations often don't know they have been victimized until well after the executed transactions or occurrences, and some never know they were a victim of white collar crime. The element of concealment keeps your company in perpetual ignorance of its victimization, or delays that realization.

The discussion of misrepresentation earlier in this chapter concerned evidence on the use of guile and deception to gain victim acquiescence (i.e., to get your company's signature or money). In contrast, this discussion of concealment concerns the evidence you should seek to show that the white collar criminal covers up a crime or wrongful act.

Acts in furtherance of concealment may simply be another aspect of, or implicit in, the steps an offender uses to obtain victim acquiescence. Or they may be an entirely separate and distinct series of deceptive acts, a continued cover-up of what has happened. In either situation it is important that you ask what the perpetrator did to conceal or cover up the act, both while victimizing your company and after obtaining the proceeds of the fraud. The U.S. Supreme Court has stated, for example, the act of lulling the fraud victim after the victim has fully parted with its money can be part of a scheme to defraud.

Despite the type of scheme or method of concealment, you should use the same basic sources of leads in gathering evidence of white collar crime concealment (i.e., complaints; intelligence about suspects, offenders, and possible criminal activities; financial investigations; and affirmative searches for violations and weaknesses using investigative audits). Your corporate white collar crime management unit must stay continually alert to the hidden nature of most sophisticated white collar crime. You should consider the following circumstances when gathering and organizing your evidence of white collar crime concealment:

Crimes Too Small for Recognition

The ideal white collar crime, from the offender's point of view, is one that will not be recognized as a crime. A classic example is charity fraud. A charity fraud may involve a large amount of money that your company contributes on appeal from the offender but is rarely noted by the company after making the contribution. When you detect a charity fraud victimizing your company, or when intelligence efforts indicate that your company might become the target of such a scheme, you must collect evidence such as (1) data on the applications for permits (fraudulent charities will often not obtain permits); and (2) the financial trail of the collected funds (i.e., how they were used or failed to be used). Analyze the cancelled corporate check to obtain leads for this activity.

Lulling the Victim Corporation

There is another type of concealment prevalent in white collar crime frauds, and this concealment must be continuous. For example, bankruptcy frauds and "bustouts" require that over time the criminal establishes sufficient credit with suppliers to enable purchasing large quantities of materials without payment. To conceal such frauds during the weeks or months of their perpetration, the offender may lull your company with a series of official-sounding letters or telephone calls, reassuring your company and explaining why the particular payment due cannot be made at this time. The letters and telephone calls will often come from persons who have previously established a relationship of trust with your company. The letters and calls might involve fronts for organized crime that have hooks into ostensible owners of business, and they will frequently result in the granting of added credit. Token payments to your company, comprising only a small percentage of the amount due, may also lull your company into delaying any contemplated action. Finally, the perpetrator goes bankrupt or closes the doors of the company and disappears.

In such cases, you must carefully investigate representations made by the perpetrator that lulled your company; the falsity of such representations will be strong proof of fraud. When fraud is established, consider the alternative I noted earlier about piercing the corporate veil and recovering from personal assets of the offender. Even when perpetrators "disappear" it's often possible to recover using the techniques I noted above regarding finding both the offender and their personal assets.

Crimes of Overwhelming Size and Complexity

Extremely large-scale white collar crime operations may be complex and may seem like legitimate, competitive, normal businesses. The sheer size and character of the sponsorship make crime seem like an incredulous possibility. A single complex scheme of this type may involve many different categories of white collar crime and peripherally may involve many common crimes. The connection between the perpetrators of the common crimes and white collar offenders will rarely be evident to any outside observer, and the entire process may include a variety of transactions into which your corporate white collar crime management unit investigators must dig.

For example, the establishment of a monopoly of material suppliers by an organized crime enterprise creates a sole source that your company must deal with, despite high prices, to stay in business. You need to buy from the company or try to get the same materials outside the area. However, your company finds that to truck or ship the materials from the nearest company not controlled by organized crime will cost more than the high prices that the organized crime enterprise charges. The process through which the organized crime monopoly occurred may take a variety of forms, such as the gradual takeover of competitors by first undercutting their prices and then buying out the failed companies.

To develop proof in such situations, you will need imaginative searches for evidence on issues such as (1) the true identities of company owners, (2) the sources of finance (i.e., possibilities of criminal funds laundered through investment in this business), (3) the pattern of bids by alleged competitors, and (4) other relationships that create a situation that will prompt legal action by your company, the government, or both.

■ A SUMMARY OF THE ELEMENTS

The elements I've discussed in this chapter cannot be separated one from the other, with each provable by a showing of entirely different sets of facts. Neither must there be evidence for each of these elements in every case. You should view the elements instead as different lenses through which the white collar crime scheme can be seen. The different perspectives these lenses offer will help you identify the evidence needed to ensure that a court or jury will understand what happened, the criminal design that made it happen, how your company was manipulated, and what losses at your company resulted from the scheme.

Through establishing a sound investigative policy and procedure for your WCC management unit staff, identifying the types of evidence needed to make a credible case, and making such identifications, your unit will be in a good position to use the investigative techniques discussed in Chapter 17.

Chapter Seventeen
Special Investigative Techniques for White Collar Crimes

For years, criminal investigators relied on six basic investigative techniques to solve crimes: (1) development of informants, (2) use of undercover agents, (3) laboratory analysis of physical evidence, (4) surveillance, (5) interviews and interrogations, and (6) legal wiretapping (with a court order). However, successful investigation of white collar crimes calls for another, often more important, technique of financial investigations that encompasses the suspect or offender.

This special technique often becomes important in detecting and proving a case, such as those involving internal corporate white collar crimes of embezzlement. In this chapter, I will introduce you to this important investigative technique, which can greatly enhance your success of investigating white collar crime cases. Too often this important technique does not find its way into the skills of the corporate white collar crime investigator, who generally relies only on available documentary proof within the victimized company. Although documentary proof (such as altered or forged books, records, inventories, and expense and travel claims) is important, proving monetary gain or intent often must rely on showing without doubt that the suspect developed unexplained assets that trace directly to the crime he or she committed against your company.

The reluctance to pursue financial investigations stems mostly from beliefs that this type of technique is too difficult without an extensive accounting background. Instead of taking positive action to overcome this inhibition, most corporate criminal investigators and public police take a negative approach and dismiss the need to investigate financial leads. This reluctance often leads to an unsuccessful investigation or losing an otherwise winnable case in prosecution or civil litigation.

This special financial investigative technique emerged from the Internal Revenue Service, which faces problems similar to those the corporate investigator faces when probing into federal tax fraud. This technique of financial investigation proved so valuable in financially motivated cases that it now enjoys widespread use and is adapted as necessary to the situation and the specific type of white collar crime. The financial investigation technique I discuss here traces from the IRS technique as well as those I have added over the years. This unique style of financial investigation will enable you to explore, develop, and follow the important financial transactions of those who victimize your corporation and successfully tie their personal gain to the documented white collar crime.

You need to consider the corporate reaction to a white collar scheme that targets your company assets. Even firing an employee who embezzles might not be without reverberations considering the contemporary labor laws and other laws that enable an employee to bring detrimental actions that further the loss. You must ensure that your white collar crime investigations leave no room for recourse for persons who are obviously responsible for the wrongdoing. The techniques discussed in this chapter will bring you that investigative success. Remember, you must not only safeguard company assets through a variety of investigative, detection, and prevention techniques discussed earlier, but also ensure that the suspect or offender has no means to further the loss through endless litigation and adverse publicity.

■ THE NET WORTH–EXPENDITURES PRINCIPLE

Before explaining how you can apply the net worth–expenditures principle, I want to explain and define the principle of this valuable and important investigative technique.

The net worth–expenditures principle emerges from a mathematical computation designed to determine the total accumulation of money and property as well as the annual expenditures made by the white collar crime suspect or offender. The U.S. Internal Revenue Service successfully uses this principle when investigating suspected tax fraud, even when there are no books or records of income and expenses maintained by the suspect taxpayer.

This special technique is not complex or difficult, and you can develop the skill and the technique with comparative ease in most cases you investigate. You can apply the net worth–expenditures principle when appropriate to

(1) Gather intelligence (related to financial transactions)

(2) Enhance the successful interview or interrogation of the suspect or offender

(3) Corroborate other evidence of a white collar crime for presenting facts to

- a prosecutor
- a grand jury
- a trial jury
- a court in civil litigation cases

(4) Determine what other white collar crimes, if any, the suspect may also use in stealing from your company

(5) Determine havens where a suspect may hide assets

(6) Identify or locate assets for restitution.

You can present your computation in two formats. One of the formats is commonly called a net worth–expenditure schedule, while the other format stems from a more readily recognized technique and is called the source and application of funds format. Either format will produce essentially the same result. You should normally use the net worth format when a suspect's spending habits appear to include the acquisition and disposal of real estate, jewelry, furs, bank accounts, life insurance policies having a cash value, and periodic reductions of mortgage loans. You can use the source and application of funds schedule when your suspect's expenditures have been of a more transient nature, such as high personal living expenses.

■ THE NET WORTH–EXPENDITURES TECHNIQUE

The net worth–expenditures investigative technique supplies an indirect method of proving income from an illegal or unknown source and, coupled with supporting documents of loss attributed to the suspect's embezzlement of company money or goods, can supply conclusive evidence in your white collar crime investigation. To arrive at this unique approach, you must show that the suspect had the opportunity to embezzle the money, and then you can show the where the same amount went, thus establishing the crime, motive, and intent. This technique stems from the difference between a suspect's personal and business assets and liabilities at a particular time. When you compare a suspect's net worth at the beginning and end of a calendar year, for example, the increase or decrease becomes apparent. If, for example, an employee embezzled money through fraudulent expense and travel claims and you can develop the amount of money stolen through this fraud, the net worth–expenditure technique should enable you to trace that amount (often, surprisingly, almost dollar for dollar).

You begin this computation by collecting information about the known and legitimate income of the suspect. For example, you can determine the suspect's take-home salary from the company plus any other sources of income, such as a spouse who works, a side business, and so on. This effort will probably call for you to use some creative investigative skills.

You have some restrictions on what you can legally investigate, even when you know that the employee embezzled company funds, or other items of proven value. For example, you need clear documentation of the theft from company records. Next, you need to link any other person such as a spouse to the scheme before you can investigate that person and their assets. Ensure that any investigation of the perpetrator remain strictly focused on the specific crime he or she is suspected of committing. I recommend the following investigative technique as your first step. Develop as much of the suspect's total assets and liabilities, such as cars, homes, land, etc., and then determine the suspect's income during the time he or she acquired the assets. The difference will usually be about the same as the company's loss resulting from the suspect's scheme.

Exhibit 17-1 shows you a formula to use in this phase of your investigation that leads to determining the net worth–expenditures of your suspect.

Exhibit 17-1
Formula for Computing Funds from Unknown or Illegal Sources

The Net Worth–Expenditures Investigative Technique

	Assets
	Assets
Less:	Liabilities
Equals:	Net Worth
Less:	Prior Year's Net Worth
Equals:	Net Worth Increase (Decrease)
Plus:	Living Expenses
Equals:	Income (or Expenditures)
Less:	Funds from Known Sources
Equals:	Funds from Unknown/Illegal Sources
Compare:	Funds Embezzled from Corporation

Sources to Determine Assets and Liabilities

Although there's a common belief that to find a suspect's assets and liabilities you need to probe into the suspect's credit background, that is largely a myth. Although consumer credit reports do reveal some information regarding liabilities, they also have the protection of the federal government, which restricts access to several legitimate needs. Investigating a suspect in a crime does not fall within that legal access. These reports also do not serve your investigative purpose because often they have flaws and they rarely go beyond basic information, which would serve little or no purpose in your case.

However, public records (those anyone can legally access) *do* serve your purpose, and I will list many of them in this section. Depending on the state, you can also obtain others that might be restricted in other states. Those listed here will serve your needs despite your location.

The sources of information shown here can aid your investigation of company employees, companies that victimize your company, vendors, companies that your company might consider doing business with, and so on. They can help you develop validity, identify owners, determine financial stability, and determine a financial motive as well as the amount of assets stolen.

Real Estate Records. Two legal sources of real estate ownership legally accessed as public records include those in the county courthouse and those provided by legitimate companies that have computerized systems that search databases nationwide. The first example costs you nothing except the time to browse through the huge recording books and files found in courthouses, usually in the Registry of Deeds section. These records date back to the founding of the county and show all real estate transactions that have occurred. You may discreetly determine if your suspect has made recent purchases of real estate. Such purchases are often made as a way of concealing a suspect's new source of income—theft of your company's money or assets.

Judgment and Lien Records. These records are also found in the county court house. Judgments (which are an effort to collect delinquent debts by presenting proof of the debt to a court, which issues a court order to the debtor ordering him or her to settle the debt) become public record in the Clerk of Court office and are available to any person. You can get copies of the court transcript and the judgment decree, which might be necessary to supply your investigation with clear motive (i.e., a desperate need for money). When your suspect pays the judgment amount to the creditor, as well as court costs and fees, but has no financial capability to do so, the suspect may have stolen the money from your company. You might find that the two amounts are the same. Legitimate companies can also conduct searches for judgment and lien records statewide or across the country. For example, if a suspect is the subject of a lawsuit in a county that is not where he or she lives or near the company location, the court house in your area would not have the records. You will find them only in the court house where the action was taken.

Liens on personal property or property involving a suspect's business are also kept on public record in the court house. A lien can include the purchase of a new car when a person still owes money for it or has not paid a creditor. The creditor files notification at the court house, an act that ensures the creditor's right to notify others that the person cannot sell the property until after settling the debt for it. When you find that a lien was filed and suddenly paid, the amount might correspond with the amount stolen from your company. You can also look for filing of tax liens by federal, state, or local tax agencies (including personal property tax not paid and recording the attachment of the suspect's property until payment of the debt). Even after the person pays the amount due plus any costs or fees, the record stays on file for public viewing.

Within this category, also check for UCC (Uniform Commercial Code) filings that show a lien on items purchased (normally for business but sometimes including personal property). The UCC filing stays on record permanently even after paid in full but will show that the person paid the balance due. These filings go back for years and, like the other items discussed in this section, may supply you with motive and amounts corresponding to the amounts stolen.

Judgment and lien records might supply you with evidence of money concealed or property stolen from your company, but also might tip you to other addresses, associates, and sideline businesses of an employee. For example, you might find an employee embezzling property through diversion or other means. The type of property stolen could establish or support a business, but you have no indication about the business's location or your suspect's involvement. You might find that a UCC filing occurred when the business bought equipment for which it owes money. The record would also show if the filing included others, such as a partner or corporation. It would supply you with the address of the business, and further investigation would continue to tie the suspect with it. With that information, you can continue to develop motive and often collate amounts embezzled or otherwise stolen to the amounts poured into the business venture.

State Corporate, Partnership, or Sole Proprietor Filings. Another valuable public record resource is the necessary filing to create a corporation, partnership, or sole proprietor business. Your investigation of a suspected embezzler or another company should include checking information available from this source. Even bogus companies will establish a corporation to appear legitimate or to obtain necessary licenses, bank accounts, and other items while hiding the true identity of the owners. A corporation also can reduce or eliminate personal liability, and you need the skill of identifying the true owners, tracing their associations, and tying all the investigative information together.

Each state has a corporation or partnership filing and records office. Sometimes it will fall within the Secretary of State's office, but other states place it under the State Department of Commerce or other agency. Copies of these filings are available to any person on request for a small fee. Some states have an alphabetical listing of names involving the persons who created the corporation or partnership and their association with the business. Many states do not have that type of listing, however, and you will need to learn the company name first.

A sole proprietor does not have to establish this filing; however, he or she can often be identified through other sources, such as state sales tax agencies. Although tax information is usually confidential and protected by law, most states will give you a verification that a business or person does have a tax number and supply you with the business name and address. Other sources can include a filing for a license to do business (normally at a local level). If you find such a business operation, you can assess the type of business and may recognize equipment or other items that the person stole from your company.

This technique also serves your investigative efforts when validating another business your company does business with or plans to do business with (to determine its legitimacy).

Informants and Other Sources of Personal Information. People rarely keep their personal lives secret. That applies to embezzlers or others who victimize your company through a white collar crime scheme. They don't usually brag to others about what they are doing or have done; however, they reveal it in other ways. For example, few white collar crime perpetrators can commit their crime and continue with a frugal lifestyle. Most will succumb to the added income and buy new cars, a new home, jewelry and wardrobe. Some go on costly vacations or start up a side business. Whatever they do will rarely coincide with their income from the corporation. Because WCC perpetrators usually show clear signals of wealth, others in the company, acting out of curiosity, jealousy, and envy will normally candidly ask the person how he or she can afford such a lavish lifestyle. The person will normally reply with an preconceived answer that rarely satisfies the other employees. Some of the employees will suspect but not want to get involved in exposing the WCC criminal. However, others will come forward as informants, while still others are eager to tell what they believe or know, but wait to be asked. You can use these human frailties to your investigative advantage because people within the corporate (or government) workplace enjoy gossip about fellow workers. Use caution in accepting gossip as truth, but often you will find the leads necessary to continue your investigation.

When you have a suspect of embezzlement or some other crime, or when another company victimizes yours or there is a takeover involving organized crime, you can find people within a company who will tell you a great deal about the suspect. For example, last year the person noticeably struggled to "make it" and talked about their hardship to fellow workers. Employees tend to share their problems, and the corporate grapevine spreads people's troubles. Embezzlers find a way to increase their income by stealing company money or property and have to create a plausible reason to satisfy observers. Their excuse for increased wealth can be an inheritance, winning a lottery, a spouse getting a high-paying job, or a variety of other justifications. This information will help you narrow your field of suspects.

Informants and other forms of personal information might also become valuable when you are investigating another company that appears to victimize yours or when organized crime groups move in on a company your company holds an interest in. The ordinary employees in these companies will have a good idea of what is happening, they will know who in their company collaborates with the organized crime group, or they will know of company financial trouble or that their company exists only to rip off other companies. The trick is to develop sources inside that will talk about the underhanded activities, even if only in a form of gossip.

Informants, however, normally are motivated by some personal gain (e.g., revenge for not getting a promotion or salary increase they believed they were entitled to, or because a "favorite" employee received something they perceive should have been theirs). In such cases, informants might tell all they know just to get back at the company or another employee. Such informants might also want to receive money, the promise of a better job, and any number of other advantages for their information. They might also want assurances that although they took part in the scheme they will be granted immunity. Whenever you develop informants, ensure that you understand their motives. Unless it's clear that they have no white collar crime guilt themselves, or their involvement is trivial, discuss the matter with the corporate legal counsel, a prosecutor, or an attorney contracted by your company. You need to ensure that your procedures and assurances have a legal and corporate policy basis to proceed with your investigation and exclude the informant from any punitive action.

Personnel Records. Viewing of employee personnel records is normally restricted, and you should ensure that your corporate and legal policy enables you, in specific cases, to view these records without showing an exact need. For example, if you have a suspect of a white collar crime developed through an investigative audit or other information, his or her personnel records may be the best starting point for a criminal investigation. However, since at the onset of a criminal investigation you always need to ensure that your thoughts stay neutral and the person remains innocent until proven guilty, even the personnel director and other employees in the department should not know who your investigation concerns. Office gossip can become a detriment both to the suspected employee, the company, your corporate white collar crime management unit, and the attitude and morale of other employees.

It's best to work in an oblique way and view a suspect's personnel files through an executive or the CEO. For example, when you need the records, ask management to request them coupled with several other records as part of a review of potential promotions. This creates a positive instead of a negative perception. You can discreetly obtain the suspect's records for viewing from the requesting executive, copy them, and use them to develop your case without the suspect or others in the company knowing that an investigation has begun.

The information you're seeking in the file includes the size of the suspect's family, the suspect's address, education, and other aspects that might supply you with data that you can use effectively to develop other information. For example, the suspect's personnel file should supply you with his or her previous and current address; however, you learn from your investigation that the current address involved a leased house or a house of less value than the new one you know the employee recently bought. Or, you might use the current address and other addresses to check in the court house public records of the amount paid and the amount mortgaged. After driving by the residence, you might find that the home surpasses the income level of the suspect. Do not jump to conclusions—the money might come from another legitimate source. However, this information might supply a good lead that will help you move forward with your investigation. On the other hand, if a person lives in a poor section of a city, that does not absolve him or her from stealing. A smart white collar criminal might anticipate an investigation and conceal his or her proceeds for use much later, after resigning and moving to a distance location.

Study the personnel records carefully, and if they contain a preemployment background investigation you might find old consumer credit reports that you could use to compare income then and now, as well as assets then and now. If a suspect's assets cannot meet the net worth–expenditure test, you might have developed additional leads.

■ THE SOURCE AND APPLICATION OF FUNDS TECHNIQUE

Development of information during your investigation should not be limited to the aforementioned sources, because they supply you with public information sources that will lead to others. The source and application of funds technique depends on development of the information discussed in the preceding section. This method supplies you with an indirect means of determining unknown sources of funds.

This method stems from a theory that if expenditures for a given period exceed the suspect's known sources of income for that period, you might logically infer that the excess expenditures represent a scheme perpetrated against your company that has netted approximately the same amount of income for which you are investigating the suspect. You might also show that the influxes of income at a specific time collate exactly with the embezzlement shortages or that increased income was from unexplained sources that might have been overlooked. In other words, you might have good reason to suspect the person in one embezzlement scheme, but did not suspect him or her for other crimes that become apparent during your investigation. The general formula for computing funds from unknown or illegal sources using the source and application of funds technique is shown in Exhibit 17-2.

Exhibit 17-2
Source and Application of Funds Formula

Application of Funds (Expenditures)

Less: Known sources of income (funds)
Equals: Income from unknown or illegal sources

The techniques noted for the net worth method are also applicable to the source and application of funds method. For example, when the suspect has several assets and liabilities that stay the same throughout the period in which you have investigated, the expenditures method might be preferred over the net worth method because of a simple computation. Assets and liabilities that do not increase during the period under investigation can be omitted from the expenditures statement (e.g., a house mortgage).

The source and application of funds method will be more helpful when your suspect's income goes for noticeably lavish living and there is little, if any, net worth. Also, an expenditures statement can verify the accuracy of another method of proving income and testing the accuracy of known or reported income. Use it to compute *cash available* for the base year of a net worth computation when a cash-on-hand starting point appears in a prior year. This can be done when you investigate a business in which your company has an interest and the financial records are available to you or perhaps the working papers or report from an internal or independent audit function are available. Personal records of a suspect might also become available when the case progresses to a point at which a prosecutor or other legal action authorizes a search and seizure of records or a subpoena for legally obtaining such records.

In the source and application of funds method, the following items must be considered in making computations. Keep in mind that although these items might not apply to your investigation, they might become available later through a variety of sources (including the suspect's voluntary release of the information).

Items to Consider in Making Computations

1. Application (Expenditures)
   - Increase in cash available or bank accounts
   - Increase in other assets (both personal and business)
   - Decrease in liability balances
   - Personal living expenses
2. Known Sources of Income
   - Decrease in cash available or bank accounts
   - Sale or exchange of assets (such as real estate)
   - Salaries or business profits
   - Tax refunds, interest, dividends, or insurance proceeds
   - Loans, gifts, or inheritances received
   - Unemployment, worker's compensation, or public assistance
   - Other known sources such as spouse's employment

Any excess of the application of funds over known sources of income indicates funds from unknown or illegal sources.

■ MASTERING THE ART OF INTERVIEWS AND INTERROGATION

Many of your investigative efforts depend on your skill at interviewing people and, when necessary and applicable, interrogating suspects or collaborating persons involved in a white collar crime scheme. Few skills are as important to the effectiveness of a white collar crime investigator.

The distinction between interviewing and interrogating stems from differences in your prime objectives and the types of persons involved in the meeting. The term *interviewing* involves the systematic questioning of a person who has or may have knowledge of events, persons involved, or circumstances surrounding the case you're investigating (including obtaining documentary or physical evidence). The term *interrogation*, however, involves questioning of suspects or often uncooperative witnesses to obtain evidence or proof of important omissions, or to give the suspect in your investigation an opportunity to volunteer facts that might put the transactions you're investigating in a different light.

The line between interviewing and interrogation is often fluid. For example, an uncooperative witness you interrogate might decide to cooperate, or one of the suspects of your investigation may turn and agree to provide you with evidence against others. In such a situation, the interrogation will necessarily take on the attributes of the interviewing process and call for many interviewing techniques, discussed later. You must always be alert for sensitive legal issues regarding whether the apparently cooperating suspect or formerly recalcitrant witness has an underlying motive for cooperating or is *truly* cooperating. When interrogation edges into interviewing, you must carefully use or change your methods to satisfy the interviewee's special motivations and objectives.

The opposite may happen. During your questioning of a witness thought to have no involvement in the white collar crime you're investigating or to be an incidental party to a transaction, you may sense that the person may also become culpable. When that happens, you will want to modify your tactics or techniques in the opposite direction, or to stop the interview entirely, either because you perceive the proffered cooperation to be untrustworthy, or because you don't want to disclose more about the case in your line of questioning, or because serious legal issues may arise regarding the person's legal rights. This point about rights has several misconceptions among non-public investigators. Although most people believe that a person's rights belong in the purview of law enforcement and apply only after an arrest (based on the landmark U.S. Supreme Court's *Miranda* decision in *Miranda v.*

Arizona, 34B U.S. 436, 1966), you need to consider several factors including a jury's perception of your attitude toward and dealings with a witness or suspect.

Give Noncustodial Warnings to Suspects

The reason you supply a suspect with a noncustodial warning based on the Fifth Amendment of the U.S. Constitution stems from common sense. Although your position of a corporate white collar crime investigator does not supply you with authority to arrest a person, and the *Miranda* decision does not apply to you, it's your responsibility within ethical and moral standards to ensure that the person and the courts or juries understand that you have exercised inherent fairness during your criminal investigations. Even in a civil suit (against an embezzler or other person when seeking recovery of losses, for example) your corporate attorney will have a stronger case if you acted fairly. Otherwise, a defendant can claim that you used misrepresentation, coercion, or other tactics and the jury might believe that the corporation picked on a poor little employee and decide not to award damages or recovery of losses.

Exhibit 17-3 shows a standard noncustodial warning you should give to any suspect before an interview or interrogation. This form documents your exercise of fairness.

Exhibit 17-3
Model Noncustodial Warning to Suspects

I am an investigator for the XYZ Corporation, Any City, Any State. I am investigating a possible criminal offense against the Company. The offense is (state the offense, e.g., embezzlement of money). I would like to ask you some questions about this investigation, and because of circumstances I need to consider you as a suspect.

I must inform you, however, that under the Fifth Amendment of the U.S. Constitution you cannot be compelled to answer any of my questions or submit any information that you feel might incriminate you in any way.

Also, anything you say and any documents you surrender involving the matter I have explained or any related matter that involves an offense can be used against you in a criminal, civil, or administrative proceeding.

You may, if you wish, obtain the assistance of an attorney before responding to any of my questions. You do not have to answer my questions and you are free to leave or discontinue this interview whenever you want.

Do you understand these rights as I have read them to you?

Record answer: _____

Do you wish to contact your attorney now?

Record answer: _____

Do you wish to answer my questions voluntarily now?

Record answer: _____

Do you read, write, and understand the English language?

Record answer: _____

                                        _____
                                        Corporate Investigator

Date: _____Time: _____ Location: _____

I have read the above statement and understand my rights as explained to me. Knowing these rights, I voluntarily and willingly waive my right to call my attorney and agree to answer questions. I also affirm that no coercion, threats, or promises were made to me by the investigator.

                                        _____
                                        Signature of Person Being Questioned

Date: _____Time:_____

File this form with your case report and retain a copy for your files.

■ TECHNIQUES OF INTERVIEWING

At the onset of a criminal investigation, you will normally have limited information about the white collar crime. In some instances, the information may become complete during an investigative audit or conventional audit, which supplies the basis for continued investigation.

Most likely, you will face one of the following situations:

(1) A white collar crime was committed but the proof of its commission must be established to a degree sufficient for prosecution, even when that isn't the intent of your company. (As discussed earlier in this book, always supply company management with all possible options.)

(2) An employee, another person outside the company, a combination of both, another company, or a fraudulent enterprise has victimized your company causing losses (e.g., finances, reputation, or in other losses).

(3) There may be some physical evidence of the crime, such as documents or computer data.

(4) There may be some intelligence regarding a white collar crime, and there may be a suspect.

In white collar crime, the interview is one of the major investigative tools to close the gap between these often fragmentary items of information and to support a prosecution or other legal action. From the interview, you generally obtain the following advantages:

- Information that establishes the essential elements of the crime
- Most of your leads for developing the case and gathering other evidence
- The cooperation of victims and witnesses in recounting their experiences.

Although there's no specific universal technique in the approach to and conduct of an interview (a process strongly dependent on the personalities of an instigator and interviewees), you should follow a system of guidelines that will ensure maximum probability of achieving your objectives.

Plan Your Interview

Proper interview planning enhances the probability of your success and effectiveness throughout a criminal investigation. You should ascertain as many facts as reasonably available before conducting any interview (including careful review of relevant documents). Rarely will you follow a format that is routine and committed to memory. I recommend preparing your questions in advance (this is particularly important when your investigation involves new schemes that might be unfamiliar to you). Without proper planning, you might find yourself over your head or not understanding the interviewee's responses. Not planning can also cause you to miss an opportunity to learn information that will help in later investigative efforts. I recommend the following planning process as a minimum:

Time and Place

You gain real advantage when you conduct the interview at your own office or other setting of your choosing. It's always best to remove witnesses from their own surroundings, where they will feel either more secure or embarrassed by your presence. A witness in a setting with other employees in the area might believe that others will think of him or her as a snitch. However, you might want to conduct the interview in two phases when the need arises, first calling on the person in his or her setting for a cursory discussion and later having a more detailed interview in a setting of your choice away from the interviewee's workplace. The first meeting at the workplace or home might prove beneficial or detrimental for the following reasons:

(1) The interviewee might have handily accessible papers, appointment books, and other documents available that are relevant to the interview. The interviewee may also immediately call on a family member or other employees for more information and corroborative evidence.

(2) It might be more convenient for the interviewee initially and make it more likely that he or she will agree to the meeting for the detailed interview later in your choice of settings.

(3) You may catch an interviewee off guard, before he or she can have second thoughts about talking to you. If you can get the person's candid and helpful answers in the first meeting, later you will have a base from which to expand the interview.

(4) You will probably be at a disadvantage when conducting an interview out of the setting of your choice because you will have trouble freeing the person from workplace distractions such as other employees and telephones.

When you conduct an interview aside from the aforementioned two-phase process, it is best to make a specific appointment for the optimum convenience of your interviewee and yourself. For example, try to avoid a tight schedule arrangement in which either you or your interviewee has only a specified amount of time. This creates a hurried session that focuses more on the time than on gathering needed information. Unless you have some special reason not to do so, the following tips will help you experience greater success:

(1) Arrange your interview to supply enough time for a full interview. It's always better to have extra time than to stop an interview early or be late to meetings following an interview that ran longer than you expected.

(2) When you attempt an interview without prior appointment, you risk not finding the person prepared (assuming that you need certain documents and want to ask the person to bring them to the interview).

(3) You should consider the special characteristics of your interviewee. For example, when dealing with a witness whose native language is not English (and you do not speak the interviewee's language), ensure that the

person understands the reasons for the interview generally and, when necessary, have an interpreter to clarify questions and responses.

(4) Schedule your detailed interview within twenty-four hours, whenever possible, after the first contact with an interviewee to prevent a decline in cooperativeness and avoid misunderstandings that could trigger confusion and loss of confidence by the interviewee.

Control Your Interview Setting

Whenever possible, control the setting and interview environment. Ensure that the setting provides a minimum of roadblocks for talking and listening. Distractions such as telephones, other voices, other conversations, and other persons in the area can have a disastrous affect on the interview. Interruptions unrelated to the problem at hand will often convey to the interviewee that you don't really have an interest in what he or she has to say. Try to arrange for the interview to be held in a private room.

In addition, consider other possibilities for creating an environment that will help you obtain useful information, put the interviewee at ease, and increase his or her trust in you. For example, you should first ask witnesses to tell their story in their own way even if it rambles. You should only interrupt for clarifications and refrain from pointed questions until interviewees unburden themselves and drop their guard. Later, you can come back to narrow the interview and focus the interviewee on the information connected to the situation.

Know What Information You Need

You must know the type of information needed from witnesses before you begin scheduling interviews, and try to have them talk with you in an escalating process. You need to build on the information from interviews in the same way that you build your case whenever possible. Exhibit 17-4 provides guidelines to ensure that you obtain the necessary information about a white collar crime scheme from interviewees. It lists the types of information from company representatives, such as the victim, potential witnesses, or third parties who may have peripheral information or expertise relating to your case. You can modify these guidelines to fit your specific situations or needs.

Exhibit 17-4
Guidelines for Collecting Information in Interviews

About the Interview
- ☐ Location, date, and time
- ☐ Choose your location carefully to obtain maximum advantage.

About the Suspects You are Investigating
- ☐ Names of persons involved
- ☐ Addresses of persons involved
- ☐ Telephone numbers of persons involved
- ☐ Names of companies involved
- ☐ Addresses of companies involved
- ☐ Telephone numbers of companies involved
- ☐ Legal status of companies (corporations, partnerships, etc.)
- ☐ Physical descriptions of persons involved
- ☐ Title, salary, tenure, duties, and responsibilities of suspects

About Contact Between Suspects and Witnesses
- ☐ How was first contact made?
  - —Advertisement in newspaper, trade magazines, radio, television (Get name of publication or station, including times and dates.)
  - —Sales letters or brochures (Get copies of letters, brochures, envelopes, and other material involved.)
  - —Personal contact (Telephone or in person? Get dates, times, names, locations, and content of conversation.)
  - —Reference through third party (attorney, friend, other employee, etc.)
- ☐ Were there any previous relationships between the suspect and victim company or representative of your company?
- ☐ How did the suspect or his or her representatives determine to target your company? (i.e., employee, vendor, another company, etc.; explain details)

About the Situation and Transactions (When Applicable)
- ☐ Date, location, and time of event
- ☐ Names, addresses, titles, etc. of persons present (other witnesses)

☐ Full details of all representations

—Method of representation

—What was said?

—What was shown? (letters, brochures, lists, prospectuses, contracts, etc.)

☐ Which person made each representation?

☐ Level of reliance on representation

—Did witness (victim) have reservations?

—Did witness (victim) express the reservation?

—Did witness (victim) ask any questions?

—What were the answers? Who made them?

—How were the witness's (victim's) reservations overcome? By whom?

—Was anything done to discourage witness (victim) from consulting with others?

☐ Representations that witness (victim) believes were false

☐ Representations that witness (victim) believes were omitted but should have been told

☐ Was witness (victim) put under any time or other severe pressure to enter into the transaction? How?

☐ Full details of transaction

—Amount of dollars

—Method of payment (check, cash, agreements, or contracts)

—Date and circumstance of payment (in person, by mail, to whom, etc.)

About the Representative of the Victimized Company

☐ Name, address, telephone numbers

☐ Representative's background (may help in finding out how defrauder got their name and position in the company)

☐ How and when representative discovered representations by the perpetrator were false

☐ Has the representative complained to defrauder?

—What did representative do or say?

—Did the company representative personally complain or refer to others in the company?

☐ Financial losses suffered by the company

☐ Representative's willingness to assist in investigation and testify in court

☐ Will the representative sign statement or affidavit?

About Physical Evidence

☐ Collect all physical evidence (brochures, letters, contracts, envelopes, etc.)

☐ Give witness a receipt for items obtained from him or her

☐ Ensure that witness (interviewee) initials and dates each page of item

---

Techniques for Investigator's Conduct During the Interview

A corporate white collar crime investigator must always be efficient, courteous, polite, and careful about the use of language when dealing with witnesses, suspects, or any other person during the criminal investigation. A negative impression can lead to problems in development and later disposition of the case. I suggest the following tips:

- Never talk down to the person you interview.
- Never assume the person has less intelligence than you.
- Any hint of disrespect or condescension can quickly turn a cooperative person into an uncooperative person.
- Never use language that disparages the intelligence or competence of the interviewee.
- Be sensitive to the personal interest of the interviewee.
- Be businesslike and conduct the interview in a professional manner.
- Be friendly, but not familiar. Certain pleasantries are necessary, but your interview must not become a social occasion.
- Do not be authoritarian.
- Do not be judgmental.
- Do not dominate the interview.
- Make it clear that anyone, no matter how smart or well trained, can become a victim of a white collar offender.
- Be sympathetic and respectful.
- Never suggest that the interviewee created the loss due to his or her incompetence.

- Avoid using jargon during the interview.
- Compliment the interviewee for cooperating in your investigation.
- End every cooperative interview on an appreciative note.

The Importance of Taking Notes

The method you use to take notes during an interview is a matter of personal style. However, regardless of style, you *must* take notes. Your notes must reflect accurately the data obtained during the interview.

If you use a tape recorder during the interview, continue to take notes. Recording an interview does not create a substitute for note taking. A word of caution on the use of a tape recorder during interviews: First, always ensure that the interviewee consents to the use of a recorder. If you surreptitiously record your interview and later the interviewee learns of it, you could lose a valuable witness. Always assure that the first thing on the interview tape is your request for permission from the interviewee to tape the interview, and that the person's oral consent is clear and loud enough to record. A second caution stems from an uneasiness for interviewees about the microphone and recording of what they say. Most people don't like to have what they say recorded, and using a recorder will probably net you far less information than the person would otherwise have provided. I have found tape recorders to be a major detriment to drawing out valuable information from an interviewee, and I have never used them for that reason. The interviewee expects you to take notes because that shows you have a sincere interest in what he or she says. A recorder, however, gives the interview type of "stage fright." Interviewees will believe you have some type of trick in mind to get them in trouble with a recording of what they said. The outcome is often cursory answers and little information.

When you conduct interviews that may contain complex, technical, or crucial information, consider (with the interviewee's concurrence) having another investigator present to take notes.

Remember that your interview notes may eventually lead to a memorandum or signed affidavit that could become evidence in a trial, and the defendant may have the right to inspect the notes or memoranda.

Converting Your Notes to a Written Statement

Whenever you conduct an interview, to the extent possible, develop a focused written statement of the information and have the interviewee read it and sign it. Having a written statement at the time of the interview protects you from embarrassing conflicts later. Witnesses tend to become fickle when they have to repeat what they have told you in a trial or other administrative proceeding. If witnesses refuse to sign a written statement, you should not rely on what they told you because in a more formal setting they will probably claim that you misrepresented what they said and leave your integrity in doubt. Although their written statement cannot in itself become evidence in a trial without their personal appearance and testimony, you can have a reliable certainty that once signing a written statement they won't change their story. If they do change their story for whatever reason, the written statement signed at the time of the interview shows calls their integrity into question—not yours.

Other Important Considerations during Your Interview

There are a variety of other aspects to consider when you conduct an interview. The success of your investigative effort may depend on the following suggestions.

(1) You must consider the emotional state of the person you're interviewing. This is especially important when the person feels responsible for supplying an opportunity for losses to the company or feels he or she has snitched on a fellow employee. The person may fear for his or her personal safety or have apprehensions about becoming involved.

(2) People you interview might have unsupported opinions or perceptions regarding the circumstances connected with the white collar crime. You should not disparage these views, but try to move them to a logical conclusion. Remember that unsupported opinions often prove justified; people's feelings often have some logical basis although they may not be able to articulate that basis.

(3) An interviewee might feel that if you had stayed out of it, everything would have been okay. Interviewees often show a certain sympathy to the suspect. They believe the suspect has done something wrong, but they believe you have blown it out of proportion.

(4) Concentrate on what the interview is saying—and not saying. Think about one topic at a time, and not about your next question. Follow each topic to its logical conclusion. When interviewees wander from the question do not stop them; their response may lead to other valuable topics. When the time is right, bring the interviewee back to the original topic with a specific question.

(5) Remember that when you interview a person you necessarily give some information about what you know and what you suspect. If you don't

want a piece of information to surface, be cautious and think about how you use it. Such information may inadvertently get back to the suspect in your investigation.

(6) Try to determine whether the interviewee is telling you the truth. When you suspect untruthfulness, you must judge whether to confront the interviewee with that perception. When you decide to do so, you must ensure that you have prepared the facts sufficiently to refute the untruthfulness. It is better to stop an interview than to lose control of it by a confrontation without enough evidence. Remember, an untruthful interview can become useful later, after you develop more evidence. People confronted with proof of their untruthfulness might realize that it's in their best interest to cooperate with you.

(7) When you suspect the interviewee is untruthful, or may become culpable, consider the following options:

- Stop the interview immediately and make a written record of the reason.
- Allow the interviewee to talk, on the theory that by confronting interviewees with their own falsities, it may push them into giving valuable information or evidence.

(8) Observe the demeanor of persons you're interviewing. You should put the interviewee at ease from the first and maintain this ease throughout the interview.

(9) Your discussions should continually and systematically go into depth more. When it appears that the pressures on the interviewee have become intense and will lead to lack of continued cooperation, you should remove the pressures immediately. You can do so by bringing the interview temporarily around to other subjects, or sincerely confirming the importance of the information by explaining your role and the goals of your investigation before getting back to the subject of the interview.

Important Obstacles to Successful Interviewing

You may face problems and obstacles that relate to certain characteristics of the interviewee or the situations they find themselves confronting. The following are some of these problematic situations.

Personal Embarrassment of the Person: The interviewee, especially when perceiving that he or she has some responsibility in the success of a white collar crime perpetrated against your company, might have a deep sense of guilt and embarrassment.

Institutional Embarrassment: When the interview involves management or a company in which your company has an interest, the interviewee might prefer to rationalize or conceal the crime instead of risk appearing incompetent.

Previous Denials and Inconsistent Stories: The interviewee might have earlier denied knowledge of a white collar crime and made a statement inconsistent with information or evidence you have developed during your investigation. The person might try to stick with his or her original story or come to believe it.

Nothing to Gain: Most persons do not welcome appearing in court despite the circumstances. Interviewees might believe they can avoid that eventuality or feel they cannot gain anything personally by cooperating. They might also harbor fears of incriminating themselves because of some unrelated situation or because they didn't come forward to report a situation they knew about for a long time.

Four Techniques for Overcoming Interviewee Obstacles

You should consider my following suggestions as potential tools and guidelines for overcoming the obstacles you might face during interviews. You must determine the specific approach that fits the demands and needs of each case you investigate.

(1) With regard to situations involving previous denials and inconsistent stories, you need to develop the following approaches:

- Persist in following up every question or topic under discussion to a logical conclusion.
- Follow the same topic from a variety of perspectives, any of which might generate responsiveness (e.g., a discussion from a technical perspective of how the fraud under consideration is generally perpetrated might trigger responses that would otherwise stay dormant if you just repeated the who, what, when, where, how, and why questions).
- Be ready to use all information obtained earlier, whether from file documents or memory, to refute denials and inconsistencies and impart variable degrees of damaging information about the scheme and the suspects. This cultivates cooperation from the interviewee.

(2) Explain to the interviewee what steps may be taken to help the person remain free from embarrassment, being scorned by other employees

or being in fear of reprisal. When applicable, you should also demonstrate to the interviewee that credit will come to those who help with your investigation. However, ensure that the company agrees and supports whatever promises, assurances and consulations you extend to the interviewee.

(3) Always try to encourage interviewees to cooperate because it is their duty and responsibility to their company and employer, or demonstrate a public duty to cooperate in a white collar crime investigation.

(4) When you attempt to gain cooperation, it's always prudent early in your interview to stay sympathetic to the interviewee's fears, situation, and attitudes. In addition, express your thanks and make the interviewee feel that he or she is an important part of the team.

■ TECHNIQUES FOR INTERROGATING SUSPECTS

Your obvious purpose when talking to an offender or suspect in a white collar crime is to persuade him or her to supply you with information (evidence) about the problem you're investigating, or to obtain admissions that will become persuasive in a criminal prosecution, civil litigation, or administrative proceedings. Your interview with a suspect may arise from either a request of a suspect, the suspect's attorney, or from your desire to get the other side of the story or an admission of guilt.

In the first situation, the suspect, his or her attorney, or both request or even clamor for an interview because word of an actual or possible investigation has reached them and (they claim) it is important to the suspect's interest that the matter is settled (e.g., to safeguard their corporate position, their reputation, or their business interests). You need to remain neutral in your investigation and remember that the suspect is innocent until proven guilty in a legitimate proceeding. In such a situation your sole objective is to get suspects to talk extensively about their role or other apparent defrauding activities. Remember that the suspect and his or her attorney may try to get information about the status of your investigation. You must be extremely cautious about inadvertently supplying information to the suspect that could create problems in the investigation or eventual actions. You should assume that since the interview happened at the suspect's request, the suspect also has the same objective (i.e., trying to learn the status of the situation and get information on what the other knows).

In the second situation, in a meeting with a suspect that you initiated, the objectives may include any of the following points, depending on your case:

(1) To complete any missing pieces of your investigation.

(2) To elicit incriminating statements from the suspect. While these incriminating statements will rarely take the form of admissions of guilt, the suspect may make false or inconsistent statements, especially if your investigation takes him or her by surprise and the facts confronting the person dramatically and conclusively point to guilt.

(3) To foresee the suspect's possible defenses. During the suspect's responses to questions regarding the nature, characteristics, and specific methods used in the white collar crime venture under investigation, you may learn about contrived defenses that will help you develop tactics and further investigative steps.

(4) To confront the suspect with the evidence and provide an opportunity for exculpatory explanations or admissions.

The possibility of achieving the aforementioned purposes or objectives in an interrogation is subject to debate. Many experienced investigators (including myself) express serious doubts about the worth of interrogation—though all recognize its usefulness in specific situations. You must consider the unique aspects of each case before making a judgment regarding the value of interviewing or interrogating the suspect. You should consider the following:

- The type of white collar crime you're investigating (e.g., internal corporate frauds by employees, victimization of your company by another company, victimization of a company that your company owns or has an interest in, misrepresentations about products and services, and a variety of other situations discussed earlier in this book)

- The type of suspect (e.g., age, experience, history, etc.)

- The scheme itself (e.g., embezzlement, charity fraud, planned business bankruptcy, collusion with your company with white collar enterprises outside the company, etc.).

Each of these factors presents you with different criteria for making judgments regarding whether to interview or interrogate a suspect or offender, and when and how to do it.

When considering the arguments pro and con interrogation, you should know that you tread on dangerous legal grounds that may not only imperil your entire case but also damage your credibility with a prosecutor and the corporation or others important to the resolution of the situation. When you adopt this tactic against a suspect, there can be no doubt in the suspect's mind that he or she might have to face prosecution for the white collar crime.

You should also consider whether it is desirable to conduct such an interrogation if the suspect wishes to have his or her attorney present. Under no circumstances should you allow yourself to be placed in the position of seeming to deny a suspect the opportunity to consult with or be accompanied by counsel, but remember that as the risks of interrogation go up, the prospective benefits go down if the suspect does have a counsel accompanying him or her to the interview. In such cases, you will be wise to defer an interrogation until after the prosecutor or your corporate legal counsel gets into the case.

Interrogations: Positive Considerations

You might consider that confronting a suspect with overwhelming evidence already accumulated during your thorough investigation will induce the suspect to plead guilty. Often, in this situation, you will induce a confession of guilt. However, remember that often white collar crime offenders will have particularly astute and skilled attorneys representing them. This is no place for slipshod investigative or legal work that will regularly cause the interrogation to backfire. When you use interrogation will largely depend on corporate policy and legal counsel or a prosecutor who advises you to interrogate and make a full disclosure of the evidence against a suspect so the company and its attorneys can intelligently weigh the risks and benefits of a public trial and the attendant publicity.

The high plea ratio in white collar crimes is important to your corporate white collar crime management unit and corporation since the resources saved when a suspect pleads guilty enable you to investigate and prepare other cases.

While the use of confrontation as a means of inducing guilty pleas has often been effective, you should be able to reap similar benefits from confronting a suspect in an interrogating manner with overwhelming evidence of guilt for civil litigation preparation or administrative proceedings. Such evidence may provoke an admission of guilt or create the first step in a series of steps leading to a plea of guilty.

Finally, in some specific cases, an interrogating confrontation with a suspect that induces any type of substantial demoralization will benefit the prosecutor of the case. The suspect's demoralization will sometimes heighten the possibility that he or she will plead guilty to the white collar crime.

When weighing the advantages and benefits of interrogation as opposed to interviews, consider the following suggestions:

(1) A meeting with a suspect before completion of evidence gathering will rarely elicit an admission of fraudulent intent, but it may serve as a means for learning about the suspect's activities. Because such meetings often will happen at the suspect's request, the suspect may discuss the scheme or

business enterprise fully. By assuming an objective approach (i.e., a professional attempting to determine facts in a situation that has provoked certain complaints), you might get the suspect to talk, and talk extensively, about the white collar crime operation. However, when you're not familiar with the facts and modus operandi of the crime, you may be misled or supplied with blind investigative leads.

(2) One rule of thumb that serves well when deciding whether interrogation would be a wise tactic is to evaluate the experience of the suspect. Experienced suspects who have taken steps to develop a fraudulent scheme will normally also develop contingency plans and explanations if the scheme comes under investigation. Interrogating that type of suspect would possibly give the suspect more information than it would give you. Inexperienced suspects, however, may not have planned for interrogation or developed enough occupational experience to handle either an interview or interrogation. This will lessen the danger that the suspect will learn something from the interrogation, and lack of a contingency plan may prevent the suspect from exploiting what he or she learns in the session. The shock of discovery and resulting fear may lead the suspect to making incriminating admissions or surrendering incriminating documents.

(3) You need to remember that you have no power or authority to confer immunity or make any promises regarding penalties. Avoid any speech or other conduct that could be misunderstood in this regard. Be particularly on guard when the suspect's attorney is present at the interrogation. Immunity or perception of immunity can often develop inadvertently. Remember that only the prosecutor in a criminal case, or your corporation legal counsel, can decide and confer any forms of immunity for information or admission of guilt, and they must make that offer to the suspect personally.

Interrogations: Negative Considerations

A number of pitfalls face you when meeting with and questioning a white collar crime suspect or offender. These pitfalls generally emerge when the evidence of the suspect's guilt in the white collar scheme is inconclusive and particularly when the suspect has his or her attorney at your meeting. For example,

(1) The investigation and prosecution or other action might become stymied by disclosing that an investigation is under way and that action of some type detrimental to the suspect is planned.

(2) The suspect may learn something during the interview or interrogation that enables him or her to figure out how to obscure evidence or manipulate witness attitudes and willingness to cooperate.

(3) The suspect might flee the jurisdiction before any action can happen.

(4) You might become deceived by the suspect and consequently either waste investigative resources on a false lead or allow the suspect more time to put together a scheme to counter your investigative process.

(5) You might become intimidated by the suspect's position, image, and demeanor (especially when the person is an executive or professional). For example, when you're confronted by a well-educated and respected person accompanied by an attorney, you might develop inappropriate feelings of deference and respect for the image presented, resulting in a loss of your confidence and loss of control of the situation.

(6) The character of a suspect might become a factor that would make interrogation a waste of your time. The likelihood of most white collar criminals admitting guilt during an interview or interrogation or supplying useful information in your case is remote. Often, white collar criminals become proficient and convincing liars. Many of them thrive on the challenge of their ability to deceive people, and it is their stock in trade. You cannot think of yourself as immune from these skills. However, when you expect the suspect to lie, you might be able to use the lies as evidence against the suspect.

Setting and Conduct of Your Interrogation

Most of the principles and methodology of interviewing discussed earlier will apply to interrogation situations. Courtesy and consideration will also be in order and can pay off if a suspect decides to cooperate against his or her confederates. However, you must consider several other factors when interviewing or interrogating a suspect in a white collar crime investigation.

When Interrogation Stems from the Request of a Suspect: The suspect who asks you for a meeting might be motivated to clear up the situation, or may wish to influence you or learn how much you know about the scheme. Despite the suspect's motivation, his or her request for the meeting puts you in a favorable position to get the suspect to discuss the scheme and crime. You should adopt the objective attitude of a professional seeking to understand the suspect's motives in the fullest detail possible. You should avoid denunciatory questioning, even if the suspect makes untruthful statements. Your questioning will inhibit the type of free discussion desired and may lead to disclosure by you about what you know. Also, false statements made by a suspect during such an interview may prove to be the most significant evidence of criminal intent developed in your investigation.

When an Interview Stems from the Request of the Investigator: When you elect to begin an interview with a suspect or noncooperative witness, you must be aware that the person you're interrogating will probably lie, but more often will simply evade your questions with nonresponsive or misleading answers. Many suspects of white collar crimes have considerable skill in misdirecting you and distracting you from the salient points. You must stay alert, maintain your concentration, and refuse to allow the suspect to sidetrack your efforts. To do so you must listen carefully but never forget the central question. Often, you will have to rephrase a question to elicit any useful response. Do not be afraid to look stupid if the first question must be repeated. Your failure to "understand" is more likely to reflect a nonresponsive answer than your lack of comprehension.

■ SUMMARY

No textbook formulas exist for conducting an interrogation. Neither is there any dependable and invariable guide to inform a corporate investigator about whether or when to interrogate a suspect or hostile witness. The infinite variation in personalities and backgrounds of investigators and suspects, as well as the different character and status of investigations, make such universal guidebooks impossible.

Chapter Eighteen
Training Program for White Collar Crime Investigators

The selection of investigators for your corporate white collar crime management unit is important, but it marks only the beginning of the process of developing first-rate investigators. These important corporate positions require further training to develop a high level of professional skill even when the individuals selected have prior investigative experience. Some investigators may have experience only with certain limited types of white collar crimes (such as embezzlement) and may not be attuned to the other types of criminals and crimes that victimize your company.

Corporate resources or other factors will often prevent a recruiting procedure that capitalizes on the personal motives of candidates (e.g., personal motivations and qualifications to deal with white collar crime targeting corporations from internal and external sources). Your investigative staff often must be educated about the importance of white collar crime and the losses it will impose on your company when left unchecked or not detected through techniques such as investigative audits and intelligence collection efforts. You need to stress the importance of an effective and fair white collar crime management effort within your company and the corporate policies, procedures, and parameters that your unit must follow.

In this chapter, I supply you with a variety of approaches to training your corporate white collar crime management unit staff. Not all approaches serve each conceivable situation, but the programs discussed here will serve as a matrix with which you may tailor your training program to serve your company needs. You must also recognize that your training program will be limited by the resources available to you; however, often you can merge your training with parts of the company's training program to conserve those resources and achieve the maximum results.

In the following pages, I emphasize active, participative learning in which staff investigators practice various techniques. I discuss various issues, including performance evaluation. This performance-oriented approach is somewhat in contrast to many of the concepts of traditional training, but it brings you the best results with a minimum of time and resources. The guidelines I offer will help you achieve a better balance between the listening and learning approach and the active (participatory) or performance-oriented approach. In line with this approach, you will note at least three ways to train your staff investigators: (1) informal on-the-job training (OJT), (2) informal cross-department training, and (3) formal performance-oriented training.

◼ INFORMAL ON-THE-JOB TRAINING

This training is especially effective for new investigators in your corporate white collar crime management unit. It conserves resources otherwise needed to conduct formal training for only one or two persons. The OJT technique also serves well to bring experienced investigators into line with corporate policy and procedure for handling specific categories of white collar crimes.

OJT is also become especially useful as a training technique for your unit if you recruit persons from other investigative disciplines, such as corporate and industrial security forces, law enforcement departments, and others with experience in investigating more traditional and common crimes. In such cases, the person is already a professional investigator but may not have the particular expertise needed for white collar crimes that target corporations.

OJT creates a comfort level in the person who needs to work with and around executives, accountants, auditors, and others in the corporate environment. There's yet another benefit for the professional investigator (especially those coming to your white collar crime unit from years of law enforcement experience). These persons have grown accustomed to exercising authority, including making arrests and conducting other activities outside the corporate investigative purview. A meaningful OJT program will enable a faster adjustment to the often labor-intensive tasks you must perform that may result only in a reprimand to an employee who is committing otherwise prosecutable white collar crimes. This adjustment is often a difficult morale problem, but it becomes more manageable when you can conduct OJT and thus relay the concepts of corporate investigation quickly.

Another problem you will face within your WCC unit at the onset involves the competition and secrecy that are commonly found within other types of investigative agencies and units but are detrimental in a white collar crime management environment. The corporate white collar crime management unit involves team management and calls for discussions, sharing of information and sources of information, and regard for the privacy of suspects and offenders. In this unique investigative setting, the faster you bring a new investigator into the team, the greater his or her productivity and the faster you will develop a team spirit.

Techniques for Beginning Effective OJT

An effective technique for implementing OJT is to bring your staff investigators together informally in staff conferences that focus on a discussion of ongoing cases and situations. This technique helps the entire staff, but also those new to the world of white collar crime. It demonstrates cooperativeness and openness among the WCC management unit staff.

You can have informal staff conferences in a variety of formats, including a brown-bag lunch in a conference room or classroom within the unit environment. However, remember that the information discussed is of a sensitive nature, and all training (including staff conferences or other gatherings of investigators) must be within a secure area where other company employees or others cannot overhear the conversation, discussion, or presentations.

Another technique of OJT is to assign a new investigator to a seasoned one. The best way to approach this is through sponsorship, in which the experienced investigator is the sponsor. Avoid treating the new person as an inexperienced investigator, because that can begin a discontent or resentment from the first day at work. Sponsorship can eliminate this problem, especially when you choose the right person to orient the new person to the company, the unit, and the policies and procedures. The sponsor should first talk about the company itself and spend as much time as needed to tour the corporation with the new person, introducing him or her to key management and others as appropriate. Within the context of the tour, your sponsor must show the new person places and equipment within the company that your staff can access and use (such as a reproduction center, mail rooms, supply centers, and others). Whenever possible, another day or two of orientation will help the person understand the environment better. This extended orientation includes conferences with internal audit, accounting, and data processing supervisors to ensure that the new person gets a solid feel for the people, facilities, and company activities. Once the new person has a solid grasp of these aspects, the sponsor can begin an orientation to the WCC management unit's role, policies, and procedures. You should allow three to five days for this sponsoring orientation.

When you believe that a new investigator has sufficient orientation to begin working independently, ensure that he or she begins with the easiest cases (normally investigative audits of areas such as control of office and administrative supplies or a comparable activity). Depending on the person's confidence and experience, you should consider having the sponsor accompany the new person to get the process started or drop in occasionally to support the effort and answer any questions that might arise. You might consider the possibility of the new investigator sitting in with seasoned investigators during their interviews and working with other staff members on a variety of different cases.

Some experienced corporate investigators may have particular skills as trainers and you should recognize their potential, using them for training tasks. The progress of the new investigators should be evaluated in periodic three-way conferences among the new investigator, the sponsoring investigator, and you. Your involvement ensures that the sponsoring investigator does not succumb to "hoarding" the new person's effectiveness by keeping him or her as an assistant longer than necessary for the training.

OJT for Your Entire WCC Unit

In a new corporate white collar crime management unit, such as bringing a group of experienced investigators together to manage the white collar crime threat to the company, you can develop an OJT program for the entire staff. This might work effectively when, for example, your staff comes together from an existing security investigative program or other efforts that did not previously specialize in white collar crimes. Your new effort and WCC staff members should begin with investigative audits of noncomplex problems in the corporation that assure productivity and successful outcome. As the investigators become more confident and settle into their new responsibilities in the company, and as intelligence programs, policies, and procedures are created, moving into more complex issues becomes possible within an OJT concept.

■ INFORMAL CROSS-DEPARTMENT TRAINING

One variation of OJT is to assign temporarily members of your investigative staff to work in other departments that have similar functions to your WCC management unit. For example, the internal audit department does not have the mission to focus on criminal activity, and instead focuses on generally accepted accounting procedures; however, it often uncovers unexplained discrepancies that indicate a possibility of fraud. The accounting department might also supply your investigators with valuable insights that can be used in future investigations. Other possibilities include the purchasing department, contract department, the corporate counsel's office, and a variety of others that can supply elements of the total corporate operation important to your unit's success.

When investigators don't have a law enforcement background, consider working out an arrangement with the prosecutor or law enforcement agency to allow your staff members to work for a time in those environments to develop a better understanding of techniques of building a white collar crime case. When you work out this type of cross-department training, the time and resources used will reap large dividends later in your unit's efficiency and effectiveness.

Another advantage of this type of OJT is the working relationships developed during the training between your investigators and other employees within the corporation. These relationships eliminate the obscurity of your unit that often breeds misunderstanding and apprehension about your true motives. When other employees understand your unit and staff, they tend to become helpful (unless they are participating in white collar crimes). Such interaction might serve well as a deterrent for those employees who have considered a scheme and may end ongoing schemes.

Your model for cross-department OJT might come from the model used in most corporations for executive training. In this process, an employee moving to an executive-level position systematically moves through several positions within the organization. However, it is important that the employee he or she works with in this trainee capacity knows about it in advance. Otherwise, the suspiciousness of the trainee being a "spy" would make the experience less valuable. The same concept applies to the WCC management staff when participating in this type program.

You should also consider making this program a continuing process that schedules staff members periodically for cross-department training (this is important for keeping your investigators current on changes, new procedures, and equipment and changes in management or to maintain contacts that might otherwise fade, particularly in large corporations). A sound OJT program also might include selected members of your staff, normally on a rotating basis, attending corporate training sessions, conferences, and other activities that help them and the entire unit maintain a close relationship to the company and what's happening inside the company.

■ FORMAL PERFORMANCE-ORIENTED TRAINING

In this section, I give you some important guidelines for the development and operation of formal training for corporate white collar crime management units. It would take an entire book to cover every possible program design and procedure, so I discuss only the key elements of a training package. Your needs might require you to use all or some of these elements, or elect to apply them in ways different from what I suggest. Or you may use these elements as a matrix to create your own version.

Much of your unit training program must involve a heavy emphasis on simulations of actual investigations or performance-oriented training. This style of training is increasingly replacing the traditional lecture-oriented style of training because it has proven superior, especially for training persons who are already professional. Performance-oriented training enables you to develop learned and new skills by doing them in a controlled training environment. It's better to make mistakes in a practice session than in an actual investigation. This style of training also enables investigators to identify their own professional weaknesses and strengths and fine-tune current skills.

Since the content of your training program depends largely on the cooperation of those attending it, you should first consider whom to train. That often depends entirely on the size and diversification of your WCC unit staff. For example, if you have clerks, intelligence analysts, investigators, and specialists in other areas including accountants, auditors, attorneys, or others, how can you develop a training program that encompasses each of the staff categories and levels? After considering these issues, I will supply the guidelines for controlling the training. Remember, however, that the selection of the training content will depend largely on the composition of the staff and your unit's particular mission in light of what the corporation wants and expects from it. Also remember that there's no one way to accomplish formal training.

Selection of Trainers

When counseling companies or law enforcement agencies about training, I always begin with the first important consideration: You must select trainers from within your staff for the training or contract with professional trainers. Selecting a staff member at random and giving him or her an assignment of conducting training will result in a waste of time and resources. Selecting a trainer based on the person's expertise and accomplishments might also be a great mistake. Although the latter has strong merit, one ingredient is essential: the trainer's ability to communicate with others in a training environment. I have known criminal investigators who repeatedly solve and present winning cases that always ensure successful outcomes. However, they cannot explain to others how they do it. This is similar to the problem that some people, who are proven experts in their field, have with written tests. I've given tests to experts that an nonexpert could easily pass, yet the expert failed the test miserably.

However, using a performance-oriented training style, you can avoid these often perplexing problems because the trainer does not need expert training skills, and an expert who has trouble giving a meaningful lecture can share his or her knowledge using this technique.

How Performance-Oriented Training Works

The performance-oriented approach to training lends itself to a training session (i.e., a class or block of instruction) consisting of three phases. I explain each term and its mechanics; however, this overview focuses on the concept of training.

Phase I: The unit trainer states the training purpose and explains or demonstrates how to perform the objectives. Essentially, the trainer is transmitting information to the staff members attending training. Because this part of the training session involves what the trainer does (not what the staff member undergoing training must do), it should provide only essential information. This saves time that is better devoted to ensuring that staff members can perform the objectives and meet the established standards.

Phase II: The staff members practice the objective to acquire proficiency. During this phase staff members acquire skills through performance. Once they have acquired these skills, your staff may need to continue practicing them to develop the necessary degree of proficiency. The trainer must supply enough time and other resources (training aids, devices, equipment, assistant trainers when applicable, etc.) to ensure that the staff members gain an acceptable level of proficiency before moving into Phase III.

Phase III: The staff members attending training are tested by performing the objective. The results show whether they can or cannot meet the established training standard.

Performance-oriented training relies on three important steps. In the following discussion, I will refer to the person you choose to manage the training program as a trainer. That term does not refer to a professional trainer, but instead a staff investigator who follows the performance-oriented program outlined next.

■ OVERVIEW OF THE THREE-STEP PLANNING PROCESS

Step 1: Describe the Desired Results

In this step, the trainer obtains your description of precisely what the staff must accomplish at the completion of the unit's training (the unit manager's training objective). Your guidance must include the standards of performance the staff must meet. If your guidance is lacking, the trainer must develop this information alone.

Step 2: Prepare to Conduct Training

The unit trainer develops those intermediate training objectives that your staff attending the training must perform if they are to accomplish your training objective. The trainer then organizes the training in a logical, progressive sequence. Finally, the trainer must complete the training administrative requirements such as lesson plans, rehearsals of the planned training, and other needed aspects.

Step 3: Conduct Training to Standards

The unit trainer supervises, continuously monitors, and evaluates the conduct of training to ensure that the staff members attending training meet the training objectives you establish.

■ STEP-BY-STEP ANALYSIS

Step 1: Describe the Desired Results

The important starting point is your guidance to the trainer. The trainer applies that guidance in two ways:

(1) Receives and analyzes your specific training objective(s) and other guidance

(2) Receives a vaguely stated directive to conduct formal training in a particular subject.

A specific training objective that is presented to the unit trainer is to answer the question, "What do I want accomplished?" You need to include the task the staff must perform, the conditions under which the staff must perform the task, and the training standard that specifies the proficiency the staff must attain from the training.

You must also show the trainer who will receive the training, when it will happen, where it will happen, and why you decided to direct the training.

If you issue training instructions to a staff trainer vaguely, omitting the important who, when, and where questions, the trainer will have to develop that information independently. If your unit training manager has the experience and skill to develop training alone, it's not a problem. However, you retain the ultimate responsibility for the WCC management unit, and the staff's ability to perform often depends on the training and standards you set.

Step 2: Prepare to Conduct Training

In this step, the trainer takes your specific objectives and decides how best to achieve them. The trainer will rarely have the time to complete meaningful performance-oriented training in one session, and I recommend that productive training take place over time instead of being compressed to fit limited sessions. To do so, the trainer must decide on a series of intermediate objectives that schedule the progressive phases needed to accomplish your training objective.

The Need for Intermediate Training Objectives

Why must you develop intermediate training objectives? Although you have supplied the unit trainer with an ultimate training objective describing what you expect, you have not determined how that will happen. The unit trainer needs to make that determination and have your approval, because the intermediate objectives tell you how long the training will take to reach your training objective.

What is the intermediate training objective? Like your training objective, an intermediate training objective contains three elements:

(1) A task statement describing the action to perform

(2) A conditions statement describing the performance conditions for the task

(3) A training standards statement describing the necessity of performing the task under given conditions.

How to Develop These Objectives

The need for and number of intermediate training objectives stems from the complexity of your objective. If your objective is simple, then it's easy to determine how your trainer will accomplish that objective. However, if your objective is complex, then what the investigative staff attending the training must do, and how the training will lead them to do it, is far more difficult to determine.

You develop the intermediate training objectives largely through "talking" yourself through how to perform the objective, including identifying the tasks necessary to accomplish your objective. When you or a trainer knows how to perform the objective or if the objective is simple, then talking yourself through it should not be difficult. The number and complexity of the tasks will give you a sound basis for determining if you must develop intermediate training objectives. Remember, you are not concerned, for the moment, with how to teach the subject matter inherent in this objective; you are only determining all the separate tasks a staff member must do to perform your ultimate objective.

Developing a Task List

When the trainer's analysis of your objectives shows the needs for intermediate objectives, he or she must first identify the specific tasks needed to accomplish your objective. Doing this will rely on personal experience or consulting with an experienced staff member. The task list must include only those tasks essential to the staff members' achievement of the training objective. Expertise in judging how detailed you should make the task list will improve with experience. The task list also relies on how well you know the subject (i.e., it should neither separate nor reduce tasks excessively nor retain tasks that are too complex).

Establishing Conditions for Performing Each Task

The conditions element of a training objective is necessary to communicate clearly how staff members must perform a task in the work environment. Conditions specify the personnel, equipment, and procedures used and the environment in which staff members must work while performing a specific training task.

Developing a Training Standard for Each Task

The training standard will be the last element of the training objective. These standards are necessary to ensure that the staff members receiving training will understand what they must achieve or exceed if their training is to increases their personal skill. Training standards serve the training program best when expressed in terms of measurement (e.g., time, distance, accuracy) or in terms of specific procedures.

Developing training standards for intermediate training objectives calls for examination of the end training objective to ensure that the intermediate objectives will not be more relaxed or more stringent than required. For example, if you specify that staff members must develop the skill to accomplish an investigative audit of travel and expense claims on each employee filing them in two days, it is inappropriate to train the staff to accomplish that objective in three days. Conversely, it would also not be appropriate for the training to specify that the audit will take one day. Remember, the standards for intermediate training objectives must correspond with the progressive movement to the end objective.

With your training objective and the appropriate intermediate objectives established, the unit trainer can translate them into orderly, progressive training. Two important steps lead to that goal: (1) determining how much training to supply, and (2) organizing the training required. This will enable the staff undergoing training to progress from easier to more difficult tasks efficiently and effectively using the available resources.

Determine How Much Training is Required. The intermediate objectives establish what the staff members attending training must be able to do to perform your objective. The trainer should determine how well the staff can perform the intermediate objectives before beginning training. This determination allows you to (1) select for training only those objectives that the staff cannot perform without further training, and (2) determine how much training is required to ensure that the staff can meet the standards of intermediate training objectives (e.g., staff investigators may need only a brief refresher or brush-up or may need extensive practice to become proficient). To determine how well the staff can perform each intermediate training objective (i.e., their current proficiency), you can obtain and evaluate past performance results or you can conduct diagnostic testing.

Using Diagnostic Testing to Determine Training Requirements. When your staff proficiency in a specific investigative role is doubtful, you should consider diagnostic testing. A diagnostic test will determine how well your staff can perform a specified objective (task, conditions, and training standard) before the start of training. This procedure will help a trainer determine how much, if any, training is needed to ensure that investigators can perform an intermediate objective and meet its training standard.

Intermediate training objectives can serve as a diagnostic test by randomly selecting a few of the staff members scheduled for training and having them perform each intermediate training objective. The results will give you a good indication of whether they can meet the established training standard or how close they are to achieving the training standard of each objective. Random selection means that you do not need all the staff to perform each objective; only choose a few of the staff investigators, in a manner similar to drawing names out of a hat. This will ensure that a valid cross section of the staff scheduled for training will be evaluated instead of evaluating only the most proficient or least proficient in a particular subject. Guidelines for diagnostic testing evaluation include the following:

(1) If most of the staff members chosen can successfully perform an intermediate training objective, no further (or very little) formal training must be considered for the objective.

(2) Conversely, if most of the staff does not meet the training standard established for a particular objective, you have determined a gap between current proficiency and desired proficiency. This gap represents the training needed.

Organizing Performance-Oriented Training

Your corporate white collar crime management unit trainer organizes training by doing the following:

Determining the teaching order for the objectives. Once you have determined the quantity of training needed, you're ready to arrange the intermediate training objectives into the order in which training will be conducted (i.e., a sequence that will lead to an orderly, progressive training session).

There are two considerations: (1) Are any of the intermediate objectives a prerequisite to beginning training in the others? (2) Do your resources dictate how you must organize the intermediate training objectives? If the answer is yes, that objective must receive the first training priority.

Estimating the resources needed and selecting the training techniques for each objective

To choose the best possible aids, devices, and techniques for each phase of training, the trainer must know what is available and how to obtain and use it. From the training objectives, you know what needs to be practiced and tested. You must select from the available techniques, aids, and devices those which best accomplish this training.

The resource of time for each phase of performance-oriented training cannot be discussed in unchanging terms. The trainer must consider several factors when allocating the time. Although these factors can be categorized and listed, they are variable; that is, they change with every training situation. These factors include the following:

Phase I: The trainer states the training objective and explains or demonstrates (if needed) how to perform the objectives.

■ Factors for Consideration:

(1) Current proficiency of staff members (influences the time needed for explanation and demonstration)

(2) Number and complexity of objectives

(3) Number of staff members to be trained versus resources available (resources available include training aids, devices, equipment, facilities, and other factors involved in the situation)

Phase II: The staff members attending training practice the objectives to achieve proficiency called for by the training standards.

■   Factors for Consideration:

(1) Current proficiency of staff members related to the objective (influences the time needed to learn the skill). Other factors difficult to determine include human elements such as motivation, intelligence, morale, etc.

(2) Number and complexity of objectives (influence the time necessary to acquire proficiency). How quickly staff members achieve proficiency also depends on their current proficiency.

(3) Number of staff members to be trained versus resources available. How many of your staff members can practice simultaneously depends on the ratio of available resources to the number of staff members scheduled for training (e.g., one aid or device per person to practice with versus one aid or device per ten persons). Resources include training aids, devices, facilities, equipment, and other factors.

Phase III: The staff members are tested by performing the objective to established training standards (i.e., the objective equals the test).

■   Factors for Consideration:

(1) Current proficiency of staff members
(2) Complexity of objective
(3) Number of staff members to be trained versus resources available

You can estimate and allocate the needed resources in Phase I because you control most of the factors that influence the decision. Specifically, your intermediate objectives enable you to reduce a complex task to a logical series of smaller, simpler tasks. You use the aids and devices and facilities noted. Through rehearsal of presentation, you can determine the time you need to explain the objectives. You can even allow time for questions. Adding diagnostic testing procedures, you also have determined the current level of proficiency of the staff members attending the training.

Determining the resources (including time) in Phase II is the most difficult of the three phases. The staff member performs or practices the subject of training. Because you have little control over these factors, the time staff members need to learn and practice (Phase II) often cannot be determined until after you have determined the time for Phase III.

The resources needed for Phase III are fixed because after sufficient practice, the staff members will be able to perform the objective to the established training standards. Because the objective states what the person will use in performing the task and usually the time frame he or she must do it in, you can determine the resources accurately.

Based on this discussion, you now have an accurate method for estimating the time needed for Phases I and III. To estimate better the time needed for Phase II, do the following:

Start with the total amount of time supplied for the training session (for example, two hours). Subtract the estimated time needed for your explanation (Phase I) and the testing (Phase III). You must also consider the administrative time required to conduct the training. Do not forget the time necessary to move the staff between practice stations (when applicable), rest or break periods, time delays peculiar to the training, and any other added events that will keep the staff members from training. The time remaining will be the time available for Phase II (practice).

If this amount of time is too short, then you must consider the following steps:

(1) Reduce the time expended in Phase I. One way to save time is to have staff members prepare for the training (a type of homework assignment). These assignments (maybe using prepared handouts distributed a few days before training) should provide them with the purpose for training (i.e., training objectives and reasons for the training), an explanation, if necessary (i.e., procedures they will follow during Phases II and III), and the knowledge they will use during Phases II and III.

(2) Try to increase resources as needed.

Completing Administrative Requirements

When all planning is approved, it's time to develop a lesson plan. In the performance-oriented training approach, the most useful lesson plan should contain the following elements:

- The final training objective
- The intermediate training objectives, if any
- When and where training will happen and who will supply the training (the trainer)
- Time-phased sequence of how training is to be conducted
- Any restrictions and other measures
- Administrative information required.

These elements should supply the type of information needed to evaluate the training. However, you must do two things before training begins:

- Check the administrative support requirements.
- Conduct your rehearsal as needed.

A good rule of thumb for the administrative support requirements is, "Don't take anything for granted—check everything." Administrative requirements vary with each training period. For example, if you need a chalkboard, confirm that it's in place before the training session. See Exhibit 18-1 for a checklist of administrative support requirements.

Exhibit 18-1
Checklist of Administrative Support Requirements

☐ Check facilities where your training will take place.
☐ Obtain or make your training aids.
☐ Notify your guest speakers or assistant trainers (when applicable).
☐ Supply information before training if staff members need to bring items for training.
☐ Prepare and reproduce handouts (when used).
☐ Coordinate for special items needed (i.e., slides, projectors, screens, etc.).
☐ Coordinate any support needed.
☐ Conduct a rehearsal of your presentation and arranged training.
☐ Make a final check of any other aspect.

Before conducting your training, but with enough time to take corrective action, check the following items:

☐ Arrangement of the classroom
☐ Special equipment and other equipment (i.e., that it operates properly)
☐ Any restrictions, such as that privacy is assured
☐ Any other important aspect for the situation that would delay or weaken the training

---

Step 3: Conduct Training to Standards

Step 3 includes conducting, monitoring, and evaluating the training to ensure that the corporate white collar crime management unit members can perform the designated training objective.

The benefits of the hard work you have done in Steps 1 and 2 can be realized if you and the unit trainer remember to be an effective manager and leader.

If you want the WCC management unit staff to be enthusiastic about their training, you must approach the conduct of training in a professional manner. Your expertise in the subject, your bearing, appearance, manner, and desire to create a meaningful training environment will cause the staff to want to learn.

Ensure that established standards are met: Training is the key to professionalism. You and your trainer have taken great care to establish realistic, attainable training standards that your staff investigators or others must meet. You must be continually involved in the training, supervision, and critiquing to ensure that the staff met these standards. To facilitate learning, let the faster learners help the slower learners.

Verify that staff members can execute the fundamentals: If your staff undergoing training cannot perform each intermediate objective and meet the established standards, it does little good to press on with the training. Only by ensuring that the staff is well drilled in the fundamentals can you ensure that they will be able to perform the final objective.

■ THE IMPORTANT FUNCTION OF POSTTRAINING EVALUATION

Both the trainer and staff member receiving the training need to know how they're doing during and after the training. Using the performance-oriented approach to training, this evaluation is fairly simple. Because the staff members know what they must do, they have an established benchmark from which they can evaluate their performance throughout the training session.

Trainers must also supervise and evaluate training. Supervising training helps determine student performance of the intermediate training objectives. This is essential to ensure that the staff can properly execute the fundamentals and meet established standards before they perform the final training objective.

Evaluation is more comprehensive and involves two important aspects of the training process: training effectiveness and training efficiency. Training effectiveness involves how well the staff members perform the final objective, while training efficiency involves how well the trainer used the available training resources. When the staff members can meet the training standard of the final training objective, the effectiveness of training can be judged a success. If that doesn't happen, the trainer must try to pinpoint the reasons.

■ ALTERNATIVE TRAINING PRESENTATION AND TECHNIQUES

The learning process (how people learn) is only partly understood. We do know, however, that learning only takes place when there is some mental and physical activity by the persons receiving the training. Further, we cannot see the learning process, but we can observe its effects (i.e., whether, as a result of the training, the persons can perform specified training objectives). It is critical for each manager and trainer to identify precisely what is to be learned (the training objectives) and then choose those techniques, aids, or devices that will enable the students in training sessions to perform the objectives successfully. There are techniques of training other than performance-oriented training. Remember, however, that you can mix the training techniques, and often it's necessary to do so. In the following sections, I discuss other types of training. Each can serve your needs without the use of practice or performance techniques.

The Lecture Technique

One of the presentation techniques used to convey information during a training session is the lecture (such as Phase I in performance-oriented training). The instructional technique of lecturing began in medieval universities, where professors read from their prepared notes in an effort to disseminate information as widely and quickly as possible. Through this "telling" method, staff members of your WCC management unit receive information principles, procedures, theories, and relationships (compare to Phase II, practice, of performance-oriented training). Essentially, the lecture is a one-way, oral explanation by the trainer to an audience. Staff participation is limited to asking and answering questions. The most effective lecture stems from a trainer who knows the subject well enough to present the necessary information without using a prepared manuscript. The "off the cuff" telling method permits trainers to be themselves and to maintain better contact with the persons they train.

Advantages

- This technique provides an economical method of presenting information rapidly.
- The trainer can place emphasis where he or she wants.

- The trainer can address any size group.
- The trainer can control the time.
- This technique can cover material not otherwise available.
- It poses minimal threat to the learner, who need only listen or pretend to listen.
- It places total control in the hands of the trainer.

Limitations

- When used alone, the lecture technique normally is an ineffective means of achieving the desired learning. Passive, uninvolved staff members become bored easily.
- The lecture does not permit active participation by the staff members attending training.
- When used alone, the rate and amount of learning cannot be evaluated easily. Questions asked by the trainer hit only a small part of the audience.
- It does not affirm the staff members' proficiency in performing a specific task.

Lecture Technique Tips

- Present only the information necessary to permit student practice when using this technique in performance-oriented training.
- Training time has limits, and lectures are better used in Phase II (practice) when the lecture precedes performance-oriented training.
- Know the subject well enough to use the "off the cuff" method of presentation. Manuscripts read aloud might supply factually complete information, but they are rarely effective in achieving desired learning.
- If you have trouble remembering key points, jot them down as informal trainer notes. A quick glance to refresh your memory is a better presentation technique than reading a manuscript. It's better to miss a few words and be yourself while maintaining eye contact with the persons receiving the training.
- When using the lecture technique, use examples, present more than one side, stress important points, and use visual aids and humor to maintain audience interest.

The Conference Technique

A conference is a variation of the lecture. Its design permits and encourages greater audience participation. The conference method supplies a vehicle for group problem solving and decision making. It also provides a technique to stimulate staff member interest during Phase I of performance-oriented training. More important, the conference technique takes advantage of the ideas and experiences of the persons attending training.

When using the conference method, your trainer must initiate, stimulate, and guide the discussion. When sufficient discussion occurs, the trainer must highlight (reinforce) key concepts to ensure meaningful training and focus on principles, procedures, and other aspects the staff must learn.

Advantages

- Encourages the type of staff member involvement that will help them learn.
- Permits persons in training sessions to share their personal ideas and experiences.
- Permits greater opportunities to evaluate the rate and amount of learning (comprehension of the material presented).
- Stimulates, when used properly, staff interest in areas that otherwise would create a confused, boring environment.

Limitations

- The trainer must have skill in guiding discussions. Too much trainer control inhibits staff participation. Too little can allow the discussion to be sidetracked into areas that contribute little to the objectives of the training.
- The conference technique requires more time than other presentation methods.
- There's no assurance that the quality of staff participation will permit training objectives to be accomplished.

Conference Technique Tips

- Use this technique only for those parts of Phase I of performance-oriented training that have significant, controversial, or difficult to learn or accept segments.

- The conference technique works best with small groups. As the size of the group increases, the effectiveness of this technique decreases.

- Be certain that staff members have some knowledge of the subject presented and discussed before deciding to use the conference technique. Advance study assignments or information about the topics discussed can help.

- Prepare thought-producing questions to stimulate discussion and understanding before training. Consider and prepare to discuss likely staff responses by highlighting important points or by asking follow-up questions.

- Consider the uses of training aids and devices to help stimulate discussion and understanding.

- Summarize discussion points and highlight lessons learned. Ensure that all pertinent information has been covered to permit staff member practice of each objective covered in the training. A good summarization will briefly point out ideas expressed, resolve conflicting points of view, and relate the ideas to the training objectives. If more than one training objective is covered, use subsummaries to move from one objective to another.

The Demonstration Technique

Combined with the lecture or conference techniques of training, the demonstration shows staff members what they're expected to do and how to do it. When appropriate, the demonstration becomes an important part of Phase I in performance-oriented training techniques. Three key forms of demonstration that will supply your corporate white collar crime management unit with training options include the following:

Procedural demonstration Used to show the operation or function of equipment. This type of demonstration serves well in technical training.

Displays This technique calls for arranging display materials so that all staff members attending the training can view them quickly. For large groups, you can duplicate displays, or divide the attendees into sections and have each section rotate from one display to another. This sometimes is called the "county fair" method of demonstration.

Training films, Videotapes, and Slide Presentations Training films, videotapes, and slide presentations supply ready-made demonstrations often performed by experts. Motion pictures, videotapes, and slide presentations supply an economical form of demonstration, but make sure that they relate to your specific training objectives.

Advantages

- Demonstration training techniques save training time.
- A brief demonstration of the proper method of performing a particular task will help the learning process more rapidly than lengthy discussions that have no visual impact. A variety of studies show that demonstration techniques have a positive learning effect.
- Demonstrations tend to stimulate staff interest by supplying a realism in the training experience that other presentation techniques do not offer.
- Demonstrations set the stage for staff practice of the particular objectives, including visually explaining performance standards the staff must meet.

Limitations

- By themselves, demonstrations do not provide for active student participation. You can overcome this problem, however, by allowing staff members to "walk through" the task either during or immediately after the demonstration.
- Some tasks are too expensive or difficult to demonstrate. They call for a large number of personnel and equipment.
- Demonstrations can be affected adversely by the training environment (e.g., a small classroom or conference room that doesn't supply enough space for demonstrations).

Demonstration Technique Tips

- When demonstrating something, consider the staff member's viewpoint. If possible, rehearse your demonstration in front of someone watching from where the staff members who will attend training will see the demonstration.
- Carefully explain each step as you demonstrate it. You must plan the details of your demonstration carefully and in sequence. Start with the training objectives, and then demonstrate one intermediate training objective at a time. Your staff members should recognize distinct breaks between the steps of the performance you're demonstrating. If it is necessary for your staff to lean more than one way of performing an operation, a separate and distinct demonstration of the alternate method should be considered. If you have several intermediate training objectives, you should avoid demonstrating all of them simultaneously.

Demonstrate only the number necessary to complete a training session. Once staff members have practiced these, move onto other intermediate objectives.

- Emphasize key points during the demonstration. One way you can do this is to ask questions about key points. Obtain and use added training aids that further clarify your explanation.

- Position yourself to one side or behind your aid or device so you will not obstruct the staff members' view. You want your audience to watch the demonstration and listen to your explanation, so while demonstrating a procedure or item of equipment, speak to the audience, not to the item.

■ IMPORTANT COMMUNICATION TECHNIQUES IN TRAINING

Effective white collar crime trainers know when and how to use a variety of communication techniques. These techniques include the following guidelines:

(1) Display a Positive Attitude. An enthusiastic attitude is generally contagious. When the trainer shows enthusiasm for the subject, so do staff members.

(2) Control Your Nervousness. Stage fright and "butterflies" are common occurrences for trainers, especially in their first training sessions. These problems usually mean you're concerned about doing a good job. Solid preparation and rehearsal give you the confidence to overcome nervousness. Having your first remarks well in mind will help you to get off to a good start. The best advice is to be natural, relax, and move briskly and purposely. As you do in everyday conversation, use gestures to strengthen your words. However, guard against distracting mannerisms such as remaining glued to one spot or jiggling your pocket change. During rehearsal, have someone objectively note any distracting mannerisms so you can correct them.

(3) Speak Clearly. Avoid a dull, boring monotone. Change the pitch of your voice for emphasis and to hold your audience attention. This raising and lowering of your voice is called inflection. It should be natural, not forced.

(4) Speak loud enough for all to Hear without difficulty. The proper volume is especially important when you conduct training in an environment with poor acoustics. By watching the staff members' reaction, you can often tell if they have difficulty hearing you. If you are uncertain, ask them if they can hear you. Do not speak too loudly; no one likes to have someone shout at them.

(5) Your rate of speech should be governed by the thought, idea, or emotion you are trying to communicate. If you speak too rapidly, you may confuse the audience; on the other hand, speaking too deliberately or slowly may irritate the audience. A delivery that is too fast or too slow (unnaturally fast or slow) is distracting to most people; staff members stop paying attention to what's said and pay more attention to how it is said.

(6) Use pauses properly. We all pause during our speaking. Sometimes we pause for effect; sometimes we pause to take a breath. Pauses are to speaking what punctuation is to writing. The proper use of pauses allows staff members to absorb ideas and take notes; it allows you to add emphasis, meaning, and interpretation to what you say.

(7) Speak as clearly as possible. Concentrate on pronouncing or accenting each syllable distinctly and correctly. It may be necessary to speak more forcefully and deliberately when instructing a large group than it is when carrying on a normal conversation.

(8) Use humor. The proper use of humor can improve your rapport with staff members attending your training session. However, do not use humor as a crutch. Jokes cannot serve you well as fillers; instead they should add interest and relate to the ongoing training. Do not waste valuable preparation time trying to think up a few good jokes for your training. You want the staff members to remember the major points and not your stories. Especially, do not use jokes that will be as in poor taste, such as ethnic stories and crude jokes. A rule of thumb is, if a joke may offend someone in your training audience, don't tell it. Spontaneous, witty, self-directed comments will succeed better than planned, contrived jokes. If the joke is on you, laugh and enjoy it with your audience. In this way you will add a human touch to your training and increase your rapport with your audience.

(9) Ask questions. Asking and answering questions is important in communication. Questions stimulate thought and encourage or force participation. They also help you adjust your presentation to the training audience. Questions may reveal misunderstanding and thus allow you to clarify something before practice sessions begin.

(10) Use Questions to Your Advantage. Questions and responses from staff members attending training will often supply you with good indicators about their interest in and attitude toward the subject presented. Questions allow you to emphasize key points and involve the audience during your explanation.

(11) Ask thought-provoking, meaningful questions. This is not easy to do; it calls for preparation and knowledge of your subject. Questions should be asked for a specific reason, to elicit a specific response.

(12) Properly Phrase the question. The question must have a purpose. Its purpose may be to emphasize a point, keep staff members alert, check

understanding of a key point, review material, or stimulate thought. The staff must understand the question. It should be direct, simply worded, and limited to one point or topic. Your questions should require a definite answer, but should be phrased to disallow a simple yes or no response. An incorrect answer may show that a staff member does not understand what you are explaining, or that your question was confusing.

(13) Ask the question in a forceful tone, assuring that it's heard by everyone. If you have the audience attention and you ask the question loudly enough, there should be no excuse for a response such as, "I didn't hear the question," or "Would you please repeat the question?"

(14) Address the Entire Group. Address the question to the entire group before designating one particular person to answer. This technique calls for each person to think, as they may be the one you call on for the answer. Pause briefly after asking to allow the person time to think about the question and formulate an answer. A simple rule for allowing enough time is to ask yourself silently the same question three times. After pausing, call on someone to answer. This is known as the ask-pause-call technique of asking questions.

(15) Distribute Questions among the Group. Contrast this procedure to one in which a particular person is called on, asked the question, and allowed to answer. Once the trainer chooses a staff member to answer a question, the rest of the audience stops thinking and starts congratulating themselves for not having to answer. Distribute questions among the group for full group participation in the discussion. Avoid calling on persons in any set order or limiting questions to the most alert audience members.

(16) Encourage Full Responses. How you react to a response is important. Your attitude can be the deciding factor in maintaining rapport and in coaxing added responses from the audience. Encourage staff members to respond to the best of their ability even though they may seem uncertain of their knowledge or ability to speak before a group. How do you do this? Avoiding questions that evoke a yes or no answer is your first step. Ensure that your question is stated simply and heard by everyone. Do not accept "I don't know" without some effort to elicit a positive response. Rephrase the question when necessary.

(17) Evaluate and respond to each answer according to its merit. If the answer is wrong, do not strengthen it by nodding your head in approval or falsely praising the answer. Do not infer that the staff member was dumb because the answer did not meet your expectations. If necessary, elaborate on the answer or have the person clarify a vague answer, or ask a follow-up question.

(18) Don't become sidetracked. Sometimes a staff member will try to throw you off by answering your question with one of his or her own. Answer the question, but don't let the staff member off the hook; he or she owes you

an answer. In fact, you may call on someone else to answer the staff member's question and then return to the person for an answer to your own question. Don't bluff if you cannot answer the question. Tell the group that you will find the answer and give it to them later; then keep your promise.

(19) Tactfully Handle Embarrassing Questions. Occasionally a staff member will attempt to embarrass the trainer with a question meant to place the trainer in an awkward situation. If you're asked such a question, tactfully dismiss it or demand an explanation of the question's purpose or intent. If the question is relevant but tricky or sensitive, answer it to the best of your ability.

▪ IDENTIFY YOUR WCC MANAGEMENT NEEDS AND PROBLEMS

Defining the problem you need to tackle is not difficult if current performance is regarded as substandard. This can mean that with the same resources, the staff member or unit achieved a better performance earlier, or that your goals exceed what the performance of the unit accomplishes. When your unit performance stagnates, the problem is clearly defined if you accept that it is necessary to achieve a better performance through an aggressive training program.

Not all problems you face can will be defined in clear-cut ways. However, when you focus on immediate, short-term, and easily measurable results from your training program, the unit performance as a whole will begin to improve and come in line with your expectations and standards.

When you focus your needs assessment on results, both immediate and future, it's necessary to understand the context in which a particular needs assessment exercise occurs. For example, you need to determine what results are expected of the unit in relationship to the needs of the corporation, and that will supply you with an accurate view of the unit needs required to fulfill that expectation. Exhibit 18-2 shows you one technique of determining your results-oriented training program though assessing needs and problems.

▪ EVALUATION OF YOUR TRAINING PROGRAM

Corporations have turned their attention to quality in recent years because of an increasingly competitive atmosphere to satisfy a global marketplace. This quality-oriented view spreads throughout the company, and your corporate white collar crime management unit does not escape the trend. Corporations

Exhibit 18-2
Results-Oriented Planning Guide

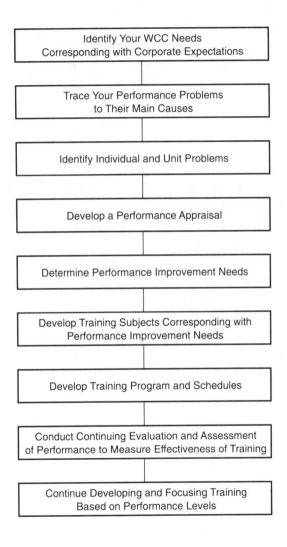

Identify Your WCC Needs
Corresponding with Corporate Expectations

Trace Your Performance Problems
to Their Main Causes

Identify Individual and Unit Problems

Develop a Performance Appraisal

Determine Performance Improvement Needs

Develop Training Subjects Corresponding with
Performance Improvement Needs

Develop Training Program and Schedules

Conduct Continuing Evaluation and Assessment
of Performance to Measure Effectiveness of Training

Continue Developing and Focusing Training
Based on Performance Levels

also are spending more than ever before on training and expect quality results from the training. Your unit training does not escape that responsibility. Former concepts of "train and hope" have changed to a long-term strategy of "train, measure, and improve." Throughout this chapter, I've discussed the options you can use to train your staff investigators to achieve higher productivity in protecting your corporation's assets and tackling tough white collar crime threats and problems. How well you evaluate your training results through assessment techniques and careful planning, will bring you the quality of performance you expected. With effective training, you can build your WCC management unit into an efficient, effective corporate asset.

To define quality in training, you must begin with clear, concise definitions that everyone in your staff can agree on. Operations definitions consist of a criterion applied to a dimension of training, a test of the dimension, and a decision on whether that dimension meets the criterion. For example, you need to determine the correct procedures tailored to the problems to achieve the quality expected. The following formula will help you achieve that task.

Criterion: Staff agreement on a training program and procedure helps the staff improve.

Test: A draft of the training program and procedure creates enthusiasm within the staff.

Decision: Allows the revision of the training program and procedure if it does not meet the criterion.

Most managers and trainers have varied opinions about quantity of training and what creates quality training. Variation is normal and ensures that training standards don't become unrealistic or self-defeating. Realistic quality control calls for a certain tolerance, and, with operational definitions, standards of quality training can develop that everyone on your staff agrees with.

■ THE EIGHT CHARACTERISTICS OF QUALITY ASSURANCE

Exhibit 18-3 will help you determine and measure the quality of your training program and needs to ensure that your corporate white collar crime management staff grows in proficiency and satisfies the needs of the corporation.

Exhibit 18-3
The Eight Characteristics of Quality

(1) Performance

- ☐ Results of your training need on-the-job measurement (performance).
- ☐ Investigator competency must be your highest training priority.
- ☐ Performance and quality combine as a documented dimension of your training program.

(2) Features

- ☐ Each feature (subject) of your training relates directly to a corporate need.
- ☐ Features or subjects must focus on performance and quality achievement.

(3) Reliability

- ☐ Your training program must produce stable and predictable results.
- ☐ Training procedure is crucial to reliability.
- ☐ Systematic monitoring improves reliability of training.

(4) Conformance

- ☐ How closely does final training match preset standards?
- ☐ Successful action by the WCC unit shows conformance to company standards.
- ☐ Precise specification in training design.

(5) Durability

- ☐ Is your training out of date?
- ☐ Will your training ensure career growth of the staff members?
- ☐ Will your training satisfy growing threats to the company?

(6) Serviceability

- ☐ Can your training program be updated easily?
- ☐ Monitor training often and make changes efficiently.

(7) Aesthetics

- ☐ Are corporate management satisfied with your unit's performance and results?
- ☐ Are corporate management satisfied with investigator working relationships internally?

(8) Perceived Quality

- ☐ The final test of quality in training: If training features and aesthetics conform to the corporation's needs and preference, perceived quality will stay high.

Corporations that have started company-wide quality assurance programs reap long-term benefits within their operations. You can reap similar benefits by determining which quality dimensions will be crucial to meet the company needs regarding white collar crime threats. You create that quality by implementing excellent systems of training measurements and standards for improvement through quality training.

■ SUMMARY

Performance improvement measures that produce results do not happen because of good program design alone. The implementation of your training program intended to improve on-the-job performance requires careful engineering to create the best possible environment for success. The same key elements that were used to analyze and solve performance problems are appropriate for planning. Implementation demands management participation instead of only support.

Whatever program designs, techniques of presentation, schedules, or quality control measures you use, remember that training is the key to excellence. Without quality and consistent training, you cannot expect your corporate white collar crime management unit to function as a team or successfully tackle the diverse threats of white collar crime against your company.

INDEX